FROM FAILING HANDS

FROM FAILING HANDS

The Story of Presidential Succession

John D. Feerick

Foreword by

Paul A. Freund

FORDHAM UNIVERSITY PRESS

New York

The title of this book and the epigraph on page xv are taken from "In Flanders Fields," *reprinted by permission of* Punch.

To My Dear Parents and Emalie

CONTENTS

Contents

IV. OTHER SYSTEMS

FOREWORD

In the year 1800 John Jay declined President Adams' invitation to return to a place on the Supreme Court, from which he had resigned to become Governor of New York. Writing to Adams, Jay expressed his low opinion of the status of the Court: "I left the bench perfectly convinced that under a system so defective it would not obtain the energy, weight, and dignity which are essential to its affording due support to the national Government." Did Adams perchance remember his own similar low view of the office of Vice-President, which he had bluntly expressed on assuming that office in 1789? "Unaccustomed to refuse any public service," he said, "however dangerous to my reputation or disproportionate to my talents, it would have been inconsistent to have adopted another maxim at this time."

Under John Marshall the Court achieved a stature and strength that seemed to Jay beyond reach; and the vice-presidency for Adams and for Jefferson after him was a stage on the electoral road to the chief magistracy. But while the judiciary has maintained its prestige over the years, the vice-presidency soon became for most of our history a difficult anomaly, an office in search of a role, a constitutional hybrid whose predominant function in the executive or the legislative branch failed of clarification.

And yet the relation of this ill-defined office to the presidency has been of critical importance to the vitality and continuity of our Government. Eight times a Vice-President has succeeded to the highest office on the death of the President. Seven times a Vice-President has died in office, leaving the succession to be governed by an act of Congress that at one time or another has focused on the president pro tem of the Senate, the Secretary of State, or the Speaker of the House. If such a vacancy occurs in the vice-presidency, either through his succession to the presidency or his death, and it is desired to avoid the statutory line of succession by filling the office of Vice-President, how can this be accomplished? At still other times,

ix

the disability of a living President—notably in the case of Garfield, Wilson, Cleveland, and Eisenhower—has raised inevitable questions of the powers and duties of the Vice-President in that contingency: on whom does responsibility rest for determining the disability; and if the Vice-President were to assume the responsibilities of the presidency would he be acting on an interim basis, until the disability was removed, or would the office, as Mr. Truman believes, be vested in him absolutely for the remainder of the term. The Constitution left all these questions unanswered.

These chances and changes and doubts have created geologic faults in our governmental structure that under pressure could produce upheaval and grave disorder. The repair of these faults has become a matter of urgent concern. Wise and constructive solutions must rest on historical knowledge, an appreciation of the constitutional possibilities, and a feel for the political processes in a government of separated powers functioning in a time of crisis.

These qualities are admirably manifest by the author of the present volume. After publishing a notable series of scholarly articles on the subject, John Feerick was invited to serve on a special committee of the American Bar Association appointed to consider presidential disability and succession. He contributed valuably to the work of that committee, which reached a consensus now embodied in substance in Senate and House resolutions proposing a constitutional amendment. The amendment, analyzed thoroughly in this book, is designed to resolve the congeries of problems of disability and succession with a view to certain basic aims: unfaltering authority in the executive office, efficiency of transition, clarity of procedure, avoidance of intrigue on the one hand and excessive hesitation on the other. Shortly before the adjournment of the Eighty-eighth Congress the Senate resolution, under the expert and assiduous guidance of Senator Birch Bayh, was passed unanimously in that body.

In one sense, then, this book is a tract for the times. It is an intelligent citizen's guide to an issue which may soon reach every state through the submission by Congress of a constitutional amendment. But like any superior tract for the times, it is of more than topical or passing interest. In the fullness of its historical narrative and the sharpness of its analysis it is a contribution to the literature of our political-constitutional order. If there is a sense of urgency about Mr. Feerick's exposition, matching the nature of the problem under discussion, there is withal an unhurried narrative, in particular a

Foreword

savory account of the vice-presidency from John Adams to Lyndon Johnson. Mr. Feerick, in short, has approached the subject of presidential disability and succession in a broad-gauged way. He has given us vivid history, careful constitutional analysis, and a cogently argued program for action.

Harvard Law School   PAUL A. FREUND

PREFACE

The operation of the provisions relating to presidential succession is one of the most important and fascinating aspects of the Constitution of the United States. It is an integral and dramatic part of the story of Presidents and Vice-Presidents of this country. This book attempts to set forth a detailed account of presidential succession as reflected in the deaths and serious illnesses of Presidents, in the crises implicit in these events, and in the continuing growth in importance of the second office of the land—the vice-presidency.

Opening with a summary of the assassination of John F. Kennedy and the succession of Lyndon B. Johnson to the presidency, the book traces the history of presidential succession from the colonial governments in which our form of government is largely rooted, through the deliberations of the Constitutional Convention of 1787, the state ratifying conventions and the early congresses, and on to the many occasions when the torch of presidential authority passed from the hand of the President to his constitutional successor and to those occasions when the torch should have passed but failed to pass to the successor. Because a history of presidential succession requires it, the book also treats the development of the office of Vice-President. Improvements in the succession mechanism and the vice-presidency are discussed, and the succession provisions of state and foreign governments are examined in the context of succession crises involving state governors and world leaders.

In the writing of this book my greatest debt of gratitude is to my wife, Emalie, without whose suggestions, research, editing, footnoting, and constant encouragement the book would not have been written.

I am deeply grateful to Professor Paul Freund of the Harvard Law School, one of the foremost constitutional authorities in the United States, for consenting to write the Foreword.

To my close friend, Joseph T. C. Hart, who painstakingly read and criticized the manuscript and assisted with many of the details,

Preface

I wish to express my special thanks. I am deeply grateful to my father-in-law, William B. Platt, Jr., one of the most creative lawyers I have ever met, for reading the manuscript and making suggestions which improved it. I also wish to express my gratitude to Professor Leonard F. Manning of the Fordham Law School for suggesting that I write a book on presidential succession.

To the secretaries of my office, especially Miss Linda Plaza, I owe a special debt of thanks for typing the manuscript during their free time.

Portions of this book have appeared in articles of mine in Volume 32 (1963–1964) of the *Fordham Law Review,* and I am grateful for permission to reprint that material here.

All errors of fact and judgment are, of course, wholly mine.

JOHN D. FEERICK

To you from failing hands, we throw
The torch—Be yours to hold it high!
If ye break faith with us who die
We shall not sleep. . . .

JOHN D. MC CRAE

In Flanders Fields

INTRODUCTION

1

A President Dies in Office

I will do my best. That is all I can do. I ask for your help—and God's.

LYNDON BAINES JOHNSON

Friday, November 22, 1963, will be remembered as one of the saddest days in American history. On that day, John Fitzgerald Kennedy, the youngest man ever elected to the office of President of the United States, met his death by assassination.

The President and Mrs. Kennedy had arrived in San Antonio, Texas at 1:30 P.M., C.S.T., the day before, Thursday, for a three-day tour of the State. The main purpose of the visit was to unite the Texas Democratic Party and win support for the Party in the 1964 presidential election. Planning for the trip had begun as far back as June, 1963. Not until November 19, however, had the details been made public. The receptions accorded the President on Thursday in San Antonio, Houston, and Fort Worth clearly demonstrated his tremendous popularity. Friday opened with a breakfast at the Texas Hotel in Fort Worth for President and Mrs. Kennedy which was sponsored by the Fort Worth Chamber of Commerce. Afterwards, as they were preparing to leave for Dallas, a strangely prophetic conversation took place between the President and his wife and Kenneth P. O'Donnell, a White House aide and close friend of the President. They were discussing the risks involved in public appearances of the President. Kennedy commented that there was "nothing anybody could do" if someone "really wanted to shoot the President" and had access to a high building and a telescopic rifle.[1]

3

From Fort Worth, the presidential party flew to Dallas, arriving at Love Field at 11:37 A.M., C.S.T. They were bound for the Trade Mart where the President was scheduled to deliver a luncheon speech to a group of prominent Dallas citizens. After the luncheon they were to fly to Austin for a fund-raising dinner and from there they would proceed to Vice-President Lyndon B. Johnson's ranch in Johnson City. They were met at the airport by a Dallas reception committee. Before entering their automobile, President and Mrs. Kennedy left the receiving line and walked over to a fence to greet the large crowd which had assembled to witness their arrival. About ten minutes later, they took their places in the rear seat of the famous presidential limousine for the ten-mile trip by motorcade to the Trade Mart. Governor and Mrs. John B. Connally of Texas sat in front of them in the jump seats. At the President's request the limousine was, on this day, without the plastic shield popularly known as the "bubble top." Secret Service Agent William R. Greer drove the car and Agent Roy H. Kellerman sat next to him. An open sedan carrying eight other Secret Service agents, whose duty it was to scan the crowds and buildings for unusual movements, followed immediately behind. Next, in an open convertible, rode Vice-President and Mrs. Lyndon B. Johnson and Texas' Democratic Senator Ralph W. Yarborough, accompanied by a Secret Service agent and a Texas State Highway patrolman who was driving.

Despite apprehension that Dallas' reception of the President might be cool because of some recent manifestations of anti-administration sentiment there, all along the route crowds waved and cheered enthusiastically. So impressive was the reception that Mrs. Connally turned and remarked, good-naturedly, to the President: "Mr. President, you can't say Dallas doesn't love you." Just then, at approximately 12:30 P.M., as the motorcade was passing through downtown Dallas at a speed of about eleven miles per hour, three shots rang out. One bystander, Howard L. Brennan, a Dallas steam fitter, later told police that he had seen a man with a rifle take aim and fire in the direction of the President's car from a sixth floor window of the Texas School Book Depository, an orange brick warehouse and office building which was behind the President's car.[2] At the first shot the President grabbed at his throat and lurched forward, saying, "My God, I am hit!" As Governor Connally started to turn in his seat he felt something strike him in the back and as he fell over into his wife's lap, he cried out, "Oh, no, no, no. My God, they

4

are going to kill us all." Mrs. Kennedy, who had turned toward her husband, now saw him hit in the head. She cried, "Oh, my God, they have shot my husband. I love you, Jack." President Kennedy slumped over, his bleeding head coming to rest on her lap. Two bullets had found their mark. One had passed through his neck. The other had shattered his skull. One of the three bullets, perhaps the same one that passed through the President's neck, had hit Governor Connally in the back, passed through his chest and wrist and lodged in his thigh. Secret Service agent Kellerman, when he realized what had happened, yelled to agent Greer, "Let's get out of here; we are hit." He then radioed ahead to the lead car, saying, "Get us to the hospital immediately." Greer, who was driving, immediately stepped on the accelerator and the car, which had come to a near stop, pulled away from the scene, headed at top speed for the Parkland Memorial Hospital, several miles away. As the vehicle started to pick up speed, Secret Service agent Clinton Hill, who had dashed up from his position on the running board of the vehicle behind the President's, climbed to one of the special steps on the back bumper of the President's car and then up to the flat trunk, pushing the dazed Mrs. Kennedy down into the rear seat. She had crawled up on the back of the car as if to get help.* Possibly, he saved her life. Other cars in the presidential motorcade also sped away. As soon as the shots had sounded, Vice-President Johnson was pushed to the floor of his car by Secret Service agent Ralph Youngblood, who was riding in the front seat of the car. Youngblood then leaped over the seat and threw himself on top of the Vice-President.

Almost ten minutes had elapsed by the time the President's limp form was carried into the emergency room. Physicians later said he was "moribund"—or beyond medical help—when he arrived, although Dr. Charles J. Carrico, who was the first physician to see him, concluded from some uncoordinated breathing movements and chest sounds that he was still alive. A quickly assembled team of about fifteen doctors, headed by Doctors Malcolm O. Perry, thirty-four-year-old attendant surgeon at the hospital, and Kemp Clark, the hospital's chief of neurosurgery, worked feverishly over the President for almost half an hour. First a breathing tube was pushed down the President's throat. Then a tracheotomy was performed in

---

* The President only several days before, in connection with a trip to Tampa, Florida, had requested that Secret Service agents not ride on the rear steps of his automobile.

5

an attempt to help his breathing. Blood and fluids were infused intravenously. Hydrocortisone was administered. A chest tube was inserted for drainage of the chest cavity. Finally, in a last desperate effort to revive the President, chest massage was attempted. But it was too late. After all efforts to obtain response had failed, Dr. Clark pronounced the President dead. The exact moment of death could not be determined. It was set arbitrarily at 1:00 P.M. Admiral George G. Burkley, the President's physician, had been in about the tenth car of the motorcade and had not arrived at the hospital until emergency treatment was underway. Later he said: "My direct services to him at that moment would have interfered with the action of the team which was in progress."[3]

John Fitzgerald Kennedy, slain in the forty-seventh year of his life in the service of his country, was the first President born in the twentieth century and the first of Roman Catholic faith. He was the eighth President to die in office, the fourth by assassination. He had served only thirty-four months of his term of office.

The nation had first learned of the shocking events in Dallas shortly after 12:30 P.M., C.S.T., when the United Press International teletype spelled out these incredible words: "Kennedy seriously wounded; perhaps seriously; perhaps fatally; by assassin's bullet."[4] Within minutes the news was being announced on radio and television. The immediate reaction of the people was horrified disbelief—disbelief that such a thing could actually have happened. This was followed, as the fact of the shooting was indisputably confirmed, by the desperate hope that the wound was not fatal, that the President would recover.

As the nation awaited further word, it received yet another jolt. It was reported that Vice-President Johnson had suffered a heart attack. This report, which was immediately denied, seems to have arisen from the fact that when Johnson entered Parkland Hospital after President Kennedy had been carried in on a stretcher, he was holding his hand over his heart.[5] Since the Vice-President had suffered a massive heart attack in 1955, there were grounds for believing the rumor.

When the news of the shooting was received in Washington, the House of Representatives was not in session. The Senate was discussing an amendment to the Library Services Act. Only a few Senators were in attendance. Senator Edward M. Kennedy of Massachusetts, brother of the President, was presiding when Richard L. Riedel, the press liaison officer for the Senate, rushed up to him and said, "Senator, your brother, the President, has been shot." The Senator, exclaiming, "No!" grabbed his papers and quickly left the Senate chamber.[6] Senator Spessard L. Holland of Florida took over as presiding officer and the debate continued. Shortly thereafter, the Senate recessed. Upon the Senate's reconvening, majority leader Mike Mansfield of Montana, joined by minority leader Everett McKinley Dirksen of Illinois, moved that the Senate be adjourned until Monday at noon. Before the adjournment, the leaders called upon Reverend Frederick Brown Harris, the Senate chaplain, for a prayer: "[W]e gaze at a vacant place against the sky, as the President of the Republic goes down like a giant cedar. . . . We pray that in Thy will his life may still be spared. . . . Hold us, we pray, and the people of America, calm and steady and full of faith for the Republic in this tragic hour of our history."[7] Unknown to all present, the fate of John F. Kennedy had already been determined.

John W. McCormack, the seventy-one-year-old Speaker of the House of Representatives and second in the line of succession, was having lunch (as were so many other Americans at that hour) in the House dining room when he received news of the shooting. "My God, my God," he moaned, "What are we coming to?"[8] He hurried to the House press gallery to keep abreast of the news regarding the fallen President.

The Joint Chiefs of Staff were having their regular Friday meeting when news of the shooting reached them. They quickly ran to the nearest television or radio. The situation was no different in the White House. Theodore C. Sorensen, the President's top aide, and McGeorge Bundy, presidential assistant for national security affairs, were, like millions of other Americans, dependent on the television and radio for information about what had happened.

A number of Cabinet members and other key figures in the Kennedy administration were then more than an hour out of Honolulu over the Pacific—almost at the point of no return—en route to Japan for the third annual United States-Japan economic conference. The group included Secretary of State Dean Rusk, Secretary of Treasury Douglas Dillon, Secretary of Labor W. Willard Wirtz, Secretary of Interior Stewart L. Udall, Secretary of Agriculture Orville L. Freeman, Secretary of Commerce Luther H. Hodges, White House Press Secretary Pierre Salinger, Walter Heller, chairman of the President's Council of Economic Advisers, and Robert Manning, Assistant Secretary of State for Public Affairs. Upon learning of the assassination, Dean Rusk ordered the plane to return to the United States.

The President's brother, Attorney General Robert F. Kennedy, was home having lunch with Robert Morgenthau, United States Attorney for the Southern District of New York, and Silvio Mallo, a Morgenthau assistant, when FBI Director J. Edgar Hoover called to tell him about the shooting in Dallas. All the Attorney General or anyone else could do was to pray and hope.

This aching hope that the President would recover practically vanished with the news that "two priests [Reverend Oscar Huber, pastor of near-by Holy Trinity Church, and his assistant, Reverend James Thompson] who were with Kennedy say he is dead of bullet wounds."[9] The priests had just administered the last rites to the President. Then, at 1:36 P.M., C.S.T., Malcolm Kilduff, an assistant White House press secretary, struggled to retain his composure as he announced to members of the press who had gathered at Parkland Hospital: "President John F. Kennedy died at approximately 1 o'clock, Central standard time today here in Dallas. He died of a gunshot wound in the brain. I have no other details regarding the assassination of the President."[10] In answer to a question, Kilduff stated that he had died without regaining consciousness.

This tragic news stunned the nation. The national pulse could hardly be felt. The stock market—always a barometer of the nation's spirits—took a deep plunge. For the first time since August 3, 1933, the Board of Governors of the New York Stock Exchange ordered it closed in mid-session. The American Stock Exchange and the Cotton and Wool Exchanges quickly followed suit. The shock and grief which had so suddenly shrouded the American people could be poignantly seen in the milling of small groups on almost every street corner, in the filling of places of worship to capacity, and in the tear-filled eyes of men and women, young and old.

The feeling of the nation as a result of the tragedy received eloquent expression in the words of its greats.[11] Former President Harry S. Truman said that he "was shocked beyond words at the tragedy that has happened to our country and to President Kennedy's family today. He was an able President, one the people loved and trusted." Former President Dwight D. Eisenhower stated that he "shared the sense of shock and dismay that the entire nation must feel at the despicable act that took the life of the nation's President." He declared that "the entire citizenry of the nation will join as one man in expressing not only their grief but indignation at this act and will stand faithfully behind the Government." President Kennedy "loved America," said the late President Herbert Hoover, "and has given his life for his country." Former Vice-President Richard M. Nixon called the assassination of the President "a terrible tragedy for the nation." "Our country and the entire world will never forget President Kennedy," said Speaker John W. McCormack. House Republican leader Charles A. Halleck of Indiana stated that "the world should know that in this hour of national tragedy, Americans stand together as one—shocked and grieved at this unbelievable news." Senator Mike Mansfield, Senate majority leader, stammered, "This is terrible. I—I can't find the words." "There are some things that are simply incredible," declared Senate minority leader Everett McKinley Dirksen, "and leave one absolutely speechless. This is one of them." Hubert H. Humphrey, then Senate Democratic whip, said: "America has lost a great President. The world has lost a great leader." "The assassin's bullet has stricken a brilliant and dedicated statesman at the very height of his powers," exclaimed Senator Richard B. Russell of Georgia. "It is both shocking and dreadful," stated Senator Barry Goldwater, "that a thing like this could happen in a free country." Chief Justice Earl Warren prayed: "May God protect our nation in this hour of crisis." Adlai E. Stevenson, chief United States delegate to the United Nations, said: "The tragedy of this day is beyond instant comprehension. All of us who knew him will bear the grief of his death to the day of ours. And all men everywhere who love peace and justice and freedom will bow their heads."

A potentially grave crisis now faced the government. It was imperative that its stability be maintained. Whether it would be depended on President Kennedy's Vice-President. Lyndon B. Johnson was notified of the President's death by Kenneth O'Donnell at about 1:20 P.M. Fearful that an international plot or conspiracy directed at himself or Speaker John W. McCormack or President pro tempore Carl Hayden might be in progress, he ordered Kilduff to delay the public announcement until such time as he had left the hospital for Love Air Field on the outskirts of Dallas.[12] Johnson decided to take the presidential oath of office as quickly as possible. It is reported that Johnson conferred by telephone with Attorney General Robert F. Kennedy about taking the presidential oath in Dallas. He was advised to do so.[13] Accordingly, he asked one of his aides to

9

summon his friend, Judge Sarah T. Hughes of the United States District Court for the Northern District of Texas. Judge Hughes, who had been appointed to the federal bench in October, 1961, by President Kennedy, was present at the Trade Mart to listen to President Kennedy's speech when she learned of the shooting. She immediately returned home, and called her Court to make known her whereabouts, at which time she was told by an assistant United States Attorney that Johnson wanted her to proceed to Love Air Field. She arrived a little after 2 P.M. and was handed a piece of paper on which the presidential oath had been transcribed. Mrs. Kennedy arrived a few minutes later, accompanying the body of her husband.

At 2:39 P.M., some ninety-nine minutes after President Kennedy's death, Lyndon B. Johnson, with his right hand raised and his left hand resting on a black leather Bible, uttered these historic words in the Executive Conference Room of the presidential plane, Air Force One: "I do solemnly swear that I will faithfully execute the Office of President of the United States, and will to the best of my Ability, preserve, protect and defend the Constitution of the United States." Judge Hughes, who wept—as did others—as she administered the oath, added, and the President repeated, the words "So help me God." "It seemed that that needed to be said," she later stated.[14] Present at this solemn moment were close to thirty people. Among these were Mrs. Kennedy, Mrs. Johnson, and four close friends of the late President—David Powers, the White House receptionist, Kenneth P. O'Donnell, the President's appointments secretary, Lawrence F. O'Brien, his congressional liaison, and Evelyn Lincoln, his personal secretary. President Lyndon B. Johnson, at fifty-five years of age, thus became the thirty-sixth President of the United States, the eighth by succession.*

Upon taking the oath of office, President Johnson ordered Air Force One back to Washington. The plane took off at about 2:45 P.M. Some of the thoughts that passed through the President's mind

---

* The question of whether a Vice-President becomes "President" upon a President's death continues to plague some citizens. Shortly after Johnson took the presidential oath, Leonard C. Jones, a New Mexico attorney, unsuccessfully requested Attorney General Robert F. Kennedy and the United States Attorney for the District of Columbia to institute a suit to clarify the matter. Finally, in June, 1964, Jones instituted his own suit in the United States District Court for the District of Columbia, seeking an ultimate determination that Johnson's becoming President was unlawful, illegal and unauthorized by the Constitution. The suit was dismissed in September, 1964.

as he traveled back to Washington were later summarized by him as follows:

I recognized that our first great problem was to assure the world that there would be continuity in transition, that our constitutional system would work. I realized the importance of uniting our people at home and asking them to carry forward with the program, so I immediately planned to have the bipartisan leaders come to the White House upon my arrival.[15]

As Air Force One headed eastward, the President was already tackling the momentous task before him. He placed calls to Washington, D.C., asking the members of the Cabinet who were in town and others to meet him at Andrews Air Force Base near Washington. He spoke with the doctors caring for Governor Connally and he called the late President's mother. "I wish to God there was something I could do," he is reported to have said to her.[16] He worked on a brief statement that he intended to make to the nation.

The presidential plane arrived at Andrews Air Force Base at 5:58 P.M., E.S.T. Over a thousand people were on hand to mourn their dead President and to greet their new President. Among them were Attorney General Robert F. Kennedy, Secretary of Defense Robert S. McNamara, the leaders of both Houses of Congress, White House aides, and foreign ambassadors. The President alighted from the plane, and made his first public statement. Still visibly shaken by the events of that fateful day, he said:

This is a sad time for all people. We have suffered a loss that cannot be weighed. For me it is a deep personal tragedy. I know the world shares the sorrow that Mrs. Kennedy and her family bear. I will do my best. That is all I can do. I ask for your help—and God's.[17]

President Kennedy's body was taken to Bethesda Naval Hospital in Maryland for an autopsy. President Johnson proceeded by helicopter to the White House south lawn. In the flight he was accompanied by and had his first official conference as President with Secretary of Defense Robert S. McNamara, Acting Secretary of State George Ball, and McGeorge Bundy, specialist on national security affairs. From there, he walked from the White House to his office suite on the second floor of the Executive Office Building across the street. William D. Moyers, Johnson's top aide in the 1960 campaign and deputy director of the Peace Corps, Walter Jenkins, administrative

11

assistant to Johnson as Vice-President, and George E. Reedy, his press secretary, were already at work.

In the next few hours, President Johnson spoke by telephone with former Presidents Eisenhower, Truman and Hoover, met with the legislative leaders of both parties and some members of the Cabinet to ask for their "united support in the face of the tragedy that has befallen our nation," spoke with FBI director J. Edgar Hoover regarding the investigation of President Kennedy's assassination, and arranged to meet with the Cabinet the following day to ask them to remain in office. At 9:25 P.M., the new President left for his home in Spring Valley, Washington, where he continued to make decisions and telephone people into the late hours of the night. Johnson called Secret Service Chief James Rowley to his home where he told him of the heroism of agent Rufus Youngblood, and suggested that an appropriate award be given him. Sometime that evening he took time to write notes to the three-year-old son and six-year-old daughter of the late President, in which he attempted to explain the meaning of that tragic Friday when a bullet took the life of their father.

The President's constant theme during the early hours following his ascendancy was that he would need the help of all in order "to assure the rest of the world that we did have continuity and assure the people of this country that we expected them to unite."[18] "The first priority," said President Johnson

was to try to display to the world that we could have continuity and transition, that the program of President Kennedy would be carried on, that there was no need for them to be disturbed and fearful that our constitutional system had been endangered. To demonstrate to the people of this country that although their leader had fallen, and we had a new President, that we must have unity and we must close ranks, and we must work together for the good of all America and the world.[19]

The state of world and domestic affairs posed great, though fortunately not critical, problems for the new President. In the foreign sphere, the war in Vietnam, the split in the Communist World between Russia and China, the differences among the countries of the Atlantic Alliance, and problems regarding Cuba, Latin America, and Berlin would have to be dealt with by the President. Curiously enough, the leadership of two staunch allies of the United States, Great Britain and West Germany, had changed hands within the last month. Prime Minister Harold Macmillan of Great Britain had been succeeded by Sir Alec Douglas-Home and Chancellor Konrad Adenauer by Ludwig Erhard. On the domestic front, the major proposals of the Kennedy administration, the civil rights and tax bills, were pigeon-holed in committee. Decisions relating to the new budget had to be made and the annual Economic Report and State of the Union messages had to be prepared. The success of the transition would depend on how President Johnson handled these matters.

Saturday, November 23, 1963 found the new President actively at work in carrying forward the business of government. He arrived at the White House slightly before 9:00 A.M. and spoke briefly with Attorney General Robert F. Kennedy. He then received intelligence briefings from McGeorge Bundy and CIA Director John A. McCone in the highly secret Situation Room in the basement of the White House. Returning to his desk in the Executive Office Building, Johnson conferred separately and at some length with Dean Rusk and Robert S. McNamara. He telephoned FBI Director Hoover about the assassination inquiry.* He spoke with George Meany, President of the AFL-CIO, and with Frederick R. Kappel, President of the American Telephone and Telegraph Company and President of the Business Council, requesting their united support. He conferred briefly with the legislative leaders of both parties, and then met and lunched with former President Dwight D. Eisenhower.

At approximately 2:30 P.M. President Johnson held his first Cabinet meeting.[20] In addition to the heads of the ten executive departments, there were in attendance Adlai E. Stevenson, Jerome B. Wiesner, the President's science adviser, Walter W. Heller, Kermit Gordon, Director of the Budget, Timothy Reardon, a special assistant to the late President, Theodore C. Sorensen, George E. Reedy, Pierre Salinger, and William D. Moyers. The meeting opened with a prayer for the late President. Then Johnson spoke briefly about the events of the last day and asked the group to continue to serve in their present positions. He stressed his need of help from all in the time ahead. In a moving statement, Secretary of State Dean Rusk, speaking in the name of the Cabinet, pledged the full support of its members. He said that all were prepared to serve Johnson as long

---

* Lee Harvey Oswald of Dallas, a twenty-four-year-old warehouse worker and a professed Marxist, had been formally arraigned for the President's murder on Friday evening.

as he should desire. Ambassador Stevenson similarly promised his wholehearted cooperation.

After the meeting, Secretary of Agriculture Orville L. Freeman, Supreme Court Justice Arthur J. Goldberg, and R. Sargent Shriver, Director of the Peace Corps, made calls on the President. Shortly thereafter, Johnson conferred with former President Harry S. Truman in his Executive Office Building suite. One of the President's final visitors that day was Secretary of Labor W. Willard Wirtz. He spent almost two hours with the President in discussion of the railway labor crisis. Johnson left his office for home at 9:15 P.M.

During the course of that first full day in office, the President had also issued a proclamation designating Monday, November 25, the day of President Kennedy's funeral, as a day of national mourning throughout the United States. He had announced that he would meet at 3 P.M. on Sunday, November 24, with Henry Cabot Lodge, United States Ambassador to Vietnam, Dean Rusk, Robert S. McNamara and McGeorge Bundy, to discuss the situation in Vietnam. (The conference had been scheduled by President Kennedy.) He had also announced that he would address a joint session of Congress at 12:30 P.M. on Wednesday, November 27, 1963. Theodore C. Sorensen had been asked to prepare the first draft of that vital speech to Congress. Ambassadors overseas had been requested to remain in their posts, not to submit the usual letters of resignation, and to emphasize the continuity of American foreign policy. Dean Rusk had informed senior officers in the State Department that they should stay on. The President had made visits to Mrs. Kennedy, to the East Room of the White House where President Kennedy's body reposed, and to St. John's Episcopal Church. He had also made a telephone call to the widow of J. D. Tippett, the patrolman killed in the search for the President's murderer.

On Sunday, November 24, 1963, President Johnson's official activities were kept to a minimum. He received the usual intelligence briefing from McGeorge Bundy and CIA Director John A. McCone at his Spring Valley home at 10:00 A.M. He and Mrs. Johnson then attended services at St. Mark's Episcopal Church at 11:00 A.M. At 1:00 P.M., President and Mrs. Johnson rode with Mrs. Kennedy and her children to the Capitol for memorial services in the Rotunda.

Sunday, November 24, found the President asking the entire White House staff to remain on the job. Following the Vietnam meeting in the afternoon, Presss Secretary Pierre Salinger stated that the President had pledged continued United States aid to Vietnam and had called for a "complete unity of purpose" toward that end by all governmental agencies. Johnson left his office for home at 7:10 P.M. That day was marred by the killing of President Kennedy's alleged murderer at the hands of a Dallas nightclub owner, Jack Ruby.

On Monday, November 25, 1963, President Johnson attended the funeral of his predecessor. Despite objections of the Secret Service, he insisted on walking in the funeral march, saying that he would "rather give . . . [his] life than be afraid to give it."[21] Walking with him in the funeral procession were a king, an emperor, a queen, princes, princesses, presidents, chancellors, premiers, prime ministers, foreign ministers, and foreign ambassadors Almost one hundred countries of the world were represented. Late in the afternoon, President Johnson took advantage of the opportunity provided by this historic assemblage of global figures and received the visiting dignitaries (over two hundred in number) in the State Department's eighth-floor reception room. The people of the country and world were witness to this impressive reception by way of television. The President sought to make it clear to the world, through its leaders, that he had been a participant in the Kennedy program and that the new administration was fully committed to it. During the course of the reception he conferred privately with several, including President Charles de Gaulle of France, Prime Minister Lester B. Pearson of Canada, and Premier Hayato Ikeda of Japan. The meeting with de Gaulle, in particular, demonstrated that although there were policy differences between the two countries, these differences were forgotten in time of crisis.

From the reception, the President hurried to the Executive Office Building to meet with over thirty governors who had attended the funeral. In a moving talk, he pledged himself to fight for the civil rights and tax measures of the Kennedy administration and emphasized that "continuity without confusion has got to be our password and has to be the key to our system." Later that evening he spoke with Secretary of Treasury Douglas Dillon, Walter Heller, and Kermit Gordon. They discussed the country's economic problems and the budget which had to be submitted to Congress in January, 1964. That day he also directed the Department of Justice and the

FBI to handle the investigation of all the circumstances surrounding the assassination of President Kennedy and the murder of his alleged assassin. He sent a message to the Armed Forces in which he stated that the "powers and purposes of your country are unchanged. . . ."[22]

Tuesday, November 26, 1963 marked the President's first working day in the White House.* He met with Lawrence F. O'Brien, congressional liaison for President Kennedy, and indicated that Kennedy's legislative priorities would be followed. He spoke by phone with the country's foremost labor and business leaders. He signed his first two bills, which had been passed on Thursday, November 21, after President Kennedy had left for Dallas. One dealt with an increase in the statutory debt ceiling for one year, and the other authorized funds for the Arms Control and Disarmament Agency. He received, throughout the day, various world leaders, including Emperor Haile Selassie I, of Ethiopia, Great Britain's Prime Minister Sir Alec Douglas-Home, President Diosdado P. Macapagal of the Philippines, Prime Minister Ismet Inonu of Turkey, Soviet First Deputy Premier Anastas I. Mikoyan, President Heinrich Lubke and Chancellor Ludwig Erhard of West Germany, and President Eamon de Valera of Ireland. In the afternoon, he was accompanied by Mrs. Kennedy to a reception in the East Room of the White House for almost one hundred Latin American leaders. He said that he fully supported a continuation of the Alliance for Progress, a program inaugurated by President Kennedy. Following this meeting, he issued a report on the Alliance—his first statement on foreign policy.

The continuity of the government was being manifested in other areas. Numerous letters indicating that there would be no changes in American foreign policy were sent to foreign leaders. Ambassador Adlai Stevenson informed the United Nations that the policy of the United States toward the world organization would be unchanged under President Johnson. Said Stevenson: "[T]here will be no 'Johnson policy' toward the United Nations—anymore than there was a 'Kennedy policy.' There was—and is—only a United States policy. . . ."[23] In Congress, the new administration received a vote of confidence when the Senate decided, 57 to 35, to oppose a bill

---

* He was not to move into the White House until December 7.

16

that would have rendered ineffectual a proposed sale of wheat to Russia recommended by the late President. President Johnson requested that the Thanksgiving Proclamation prepared by President Kennedy be read throughout the nation. The effectiveness of Johnson's succession at this point could readily be gauged by the fact that the stock market had returned to normal.

Wednesday, November 27, 1963, was a monumental day in the period of transition from Kennedy to Johnson. President Johnson appeared before a joint session of Congress and, after being introduced by Speaker John W. McCormack, delivered a forceful address on what the nation could expect of his presidency for the remainder of the term. In that address, he asked for the early passage of the civil rights and tax bills, the major measures of President Kennedy's domestic program. He embraced the Kennedy foreign policy, saying he would honor all American commitments "from South Vietnam to West Berlin." The underlying theme was that "this is no time for delay. It is a time for action." President Kennedy had said on January 20, 1961: "Let us begin." President Johnson urged: "[L]et us continue."[24] Throughout the nation and the world the President's words established new confidence. There was now little doubt that the United States was in able hands.

The tempo of activity set in the government during the first few days after President Kennedy's death quickened following President Johnson's address to Congress. On Thursday, November 28, 1963, Johnson went on television with a Thanksgiving message, in which he called for a turn "from this midnight of tragedy" to "a new American greatness."[25] On Friday, November 29, he met with Pakistan's foreign minister Zulfikar Ali Bhutto and Indonesian Defense Minister General Abdul Haris Nasution; with Dr. Glen T. Seaborg, Chairman of the Atomic Energy Commission; with Roy Wilkins, executive secretary of the National Association for the Advancement of Colored People; and with Charles A. Horsky, special assistant for District of Columbia affairs. He issued an executive order whereby Cape Canaveral became Cape Kennedy and announced the appointment of a Special Commission to make a full scale investigation of the assassination. Its members were Chief Justice Earl Warren, as head, Senators Richard B. Russell of Georgia and John Sherman Cooper of Kentucky, Representatives Hale Boggs of Louisiana and Gerald R. Ford of Michigan, Allen W.

Dulles, former director of the CIA, and John McCloy, former disarmament adviser to President Kennedy.* The President also held his first meeting with the Joint Chiefs of Staff.

On Saturday, November 30, 1963, the President called upon all federal departments and agencies for thrift in government, held numerous meetings with members of his staff, and signed two bills into law—one dealing with provisional appropriations for certain governmental agencies, the other with authority for the safeguards program President Kennedy had promised in connection with the nuclear test ban treaty.

The week of December 1 found the President meeting with civil rights leaders, leaders of both parties in the Congress, leaders of the Executive Board of the AFL-CIO, and with members of the Business Council; holding his first meeting of the National Security Council; emphasizing the need for economy in government; obtaining an agreement from Senator Harry Byrd of Virginia, chairman of the Senate Finance Committee, not to stop action on the tax bill and a pledge from Representative Howard W. Smith, chairman of the House Rules Committee, to hold early hearings on the civil rights bill in January; communicating to the United Nations through Stevenson his intention to back President Kennedy's offer to Russia to join in a solar project; awarding Presidential Medals of Freedom to President Kennedy, Pope John XXIII, and former Governor of New York Herbert H. Lehman, posthumously, and thirty others designated under President Kennedy. He announced that he would speak to the United Nations on December 17, 1963, that Chancellor Ludwig Erhard would visit with him at Christmas time and that other leaders would do so early in the new year, and that Secretary of Defense Robert S. McNamara would go to Vietnam to review the military situation. He praised Secretary of State Dean Rusk at a Foreign Service Officers meeting at the State Department and conferred the Atomic Energy Commission Enrico Fermi Award on Robert F. Oppenheimer, former adviser of the Atomic Energy Commission who had lost his security clearance in 1954. President Kennedy's confidants, Pierre Salinger, Kenneth P. O'Donnell, Lawrence F. O'Brien and Theodore C. Sorensen announced that they would continue to serve as long as Johnson wanted them, indicating

---

* The so-called Warren Commission rendered its report to the President in September, 1964, and concluded that Lee Harvey Oswald assassinated President Kennedy and that he acted alone.

that there would, indeed, be little deviation from John F. Kennedy's ideals and purposes.

Two important developments during the week of December 1 were President Johnson's announcement on Tuesday, December 3, to include his possible successor, Speaker John W. McCormack, in key decision-making meetings at the White House and his issuance, on Thursday, December 5, of an arrangement to cover a case of his becoming disabled. Although the President had suffered a heart attack in 1955, medical reports had already been published after President Kennedy's assassination attesting to Johnson's complete recovery and present excellent health.[26] The President's amazing pace from early morning to late at night left little doubt on this point.

As the weeks passed, President Johnson continued to discharge the powers and duties of the presidency with remarkable efficiency. He worked from early in the morning to late in the night, going from one problem to another. One by one the measures of his predecessor became law—the tax bill in February, 1964, and the civil rights bill the following July. New laws on housing, poverty, conservation, wilderness preservation, mass transit and salary increase for federal employees were passed, and the National Defense Education Act was expanded and extended. Many of these programs had been instituted by President John F. Kennedy. It was largely the leadership of President Lyndon B. Johnson which made their passage possible. The effectiveness of the President's leadership was not confined to domestic problems. Riots in Panama and a crisis in Vietnam, where North Vietnamese PT boats attacked an American destroyer, were met with firmness. In outer space, America launched a spacecraft, Ranger 7, which succeeded in reaching the moon and sending back historic pictures of its surface. In the year between November, 1963 and November, 1964, Lyndon B. Johnson so proved his ability to lead the United States that he was nominated by acclamation for the presidency by the Democratic Party in August, 1964, and easily elected by the people to his first full term as President in November, 1964.

Thus, in the United States of America, a shocking event, which would have destroyed the very foundations of some governments of the world and shaken many others, resulted in a smooth and orderly transfer of power. The United States was fortunate, indeed, to have both a Vice-President of Lyndon B. Johnson's capabilities and a recognized rule which made him President upon the death of the President.

The smooth manner in which presidential power changed hands upon the death of President John Fitzgerald Kennedy was not entirely unlike what had happened on seven other occasions in American history. Four times in the last century and three times in this century Presidents had died in office.* Each time a Vice-President became President and led the country safely through the tragedy and crisis of losing its leader.

One wonders what would have happened if on November 22, 1963, President John F. Kennedy had not died—but had lingered on, unconscious for days or even weeks. On several occasions in our history when the President was disabled, the Ship of State simply drifted. Each time the Vice-President stood by powerless while strangers to the helm, as it were, sought to give it direction.

The failure of the Vice-President to assume the presidential responsibilities was due to certain ambiguities in the United States Constitution. As written, the Constitution did not answer these vital questions: What happens when the President of the United States becomes incapable of discharging the powers and duties of his office? Does the Vice-President become President for the remainder of the term or does he merely act as President† for the period of the inability? Who can declare a President disabled? Who can declare the end of the inability? Presidents Dwight D. Eisenhower, John F. Kennedy and Lyndon B. Johnson tried to supply temporary answers by working out informal arrangements with their immediate successors. These arrangements, however, were not adequate as a permanent solution to the problem.

The vice-presidency and the constitutional provisions for presidential succession are usually taken for granted until times of national crisis. At such times they come into focus and their true value is more fully appreciated.

This book is a study of these institutions and how they have functioned in history.

---

* See Appendix A.
† See Appendix B.

20

I. THE BEGINNINGS

(1607–1804)

2

Succession Before the Constitution

*If no use is made of the labors of past ages, the world
must remain always in the infancy of knowledge.*

CICERO

When the Founding Fathers met at Philadelphia in May of 1787
to write the Constitution of the United States, they brought with
them a treasury of political experience including over a century and
a half under various types of colonial governments, twelve years
with their state governments, and eight years of national government under the Articles of Confederation. From this heritage they
selected for their new government those elements which had proven
valuable in their past. The need for executive succession machinery
in case the chief executive should become immobilized was one
thing the past had proven, having been demonstrated time and
again during the colonial years. It is appropriate, therefore, that
this study start with the colonial origins of the vice-presidency and
the succession provision of the Constitution.

Establishment of the Colonies

Private enterprise was perhaps the single most important element
in the establishment of settlements on the North American continent
in the seventeenth century. When the century opened, North America was a vast wilderness populated sparsely by Indians. But through
the activity both of joint-stock trading companies, in which various
individuals pooled resources and distributed risks, and that of individual proprietors, usually court favorites, the making of a great

23

nation began. These trading companies and proprietors obtained charters granting them land in North America and extensive rights and powers within the land granted.

Five of the thirteen original colonies—Virginia, Massachusetts, New York, New Jersey and Delaware—were established under charters granted to trading companies.* Six—Maryland, New Hampshire, North Carolina, South Carolina, Pennsylvania and Georgia —were established under charters given to a single proprietor or a group of proprietors. Two—Rhode Island and Connecticut—were established independently of any legal authorization in the form of a charter, although such authorization was acquired after the Restoration.

As the colonies developed they gradually fell into different categories. One by one the charters of the trading companies and of some proprietors were revoked and the colonies under them royalized. By the mid-eighteenth century, the colonies could be distinguised as royal, proprietary and charter colonies. The royal colonies, which included Virginia, New Hampshire, New York, Massachusetts, New Jersey, North Carolina, South Carolina and Georgia, were administered by the English monarch. Maryland, Pennsylvania and Delaware were the only remaining proprietary colonies. The charter colonies, Rhode Island and Connecticut, remained self-governing.

The Colonial Governor

In each of the thirteen original colonies there was a chief executive (the governor) and, with the exception of Pennsylvania, a bicameral legislature. A governor's council, which acted as an advisory cabinet, the upper house of the legislature and the highest

---

* In the case of New York, New Jersey and Delaware, the trading companies were non-English in origin. In 1621, the States General (the ruling group of the Netherlands) issued to the Dutch West India Company a charter, pursuant to which the colony of New Netherland (which included New York and New Jersey) was formed. In 1642, King Gustavus Adolphus gave a charter to the Swedish West India Company, and New Sweden (or Delaware) was established under it. All three of these colonies eventually came under English control in 1664 when the English took the Dutch holdings for the Duke of York, later King James II. (Peter Stuyvesant had driven the Swedes out of Delaware in 1655 and had taken it for the Dutch.)

court, was found in the various colonies.* The chief distinguishing feature among the colonies was the manner in which the governor was appointed. In the royal colonies he was appointed by the crown and in the proprietary colonies by the proprietor (subject to ratification by the crown after the end of the seventeenth century). Both royal and proprietary governors served at the pleasure of the appointing authority in England, some three thousand miles and an ocean away from the community to be governed. In the chartered colonies of Connecticut and Rhode Island the governor was elected annually by the colonists.

The royal and proprietary governors received a commission, a formal but brief statement of authority, from the crown or proprietor. The manner in which they were to execute that authority was delineated, sometimes at great length, in another document—the instructions.[1] Additional instructions were issued from time to time during the course of an administration.

The arrival of a governor in the colony (usually several months after his appointment) was an occasion for great celebration.[2] Upon arrival he was escorted to the local government building, where he opened and published his commission in the presence of the council and those assembled. Unlike the commission, the instructions were usually considered confidential and, therefore, would not be read in public. It was not uncommon for the chief executive to keep even his council ignorant of certain instructions, although not those articles relating to his powers. "To let the councillors know just what directions he had received from home might provide his opponents ammunition with which to attack his administration."[3] It was good politics to let everyone think he had more power than he actually had. Following the publication of the commission, various oaths were administered to the governor—the usual oath of office, oaths of supremacy and allegiance to the crown, ecclesiastical oaths, and the oath to enforce the various acts of Parliament relating to the colonies, in particular, the Navigation

---

* In the royal and proprietary colonies, the members of the council were chosen by the authorities in England, principally upon the recommendation of the governor. The exceptions were Massachusetts where, after 1691, the council was elected by the local legislature subject to the governor's veto, and Pennsylvania where the governor's nomination was submitted to the council itself. In the self-governing colonies the council was chosen by the voters.

Acts.[4] The governor then administered the oaths to the council. Finally, he issued a proclamation announcing his arrival and inauguration.

In many respects the colonial governor was to the colony what the modern governor is to the state or the President is to the United States. He enforced the laws, appointed persons to civil and military offices, commanded the military and naval forces, granted pardons and reprieves and remitted fines and forfeitures. In the royal and proprietary colonies he had the power to summon, adjourn and dissolve the legislature and, except in Pennsylvania, a power of veto over legislation.

The royal or proprietary governor was the personal representative of the crown or proprietor in the colony, but he was expected to guard the interests of the colonists as well. This dual obligation was expressed by Governor Benning Wentworth of New Hampshire as follows: "My firm attachment to his Maj[tys] Person family & Government challenges my first attention—my next Pursuit shall be the Peace & Prosperity of his Maj[tys] good subjects of this Province."[5] This obligation often put the governor in a difficult position, since the interests of the crown or proprietor often collided with those of the colonists. It is not surprising, therefore, that the history of eighteenth-century colonial America is replete with cases of governors battling with local assemblies regarding the crown's or proprietor's interests. The governor was more often the loser since, with few exceptions, he was dependent upon the assembly for his salary and other finances. This struggle ended with the overthrow of the then existing order in the 1770s.

The Governor's Successor

The necessity of having someone available to act in the governor's place should he become ill, be absent from the colony, die in office, be removed, resign, or be otherwise prevented from discharging his duties was early recognized in the colonies. In Jamestown, Virginia, the first permanent English colony in America, the original government consisted of an executive council appointed by a council of the Virginia Trading Company resident in England. The latter was, in turn, appointed by the crown. The local councillors in the colony elected a president from among themselves and if he resigned or were deposed, as did happen, they chose another president.[6]

This system of plural executive was changed to a single executive after the Virginia Charter of 1609. "One able and absolute governor" assisted by an advisory council of his choice was appointed by the parent council in England, which was thereafter to become a company-appointed council. Sir Thomas West, Lord Delaware (De la Warr), was commissioned for life as first governor of Virginia. Since he was not able to leave England at the time, Sir Thomas Gates was directed to proceed to Virginia to act as ad interim governor. Delaware finally arrived in February, 1610 but he had to return to England in the spring of 1611 due to illness. From then until he died in 1618, Delaware governed Virginia through deputies—Captain George Percy (1611), Sir Thomas Dale (1611), Sir Thomas Gates (1611–1614), Dale again (1614–1616), George Yeardley (1616–1617), and Samuel Argall (1617–1619).[7]

A most significant development occurred in the Plymouth colony.[8] The Pilgrims who landed at Provincetown in 1620 had no charter, as they had been authorized by the Virginia Company to settle in Virginia and had strayed from their course because of bad weather. Consequently, they had to establish a government on their own initiative, and the result was the famous Mayflower Compact, a simple agreement to frame just laws and obey them. It was to serve as the constitution of Plymouth until Plymouth was joined to the Massachusetts Bay Colony in 1691. Plymouth's first governor, Deacon John Carver (who holds the distinction of being the first popularly-elected governor in America), died during the Pilgrims' first winter in America. William Bradford, an energetic young man in his early thirties, was thereupon chosen governor. Since he was recovering from an illness, the Pilgrims selected Isaac Allerton, a shrewd businessman, to assist him. Bradford and Allerton served together as governor and deputy governor, respectively, for many years. Bradford was re-elected thirty times, serving every year except five between 1621 and 1656.

The existence of a deputy governor is also found in the early history of other colonies. The Massachusetts Bay Charter of March 4, 1629, provided for the annual election, by the freemen of the colony, of a governor, deputy governor and eighteen assistants.[9] This charter remained the fundamental law of the Massachusetts Bay Colony until it was annulled in 1684.

The Hartford and New Haven colonies, which united in the 1660s to form the colony of Connecticut, each elected annually a governor and deputy governor. No mention was made of a deputy governor in the Fundamental Orders of Connecticut adopted by the freemen of the towns of Hartford, Windsor and Wethersfield on January 14, 1639. The Orders, the first written American constitution, called for the election of a governor and at least six magistrates to assist him. At the first election under the Orders, the freemen chose one of the six magistrates as deputy governor, and continued to do so thereafter at each annual election.[10] In the New Haven colony, however, the Fundamental Orders of 1643 specifically provided for the annual election of a deputy governor.[11]

When the Rhode Island settlements of Portsmouth and Newport united in 1640, they agreed to be jointly ruled by a governor and deputy governor and four assistants, all to be chosen annually. It was provided that the governor and two assistants must come from one town and the deputy governor and two assistants from another.[12] Under the confederation of 1647 consolidating the settlements of Providence, Newport, Portsmouth and Warwick, from the union of which the colony of Rhode Island was formed, provision was made for a deputy governor.[13]

It was logical, therefore, that the Connecticut Charter of 1662 and the Rhode Island and Providence Plantations Charter of 1663 recognize what had earlier taken place. These charters, obtained from Queen Anne, were to serve as the constitutions of these colonies until many years after the American Revolution. Both specifically provided for the annual election of a governor and deputy governor, and both empowered the deputy governor to act in the "absence of the governor by occasion of sickness, or otherwise by his leave and permission."[14] As an additional safeguard it was provided that the legislature could fill a vacancy occurring in either of these offices. This power was exercised time and again in both colonies.[15] In Connecticut, when Governor John Winthrop died in 1707, Gurdon Saltonstall was selected by the legislature (which was convened by Deputy Governor Robert Treat) to fill the vacancy. Saltonstall subsequently became governor in his own right and when he died in office in 1724, his deputy governor, Joseph Talcott, was selected to fill the vacancy. Jonathan Law was appointed as the interim deputy governor. In 1741 Law was elected governor. Upon his death in office in 1750, deputy Governor Roger Wolcott was chosen by the legislature to fill the vacancy, and Thomas Fitch was appointed to fill the resulting vacancy in the office of deputy governor.

In Rhode Island, when Governor Benedict Arnold died in June,

1678, after several months of illness, William Coddington (then in his late seventies) was selected to fill the vacancy. He died in November, 1678 and John Cranston, who was deputy governor all the while, was appointed to fill the vacancy. James Barker was chosen deputy governor. Other Rhode Island governors who died in office and were replaced include Caleb Carr (1695), Samuel Cranston (1727), William Wanton (1733), John Wanton (1740), and William Greene (1758). Among the deputy governors are Walter Clarke (1714), Jonathan Nichols (1727), George Hassard (1738), Jonathan Nichols (1756), and John Gardner (1764).

In Dutch New York (New Netherland), the chief executive was a director general appointed and instructed by the Dutch West India Company. With Peter Stuyvesant's appointment as director general in 1645, there was also appointed a vice-director, Lubbertus van Dincklage, to be "second to, and first counsellor of, the Director in New Netherland." His commission provided that he was to fill the director's place "in the absence of the said Director" and was "to perform all that a good and faithful Vice Director is bound to do."[16]

Succession in the proprietary colonies must be viewed from two aspects: (1) the demise of the proprietor, and (2) the demise of his appointed representative in the colony. The proprietor possessed supreme political authority, subject to certain limitations, and such authority was passed to his heir upon his death. If he became disabled, the authority might be exercised for him by another. For example, when William Penn, the founder of Pennsylvania, suffered an inability during the last years of his life, his second wife, Hannah, wielded his authority, and continued to do so after his death until his children were of age.*[17]

The actual chief executive of the proprietary colonies was not the proprietor but his appointed deputy or lieutenant. This official (who was many times referred to as deputy or lieutenant governor) was, for all intents and purposes, the governor of the colony (except when the proprietor was present in the colony). The manner of succession to this office followed no fixed lines. Unlike other colonies, there was no office of deputy governor as such. However, many early proprietary commissions permitted the proprietor's appointed deputy to select a substitute should he become disabled, depart from

---

* This role is strikingly similar to that played by the wife of one President upon her husband's disability, as will be seen later in this book, pp. 172–73.

the colony, or be dying. For instance, when Governor Leonard Calvert of Maryland, who was the brother of the proprietor, returned to England in 1643, he deputized a relative, Giles Brent, to act in his place for the time being. When Leonard Calvert was on his deathbed in 1647, he deputized one Thomas Greene, a Catholic royalist, as his successor. Greene was removed in the following year by the proprietor for mishandling certain matters. Greene came into power again when the new governor, William Stone, deputized him before going to Virginia. Stone was quickly forced to return inasmuch as Greene used his newly acquired power to proclaim Charles II heir to the throne of his father, Charles I, at a time when Cromwell and Parliament were in power, a politically inexpedient action under the circumstances.[18]

This method of succession—empowering the governor to deputize a successor—was specifically provided for in the Concessions and Agreements adopted by the New Jersey proprietors in 1664.[19] When Governor Neil Campbell of East Jersey returned to Scotland in 1687, he nominated Andrew Hamilton as his deputy, and Hamilton was thereupon commissioned by the proprietors.[20] Hamilton was replaced by Jeremiah Basse in 1697, and when Basse returned to England in 1699 to consult with the proprietors, he deputized Andrew Bowne, a member of the council.[21] The Carolina proprietors' Concessions and Agreements of 1665 prescribed a similar manner of succession.[22]

In the later proprietary colonies, the death or absence of the proprietor's deputy would often find the senior councillor or president of the council acting as governor until a new governor had been appointed or the incumbent had returned to the colony. Hence, when Governor Andrew Hamilton of Pennsylvania died in 1703, Edward Shippen, the president of the council, served as acting governor for almost a year until the new governor, John Evans, arrived.[23] Similarly, when Governor George Thomas of Pennsylvania resigned in 1746 because of ill health, Anthony Palmer, president of the council, acted as governor until a new one was appointed.[24]

In the royal colonies, the matter of succession came to be carefully prescribed. An office of lieutenant governor was found in some of these colonies, especially in Massachusetts, New Jersey, New York and New Hampshire. Like the governor, the lieutenant governor was commissioned by the crown to hold office at its pleasure. His primary function was to act as governor during the governor's absence or, in case of the death of the governor, until a new governor was appointed and had arrived in the colony. His commission normally provided that:

[I]n case of the Death or absence of the said . . . [Governor], We do hereby authorize and empower you to execute and perform all and singular the Powers and Directions contained in our said Commission to the said . . . [Governor], and such Instructions as are already or hereafter shall, from time to time be sent unto him, so nevertheless, that you observe and follow such orders and Directions as you shall receive from us, and from the said . . . [Governor], or any Chief Governor of our said Province of . . ., for the time being.[25]

The arrival of a lieutenant governor in the colony usually was not an occasion for great celebration. He took the required oaths of office and took up the meager duties of his office, depending, as it happened, upon the governor for work. He was at times, but not always, a member of the governor's council. If he was a member, it was the rule in the royal colonies that he preside over it when the council sat as the upper house of the legislature.[26] The question, whether he could sit with the council by virtue of his office without being elected to it, was raised in Massachusetts in the year 1732.[27] In that year, Governor Jonathan Belcher successfully prevented his lieutenant governor, William Phips, from sitting with the council, of which he was not a member by election. Phips probably had the law in his favor. The intent of the Massachusetts Charter of 1691 seems to have been that the lieutenant governor be an ex-officio member of the council. The first lieutenant governor, William Stoughton, had sat with the council without being a member, and since 1693, it had been customary for the lieutenant governor to sit with the council and to have a vote if he were elected.

The system of succession largely in operation throughout the royal colonies received formal expression in the Massachusetts Charter of 1691 as well as under individual royal commissions. The charter provided for a governor and lieutenant governor, and empowered the lieutenant governor to act as governor, in the event of the governor's death, removal or absence, until a new governor arrived or the governor returned.[28] In a case where both the governor and lieutenant governor had died, been removed, or were absent, and there was no other person in the colony commissioned to be governor, the charter provided that the council was to have the "full power and authority" of a governor or lieutenant governor as if either were present, administering the government until a new governor arrived or the governor returned.

In those royal colonies where the office of lieutenant governor was not filled, the early royal commissions allowed the council to deputize someone upon the governor's death or absence.[29] Then, this was changed to let the council itself take over.[30] In a case where the council succeeded to the reins of government,* it was usual for the senior councillor resident in the colony to preside. Not surprisingly, disputes arose over the extent of his authority. To clarify this situation, Queen Anne issued a special instruction in 1707, providing that in the absence or death of both the governor and lieutenant governor, the eldest councillor then in the colony should administer the government.[31] He was charged with executing the governor's powers, as set forth in the governor's commission and instructions. It was a while before this special instruction was followed. In Massachusetts, however, the instruction was disregarded entirely, the council taking the position that the charter of 1691 placed the right of government in the council as a whole. In the 1720's, certain limitations were placed upon a councillor who acted as governor. He could not pass any acts not immediately necessary, dissolve the legislature, or remove any officers without the consent of a certain number of councillors. When he took over, he was required to give prompt notice of that fact to the crown.[32]

The history of the royal colonies is replete with examples of lieutenant governors and councillors acting as governor when governors were absent from the colony, resigned for reasons of health, were removed, or died in office.† It has been said that of the one-hundred-thirty governors whose service had ended before the beginning of the revolution, forty, or one-third, died in office.[33] The procedures on succession functioned to meet these situations and, in general, worked effectively. On occasion, however, disputes arose, some of which are noted below.

During the period when Maryland was under royal control (1692–1716), this interesting situation arose.[34] Maryland's first royal governor, Sir Lionel Copley, was an invalid and was assisted

---

* The Council's authority was limited to the performance of such acts as were immediately necessary.

† The average length of a governor's service was approximately five years.

by Lieutenant Governor Francis Nicholson. When Copley died in 1693, Nicholson was in England. Sir Edmund Andros, who was then Governor of Virginia, seized control of the government. He claimed that a royal commission permitted him to act in such cases, since it empowered him to act as governor of Maryland if the lieutenant governor had died and the governor was absent. A question arose in the assembly as to the validity of his action. It was maintained that his commission did not embrace the case of the governor's dying and the lieutenant governor's being absent. Notwithstanding, his decisive action in taking over appears to have been accepted. Shortly thereafter, Andros left Maryland to return to England, leaving the government in the hands of Nicholas Greenbury, president of the council. Lieutenant Governor Nicholson returned to the colony the following year (1694) and relieved Greenbury of the administration of the government.

When the Earl of Bellomont, Governor of New York, died in 1701, Lieutenant Governor John Nanfan was absent from the province and the eldest councillor, William Smith, was also unavailable. The councillors on hand issued a proclamation confirming all civil and military officers in their places and sent messages of Bellomont's death to the other councillors. Abraham De Peyster, the eldest councillor present, was selected to act as president of the council until the lieutenant governor or eldest councillor should arrive. Smith arrived and sought to act as chief executive but certain councillors took the position that he was powerless without the council. A governmental crisis ensued, which was not resolved until Lieutenant Governor Nanfan returned to the colony.[35]

For periods of time the crown experimented with having the same person as governor of more than one colony. This caused some confusion as to the status of the lieutenant governor of a particular colony when such a governor was not physically present in that colony. The question arose during the tenure of Edward Hyde, Lord Cornbury, as governor of both New York and New Jersey.* As Cornbury spent most of his time in New York, it was suggested that the lieutenant governor of New Jersey, Colonel Ingoldsby, should act in Cornbury's absence. Cornbury, however, was of a different opinion. He held to the view that when he was in New York, he

---

* New Jersey became a royal colony in 1702, but until 1738, when Lewis Morris of Monmouth County was appointed governor, it had the same governor as New York.

was to be regarded as legally present in both colonies. Since Cornbury was a strong individual, he prevailed in the struggle.[36]

A similar conflict took place in the New England colonies of Massachusetts and New Hampshire. Until 1741, these colonies had the same governor and he usually resided in Boston. He visited New Hampshire for brief periods and in the event of a conflict of interest between the two colonies, he usually sided with Massachusetts. It was said of the administration of Joseph Dudley: "He adopted a mode of administration for New Hampshire, which promoted his profit without disturbing his ease."[37] In 1703, during the reign of Queen Anne, Lieutenant Governor John Usher of Massachusetts sought to remove some civil and military officials for disloyalty to the crown and incompetency. He wrote to the governor, Joseph Dudley, who resided in Boston, for authority to make the removals. Dudley suggested that Usher act cautiously, remarking that " 'where there are so few persons fit for public business we must drive as we can.' "[38] Usher subsequently attempted to remove one Captain Hincks. Dudley replied to Usher that he would sign all commissions ("lest there be a quarrel between officers of two sorts," said Dudley). Dudley further stated that any request he had to make would reach Usher within twenty-four hours. The perplexed Usher complained to the authorities in England, declaring that his commission was a mere cipher, that the position of lieutenant governor meant nothing, and that he was seldom consulted by Dudley concerning New Hampshire. Usher's complaints, however, were to no avail.[39]

A similar dispute arose during the administration of Governor Samuel Shute.[40] Lieutenant Governor George Vaughan, a resident of New Hampshire, had acted as governor for a year before Shute's arrival in the colony. Vaughan took the position that he was to act as governor whenever the governor was absent from New Hampshire. Shute disagreed, stating that he was legally present in both New Hampshire and Massachusetts when present in either. Vaughan brought the matter to a head by acting in disregard of Shute's orders and by suspending one of the councillors. Thereupon, Shute returned to New Hampshire and suspended Vaughan. The suspension was approved by the assembly.

The same controversy was to recur again in New Hampshire during the administration of Governor Jonathan Belcher and Lieutenant Governor David Dunbar.[41] In every such case the governor prevailed.

Although the lieutenant governor may have been at times a discordant element in the provincial constitution and although his office may generally have been of little importance,[42] its usefulness in maintaining the continuity of government upon the governor's demise or absence was demonstrated time and again.

Succession on a National Scale

As the colonies moved toward unity, the subject of executive succession was not overlooked. In June, 1754, commissioners from nine colonies met in Albany to discuss Indian affairs and military activities. In the course of this meeting they adopted a plan of union proposed by Benjamin Franklin, calling for the creation of a Grand Council consisting of delegates chosen by the colonial assemblies and a President General appointed by the crown. It was provided in one section of the Albany Plan of Union that:

[I]n case of the Death of the President General the Speaker of the Grand Council for the time being shall succeed and be vested with the same powers and authorities & continue till the Kings [sic] pleasure be known.[43]

The Albany Plan of Union, however, was unanimously rejected by the colonial assemblies. They were not yet ready to subject themselves to an intercolonial government.

The surge toward independence from England and toward an intercolonial government gained momentum in the 1770s, starting with the Continental Congresses of 1774 and 1775 and receiving expression in the Declaration of Independence of 1776 and the Articles of Confederation of 1781. The Articles, the first Constitution of the United States, set up a national government under which the full authority was entrusted to the Continental Congress. A great weakness of the Articles was the lack of any specific provision for executive authority. They merely authorized Congress to create such "committees and civil officers as may be necessary for managing the general offices of the United States under their direction." Although Congress was permitted to appoint one of its members to preside over it as "President," he was to be little more than a presiding officer, serving for no more than one term of one year in any three years. The lack of any effective executive machinery and the fact that each of the colonies (or states) retained almost complete sovereignty doomed the first written constitution of the United States.

First State Constitutions

On the local level, changes took place in the governmental structure of the various colonies following the Declaration of Independence. The Second Continental Congress had suggested to the colonies in May of 1776 that they form independent state governments.* Accordingly, all of the colonies, with the exceptions of Connecticut and Rhode Island, adopted constitutions—the first state constitutions. The experience of a century and a half of colonial government was not discarded in these constitutions, but was reflected in them in one way or another.

Externally, the government set up by the new state constitutions continued to be the same—a governor, a legislature and a judiciary. A bicameral legislature was formed in all but two of the states (Georgia became bicameral in 1789 and Pennsylvania in 1790). The great distrust and hatred of autocratic rulers which the colonists had acquired clearly showed up in the provisions relating to the chief executive.†

The first state governors were, in most important respects, made subordinate to the legislature. In eight states, he was chosen by the legislature.‡ In four of the five states (Connecticut, Massachusetts, New Hampshire and Rhode Island) where he was elected directly, he had to obtain a majority of the votes. Otherwise, the election would be by the legislature. In ten states, his term of office was limited to one year; in two, to three years; and in one, to two years. In some states his veto power was made subject to a simple majority vote of the legislature. In others, it was eliminated (e.g., the Carolinas), while in another, it had to be shared with a council (New

---

* New Hampshire and South Carolina had adopted constitutions earlier that year.

† He was referred to as "President" in Delaware, New Hampshire and Pennsylvania, and also in the South Carolina Constitution of 1776 but not in that of 1778.

‡ In Pennsylvania, executive power was given to a council of twelve of which one would be elected "President" by joint vote of the council and the assembly.

36

York). His power of appointment was sharply curtailed, with provisos for appointments by the legislature or council.

Despite the relatively weak chief executive created by these constitutions,[44] the position of the governor was still important enough to render essential adequate safeguards for succession. All the state constitutions had succession provisions. Examining those provisions is important for the light they cast on the meaning of the succession provision of the United States Constitution.

The succession contingencies varied somewhat. The constitutions of North Carolina, Delaware and Virginia covered the contingencies of death, absence from the state and inability; Pennsylvania and New Jersey, only absence; Maryland, death, resignation, and absence from the state; New York and South Carolina, death, resignation, absence from the state, impeachment and removal from office; New Hampshire and Massachusetts, death, absence from the state and "otherwise"; Georgia, absence or sickness; and Rhode Island and Connecticut (in their charters) absence of the governor by occasion of sickness, or "otherwise by his leave and permission."[45] Most significantly, succession upon the occurrence of any of these contingencies was, in almost all the states, to the governor's powers and duties, not to his office, for a limited tenure. South Carolina's constitution was unique in its provision that the lieutenant governor of the state was to "succeed" to the governor's "office" upon the occurrence of any of the contingencies mentioned.

The immediate successor to the governor also varied. In Connecticut, Rhode Island, New York and Massachusetts he was a lieutenant (or deputy) governor elected by the people at the same time as the governor, while in South Carolina, he was a lieutenant governor chosen by the legislature at the same time as the governor. With regard to the office of lieutenant governor created by these constitutions, only the Massachusetts and South Carolina constitutions were specific that its occupant must have the same qualifications as the governor. In New York, he was made ex-officio president of the upper house, with a tie-breaking vote, and in Massachusetts, he was designated a member of the governor's council, but without any vote. The President of the privy (or executive) council was named the immediate successor in Virginia and Georgia,* the vice-president with the council in Pennsylvania, the first

* The council was chosen by the legislature and the president by the council.

named of the council in Maryland,* the presiding officer (speaker) of the upper house of the legislature in Delaware and North Carolina, the senior senator in New Hampshire,† and the vice president of the legislative council in New Jersey.

Several state constitutions specifically provided for more than one successor to the governor. New York ran the line of succession to the president pro tempore and speaker; South Carolina, to a lieutenant governor appointed by the council from its membership; and Delaware and North Carolina, to the speaker of the lower house.

Conclusion

In all the pre-Constitution influences considered, temporary succession was the usual rule. In no case (with the possible exception of the South Carolina state constitution) did the successor permanently displace the chief executive unless there was a permanent vacancy in the office (and even then the succession was often temporary). It cannot be doubted that this pre-Convention practice influenced the delegates to the Constitutional Convention when they wrote the succession provision of the Constitution of the United States.

---

* The council was chosen by the legislature.

† The governor (or president) presided over the Senate and had the power to cast tie-breaking votes.

3

The Succession Provision of the Constitution

*I agree to this Constitution with all its faults, . . . be-
cause . . . I doubt . . . whether any other Convention
we can obtain may be able to make a better Constitution.*

BENJAMIN FRANKLIN

In the autumn of 1786 the Annapolis Convention, to which five
states sent delegates to discuss trade regulation, proposed that a
convention of the states meet at Philadelphia the following May to
"devise such . . . provisions as shall . . . render the constitution of the
federal government adequate to the exigencies of the Union. . . ."[1]
On February 21, 1787, pursuant to this recommendation, the Continental Congress resolved that such a convention be held "for the
sole and express purpose of revising the Articles of Confederation,
and reporting to Congress and the several legislatures such altera-
tions and provisions therein as shall, when agreed to in Congress
and confirmed by the states, render the federal constitution adequate to the exigencies of government and the preservation of the
Union."[2] Every state, with the exception of Rhode Island, appointed
delegates to attend. In all, seventy-four delegates were named, but
only fifty-five attended. These men included many of the most
prominent and influential of the day. Among them were George
Washington, James Madison and Edmund Randolph of Virginia,
Alexander Hamilton of New York, Benjamin Franklin, Gouverneur
Morris and James Wilson of Pennsylvania, Elbridge Gerry and
Rufus King of Massachusetts, the two Charles Pinckneys and John
Rutledge of South Carolina, Oliver Ellsworth and Roger Sherman

39

of Connecticut, William Paterson of New Jersey and John Dickinson of Delaware. Thomas Jefferson, who was on a diplomatic mission to Paris at the time, referred to the group as "an assembly of demi-gods."

The great majority (about thirty-six) of the delegates were lawyers.[3] There were at least four lawyers each from Delaware, New Jersey, Pennsylvania and Virginia, and at least two each from all the other states except New Hampshire and Rhode Island. Most of the delegates had been active in the government and politics of their states. "The list included thirty-nine former members of Congress, eight signers of the Declaration of Independence, twenty-one veterans of the Revolutionary War, seven who had been governors of states, and eight who had aided in the framing of state constitutons."[4]

The Convention

The Convention was scheduled to meet on the second Monday of May, which was the fourteenth. By that date only a few of the delegates had reached the old brick State House in Philadelphia where the sessions were to be held, so that the opening session was delayed until May 25 when nine states were represented. At that session General George Washington was unanimously chosen presiding officer of the Convention and certain rules of procedure were adopted. Each state was to have one vote, and it was agreed that no reporters would be permitted to attend and that the proceedings of the Convention should be kept secret. The purpose of secrecy was to encourage complete freedom of debate and protect the delegates from outside criticism and pressure. A secretary, William Jackson, was appointed to keep an official journal of what took place. As it turned out, this journal was a mere skeleton of what occurred at the Convention. The proceedings can be reconstructed with accuracy only because of the labors of one of its most brilliant and industrious members, James Madison. He kept his own record of the proceedings, in which he noted all motions, arguments and votes. His so-called "Notes" were not published until 1840, four years after the government purchased them upon his death in 1836. Until their publication, the nation had to depend almost exclusively on the *Journal of the Convention*, published in 1819, a brief and, unfortunately, in some respects inaccurate work.

On May 29 the first plan for a national government was submitted to the Convention when Edmund Randolph of Virginia, a former attorney general, governor of his state, and a member of the Continental Congress, presented his state's fifteen resolutions (the Virginia Plan). This plan, couched in terms enlarging the Articles, seems to have been the work of James Madison. In effect, it recommended the creation of a strong national government consisting of an executive, a two-house legislature and a judiciary. One house of the legislature was to consist of representatives elected by the people of the various states. This house, in turn, would choose the members of the second house from nominations made by the state legislatures. The executive was to be chosen by Congress. His term was not specified and he was not to be eligible for re-election. The plan contained no provision on succession. On the following day, the Convention resolved itself into a Committee of the Whole so that it could discuss the Virginia Plan point by point, informally and freely.

On the same day that the Virginia Plan was introduced, Charles Pinckney offered his plan of government. Although the original of Pinckney's plan has never been found, it is understood as having called for a strong national government. To what extent, if any, the plan contained a provision on executive succession is in much doubt. Most writers on the subject of presidential succession have assumed that the plan did have such a provision.[5] The background seems to be this: In 1818, when John Quincy Adams, then Secretary of State, was preparing the *Journal of the Convention,* he could not find any copy of Pinckney's plan among his papers. Consequently, he wrote to Pinckney and asked him for a copy of the original. Pinckney replied, sending a draft which included the following succession provision:

In the case of his [the President's] removal death resignation or disability The President of the Senate shall exercise the duties of his office until another President be chosen—& in case of the death of the President of the Senate the Speaker of the House of Delegates, shall do so—[6]

After this draft was published as part of the Convention Records in 1819, the similarity between it and the Constitution, as adopted, became manifest. James Madison expressed his views on the matter as follows:

On comparing the paper with the Constitution in its final form, or in some of its stages, and with the propositions and speeches of Mr. Pinckney in the Convention, it was apparent that considerable error had

41

crept into the paper, occasioned possibly by the loss of the document laid before the Convention . . . and by a consequent resort for a copy to the rough draught, in which erasures and interlineations, following what passed in the Convention, might be confounded, in part at least, with the original text, and, after a lapse of more than thirty years, confounded also in the memory of the author.

There is in the paper a similarity in some cases, and an identity in others, with details, expressions, and definitions, the results of critical discussions and modification in the Convention, that could not have been anticipated.[7]

Those who have studied the subject of Pinckney's plan have attempted to reconstruct the original, based on the views expressed by Pinckney during the Convention and immediately thereafter.[8] As reconstructed, the plan contains no succession provision.

The Pinckney Plan, like the Virginia Plan, was referred to the Committee of the Whole. From May 30 to June 13 the delegates concentrated primarily on the Virginia Plan, reporting it out of committee on June 13, in amended form. The small states objected to its provision for proportional representation in both houses of Congress. Discussion of the plan was then briefly postponed so that another plan could be offered to the Convention. On June 15, William Paterson of New Jersey submitted to the Committee of the Whole the New Jersey Plan of government. Under it, the Articles were to be amended in various particulars. The power of Congress was to be enlarged but the national government was not to be sovereign. There would be a unicameral legislature in which each state would have one vote and a judiciary consisting of a supreme tribunal. The plan called for a plural executive to be elected by Congress. The executive was to be ineligible for a second term and removable by Congress on application by a majority of the executives of the several states. There was no provision on executive succession.

On June 18, Alexander Hamilton of New York, a leading advocate of a strong national government, advanced a brief sketch of his frame of government which was patterned after the England of George II. "He had no scruple in declaring . . . that the British government was the best in the world," "and he doubted much whether any thing short of it would do in America."[9] His national executive was to be chosen by electors and was to serve for life. Provision was made for succession in the event of his death, resignation, impeachment, removal, and absence from the country:

The Succession Provision

The President of the Senate shall be vice President of the United States. On the death, resignation, impeachment, removal from office, or absence from the United States, of the President thereof, the Vice President shall exercise all the powers by this Constitution vested in the President, until another shall be appointed, or until he shall return within the United States, if his absence was with the Consent of the Senate and Assembly.[10]

Hamilton's plan seems to have received little serious consideration by the delegates and was never formally discussed. The New Jersey Plan was rejected on June 19, by a vote of seven to three, with one state divided, and discussion of the Virginia Plan was resumed. During the next few weeks, the question of representation in the legislature was the main subject of discussion. By July 16, by a vote of five to four, with one state divided, the Convention had accepted the idea of two houses, with proportional representation in the lower and equal representation in the upper.

On July 23, a Committee of Detail was formed and given the responsibility of considering the matters that had been discussed up to that time. Its members were John Rutledge, Edmund Randolph, Nathaniel Gorham of Massachusetts, Oliver Ellsworth, and James Wilson.[11] On July 24, the Committee of the Whole was discharged and the various plans of government were referred to the Committee of Detail. When the Convention adjourned on July 26 to allow the Committee of Detail to work on its report, the selection of the executive by the legislature seemed to have been agreed upon (the selection by presidential electors having been rejected on that day).

After considering everything which had thus far taken place in the Convention and after undoubtedly taking into account their previous colonial, state and national experiences in the art of government, the Committee presented its report on August 6. It provided for a national executive to be elected by the legislature and it included in Article X, section 2, the following succession provision:

In case of his [the President's] removal as aforesaid, death, resignation, or *disability* to discharge the powers and duties of his office, the President of the Senate *shall exercise those powers and duties, until another President of the United States be chosen, or until the disability of the President be removed.*[12] (Italics added.)

It bears noting that among the Committee's papers were found the following notes: A note in the handwriting of John Rutledge provided that "the Presidt of ye Senate to succeed to the Executive in Case of (death) Vacancy untill the Meeting of the Legisle. . . ."[13] One in the handwriting of James Wilson stated that:

In Case of his Impeachment, (Dismission) [Removal], Death, Resignation or Disability to discharge the Powers and Duties of his (Department) [Office]; the President of the Senate shall exercise those Powers and Duties, until another President of the United States be chosen, or until the President impeached or disabled be acquitted, or his Disability be removed.[14]

The parts in parentheses were stricken out in the originals, and the bracketed words in the latter note were added by Wilson. Both notes serve to show that the Committee of Detail regarded succession by the President of the Senate as being of a temporary nature and, in the case of inability, until the inability was removed—and not longer.

The Committee's draft was the subject of discussion for the next five weeks. Succession was not discussed until August 27.[15] On that day, Gouverneur Morris objected to the President of the Senate being the "provisional successor" to the President. He suggested instead the Chief Justice of the United States. James Madison believed that if the President of the Senate were next in line, the Senate might delay the appointment of the President of the United States so that it could "carry points whilst the revisionary power was in the President of their own body." Madison's recommendation was that during a vacancy the "Executive powers" should be administered by persons constituting a council to the President.* Hugh Williamson of North Carolina then suggested "that the Legislature ought to have power to provide for occasional successors. . . ." Thereupon, he asked that the question be postponed. John Dickinson, in seconding the motion for postponement, remarked that Article X, section 2 of the Committee's report was "too vague." "What is the extent of the term 'disability,' " he asked, and "who is to be the judge of it?" Unfortunately, these questions were never answered but they were to become of critical importance to the young country in its future.

On August 31, a number of matters, including succession, were

---

* There was current at the time a suggestion of a council to the President consisting of the Speaker, the President of the Senate, the Chief Justice, and the heads of certain executive departments.

referred to a Committee of Eleven which was commissioned to report on those parts of the Constitution that had been postponed or not acted upon. Its members, over half of whom were lawyers, were Abraham Baldwin of Georgia, David Brearley of New Jersey, Pierce Butler of South Carolina, Daniel M. Carroll of Maryland, John Dickinson of Delaware, Nicholas Gilman of New Hampshire, Rufus King of Massachusetts, James Madison of Virginia, Gouverneur Morris of Pennsylvania, Roger Sherman of Connecticut and Hugh Williamson of North Carolina.[16] New York was unrepresented on the committee, since Hamilton was absent and Robert Lansing and John Yates had left the Convention on July 10 to return to New York.

On September 4, the Committee presented through its chairman, David Brearley, a partial report.[17] The report was remarkable in its provisions for the creation of an office of Vice-President and the election of both the President and Vice-President by an electoral college. The President and Vice-President were to be chosen by electors who, in turn, were to be chosen in such manner as the state legislatures might establish.

The electoral college system was to work in this manner: The electors were to meet in their respective states and vote for two persons for President. The person who received the greatest number of votes would be President provided such number were a majority of the number of electors. Since each elector had two votes, it was possible for more than one person to have a majority. For example, if there were thirteen electors, they could cast a total of twenty-six votes. Since a majority of thirteen is seven, there could be three persons with a majority. If more than one person had such a majority, and they had an equal number of votes, then the Senate (the House in the Constitution as adopted), would choose one of them for President by ballot. If no one had a majority, the Senate would choose the President from the five highest on the list. The Vice-President would be the person having the greatest number of votes after the President had been chosen. If more than one had such number, the Senate would choose the Vice-President from among them.

The Committee's report specified that the Vice-President was to be ex-officio President of the Senate, except in case of impeachment of the President, when the Chief Justice was to preside, and except when the Vice-President exercised the "powers and duties" of the President. In cases of the Vice-President's absence, the Senate was to choose a President pro tempore. The report further provided that:

[I]n case of his [the President's] removal as aforesaid, death, absence, resignation or inability to discharge the powers or duties of his office, *the vice-president shall exercise those powers and duties until another President be chosen, or until the inability of the President be removed.*[18] (Italics added.)

After the report had been made, several delegates commented on it.*[19] Nathaniel Gorham of Massachusetts objected to the lack of a requirement that the Vice-President have a majority, stating that a "very obscure" man could be elected. Roger Sherman commented that the object of the provision for an electoral college was to make the President independent of the Congress. He felt that the possibility of "obscure characters" becoming President was remote in view of the provision that the choice was to be made from the five highest candidates. Madison feared that under the provision the attention of the electors would not be directed to making a definite choice. He believed that the election would probably be "consigned" to the Senate altogether. James Wilson, an able lawyer from Pennsylvania, thought, as did others, that the mode of election would eliminate cabal and corruption. "Continental Characters," he said, would multiply as the country grew. Further discussion of the committee's report was postponed until September 7 when the subjects of the vice-presidency and succession occupied full attention.

The September 7 session opened with a motion by Edmund Randolph to add the following clause to the report:

The Legislature may declare by law what officer of the U.S.—shall act as President in case of the death, resignation, or disability of the President and Vice-President; and such officer shall act accordingly *until the time of electing a President shall arrive.*[20]

James Madison objected to the inclusion of the italicized words on the grounds that they would prevent the filling of a vacancy by means of a special election. Accordingly, he moved to substitute

---

* James McHenry of Maryland recorded in his notes for September 4 that there was "no provision . . . for a new election in case of the death or removal of the President." 2 The Records of the Federal Convention of 1787, at 504 (Farrand ed. 1911) (Yale University Press).

the words "until such disability be removed, or a President shall be elected."[21] Some of the delegates objected because they thought it would be difficult to hold an election other than at the fixed periods. Others objected to the motion since it would limit the Congress to appointing only officers of the United States while it should be at liberty to appoint other successors. Randolph's motion, as amended by Madison, was carried by a vote of six to four, with one state divided. The delegates then turned their attention to the vice-presidency, concentrating on his position as President of the Senate and its relation to the principle of separation of powers.[22]

Elbridge Gerry thought that the office, as proposed (i.e., combining the functions of succeeding to the presidency and presiding over the Senate), violated the principle of separation of powers by permitting executive interference in the Legislature and was therefore against having a Vice-President. Gouverneur Morris dismissed this objection, arguing that the Vice-President could be expected to be independent of the President ("the vice-President then will be the first heir apparent that ever loved his father"). He added that "if there should be no vice president, the President of the Senate would be temporary successor which would amount to the same thing."[23] Roger Sherman was concerned that, without a Vice-President, some member of the Senate would be deprived of his vote, except in cases of ties, by being made President of the Senate. He also felt that the Vice-President "would be without employment" if he were not President of the Senate. Edmund Randolph concurred in opposition to the clause that the Vice-President be President of the Senate. Hugh Williamson of Delaware stated that "such an officer as Vice-President was not wanted. He was introduced," said Williamson, "only for the sake of a valuable mode of election which required two to be chosen at the same time."[24] George Mason of Virginia, an authority on matters of public law, viewed the vice-presidency as an encroachment on the rights of the Senate—as mixing "too much the Legislative and Executive."[25] At the conclusion of these debates, the clause providing that the Vice-President be President of the Senate was approved by a vote of eight to two. New Jersey and Massachusetts voted against it, North Carolina abstained, and New York was absent. What is surprising is that the delegates gave little attention "to the chief part which the Vice-President has, in fact, played in history, that is, to his succession in case of the death of the President."[26]

On September 8, a committee was formed to "revise the style of and arrange the articles agreed to by the House." All its members were lawyers—Alexander Hamilton, William S. Johnson of Connecticut, Rufus King, James Madison and Gouverneur Morris.[27] This so-called Committee of Style was given no power to effect substantive change in the matters submitted to it. On Wednesday, September 12, the committee returned a draft to the Convention which, except for a few changes, was to become the Constitution of the United States. When the draft submitted to the Committee is compared with the draft returned to the Convention, it becomes evident that in the process of revising and arranging some confusing changes were made in the provisions relating to presidential succession.

As submitted:[28]	As returned:[29]
Sec. 2: [I]n case of his removal as aforesaid, death, *absence,* resignation or inability to discharge the powers or duties of his office the Vice President *shall exercise those powers and duties until another President be chosen, or until the inability of the President be removed.*	In case of the removal of the president from office, or of his death, resignation, or inability to discharge the powers and duties of the said office, *the same shall devolve* on the vice-president, and the Congress may by law provide for the case of removal, death, resignation or inability, both of the president and vice-president, declaring what officer shall then act as president, and such officer shall act accordingly, *until the disability be removed, or the period for chusing another president arrive* (Italics added).
Sec. 1: The Legislature may declare by law what officer of the United States shall act as President in case of the death, resignation, or *disability* of the President and Vice President; *and such Officer shall act accordingly, until such disability be removed, or a President shall be elected* (Italics added).	

Thus, two separately positioned clauses were joined and the following changes were made: (1) the "absence" contingency was dropped and the term "inability" was substituted for "disability"; (2) the words "the same shall devolve on the vice-president" were substituted for "the Vice-President shall exercise those powers and duties"; (3) the clause "until such disability be removed, or a President shall be elected," which had appeared, in substance, after both the Vice-President and "other successor" clauses, now appeared only after the latter as "until the disability be removed, or the period for chusing another president arrive."

Why these changes? Only guesses and surmises are possible. The "absence" contingency was probably dropped because the Committee felt that it was included in "inability." The words "inability" and "disability" appear to have been used interchangeably. The definitions of these words in Dr. Samuel Johnson's famous *Dictionary* of 1755 suggest that "disability" was more restrictive in the situations it covered than "inability." "Disability" was defined as "want of power *to do anything*." "Inability" was defined as "want of power."

There is no clue in the proceedings of the Convention regarding the type of situations intended to be covered by the term "inability." It is suggested that it was intended to be subject to a broad construction, covering all circumstances which might cause a President to be "unable" to discharge the powers and duties of his office, such as mental and physical illness, coma, kidnapping, wartime capture, and so on. The position that a particular "inability" might subject the President to impeachment received some support at the Convention. In July, James Madison had spoken out in favor of including a provision for impeachment in the Constitution because "he thought it indispensable that some provision be made for defending the Community against the incapacity, negligence or perfidy of the chief Magistrate. . . . In the case of the Executive Magistracy which was to be administered by a single man, loss of capacity was more within the compass of probable events, and either of them might be fatal to the Republic."[30] Gouverneur Morris added that "corrupting his electors, and incapacity, were other causes of impeachment. For the latter he should be punished not as a man, but as an officer, and punished only by degradation from his office."[31] Some authorities have asserted, without either referring to or explaining these statements, that a case of inability is not impeachable.[32]

The change of the wording in clause (3) above appears to have been an oversight on the part of the Committee. As will be recalled, the words "until . . . the period for chusing another president arrive," which would prevent a special election, had been rejected on September 7 and in lieu thereof the words "until . . . a President shall be elected" had been inserted. The Convention noticed this error on September 15 and reinserted the words which had been

49

agreed upon.[33] As noted, this clause had appeared twice in the succession provision submitted to the Committee of Style. The deletion of one such clause appears to have been due to an effort to eliminate unnecessary repetition.

The change made in (2) was the most substantial of all, since its net effect was to render the meaning of the succession provision uncertain to later generations. What devolved on the Vice-President? Was it the office of President or the powers and duties of the office? If the office devolved, the Vice-President would probably become President for the remainder of the term.* If the powers and duties devolved, the Vice-President would merely become an acting President for the time being. Whatever devolved did so in all cases—removal, death, resignation and inability.

Taking a grammatical approach to the matter, it can be argued that the subject of the clause "the same shall devolve on the vice-president" is the pronoun "same," whose antecedent is the object of the verb "discharge," i.e., "powers and duties of the said office," not "office," which is the object of the preposition "of." On the other hand, it is argued that the proper rule of construction is that where there is a relative pronoun, it refers to the nearest preceding noun.[34] In the case of "same" the nearest noun is "office."

The status of the officer appointed by Congress is beyond dispute—he "acts as President." The words of limitation on his tenure, "until the disability be removed," can properly be said to apply to the Vice-President as well. This is because these words are separated from the vice-presidential clause only by commas so that they can modify it as well as the "other successor" clause.

Grammatical hair-splitting of this sort is, however, not necessary for an understanding of the succession provision.[35] The debates at the Convention clearly show that the Vice-President was merely intended to discharge the powers and duties of the President temporarily. All of the drafts before the Committees of Detail and Style were explicit in this regard. Another part of the original Constitution is consistent with this position. Article I Section 3, Clause 5, provided that "in the Absence of the Vice President, or when he

---

* The argument is that the President cannot hold the office if the Vice-President holds it, and that once the President is out of office, there is no way for him to get back in during that term.

shall exercise the office of President of the United States," the Senate shall choose a President pro tempore.* Further support can be found in the fact that Madison, Hamilton and King, who were members of the Committee of Style, were particularly notable for their advocacy of a strong, independent President. It is doubtful that they would have accepted the devolution of the "office," since it would have to be equally applicable to a case of inability. The result could be ludicrous. Suppose the President became disabled, the Vice-President replaced him, the Vice-President then became disabled, an officer was appointed by Congress to act as President, and the replaced President recovered? If the office had devolved on the Vice-President, the President, presumably, could not replace the officer appointed by Congress.

After reviewing the proceedings at the Convention, it is clear that when the thirty-nine delegates signed the Constitution on September 17, they accepted "the Same" as referring to "Powers and Duties" and the words limiting tenure, i.e., "until the Disability be removed, or a President shall be elected," as applicable to all successors, including the Vice-President.

Ratification

Post-Convention discussion of the vice-presidency was not extensive. The famous *Federalist* papers, written by Hamilton, Jay and Madison, contained only one reference—in Hamilton's No. 68 —as follows:

The appointment of an extraordinary person, as Vice-President, has been objected to as superfluous, if not mischievous. It has been alleged, that it would have been preferable to have authorized the Senate to elect out of their own body an officer answering to that description. But tw considerations seem to justify the ideas of the Convention in this respect. One is, that to secure at all times the possibility of a definitive resolution of the body, it is necessary that the President should have only a casting vote. And to take the Senator of any State from his seat as Senator, to place him in that of President of the Senate, would be to exchange, in regard to the State from which he came, a constant for a contingent vote. The other consideration is, that, as the Vice-President may occasionally become a substitute for the President, in the supreme Executive magistracy, all the reasons which recommend the mode of election pre-

---

* This provision seems to contemplate situations whereby the Vice-President would be *temporarily* absent.

scribed for the one, apply with great if not with equal force to the manner of appointing the other.[36]

Opinions varied regarding the vice-presidency. Governor George Clinton of New York, who was later to be Vice-President under both Thomas Jefferson and James Madison, expressed the opinion in the November 8, 1787 issue of the *New York Journal* that the vice-presidency was a dangerous and unnecessary office.[37] He thought that there was an improper blending of the legislative and executive powers and that the Vice-President's state would have an "unjust pre-eminence." Writing in the December 3, 1787 edition of *The Connecticut Courant,* Oliver Ellsworth, a member of the Connecticut contingent at the Constitutional Convention and a member of the important Committee of Detail, declared that the Vice-President is not an executive officer while the President is discharging his duties and that when he is called to preside, his legislative voice ceases.[38] Roger Sherman, another member of the Connecticut delegation at the Convention, expressed a similar view in the *New Haven Gazette.*[39] He stated that the Vice-President would have nothing to do in the executive department while he acted as President of the Senate. Moreover, he felt that as a nationally elected official, the Vice-President was best qualified to cast tie-breaking votes as he would consider the interests of all the states. Richard Henry Lee of Virginia, who opposed the Constitution because of its infringement on the rights of the states, regarded the Vice-President as "not a very important, if not an unnecessary part of the system—he may be a part of the senate at one period, and act as the supreme executive magistrate at another."[40] He also doubted whether the Vice-President had to have any qualifications in view of the Constitution's failure to mention any for him.

James Iredell of North Carolina, writing as *Marcus,* spoke out against George Mason, who had been a member of the Virginia delegation to the Convention and was a leading opponent of the Constitution in the Virginia state ratifying Convention. Said Iredell of the Vice-President:

[I]t appears to me very proper, he should be chosen much in the same manner as the President, in order that the States may be secure, upon any accidental loss by death or otherwise of the President's service, of the services in the same important station of the man in whom they repose their second confidence. The complicated manner of election wisely prescribed would necessarily occasion a considerable delay in the choice of another, and in the mean time the President of the Council, though very fit for the purpose of advising, might be very ill qualified, especially in a critical period, for an active Executive department.[41]

He regarded the objection that the Vice-President's state would have pre-eminence over the others as being "utterly unworthy of that spirit of unity, and rejection of local views, which can alone save us from destruction."

The vice-presidency and the subject of succession received scant attention in the state ratifying conventions which ran from the fall of 1787 to the spring of 1790 when Rhode Island, the last of the thirteen states to do so, ratified the Constitution.[42] The discussion of the vice-presidency that did occur centered mostly around the fact that the office blended legislative and executive functions.

In the North Carolina Convention, David Caldwell, a clergyman who was opposed to ratification, objected to the office on the ground that "the Vice-President is made a part of the legislative body, although there was an express declaration, that all the legislative powers were vested in the Senate and House of Representatives."[43] To this, William Maclaine answered that the Vice-President's having a casting vote was a provision of the kind that is to be found in all deliberative bodies and is highly useful and expedient, since it prevents the operation of government from being impeded. Other than that, the Vice-President has no legislative power.[44] Some other members of that convention were still not convinced that it was proper, that while the Vice-President was "not a member of the Senate, but an officer of the United States, [he] yet had a legislative power."[45] Governor Samuel Johnston of North Carolina, who was to become the state's first Senator, thought it a wise provision, because "if one of the Senate was to be appointed Vice-President, the state which he represented would either lose a vote if he was not permitted to vote on every occasion, or if he was, he might, in some instances, have two votes. . . ."[46]

The vice-presidency was also objected to on several occasions as being unnecessary. In the Virginia Convention, George Mason expressed the opinion that the Vice-President would be dangerous, since "he is, contrary to the usual course of parliamentary proceedings, to be president of the Senate. The state from which he comes may have two votes, when the others will have but one. Besides, the legislative and executive are hereby mixed and incorporated together. . . ."[47]

In answer to Mason, James Madison argued that the office of Vice-President had some peculiar advantages which should not be overlooked: "[H]e will be the choice of the people at large. . . . There is much more propriety in giving this office to a person chosen by the people at large, than to one of the Senate, who is only the choice of the legislature of one state. His eventual vote is an advantage too obvious to comment upon."[48] James Monroe, in the same convention, also thought that the Vice-President was an unnecessary officer. "The Senate," said he, "might of their own body elect a president who would have no dangerous influence."[49] He was convinced that the advantages attached to the office would not counterbalance the disadvantages.

When it was argued in the Pennsylvania Convention that the Vice-President was a useless officer and, as an executive officer, should not preside in the Senate and have a casting vote, a delegate replied that: "Perhaps the government might be executed without him, but there is a necessity of having a person to preside in the Senate, to continue a full representation of each state in that body."[50] In the North Carolina Convention when it was objected that the Vice-President possessed legislative powers, Maclaine stressed that

the Vice-President is to have no acting part in the Senate, but a mere casting vote. In every other instance, he is merely to preside in the Senate in order to regulate their deliberations. . . . [T]here is no danger to be apprehended from him in particular, as he is to be chosen in the same manner with the President, and therefore may be presumed to possess a great share of the confidence of all the states.[51]

William R. Davie of North Carolina, a delegate to the Constitutional Convention, argued that the vice-presidency was a valuable office, saying:

It might happen, in important cases, that the voices would be equally divided. Indecision might be dangerous and inconvenient to the public. It would then be necessary to have some person who should determine the question as impartially as possible. Had the Vice-President been taken from the representation of any of the states, the vote of that state would have been under local influence in the second. It is true he must be chosen from some state; but, from the nature of his election and office, he represents no one state in particular, but all the states. It is impossible that any officer could be chosen more impartially. He is, in consequence of his election, the creature of no particular district or state, but the officer and representative of the Union. He must possess the confidence of the states in a very great degree, and consequently be the most proper person to decide in cases of this kind.[52]

James Iredell, the number one advocate of ratification in North Carolina, found the Vice-President a valuable officer for the reason that: "[T]wo men will be in office at the same time; the President, who possesses, in the highest degree, the confidence of his country, and the Vice-President, who is thought to be the next person in the Union most fit to perform this trust."[53]

The succession clause as such was hardly mentioned in these conventions. It was objected to in the Virginia Convention by George Mason on the ground that it should provide for an immediate election in case of a vacancy in the office of President. In answer, Madison said that if both President and Vice-President died, another election would immediately take place.* However, he said, if it did not, the most Congress could do would be to make an appointment for the remainder of the four-year term.[54]

Aside from the above, the thinking of the delegates regarding the succession clause can only be found in their oblique references to it. In the Massachusetts Convention, James Bowdoin said that "the Vice-President, when acting as President" should take the President's oath of office before entering on the execution of the office.[55] In the New York Convention, a delegate referred to "the President of the United States, or the person holding his place for the time being."[56] In the Virginia Convention, Madison, speaking of the impeachment and removal of the President, said "the power will devolve on the Vice-President."[57] In referring to the Vice-President in an address to the Maryland House of Delegates, Luther Martin stated that in case of the death, resignation, removal, or inability of the President, the Vice-President would "supply his place, and be vested with his powers."[58] In the Virginia Convention, James Monroe, in objecting to the vice-presidency as unnecessary, said: "He is to succeed the President, in case of removal, disability, &c. . . ."[59] A delegate in the North Carolina Convention, making the point that

---

* What Madison contemplated, of course, was a double vacancy.

the Vice-President should not preside at the trial of the President in the Senate, said: "On the removal of the President from office, it devolves on the Vice President."[60]

There is no indication that anyone thought that the Vice-President whether referred to as acting as President, succeeding the President, supplying his place, or executing the office of President would actually *become* President. There seems not to have been much concern about terminology. The words "office" and "succeed" appear to have been used rather loosely. At one point the terms "acting as President" and "executing the office" are used in the same breath. It is not unlikely that those who thought the office devolved also thought it could devolve temporarily. What evidence is to be found in the ratifying conventions regarding the status of a Vice-President who succeeds a President appears to be more heavily on the side of the argument that the Vice-President was intended to act temporarily, without ever becoming the President.

4

The First Succession Law

The Secretary of State is struck out of the bill for the future Presidency, in case of the two first offices becoming vacant. His friends seemed to think it important to hold him up as King of the Romans. The firmness of the Senate kept him out.

FISHER AMES

Since the Constitution left it to Congress to establish a line of succession to the presidency, it was not surprising that the matter of presidential succession should receive attention in the First Congress. On December 20, 1790, a bill was presented to the House of Representatives providing that an officer, the name of which was left blank, shall act as President when there are vacancies in the offices of President and Vice-President.[1] It was referred to the Committee of the Whole on the next day, but did not come up for consideration until January 10, 1791. On that day, little agreement manifested itself as to who should be next in line after the Vice-President.

Representative Samuel Livermore of New Hampshire expressed his preference for the President pro tempore of the Senate. Hugh Williamson of North Carolina and James Jackson of Georgia suggested the Speaker of the House of Representatives. Representatives Theodore Sedgwick of Massachusetts and Egbert Benson of New York favored the Chief Justice of the Supreme Court. James Madison of Virginia and William L. Smith of South Carolina wanted the Secretary of State. As a result, arguments against the various proposed successors were engendered. Alexander White of Virginia argued that the President pro tempore was not an officer of the United

States, as required by the Constitution. In this view he was joined by Smith and Sedgwick and opposed by Representative Roger Sherman of Connecticut. Smith said that it would be unconstitutional to designate the President pro tempore, since it would deprive his state of its equal vote in the Senate. White felt that the designation of the President pro tempore would be contrary to the Constitution, giving one branch of Congress the power to elect a President when the voice of both branches should be equal. To name the Chief Justice, said Benson, would prevent the Vice-President from selecting his own successor, which he could do if the successor were the Secretary of State. There would be a blending of the Executive and Judiciary, Madison thought, if the Chief Justice were the successor. He objected to the President pro tempore on the ground that as a Senator, he would be subject to instruction by his state, and would also be holding two offices. Objecting to the Chief Justice, Secretary of State and Secretary of the Treasury (who then were John Jay, Thomas Jefferson and Alexander Hamilton, respectively), Livermore said that the occupants of the offices at the particular time must be overlooked, since a case of succession would not occur more than once in a hundred years. However, if any of these three officers should be designated, in virtue of his power of removal, the Vice-President could appoint his successor without consulting either branch of the Legislature. Joshua Seney of Maryland had other things on his mind. He interjected that the House had more important business. Others felt that a decision should be reached on the successor. However, the discussion ended without any consensus having been reached.[2]

The matter of providing for presidential succession was considered serious enough to be taken up again later in the year. In the Second Congress, on November 15, 1791, a Senate committee reported a bill dealing with the choice of presidential electors. On November 23, the bill was returned to the committee which was "instructed to report a clause, making provision for the administration of Government, in case of vacancies in the offices of President and Vice President."[3] The bill was reported on November 28 and ordered to be printed. On November 30, the bill, entitled "An act relative to the election of a President and Vice President of the United States, and declaring the officer who shall act as President in case of vacancies in the offices both of President and Vice President," was passed by the Senate and ordered sent to the House of Representatives for concurrence.[4] Unfortunately, the Senate met behind closed doors at the time so that there is little known as to its debates on the bill.* Section 9 of the bill provided that "in case of removal, death, resignation, or inability, both of the President and Vice President of the United States, the President of the Senate pro tempore, and in case there shall be no President of the Senate, then the Speaker of the House of Representatives for the time being, shall act as President of the United States, until the disability be removed, or a President shall be elected." On December 22, the House, in Committee of the Whole, turned its attention to the bill.[5]

Representatives William B. Giles of Virginia, Jonathan Sturges of Connecticut, Hugh Williamson of North Carolina and Alexander White of Virginia urged that these successors were not officers of the United States as contemplated by the Constitution. If the Speaker were in the line, said Sturges, there would be "caballing" and "electioneering" in the choice of a Speaker. Giles declared that "if they had been considered as such [i.e., officers of the United States], it is probable they would have been designated in the Constitution; the Constitution refers to some permanent officer to be created pursuant to the provisions therein contained."[6] Williamson stated that he was opposed to an "extensive construction" of the word "officer" on the ground that it "would render it proper to point out any person in the United States, whether connected with the Government or not, as a proper person to fill the vacancy contemplated."[7] Others, such as Representatives Theodore Sedgwick and Elbridge Gerry, both of Massachusetts, felt that they, indeed, were officers. "If the Speaker is not an officer," said Gerry, "what is he?"[8] Gerry, however, objected to the bill's blending of the Executive and Legislative. In contrast, Representative James Hillhouse of Connecticut said that he could not support a provision under which the President could appoint his own successor because it would take "away the choice from the people, . . . thus violating the first principle of a free elective Government."[9]

On January 2, 1792, the Committee of the Whole reported the bill to the House. Hugh Williamson moved to strike out the President pro tempore. His motion was defeated by a vote of 27 to 24. Included among the yeas were four delegates to the Constitutional

---

* Public galleries for regular sessions were not authorized until 1794 and newspaper reporters were not admitted until 1801.

Convention—Abraham Baldwin of Georgia, Thomas Fitzsimons of Pennsylvania, Madison and Williamson. The nays had only two— Nicholas Gilman of New Hampshire and Elbridge Gerry. A motion to strike out the Speaker was carried by a vote of 26 to 25, with Baldwin, Fitzsimons, Gerry, Madison and Williamson supporting it. The bill was laid on the table. On January 6 it was returned to the Committee of the Whole. The Committee considered it on February 9. Section 9 was stricken out in its entirety. A motion to add the Senior Associate Justice was then made but was not passed. Another motion was made, this one to substitute the Secretary of State as the person to fill the vacancy. A short debate followed, but no vote was taken. On the next day, the striking out of the President pro tempore and Speaker was confirmed by a vote of 32 to 22,* and the Secretary of State was inserted.[10] The House concurred in the substitution and on February 15, the bill was passed as amended and returned to the Senate.[11]

In the Senate on February 20, the House amendment was rejected: the President pro tempore and Speaker were again inserted and the Secretary of State removed. On the following day the bill was returned to the House, which receded from its amendment by a vote of 31 to 24.†[12] The bill became law on March 1, 1792, with the signature of President George Washington.‡[13]

The Senate's opposition to having the Secretary of State next in line after the Vice-President appears to have been due to Alexander Hamilton's dislike of Thomas Jefferson. Hamilton was then the leader of the Federalist Party which dominated the Senate. His influence was a decisive factor in the Senate's rejection of the Secretary of State as the next successor after the Vice-President. In a

---

* Baldwin, Fitzsimons, Gilman, Madison and Williamson favored this action, while Gerry opposed it.

† Fitzsimons and Gerry and Jonathan Dayton of New Jersey, also a former delegate to the Constitutional Convention, voted for receding; Baldwin, Gilman, Madison and Williamson, against it.

‡ Section 10 of the act provided that whenever the offices of both President and Vice-President became vacant, the Secretary of State was to notify the Governor of every state that electors were to be appointed within thirty-four days prior to the first Wednesday of the ensuing December. If less than two months remained before that date and if the term of the last President and Vice-President was not to end in the following March, the election would take place in the year next ensuing. If the term were to end in March, no election at all would take place.

letter to Edward Carrington, a military figure of the day, Hamilton said:

'T is evident, beyond a question . . . that Mr. Jefferson aims with ardent desire at the Presidential chair. . . . You know how much it was a point to establish the Secretary of State, as the officer who was to administer the government in defect of the President and Vice-President. Here, I acknowledge, though I took far less part than was supposed, I ran counter to Mr. Jefferson's wishes; but if I had had no other reason for it, I had already experienced opposition from him, which rendered it a measure of self-defence.[14]

William Rives, who had studied law under Jefferson, later stated:

The great zeal shown to prevent the secretary of State being declared in the line of succession to so remote and shadowy an inheritance, arose from its connection with another question of present interest and feeling. It was the pretension of the secretary of the treasury and his friends, that, in analogy to the position of the first lord of the treasury in the English cabinet, he ought to be considered prime minister and head of the cabinet here. A legislative declaration that the secretary of State should succeed to the Presidency in the event of a double vacancy in the offices of both President and Vice-President, however improbable the actual occurrence of such a contingency, would, it was thought, operate as a negative to this pretension.[15]

Fisher Ames, a Federalist member of the First Congress, noted that the Senate was intent on keeping Jefferson from being held up "as King of the Romans."[16]

Shortly after the passage of the 1792 Act, James Madison wrote Edmund Pendleton, Governor of Virginia, a letter in which he gave his opinion that the law was unconstitutional:

It may be questioned whether these [the President pro tempore and Speaker] are officers in the Constitutional sense. . . . If officers, whether both could be introduced. . . . As they are created by the Constitution, they would probably have been there designated if contemplated for such service, instead of being left to the legislative selection.[17]

He also believed that if either the President pro tempore or Speaker acted as President and retained his legislative position, as was probably contemplated, there would be a violation of the principle of separation of powers. On the other hand, if he resigned his position, he could not so act, for the powers and duties of the presidency must be annexed to another office. Said Madison:

61

[Either the Speaker or President pro tempore] will retain their Legislative stations, and then incompatible functions will be blended; or the incompatibility will supersede these stations, & then those being the substratum of the adventitious functions, these must fail also. The Constitution says Congress may declare what officers, &c., which seems to make it not an appointment or a translation, but an annexation of one office or trust to another office.[18]

Although there was not great enthusiasm for the first succession law, it was to be the law of the land for the next ninety-four years.

5

Early Days of the Vice-Presidency

[I]t is the only office in the world about which I am unable to decide in my own mind whether I had rather have it or not have it.

THOMAS JEFFERSON

The Vice-President was given only two duties by the Constitution: (1) to preside over the Senate, in which capacity he could vote when the Senate was "equally divided" and, in the presence of both Houses, open the certificates listing the votes of the presidential electors, and (2) to discharge the powers and duties of the President in case of his death, resignation, removal or inability. His was a unique office, neither strictly legislative nor executive but combining functions of both.

The Vice-President, like the President, was to hold office for four years.*[1] He was to be elected at the same time and in the same manner as the President and he was to be subject to impeachment but, while the Constitution provided that the Chief Justice would preside at a trial of the President, no presiding officer was mentioned for a trial of the Vice-President.† In contrast to its provision of an oath of office for the President, the Constitution prescribed no oath of office for the Vice-President. Nor did it mention any qualifica-

---

* There has always been some question as to whether the Vice-President has a term independent of that of the President as the Constitution provides in Article II: "He [the President] shall hold his Office during the Term of four Years . . . together with the Vice President, chosen for the same term."

† It seems that the President pro tempore would preside, since hs is the presiding officer of the Senate in the absence of the Vice-President.

tions for the vice-presidency. However, that was not due to oversight or lack of deliberation. The Vice-President would have the same qualifications as the President (i.e., be a natural-born citizen, at least thirty-five years of age, and fourteen years a resident within the United States[2]), since under the original method of election, the presidential electors would vote for two persons for President. The person having the greatest number of votes after the choice of the President would become the Vice-President. The method was designed to place in the office of Vice-President a person comparable in stature to the President.

The first presidential election under this constitutional scheme of government took place in 1789. Only ten states participated in the election.* George Washington was unanimously elected President, receiving sixty-nine electoral votes. John Adams, a fifty-three-year-old lawyer who had been the first United States Minister to Great Britain, was chosen Vice-President, with a total of thirty-four votes. Although this was one less than a majority, it was more than that received by anyone else except Washington. The remaining thirty-five votes were spread among ten different persons. The distribution was partly due to a fear that Adams might obtain as many electoral votes as Washington, which would throw the election into the House of Representatives.

Adams arrived in New York City, where the seat of government was then located, on April 18, 1789. He went to the Senate on Tuesday, April 21, to enter upon his duties and John Langdon of New Hampshire, who had been chosen President pro tempore of the Senate on April 6, introduced him to the body, saying, "Sir: I have it in charge from the Senate, to introduce you to the chair of this House; and, also, to congratulate you on your appointment to the office of Vice-President of the United States of America."[3] Adams then took his place and, accepting his election to the vice-presidency, he said:

Unaccustomed to refuse any public service, however dangerous to my reputation or disproportionate to my talents, it would have been inconsistent to have adopted another maxim at this time, when the prosperity of the country and the liberties of the people require, perhaps as much

---

* The New York State legislature chose no electors, because its Federalist-dominated Senate could not agree with its Anti-Federalist House as to how the electors should be selected. North Carolina and Rhode Island had not yet ratified the Constitution.

64

as ever, the attention of those who possess any share of the public confidence.[4]

All this occurred nine days before the inauguration of George Washington. It was not until April 30, 1789, that Washington was sworn in as the first President of the United States. His oath was administered by Chancellor Robert R. Livingston of New York. Since there was no prescribed oath in the Constitution for the Vice-President, Adams' swearing in had to await an act of Congress, although in the interim he discharged his duty as President of the Senate. On June 1, 1789, President Washington signed into law an act establishing an oath of office for the Vice-President and the members of the Senate. It provided that any member of the Senate could administer the oath to the Vice-President and he, in turn, could administer it to the members.[5] The oath, which had to be administered within three days after the passage of the law, was as follows: "I, A. B., do solemnly swear or affirm (as the case may be) that I will support the Constitution of the United States."* John Langdon administered the oath to Adams on June 3.

The Constitution and its institutions were now to be put into effect. There were no precedents to rely on—rather, they had to be made. As Adams put it, "the scene is new and the actors are inexperienced."[6] Among the questions to be answered by the first "actors" in the "scene" of the new government were questions of protocol. As was noted in the previous chapter, the Senate met behind closed doors at the time and no record was kept of its debates. However, Senator William Maclay of Pennsylvania kept a diary which provides the best (though not always objective) account of the early Senate proceedings.†

On April 24, 1789, when it became necessary for Adams to send a letter to the Speaker of the House of Representatives, he asked the

---

* The present oath of the Vice-President is: "I, A.B., do solemnly swear (or affirm) that I will support and defend the Constitution of the United States against all enemies, foreign and domestic; that I will bear true faith and allegiance to the same; that I take this obligation freely, without any mental reservation or purpose of evasion; and that I will well and faithfully discharge the duties of the office on which I am about to enter. So help me God." 15 Stat. 85 (1868), 5 U.S.C. §16 (1958).

† Maclay was not overly sympathetic with Adams' concern about the setting of precedents.

Senate by what title the Speaker should be addressed, suggesting "honorable." The question, having been put, passed in the negative and Maclay observed in his diary that "from this omen I think our Vice-President may go and dream about titles, for none will he get."[7] On the following day, a report was read that on Inauguration Day, Washington should be received in the Senate and then taken to the House to be sworn in. Thereupon, Adams made the following speech:

Gentlemen, I do not know whether the framers of the Constitution had in view the two kings of Sparta or the two consuls of Rome when they formed it; one to have all the power while he held it, and the other to be nothing. Nor do I know whether the architect that formed our room and the wide chair in it (to hold two, I suppose) had the Constitution before him. Gentlemen, I feel great difficulty how to act. I am possessed of two separate powers; the one in *esse* and the other in *posse*. I am Vice-President. In this I am nothing, but I may be everything. But I am president also of the Senate. When the President comes into the Senate, what shall I be? I can not be [president] then. No, gentlemen, I can not, I can not. I wish gentlemen to think what I shall be.[8]

Oliver Ellsworth of Connecticut paged through the Constitution. "At length," said Maclay, "he rose and addressed the Chair with the utmost gravity: 'Mr. President, I have looked over the Constitution (pause), and I find, sir, it is evident and clear, sir, that wherever the Senate are to be, there, sir, you must be at the head of them.' "[9]

Yet another problem presented itself on May 15. Adams had received a letter from a printer who sought the job of printing for the Senate. He was addressed as "His Excellency the Vice-President." Adams was perplexed about whether he should read the letter. Maclay commented that "until we had a rule obliging people to be regular we must submit to their irregularities, more especially of this kind."[10] The letter was finally opened and read. It is said that during the discussion of titles one of the Senators suggested, in a whisper, that the Vice-President be referred to as "his Superfluous Excellency." This remark has also been attributed to Benjamin Franklin, who supposedly made it at the Constitutional Convention.

Another problem requiring resolution was how the Vice-President should sign bills and messages. Adams' preference was to sign his initials, "J.A.," followed by "Vice-President." Adams called upon the Senate for advice. Some of the Senators were indifferent, while others approved the practice. Maclay, however, rose and said that the very term Vice-President carried on the face of it the idea of holding the place of the President in his absence; that every act done by the Vice-President as such implied that when so acting he held the place of the President. In this point of view nothing could be more improper than the Vice-President signing an address to the President. It was like a man signing an address to himself. That the business of the Vice-President was when he acted exactly the same with that of President, and could not mix itself with us a Senate.[11]

Continuing, he said:

Sir, we know you not as Vice-President within this House. As President of the Senate only do we know you. As President of the Senate only can you sign or authenticate any act of that body.

Adams decided that the question need not be put to a vote, since a majority seemed to favor his signing as President of the Senate. However, several days later he informed the Senate that he had checked the Constitution and that his proper title was Vice-President and he would insist on it. Thus he would sign as Vice-President and President of the Senate. This time no one objected to his signing as Vice-President.

Adams was, on many occasions, puzzled about how to conduct himself as President of the Senate. At first, he participated quite freely in the Senate's debates, often lecturing and attempting, as presiding officer, to influence its course. As Maclay's diary indicates, not a few Senators resented his so doing.[12] In the course of his two terms as Vice-President, he gradually adjusted himself to the pressure put upon him and abandoned his efforts to be more than an impartial presiding officer. In a letter to his friend, John Trumbull, dated March 9, 1790, he said: "I have no desire ever to open my mouth again upon any question."[13]

Upon entering the office of Vice-President, Adams had viewed it as "disproportionate" to his "talents," and it was not long before he was convinced that the office was "too inactive and insignificant" for him and he would be glad to be out of it. His opinion of the office did not change as his service progressed. Writing to his wife in December, 1793, he said, "My country has in its wisdom contrived for me the most insignificant office that ever the invention of man contrived or his imagination conceived; . . . I can do neither good nor evil. . . ."[14]

There were many, however, who regarded the vice-presidency as truly the second office of the land—a post of honor and dignity. The difference of opinion regarding the office became evident when the First Congress was considering the compensation to be given the Vice-President.[15]

Some members of the House of Representatives (Michael J. Stone of Maryland, for one) felt that the Vice-President's work would be so sporadic that he should be paid only on a per diem basis. Alexander White of Virginia said that the Constitution imposed no duty on the Vice-President requiring constant attendance, so that he would give him the salary of the President when he acted as President. Otherwise, he would pay him on the basis of the service he rendered in presiding over the Senate. Joshua Seney of Maryland believed that the Vice-President could absent himself the "whole time."

In contrast was the view that the Vice-President should be given a regular salary in consequence of his position. There were two main reasons for this view. First, as second officer of the government and of the nation, he should be compensated in a measure commensurate with the dignity of his station and in a way that would enable him to meet the extra expenses incurred in maintaining that standard of dignity. John Page of Virginia observed: "[A] proper proportion [should be] observed between the salary of the First and Second Magistrates. . . ." Continuing, he stated that if he had had a hand in forming the Constitution, he probably "should never have thought of such an officer; but as we have got him, we must maintain him."[16] Edanus Burke of South Carolina agreed. It was his opinion that "it was but reasonable the Vice President should receive a compensation adequate to the second officer in the Government. He will be subject to extra expenses . . . and will be obliged to maintain his dignity."[17] William Smith of South Carolina thought that "considering him as an officer in the Government, next in dignity to the President, . . . he must support a correspondent dignity in his style of living, and consequently ought to have a competent allowance for that purpose."[18] Elias Boudinot of New Jersey pointed out that "he is to be elected in the same manner as the President, in order to obtain the second best character in the Union. . . . The constitution considers him a respectable officer. . . . [C]onsequently he ought to be respected, and provided for according to the dignity and importance of his principal Character."[19]

The second reason set forth for giving the Vice-President an annual salary was the argument that, in consequence of his being the possible successor, he must give up all other pursuits in order to devote himself fully to preparing for the task he might have to undertake. Theodore Sedgwick of Massachusetts argued that:

[T]he Vice President . . . must always be ready to take the reins of Government when they shall fall out of the hands of the President; hence . . . he should . . . devote his whole time to prepare himself for the great and important charge for which he is a candidate. [Thus] he should be provided with a constant salary, to support that rank which we contemplate for him to bear.[20]

James Madison of Virginia was of the same opinion. Said he:

If he is to be considered as the apparent successor of the President, to qualify himself the better for that office, he must withdraw from his other avocations, and direct his attention to the obtaining a perfect knowledge of his intended business. . . .

[I]f we mean to carry the constitution into full effect, we ought to make provision for his support, adequate to the merits and nature of the office.[21]

An annual salary of $5,000 was finally decided upon, as against the President's $25,000.

Despite the low esteem in which some persons, including Adams, himself, held the vice-presidency, it got off to a respectable start under President Washington. Adams served as Vice President of the United States for two terms, during which time his relationship with Washington was close and cordial. He was frequently consulted and was considered one of Washington's official advisers. When Washington decided to make a tour of the southern states in the spring of 1791, he addressed a letter to the Secretaries of State, Treasury and War, directing that if any "serious and important cases" should arise during his absence, they consult and act on them.[22] He requested that the Vice-President also be consulted. It appears that Adams took part in a Cabinet meeting on April 11, 1791, which was called and presided over by Jefferson.[23] At another time Washington refused to send Adams to a foreign embassy on the ground that "it would not be justifiable to send away the person who, in case of his [Washington's] death, was provided by the Constitution to take his place. . . ."[24]

In the Senate, Adams used his tie-breaking vote twenty-nine times, more than any other Vice-President since.[25] Some of these votes were of critical importance to the administration. His first such vote sustained the President's power of removal. On April 28, 1794, he used his vote to defeat the third reading of a bill to suspend British imports which, if it had become law, might have brought on a war and would have defeated Washington's purpose in sending John Jay to England.

When Washington declined a third term as President, Adams, a Federalist, ran for the presidency. The other chief contestant was Thomas Jefferson, a Democratic-Republican from Virginia. Speaking of the possibility of his opponent's being chosen Vice-President, Adams said: "I am almost tempted to wish he may be chosen Vice-President . . . for there, if he could do no good, he could do no harm."[26] Adams was to get his "wish." In the election of 1796 Adams was elected President, obtaining the votes of seventy-one of the 138 electors.* Jefferson received sixty-eight electoral votes, thus becoming Vice-President.† The political differences between the two prevented them from having a good working relationship. Although Adams appears at one time to have been inclined to include the Vice-President in Cabinet meetings, he never actually invited Jefferson to participate in any such meetings.[27] Jefferson, moreover, had no interest in so participating. Said Jefferson: "I consider my office as constitutionally confined to legislative functions, and that I could not take any part whatever in executive consultations, even were it proposed."[28] At another time he said: "As to duty, the Constitution will know me only as the member of a legislative body."[29] William Smith of South Carolina, however, in a letter of April 3, 1797 to Rufus King, Minister to England, indicated that some of Jefferson's friends wanted him to participate in meetings of Adams' Cabinet. Said Smith: "Jacobins are flattering him [Adams] and trying to cajole him to admit the V.P. into the Council."[30]

Adams also considered sending his Vice-President on a diplo-

---

* Since he was still Vice-President when the electoral votes were counted on February 8, it was incumbent upon him to announce himself President-elect.

† He was sworn in on March 4, 1797, President pro tempore William Bingham of Pennsylvania administering the oath. Interestingly, when Washington was sworn in on March 4, 1793 to begin his second term, Adams was not sworn in until the Senate met on December 2, 1793. President pro tempore John Langdon administered the oath to Adams.

matic mission but, after Jefferson had refused, thought better of it because:

The Vice-President, in our Constitution, is too high a personage to be sent on diplomatic errands, even in the character of an ambassador. . . . It must be a pitiful country . . . in which the second man in the nation will accept a place upon a footing with the *corps diplomatique.* . . . The nation must hold itself very cheap, that can choose a man one day to hold its second office, and the next send him to Europe, to dance attendance at levees and drawing rooms, among the common major-generals, simple bishops, earls, and barons, but especially among the common trash of ambassadors, envoys, and ministers plenipotentiary.[31]

Like Adams, Jefferson was not impressed with the challenges afforded by the office. Commenting on his office in a letter to Elbridge Gerry of May 13, 1797, Jefferson said: "The second office of this government is honorable and easy, the first is but a splendid misery."[32]

Yet, the vice-presidency was to lead Jefferson to the presidency as it had Adams before him. Despite the inadequacies of the office, the method of election prescribed by the Constitution was providing men of presidential timber for it. The presidential election of 1800, however, brought about a significant change in the original method of electing the President and Vice-President.

In the election of 1800, most of the Republican electors voted for Thomas Jefferson and Aaron Burr, intending Jefferson for President and Burr for Vice-President. Of the 276 electoral votes cast, Jefferson and Burr each received 73. This was a majority of the number of electors. Since they were tied for first place, the election fell to the House of Representatives. There, balloting was by states, each of the sixteen states having one vote. In order to be elected, a candidate was required to receive a majority—or nine votes. On the first ballot, Jefferson received eight and Burr six, with two states divided. The balloting continued for seven days. Finally, on the thirty-sixth ballot, the deadlock was broken when Jefferson received ten votes and Burr four, with two states abstaining. It has been said that the Federalists, who had lost the election and were bitterly opposed to Jefferson, tried to use the opportunity to frustrate the victors by electing Burr instead of Jefferson.[33] They were unsuccessful, but the election had stirred up so much dissatisfaction with the original method of election that a change was inevitable.

The Twelfth Amendment

Proposals to change the original method of election were introduced in both Houses of Congress upon the convening of the Eighth Congress in October, 1803. On December 8, after much debate, a proposed amendment passed the House* after having passed the Senate on December 2. It provided that in future elections the electors would vote for two persons, one of whom was not to be an inhabitant of the same state as themselves. They would cast two ballots—one designating the person voted for as President; the other designating the person voted for as Vice-President. The person having the greatest number of votes for President, if that number were a majority of the number of electors, would be the President. If no person received a majority, the House of Representatives would choose the President from those candidates having the three highest numbers. The House of Representatives would vote by states, each state having one vote, and a quorum would consit of a member or members from two-thirds of the states. A majority of the states would be necessary to a choice. If the House did not choose a President, when the right of choice had devolved on it, by the following fourth of March, the Vice-President was to "act as President, as in the case of the death or other constitutional disability of the President."

The proposed amendment further provided that the person having the greatest number of votes as Vice-President, if that number were a majority of the number of electors, was to be Vice-President. If no person received a majority, the Senate would choose the Vice-President from those candidates having the two highest numbers. A quorum for this purpose would consist of two-thirds of the whole number of Senators, and a majority of the Senators would be necessary to a choice. No person constitutionally ineligible to the office of President would be eligible to that of Vice-President.

This proposal became the Twelfth Amendment to the Constitution in 1804. During the debates on the amendment there was lengthy discussion of the vice-presidency—what it was originally intended to be and what it would become under the change. In-

---

* Speaker Nathaniel Macon of North Carolina cast the deciding vote, making the necessary two-thirds.

terestingly, it was proposed in both Houses that if the method of voting for President and Vice-President were to be changed, the vice-presidency should be abolished, since the principal reason for establishing the office (i.e., to provide for a successor of stature equal to the President's) would be nullified. Senator Jonathan Dayton of New Jersey believed that under the proposed amendment there would be "all the inconveniences, without a single advantage from the office of Vice-President." "The reasons of erecting the office," he said, "are frustrated by the amendment . . . ; it will be preferable, therefore, to abolish the office."[34] He so moved, and on November 23, 1803, a vote was taken on his motion. It was defeated by a vote of 19 to 12.[35]

On December 7, 1803, a vote was taken in the House on a similar motion of Representative Samuel W. Dana of Connecticut. He said: "This amendment makes the Vice President a secondary character. The reasons, therefore, for continuing the office of Vice President are not so great under this amendment, as under the Constitution, as it at present stands. . . ."[36] His motion was also defeated, the vote being 85 to 27.

Those who thought that the office should be abolished felt that the necessity of providing for a successor did not warrant the continuation of the office. In the words of Representative Dana:

Unless some great good result from the office of Vice President, no argument for its continuance can be deduced from the necessity of having an eventual successor; that case can easily be provided for, when the Senate choose their own President, and, as in many of the States, the President of the Senate may eventually preside.[37]

The change in the method of election was vehemently argued against by those who foresaw a tremendous decline in the character and prestige of the vice-presidency. Representative Seth Hastings of Massachusetts asked, "[W]ill not the office of Vice President, in all future elections, be considered as a mere sinecure?"[38] Senator Samuel White of Delaware thought "this designating mode of election . . . will go very far to destroy . . . the personal consequence and worth of the officer. . . ." He went on to say, "[T]he Vice Presidency will either be left to chance, or what will be much worse, prostituted to the basest purposes; character, talents, virtue, and merit, will not be sought after, in the candidate. The question will not be asked, is he capable? is he honest? But can he by his name, by his connexions, by his wealth, by his local situation, by his influence, or his intrigues, best promote the election of a President?"[39] Senator William Plumer of New Hampshire agreed. Said he: "The office of Vice President will be . . . brought to market and exposed to sale to procure votes for the President."[40] Representative Roger Griswold of Connecticut also agreed. "If that principle [of designation] is adopted, of what use," he asked, "can the Vice President be?" He went on to say, "[T]he continuance of the office will be worse than useless, inasmuch as it will only tend to introduce a system of corruption."[41]

Representative Samuel D. Purivance of North Carolina, observing that "the principal reasons for creating it were to bring forward two of our ablest characters . . . and to keep all intrigue from being interwoven in the election of the Chief Magistrate," said: "This object is done away, and the office is retained at the expense of five thousand dollars a year, when the duties attached to it might as well be discharged by some other person, as is the case in every State in the Union, where there is not a Lieutenant Governor. . . ."[42] Representative Samuel Taggart of Massachusetts could not see "what end a Vice President can answer, unless it be to take a pleasant journey to the seat of Government once a year, meet with and preside in the Senate for a few weeks, possibly not more than three or four in a session, receive five thousand dollars, and go home again. This to be sure is a very pretty douceur. . . ."[43]

Although the arguments against the change were far more numerous and persuasive than those for it, the opposition was well-outnumbered on the final vote. The amendment was passed in the Senate by a vote of 22 to 10 and in the House by a vote of 84 to 42.

Interesting is the view of some members of the Eighth Congress about the meaning of this provision: if the House failed to choose a President by Inauguration Day, the Vice-President would "*act as President* [italics added], as in the case of the death or other constitutional disability of the President." This language originated in the Senate (the House version had no such provision). There, the language, which was suggested by Senator John Taylor of Virginia, was decided upon without discussion after a proposal by John Quincy Adams of Massachusetts that "the said Vice President shall discharge the powers and duties of the President," in case the House makes no choice within a given time had been defeated, as had a proposal by Samuel Smith of Maryland that Adams' proposal be amended so as to read "the Vice President shall be President" in such a case. When this provision was discussed in the House, most participants in the discussion seemed to view the Vice-President under this language as actually becoming President for the four-year term.[44]

During the course of the debates, there were frequent references to the succession provision. Little agreement on the Vice-President's status when acting under this provision revealed itself. Some members of the Eighth Congress stated that he "acts" as President or exercises the "powers" or "duties" of President.[45] Others freely used language to the effect that he "becomes President."[46] Still others used language which does not make it clear whether they thought he merely discharges the duties of President or actually "becomes" President.[47] Some, in fact, seem to have thought that discharging the duties of President or acting as President was the same as becoming President, since they used the expressions interchangeably.[48] It is significant that, already, the ambiguity inherent in the succession provision had begun to manifest itself.

II. THE SYSTEM IN OPERATION

(1805–1965)

6

Decline of the Vice-Presidency

*What end [can] a Vice President . . . answer, unless
it be to take a pleasant journey to the seat of Government once a year, meet with and preside in the
Senate for a few weeks . . . , receive five thousand
dollars, and go home again.*

SAMUEL TAGGART

From 1805 to 1841, the vice-presidency took a sharp turn
downward. The men elected to the office in that period differed
markedly from the first two Vice-Presidents in calibre. They seldom received any executive responsibilities and were not included
in meetings of the President's Cabinet. Their role as President of
the Senate became little more than a pastime and no longer did
they decide disputed questions regarding the certificates of the
presidential electors.*[1] Except for the relationships which existed
between Madison and Gerry and Jackson and Van Buren, the relationships between the Presidents and Vice-Presidents left much
to be desired. No longer was the Vice-President a sure heir to the
presidency. This distinction now belonged to the Secretary of State.
Of the six Presidents between 1805 and 1840, five were former
Secretaries of State. Only one of these, Van Buren, had also been
Vice-President. Some occurrences in this period deserve noting.

The death of George Clinton, James Madison's first Vice-Presi-

---

* This power had been used by Vice-Presidents prior to the adoption of
the Twelfth Amendment but seems to have been relinquished thereafter.

79

dent, on Monday, April 20, 1812 of pneumonia, marked the first death in office of either a President or Vice-President. Clinton was then seventy-two years of age and in his eighth year as Vice-President. His death came after several weeks of failing health. Despite his infirmity, he had been looking toward the election of 1812 and aspiring to the presidency. At the time of his death, a lively debate was being waged as to who his successor might be in the forthcoming election. "The Vice-President," Mrs. Dolly Madison wrote on March 27, 1812, "lies dangerously ill, and electioneering for his office goes on beyond description—the world seems to be running mad, what with one thing or another."[2] Clinton's tenure as Vice-President was not remarkable for achievement.

Clinton, a seven-time governor of New York, first had been elected to the vice-presidency in 1804. He had previously been a candidate for the presidency on three occasions. In 1789 three of the sixty-nine electors cast votes for him. In 1792, although he was an Anti-Federalist and opposed to Washington's policies, he had actively sought to become his Vice-President in the hope of implementing his political convictions from that vantage point. He received the votes of fifty of the 132 electors, while John Adams received those of seventy-seven. In 1796 Clinton was voted for by seven of 138 electors. At the Democratic-Republican caucus of 1804,* he received sixty-seven of 107 votes for Vice-President, which placed him on the ticket headed by Thomas Jefferson. In the election, the first under the Twelfth Amendment, each received the votes of 162 of the 176 electors.

The oaths of office were administered to Jefferson and Clinton in the Senate Chamber on March 4, 1805 by Chief Justice John Marshall. Clinton was then in his mid-sixties and it was not expected that he would have an important role in the government. It is said that upon his election in 1804 he "went into comfortable retirement. . . ."[3] In the early part of his vice-presidency, Clinton was on fairly good terms with Jefferson and used his casting vote on several occasions to support administration measures. However, he was seldom consulted and toward the end of his tenure as Jefferson's Vice-President, he became openly critical of the administra-

---

* From 1800 to 1824, presidential and vice-presidential candidates were usually nominated by the members of the party in Congress.

80

tion, particularly on matters of foreign policy.* Clinton's health sometimes prevented him from presiding over the Senate, a duty of which he was not overly fond. When he did preside, his ability was seriously questioned by some Senators. A young Senator from Massachusetts named John Quincy Adams wrote in a letter to his father, the former President:

Mr. Clinton is totally ignorant of all the most common forms of proceeding in Senate, and yet by the rules he is to decide every question of order without debate and without appeal. His judgment is neither quick nor strong: so there is no more dependence upon the correctness of his determinations from his understanding than from his experience. As the only duty of a Vice-President, under our Constitution, is to preside in Senate, it ought to be considered what his qualifications for that office are at his election. In this respect a worse choice than Mr. Clinton could scarcely have been made.[4]

A similar comment was made by Senator William Plumer of New Hampshire. Clinton, he said, "is old, feeble, & altogether uncapable of the duty of presiding in the Senate. He has no mind— no intellect—no memory."[5] But Plumer also said: "[T]he more I see & know of this man the more highly he rises in my estimation. He is an old man. . . . He is too old for the office he now holds; little as are its duties. . . . But there is something venerable in his appearance. . . . He appears honest."[6]

Clinton was renominated for the vice-presidency on a ticket with James Madison in 1808. This was, to say the least, a disappointment to Clinton, because he had entertained hopes of being nominated for the presidency. He felt that it was his right because the Vice-President had always been the heir apparent. But, as one biographer of Clinton has said: "He had had no experience with diplomacy and the times demanded a skilled diplomat at the helm of the state. He had few of the social assets that the presidency demanded."[7] It was widely felt at the time that Clinton was too old to lead the country, as he was then in his sixty-ninth year. At one point it had been suggested to Monroe, another major con-

---

* Interestingly, on April 12, 1808, Senator James Hillhouse of Connecticut proposed a constitutional amendment which, among other things, would have abolished the office altogether. He recommended the selection of the President by lot from among the members of the Senate and as his temporary successor, should one be necessary, the Speaker of the Senate.

testant for the presidential nomination, that he consider accepting the nomination for Vice-President on a ticket with Clinton, since Clinton was not likely to survive the term.[8]

After being nominated for Vice-President, Clinton continued to campaign against Madison for the presidency, maintaining that he had not been consulted and had been nominated for Vice-President against his will.[9] In the election of 1808, Madison received 122 of the 175 electoral votes cast for President. Clinton received 6 votes for President and 113 votes for Vice-President.

Clinton's relationship with Madison was, in many respects, openly hostile. During the campaign the *American Citizen,* a New York newspaper, had fanned the differences between Clinton and Madison. It claimed that Madison was responsible for Clinton's not being included in meetings of Jefferson's Cabinet. "The influence of Mr. Madison over the President is known and harmony in the cabinet probably required that his wishes should be complied with."[10] Clinton did not attend Madison's inauguration on March 4. In fact, he delayed taking his oath of office until the Senate met in special session on May 22, 1809. "Probably he preferred not to be present . . . when the man his friends had for months been busy vilifying took the president's oath from Chief Justice Marshall."[11] The differences between the two men were further accentuated when Clinton used his casting vote against renewing the charter of the national bank—a measure supported by Madison. Although his death was no great loss to the administration, the newspapers of the day expressed the country's grief over the passing of the "venerable sage." Possibly because the term was almost over, no thought was given to filling the vacancy which had thus occurred.*

On May 12, 1812, the Democratic-Republican caucus nominated Senator John Langdon of New Hampshire for the vice-presidency. Since he was then seventy-one years of age, he declined the nomination. On June 8, Elbridge Gerry of Massachusetts, who, like Clinton, had opposed the creation of the office of Vice-President, was nominated. Although he was only three years younger than Langdon, he accepted the nomination and became

---

* At the time of Clinton's death, forty-year-old William H. Crawford of Georgia, who had been appointed on March 24, 1812 due to Clinton's absence because of illness, was President pro tempore of the Senate. He thus became the possible successor to the presidency. Henry Clay, then thirty-five, was the Speaker of the House of Representatives.

82

Madison's running mate. The election brought them victory.* On March 4, 1813, Madison was inaugurated in the Chamber of the House of Representatives, while Gerry took the oath of office at his residence in Cambridge, Massachusetts.† Two years later, on the morning of November 23, 1814, while on his way to the Senate chamber, Gerry suffered a hemorrhage of the lungs and died within twenty minutes. He thus became the second Vice-President to die in office. His death was sudden and unexpected, since the day before he had sat as presiding officer during a long session of the Senate.‡

Unlike Clinton, Gerry had been pleased to be Vice-President. "[H]e felt the highest sensations of gratified ambition; and cheerfully assumed the duties of a station, which in addition to its inherent dignity, had the cheering appearance of a reward for past labours of patriotism, and a compensation for the consequences of political fidelity."[12] Relations between Madison and Gerry were cordial. Gerry was not invited to attend Cabinet meetings, but he was frequently consulted by Madison and visited him socially. In the Senate, where he was in regular attendance as the presiding officer, Gerry was a strong supporter of administration programs. During the first special session of the Thirteenth Congress, he kept his chair until actual adjournment on August 2, 1813, for fear that a faction hostile to Madison might appoint one of its own, Senator William B. Giles, as President pro tempore of the Senate. Madison was seriously ill at the time. Prior to this, it had been the practice for the Vice-President to retire before the close of the session so that the Senate could appoint a President pro tempore. The reason for this was that if both the President and Vice-President died between sessions, there would be a President pro tempore who could take over the helm of government. Gerry's action thus put the Speaker of the House, Henry Clay, next in the line of succession.§

---

* Madison received 128 of the 217 electoral votes cast for President. Gerry received 131 of those cast for Vice-President.

† The oath was administered to him by a United States District Court judge.

‡ Langdon survived Gerry by almost five years. He died on September 18, 1819.

§ On April 18, 1814, when the second session of the Thirteenth Congress came to an end, Gerry relinquished his seat in order to let the Senate choose a President pro tempore. John Gaillard of South Carolina was chosen.

Until 1890, the usual practice was for the Senate to elect a President pro

Following Gerry's death on November 23, 1814, there was considerable political activity in the Senate for the position of President pro tempore. John Gaillard was chosen by a vote of sixteen to ten on November 25. In the interim, thirty-eight-year-old Langdon Cheves of South Carolina, as Speaker, was the only one in the line of succession. As in the case of Clinton, no discussion of devising a method for filling the vacancy in the vice-presidency took place even though over two years remained in the term. This is not surprising, since the vice-presidency had come to be looked upon as a reward for party loyalty and not as the truly second office of the country.

In the election of 1816, the Federalists nominated Rufus King for President, but made no nomination for Vice-President. The Democratic-Republicans nominated James Monroe of Virginia for President and Daniel D. Tompkins of New York, a forty-two-year-old former governor of the State, for Vice-President. They won by a wide majority, each receiving 183 of the 221 electoral votes, respectively. Tompkins, who served as Monroe's Vice-President for two terms (1817-1825), was seldom seen in Washington, D.C. It is said that he would gladly have given up the vice-presidency if he could have been governor of New York.[13] When his successor, John C. Calhoun, was sworn in on March 4, 1825, Tompkins was absent from Washington.* Since there was no President pro tempore at the time, Calhoun's oath was administered to him by Andrew Jackson of Tennessee, the senior Senator present.

The subject of succession received some attention while Tompkins was Vice-President. In 1820, Senator James J. Wilson of New Jersey offered a resolution, which was passed, directing the Senate Judiciary Committee to determine whether the law of 1792 should be changed.[14] On February 1, 1821, the committee reported in the negative.[15] In the same year this interesting event occurred.

---

tempore whenever the Vice-President was absent. On March 12, 1890, a new procedure was adopted, which has continued to date: a President pro tempore is elected to hold office continuously at the pleasure of the Senate or until a successor is elected. For the practice regarding the Speaker, see pp. 90–91n.

* Up to 1860, the President pro tempore usually administered the oath to the Vice-President. Then, the outgoing Vice-President administered it, except if he had died, resigned, succeeded or been elected to a second term, in which cases the President pro tempore did so. Since the 1930s it has been administered by Senate party leaders (1937, 1953, 1957), a Supreme Court Justice (1949)and Speakers (1961 and 1965).

Decline of the Vice-Presidency

Monroe's first term ended at midnight March 3, 1821.* Since March 4 fell on a Sunday, he did not take the oath of office for his second term until March 5. Tompkins had taken his oath on March 3 at his home in Staten Island, New York, but when he learned that Monroe was to take the presidential oath on the 5th, he renewed his oath on that day.

In the election of 1824, Andrew Jackson of Tennessee received 155,872 popular votes and ninety-nine electoral votes (37.93 per cent). John Quincy Adams of Massachusetts received 105,321 popular votes and eighty-four electoral votes (32.18 per cent). William H. Crawford of Georgia was third highest, with 44,282 popular votes and forty-one electoral votes (15.71 per cent).† Since no candidate had a majority, it was incumbent upon the House of Representatives to choose a President from the candidates having the three highest numbers. In the House, Adams obtained thirteen votes, Jackson seven and Crawford four. John Quincy Adams therefore became the first President to be elected without a plurality of the popular vote and the only President to be elected without having received a majority of the electoral vote.

The vice-presidential contest of 1824 found John C. Calhoun of South Carolina the winner, with 182 electoral votes. His closest competitor was Nathan Sanford of New York, with thirty electoral votes. Calhoun's tenure as Vice-President was notable for his decision on December 28, 1832 to resign the office in order to become a Senator from South Carolina. This resignation came when he was Vice-President under President Andrew Jackson (1829-

---

* Prior to the Twentieth Amendment (see p. 190) the Constitution merely provided for a four-year term, without indicating when the term was to begin. An Act of March 1, 1792 provided that a presidential term should be measured from the fourth of March following the election. Through much of the first half of the nineteenth century, it was assumed that a President ceased to be President at midnight on March 3 notwithstanding the fact that the new President did not take his oath until around noon on March 4. Thereafter, until the passage of the Twentieth Amendment, the dominant view was that a President's term ended at noon on March 4. See Warren, *Political Practice and the Constitution,* 89 *University of Pennsylvania Law Review* 1003 (1941). The Twentieth Amendment changed the beginning of the term to noon on January 20 following the election, and it specified that the term of the outgoing President would end at that time.

† Crawford's vote was adversely affected by the fact that he had suffered a paralytic stroke during the campaign.

85

1832).* This is the only time in history when either a President or Vice-President resigned. However, the possibility of a President's resigning was discussed early in Jackson's term. This was in 1830, when Jackson proposed to Martin Van Buren, then Secretary of State, that they run on the same ticket in 1832—Jackson for President and Van Buren for Vice-President. Jackson, the proposal went, would resign after a year or, at most, two and leave Van Buren to carry on his policies. Van Buren refused to take part in the scheme, but he did run for Vice-President with Jackson in 1832 and was elected.† As Vice-President, Van Buren "proved to be an able and fair presiding officer of the Senate."[16] He had Jackson's complete confidence and when Jackson retired from the presidency he enthusiastically endorsed Van Buren for President.

In 1835 President Jackson came close to being the first President to die in office. On January 30 of that year, while he was attending funeral services in the rotunda of the Capitol for Representative Warren Davis of South Carolina, Richard Lawrence, an English-born Washington house painter, attempted to shoot him. Standing at a distance of only several feet from his intended victim, the President, Lawrence pulled the triggers of two pistols. Both misfired, and Lawrence was immediately captured.[17] He was later found to be insane. If the attempt had succeeded, Martin Van Buren would have been the first Vice-President to succeed to the presidency on the death of a President. As it turned out, Van Buren succeeded Jackson by election in 1836, becoming the first Vice-President to become President since the passage of the Twelfth Amendment.

In the election of 1836, Van Buren easily won a majority of the number of the electors (170 out of 294). His running mate, Richard M. Johnson of Kentucky, was not so fortunate. Johnson re-

---

* Calhoun transmitted his resignation to the Secretary of State as required by the Act of March 1, 1792, which provided: "The only evidence of a refusal to accept, or of a resignation of the office of President or Vice President, shall be an instrument in writing, declaring the same, and subscribed by the person refusing to accept or resigning, as the case may be, and delivered into the office of the Secretary of State." This provision remains in effect. 3 U.S.C. §20 (1958). As a result of Calhoun's resignation, Hugh L. White of Tennessee, as President pro tempore, was placed first in the line of succession and Andrew Stevenson of Virginia, as Speaker, second.

† As with President Jefferson and Vice-President Clinton, Chief Justice John Marshall administered the oaths to both Jackson and Van Buren.

ceived 147, or exactly one-half, of the votes for the vice-presidency. Francis Granger of New York received 77 votes; John Tyler of Virginia, 47 votes; and William Smith of Alabama, 23 votes. The lack of a majority brought into effect, for the first and only time in our history, this provision of the Twelfth Amendment:

... [I]f no person have a majority, then from the two highest numbers on the list, the Senate shall choose the Vice-President; a quorum for the purpose shall consist of two-thirds of the whole number of Senators, and a majority of the whole number shall be necessary to a choice.

In the Senate, Johnson obtained 33 votes and Granger 4, and Johnson therefore became the ninth person to occupy the second office of the nation.

In 1840, the Democratic-Republican Convention unanimously nominated Van Buren for re-election. Since no vice-presidential candidate, including Johnson, was able to obtain the necessary two-thirds vote,* the Convention adopted this resolution:

RESOLVED, That the Convention deem it expedient at the present time not to choose between the individuals in nomination, but to leave the decision to their republican fellow-citizens in the several states, trusting that before the election shall take place, their opinions shall become so concentrated as to secure a choice of a Vice-President by the electoral colleges.[18]

Prior to the Convention, former President Jackson had written to Van Buren, advising him to select for his running-mate a person who could obtain widespread support, rather than Johnson who "would be a dead weight upon your popularity."[19] Since no nomination for Vice-President was made by the Convention, each state proposed a nominee for the position. Among those so nominated were Johnson, Littleton W. Tazewell of Virginia and James K. Polk of Tennessee. In the election, the Democratic candidates were defeated by the Whigs. Vice-President Johnson received forty-eight of the sixty Democratic electoral votes for Vice-President.

The Whigs, in the election of 1840, had nominated for President an old war hero, William Henry Harrison of Ohio, who had become famous in the Battle of Tippecanoe. For Vice-President they

---

* The Two-Thirds Rule was put into effect at the Democratic Nominating Convention of 1832. This convention was the first of its kind and did away with the caucus method of nominating presidential and vice-presidential candidates.

endorsed John Tyler of Virginia. Tyler had served as Governor of his state and as a member of the House of Representatives (1817-1821) and Senate (1827-1836). Although he had been a Democrat for all of his political life up to 1836 and had strongly opposed the Whig programs of protective tariffs, internal improvements and the national bank, he was endorsed by the Whigs because of the feeling that, as a staunch supporter of states' rights, he could win the southern states. The 1840 Whig Convention adopted no platform. The "log cabin and hard cider" campaign that followed was, perhaps, unique in its complete avoidance of issues. Under the campaign slogan, "Tippecanoe and Tyler too," the Whig candidates easily defeated the Democratic candidates. Harrison and Tyler each received 234 of the 294 electoral votes. Tyler's tenure as Vice-President was to be marked by the most significant development in the vice-presidency up to that time.

7

The Tyler Precedent

In upwards of half a century, this is the first instance of a Vice-President's being called to act as President of the United States, and brings to the test that provision of the Constitution which places in the Executive chair a man never thought of for it by anybody.

JOHN QUINCY ADAMS

When William Henry Harrison took the oath of office on March 4, 1841, as ninth President of the United States, he was in the sixty-ninth year of his life. But there was little cause for concern that he would not serve out his term. On Inauguration Day, 1841, "his bodily health was manifestly perfect: there was an alertness in his movement which is quite astonishing, considering his advanced age, the multiplied hardships through which his frame has passed, and the fatigues he has lately undergone," the *Daily National Intelligencer* reported to its readers on the following day.[1] Moreover, the fact that all of his predecessors had lived through and beyond their allotted official terms, probably lulled people into thinking there was no reason to believe that it would not be the same in this case. Perhaps it was overlooked that seven of the eight predecessors departed the presidency younger than Harrison was at his inauguration.

On March 4, 1841, after President pro tempore William R. King of Alabama had administered the oath to Tyler in the Senate chamber,* Harrison was sworn in on the east portico of the Capitol by Chief Justice Roger B. Taney. Then, standing without a hat or coat in the cold and brisk air, he delivered the longest inaugural address in history (8,578 words, lasting almost two hours). In the days that followed, Harrison is reported to have been overwhelmed by office seekers and fatigued by numerous social activities. At 12:30 A.M., on Sunday, April 4, 1841, exactly one month after becoming President, he was dead of pneumonia.

It appears that on Saturday, March 27, the President, as was his custom, had gone for an early morning walk to the market and was caught in a shower. He returned to the White House, complained of feeling ill and, after performing a few executive chores, went to bed. By evening a physician was called. On the next day the illness was diagnosed as pneumonia. Several other physicians were called in and the diagnosis was changed to bilious pleurisy. Although the country had been kept generally informed of the President's illness, his death caused much grief and shock. According to the public announcement of the death made by the Cabinet, the "last utterance of his lips expressed a fervent desire for the perpetuity of the Constitution and the preservation of its true principles."[2] Dr. N. W. Worthington, one of the consulting physicians, said that the last words he heard Harrison utter were: "Sir, I wish you to understand the true principles of the Government. I wish them carried out. I ask nothing more."[3] With Harrison at the time of his death were the members of his Cabinet, the Mayor of Washington, the rector of St. John's Episcopal Church, the marshal of the District of Columbia, the clerk of the Supreme Court and five physicians.

Harrison's death came at a time when Congress was not in session.† It was to convene on May 31 in a special session which Har-

---

* The usual practice was for the outgoing President to convene a special session of the Senate for March 4 to act upon Cabinet nominations by the new President and such other matters as might be necessary. The administering of the oath to the Vice-President was normally the first event at this session.

† Until the Twentieth Amendment, members of Congress were chosen in November, but their terms did not commence until the following March 4. In the interim, the old or "lame duck" Congress acted, in the second of its required sessions. Unless a special session were called by the President, the new Congress would not meet for its first regular session until the first Monday in the December following March 4—more than a year after the election. Moreover, there would be no speaker between March 4 and December until one was appointed by the House on the opening day of its first session. Under the

rison had called on March 17 for the purpose of considering "sundry important and weighty matters, principally growing out of the condition of the revenue and finances of the country. . . ."[4] Vice-President John Tyler was then at his home in Williamsburg, Virginia. He had not been kept officially informed of the illness, which was not surprising, as he rarely had any contact with President Harrison.

Immediately following the death, Secretary of State Daniel Webster dispatched his son, Fletcher, who was chief clerk in the State Department, to Tyler's residence in Williamsburg with the following message:

Washington, April 4, 1841.

John Tyler,
Vice-President of the United States.

Sir: It has become our most painful duty to inform you that William Henry Harrison, late President of the United States, has departed this life.

This distressing event took place this day at the President's mansion, in this city, at thirty minutes before 1 in the morning.

We lose no time in dispatching the chief clerk in the State Department as a special messenger to bear you these melancholy tidings.

We have the honor to be, with the highest regard, your obedient servants.

DANIEL WEBSTER,
Secretary of State.
THOMAS EWING,
Secretary of the Treasury.
JOHN BELL,
Secretary of War.
JOHN J. CRITTENDEN,
Attorney-General.
FRANCIS GRANGER,
Postmaster-General.[5]

Fletcher Webster, having to travel by boat and horse, did not arrive at Tyler's residence until early in the morning of April 5. Shortly after receiving the message, Tyler set out for the 230-mile journey to Washington. He arrived about 5:00 A.M. on April 6 and went to

---

Twentieth Amendment, on the opening day of the new Congress (January 3) the majority party promptly proceeds to elect one of its own as Speaker. He then holds that position continuously, at the pleasure of the House, until noon of January 3 of the second year ensuing.

Brown's Hotel. Several hours later he took the presidential oath of office at the hotel. It was administered in the presence of the Cabinet (except for Secretary of Navy George T. Curtis), Fletcher Webster, Jesse Brown, and several hotel guests by William Cranch, Chief Judge of the United States Circuit Court for the District of Columbia. Tyler wanted Roger B. Taney, Chief Justice of the Supreme Court, to administer the oath, but Taney was in Maryland at the time. It is said that shortly after Harrison's death, Daniel Webster had sent a message to Taney in Maryland, asking him to return and discuss whether or not Tyler should take the presidential oath. Taney, the account goes, refused to do so without an official invitation from the Cabinet or Tyler.[6]

There is some dispute as to Tyler's motive for taking the oath. It is said by some that he took it because he regarded himself without it as not legally President.[7] Others believe that Tyler, certain of his status as President upon Harrison's death, took the oath in order to remove any doubt that might arise in the future.[8] This view is supported by the certification given by Cranch at the time of the oath's administration.* It stated:

I, William Cranch, chief judge of the circuit court of the District of Columbia, certify that the above-named John Tyler personally appeared before me this day, and although he deems himself qualified to perform the duties and exercise the powers and office of President on the death of William Henry Harrison, late President of the United States, without any other oath than that which he has taken as Vice-President, yet as doubts may *arise,* and for greater caution, took and subscribed the foregoing oath before me.[9]

Tyler had met informally with the members of the Cabinet before taking the oath and indicated to them that he would continue Harrison's policies and that it was his desire that they continue to serve in their present capacities. After taking the oath, he held his first official Cabinet meeting in the privacy of his hotel rooms. At this first meeting, Daniel Webster is said to have expressed himself as follows:

---

* The Vice-President takes an oath faithfully to perform his duties, one of which is the succession duty. Consequently, it is suggested that Tyler did not have to take the presidential oath as he had already taken an oath for the duty he was about to discharge. Whatever devolves on a Vice-President in case of a President's death should do so at the time of the President's death and not when the presidential oath is taken.

Mr. President, I suppose you intend to carry on the ideas and customs of your predecessor, and that this administration inaugurated by President Harrison will continue in the same line of policy under which it has begun. It was our custom in the cabinet of the deceased President, that the President should preside over us. Our custom and proceeding was that all measures whatever, however, relating to the administration were brought before the cabinet, and their settlement was decided by a majority—each member, *and the President having one vote*.[10]

Tyler answered:

I beg your pardon, gentlemen. I am sure I am very glad to have in my cabinet such able statesmen as you have proved yourselves to be, and I shall be pleased to avail myself of your counsel and advice, but I can never consent to being dictated to as to what I shall or shall not do. I, as president, will be responsible for my administration. I hope to have your co-operation in carrying out its measures; so long as you see fit to do this, I shall be glad to have you with me—when you think otherwise, your resignations will be accepted.[11]

Uncertainty about what course the new administration would take caused the *New York Herald* of April 6 to declare that:

All eyes will now be turned towards Washington, looking with doubt and anxiety to the organization of the administration, under the new President. The event has produced much consternation among the politicians. The great questions are, who is John Tyler? what are his principles? what will be his policy?

On April 9, 1841, Tyler delivered what amounted to an inaugural address, in which he stated that

This . . . occurrence has subjected the wisdom and sufficiency of our institutions to a new test. For the first time in our history the person elected to the Vice-Presidency of the United States, by the happening of a contingency provided for in the Constitution, has had devolved upon him the Presidential office. . . . I shall place in the intelligence and patriotism of the people my only sure reliance. My earnest prayer shall be constantly addressed to the all-wise and all-powerful Being who made me, and by whose dispensation I am called to the high office of President of this Confederacy, understandingly to carry out the principles of that Constitution which I have sworn "to protect, preserve, and defend."[12]

On April 13, Tyler issued a proclamation recommending May 14 as a day of prayer and fasting. On April 14, he moved into the White House. And thus it was that the *New York American* could state on April 16: "It is impossible for an American not to feel . . . great pride at the quiet, orderly, and, as it were, matter of course transition, by which so important a movement has been operated."[13]

Tyler's ascendancy to the office of President, and not merely to its powers and duties, was not without opposition. Some thought that his action was unconstitutional in that he was still the Vice-President, with the additional responsibility of discharging the powers and duties of President. John Quincy Adams, sixth President of the United States and then a member of the House of Representatives, made this notation in his diary of April 16, 1841:

I paid a visit this morning to Mr. Tyler, who styles himself President of the United States, and not Vice-President, acting as President, which would be the correct style. But it is a construction in direct violation both of the grammar and context of the Constitution, which confers upon the Vice-President, on the decease of the President, not the office, but the powers and duties of the said office.[14]

In Adams' view, Tyler was "Acting President of the Union for four years less one month."[15] Others disagreed. Daniel Webster is said to have been of the opinion that the powers and duties were inseparable from the office and that any succession by a Vice-President was to the office and title of President for the remainder of the term.[16] The Cabinet seems to have accepted Tyler as President. Although they addressed him as Vice-President in the message notifying him of Harrison's death, this probably was an oversight.[17]

In the newspapers of the day, Tyler was variously referred to as the "Acting President," "Accidental President," and "New President." Some spoke of the duties of the presidency devolving upon him; others of his succession to the office of President. There was, however, little newspaper criticism of his assumption of the office and title of President. To put an end to the confusion on Tyler's status, the leading Whig paper of the day, the *Daily National Intelligencer,* stated on April 15:

An erroneous conception of the quality and designation of the office devolving on the Vice President . . . seems to prevail in some of the public papers, in which Mr. Tyler is styled the *acting* President: as if he were still, *ex officio,* Vice President, merely acting *ad interim* as President. . . . Whereas he is, to all intents and purposes, by the appointment of the Constitution, and by election, President of the United States; in-

94

vested with the office proper of President, with as plenary right and authority as his predecessor . . .; and exercises the powers of the office, not in his quality of Vice President but of President, the office of Vice President being vacated by his accession to the office of President, or entirely merged in the superior office. By the terms of the Constitution, the *office* of President, "*devolves* on the Vice President." By his original election as Vice President, he was *provisionally* elected President; that is, elected to the office of President upon the happening of any one of the conditions provided in the Constitution.[18]

When the special session of the Twenty-Seventh Congress met on May 31, 1841, some of its members took strong exception to Tyler's assumption of the presidential office. On that day, Henry A. Wise of Virginia introduced a resolution in the House of Representatives calling for the formation of a committee "to wait on the President of the United States. . . ."[19] Representative John McKeon of New York immediately moved to strike out the word "President" and insert "Vice-President, now exercising the office of President."[20] He argued that "a grave constitutional question" was presented which should be set "at rest for all future time." The Constitution, he said, provided only for the devolution of the powers and duties, but he would have no objection to giving Tyler the President's salary. Wise stated that Tyler would claim his right and title to the office "by the Constitution, by election and by the act of God," so that Congress should address him accordingly. The House rejected McKeon's suggestion and passed the Wise resolution intact, forwarding it to the Senate, which discussed it the next day.

There, Senator William Allen of Ohio strongly urged that Tyler be addressed as "the Vice President, on whom by the death of the late President, the powers and duties of the office of President have devolved."[21] If the President were afflicted with a disease producing a mental disability and then recovered, said Allen, he could be reinstated to the powers and duties of his office. Allen said that he would have no objection if Tyler called himself President, but he wanted it understood that a man could achieve the presidency only by election. Senator David Tappan, also of Ohio, agreed, saying that under the Constitution a person could become President only through the elective route and not by succession. If a military commander is shot in battle, argued Tappan, the most senior officer takes command—without assuming the rank of the person shot.

Give Tyler the President's salary, call him President in private, but officially he must be recognized as the Vice-President, concluded Tappan.[22]

Senator Robert J. Walker of Mississippi disagreed. In his opinion the Constitution provided for two separate contingencies. He said that it was explicit that an officer appointed by Congress merely *acts* as President where both President and Vice-President are immobilized but that there is no such limitation on a Vice-President who takes over for an immobilized President. The Vice-President, therefore, must succeed to the office. "This is the language and the meaning of the Constitution," he said. "Can there be any doubt on the subject?"[23]

Senator Allen thought there was. He hypothesized a case of temporary disability, more easily conceived of by the Founding Fathers than death, he said, where a disabled President recovered to find the Vice-President in his office. "What would become of the office," said Allen. "Was it to vibrate between the two claimants?" If the country were divided into political factions and the Vice-President, having succeeded to the office, insisted on holding onto the office, he might prevail in having the President "take his place as a private citizen." If Walker's doctrine that the office devolves were established, he urged, "the most fearful convulsions might follow." According to Allen, there was no manner known to the Constitution by which "a President of the United States—unimpeached, sane, and alive"—could cease to be President.[24]

Senator John C. Calhoun of South Carolina thought that this discussion was academic since there was a permanent vacancy in the presidential office. The Senate, jumping at this opportunity to close the discussion, passed the House resolution without change, by a vote of thirty-eight to eight,[25] and the Tyler precedent became firmly established in our history.

By virtue of the law of 1792, Tyler's immediate successors for the forty-seven months he served as President were the President pro tempore and the Speaker. At the time of his accession to the presidency, Samuel L. Southard of New Jersey was President pro tempore. He had been chosen on March 11 at the special session of the Senate (convened for the Inauguration) after Tyler had retired from the chair for the rest of the session. The session adjourned on Monday, March 15. As President pro tempore after Tyler's succession, Southard was not technically the new Vice-

President though he was regarded as such by some. The *New York American,* a Whig newspaper, felt compelled to state in its issue of Tuesday, April 6: "Many journals we observe speak of Mr. Southard, the President *pro tem.* of the Senate, as now Vice-President. Not so. The office of Vice-President is vacant, and will so remain until the next election." Southard remained President pro tempore until the Senate selected Willie P. Mangum of North Carolina as its presiding officer at the special session which commenced on May 31, 1841. Between April 4 and May 31, Southard was the only available successor. On May 31, the new House of Representatives (as of March 4) met and elected John White of Kentucky as Speaker.

Neither the President pro tempore nor the Speaker had to be called upon during Tyler's tenure to take over the helm of government. There was one close call, however. On February 28, 1844, Tyler visited the *U.S.S. Princeton,* the first propeller-driven warship, with members of his Cabinet, the Congress, and the diplomatic corps. The ship departed from Alexandria, Virginia, and sailed down the Potomac River. On the return trip, the ship's "Peacemaker," the world's largest naval gun, exploded during a demonstration firing, as many of the passengers crowded around it. Killed by the explosion were the Secretary of State, Abel P. Upshur, the Secretary of Navy, Thomas W. Gilmer, and five others. Eleven, including the Captain, a Senator and members of the crew were wounded. Tyler was below deck at the time and escaped injury.[26] Senator Willie P. Mangum of North Carolina was still President pro tempore of the Senate.

Tyler's administration of the presidency was notable for his opposition to the various programs of the Whig Party,* in particular, the establishment of a national bank. His veto of a bill proposing a national bank resulted in the whole Cabinet, except Daniel Webster, resigning on September 11, 1841. Webster remained until

---

* His opposition to tariff legislation brought forth a bitter denunciation of his administration in 1842 by a House Committee investigating his reasons for vetoing a tariff-distribution bill. The Committee, the chairman of which was John Quincy Adams, recommended that the Constitution be amended to allow Congress to override a presidential veto by majority vote, and suggested that Tyler could be impeached. Impeachment resolutions were actually introduced in July, 1842, but were not acted upon. In January, 1843, the matter of impeaching him was put to a vote and was defeated, 127 to 83.

1843 to conclude the Webster-Ashburton Treaty defining the disputed boundary between Maine and Canada. On September 13, 1841, two days after the mass walkout of the Cabinet, Tyler was officially expelled from the Whig Party by a caucus of Whig congressmen in Capitol Square.

Tyler carried on without a party and, among other things, reorganized the United States Navy, established the weather bureau, negotiated a treaty with China which opened the Orient to Ameriand Trade for the first time, brought the Seminole War to an end, and succeeded in having Texas annexed by a joint resolution of Congress. Upon leaving office in 1845 and after having started and dropped an independent campaign for re-election, Tyler retired to a quiet life in Virginia (Sherwood Forest). When he died on January 18, 1862, there was no official announcement by the government that he had died. It was not until 1911 that Congress authorized the erection of a monument to his memory. No monument was really necessary for John Tyler. His had been erected at the outset of his administration—the Tyler Precedent whereby the Vice-President becomes President on the death of the elected President.

8

An Era of Tragedy

A great man has fallen among us, and a whole country is called to an occasion of unexpected, deep, and general mourning.

MILLARD FILLMORE

Harrison's death and Tyler's accession to the presidency did not have any noticeable effect on the criteria for selecting a vice-presidential candidate. "Balancing the ticket" and appeasing disappointed factions remained the principal determinants.

In 1844, James K. Polk of Tennessee, who had been Speaker of the House of Representatives from 1835 to 1839, received the presidential nomination of the Democratic Convention on the ninth ballot as a compromise candidate, and became the first "dark horse" to be nominated for President in American history. Since former President Martin Van Buren had been the leading candidate for the nomination and since it was good politics to placate his supporters, Senator Silas Wright of New York was nominated almost unanimously for Vice-President. Wright's loyalties to Van Buren, however, were of such intensity that he rejected the nomination. The Convention then turned to George M. Dallas, a fifty-one-year-old practicing Philadelphia lawyer who had been Minister to Russia under Van Buren. In the election which followed, Polk and Dallas defeated the Whig candidates, Henry Clay of Kentucky and Theodore Frelinghuysen of New Jersey.

As President and Vice-President, respectively, Polk and Dallas enjoyed a friendly relationship. Although Dallas appears to have taken part in no Cabinet meetings, he was often consulted by Polk on matters of policy and asked to comment on Polk's messages in their early draft stages.[1] As a presiding officer of the Senate, Dallas supported his Party's platform. "[H]is dignified, yet winning manners, uniform courtesy and fairness, and ample stores of information added to the authority which his official station gave him. The traditions of the Senate ascribe to no one of his eminent predecessors a superiority to Mr. Dallas, as a presiding officer."[2] When called upon to cast tie-breaking votes, Dallas would do so according to his conception of the national interest. Thus, in casting a crucial vote for the Walker Tariff Bill of 1846, which was opposed by his state, he said:

To my mind, ample proof has been furnished that a majority of the people and of the States desire to change . . . the system . . . in assessing the duties on foreign imports. . . . In a case free from constitutional objection, I could not justifiably counteract, by a sort of official veto, the general will.[3]

He went on to say: "The Vice President, now called upon to act, is the direct agent and representative of the whole people."

Polk and Dallas retired from the national scene in 1849 upon the inauguration of General Zachary Taylor and Millard Fillmore. Although Fillmore had served four terms as a Representative in Congress from New York and was partly responsible for the Tariff Act of 1842, he was not well known nationally. He won the vice-presidential nomination of the Whig Party on the second ballot, defeating Abbott Lawrence of Massachusetts, the favorite at the Convention's opening. Fillmore was chosen because he was a Northerner and because it was felt that the followers of Clay, who had lost the presidential nomination, would be conciliated. Yet, in a little more than sixteen months after Inauguration Day, March 5, 1849,*

---

* It is interesting to note that March 4, 1849, fell on a Sunday, so that Taylor did not take his oath as President until the next day. On March 2, 1849, Vice-President George Mifflin Dallas had vacated his position as President of the Senate and Senator David R. Atchison of Missouri had been appointed President pro tempore. It is therefore said by some that on March 4, Atchison was President of the United States. Thus his monument in Missouri contains these words: "David Rice Atchison, 1807–1886. President of U.S. one day. Lawyer, statesman and jurist." It is questionable whether this interpretation is correct. Both the succession provision of the Constitution and the 1792 law prescribed that the officer designated by Congress should act upon

100

Fillmore was to become the thirteenth President of the United States.

On Tuesday, July 9, 1850, Zachary Taylor became the second President to die in office. On Thursday, July 4, Taylor had attended lengthy ceremonies at the Washington Monument with his head bared to the hot sun. Upon returning to the White House, he had partaken freely of iced drinks and fruit. The following morning he was sick, the diagnosis being "cholera morbus." On the evening of July 8, this bulletin was released to the public: "The President is laboring under a bilious remittent fever, following an attack of serious cholera morbus; and is considered by his physicians seriously ill."[4] Between July 4 and July 9, when this bulletin—the first official announcement of the President's illness—appeared in the newspapers, rumors had circulated that the President was not well. At approximately 10:30 P.M. on July 9, Taylor died. His last words were: "I am not afraid to die; I have done my duty; my only regret is leaving those who are dear to me."[5]

As in the case of Harrison, the Cabinet, which had assembled in an anteroom earlier that day, immediately notified Fillmore of Taylor's death, addressing him as "President of the United States." Fillmore promptly dispatched a note to the Cabinet in which he stated:

I have no language to express the emotions of my heart. The shock is so sudden and unexpected that I am overwhelmed with grief.

I shall avail myself of the earliest moment to communicate this sad intelligence to Congress, and shall appoint a time and place for taking the oath of office prescribed to the President of the United States. You are requested to be present and witness the ceremony.[6]

Taylor's death did not take Fillmore completely by surprise, since he had known of the illness over the weekend and had been summoned to the White House from the Senate Chamber that afternoon and informed that the President was dying.

On the following day, Fillmore sent a message to the Senate saying that because of Taylor's death he would "no longer occupy the chair of the Senate," and suggesting that "a presiding officer" be

the death, resignation, removal or inability of both the President and Vice-President. None of these contingencies had occurred. Therefore, Atchison could not have acted as President. See p. 275n. It was not until 1933 that provisions dealing with the President-elect and the Vice-President-elect were adopted. See pp. 190–91.

chosen.[7] He also sent a message to Congress announcing that he would take the presidential oath in the Hall of the House of Representatives, in the presence of both Houses, at twelve o'clock that day.* Announcements of the President's death were also sent to representatives of the United States abroad, to representatives of foreign governments in the United States and to the Army.

On July 10, 1850, at twelve o'clock, the presidential oath of office was administered to Fillmore by Judge William Cranch, Chief Judge of the United States Circuit Court of the District of Columbia. Fillmore delivered no address, but sent a brief message to Congress. "To you, Senators and Representatives of a nation in tears," he said, "I can say nothing which can alleviate the sorrow with which you are oppressed. I appeal to you to aid me, under the trying circumstances which surround me, in the discharge of the duties from which, however much I may be oppressed by them, I dare not shrink. . . ."[8]

The July 11 issue of the *Daily National Intelligencer* described the accession of Fillmore:

It was the incident of the day which probably made less impression than some others on American spectators, but was precisely that which is most calculated to attract the notice of foreigners. The death of the President being announced, a citizen, plainly attired, enters among the assembled Representatives of the Nation, walks up to the Clerk's desk, takes an oath on the Bible to support the Constitution of the United States; and, by this brief ceremony, he becomes, in an instant of time, invested with the command of the whole military force of a mighty empire, with the execution of its laws and the administration of the power. No one objects or dreams of objection; the act is acquiesced in as a thing of course, and with the submission that would be rendered to a law of nature. The sceptre of the People passes into his hands as quietly and as quickly as a power of attorney could be acknowledged before a justice of the peace . . . . In some countries such a transfer of power would have cost streams of blood, and shaken the Government to its very foundations.

On the night of Fillmore's inauguration, the members of the Cabinet tendered their resignations pro forma. Surprisingly, Fillmore

---

* On the same day Daniel Webster introduced a resolution, which was passed unanimously, to have Congress assemble to witness the administration of the oath to "the late Vice-President." Cong. Globe, 31st Cong., 1st Sess. (1850), p. 1363.

accepted all of them, but asked that the Cabinet members remain in their positions for a month until he could reorganize his administration. They agreed to remain, but only for a week. In selecting men for the new Cabinet, Fillmore's major concern was whether they were men who possessed a "national outlook." His purpose was to overcome the sectionalism which was rampant at the time. Accordingly, Daniel Webster was substituted for John M. Clayton as Secretary of State, Thomas Corwin for William M. Meredith as Secretary of Treasury, Charles M. Conrad for George W. Crawford as Secretary of War, John J. Crittenden for Reverdy Johnson as Attorney General, Nathan K. Hall for Jacob Collamer as Postmaster General, William A. Graham for William B. Preston as Secretary of the Navy, and Thomas M. T. McKennan* for Thomas Ewing as Secretary of Interior.

Fillmore had enjoyed little influence in Taylor's administration. Although the idea of including him in Cabinet meetings had occurred to Taylor prior to his inauguration, he seems to have rejected it on the advice of his friend Senator John J. Crittenden of Kentucky.[9] Fillmore's succession to the presidency came at a critical juncture in history, since Congress was then embroiled in its debates over the Compromise of 1850, involving the question of slavery in the Southwest. Taylor had been opposed to the Compromise. Texas was threatening to send a force into New Mexico to establish its claims to the Rio Grande. War between the North and South over the slavery question was threatening. The question which was uppermost in the minds of many was how Fillmore would stand on the Compromise. As Vice-President, he had presided over the debates in a strictly impartial manner. It soon became clear that as President he would support the Compromise. Before the end of September, 1850, the Compromise had passed both Houses and been signed into law. The problem of territorial government which had plagued the nation for several years was thus settled under Fillmore's leadership. Although this course lost him much Northern support, it delayed war for ten years. Fillmore, like Tyler before him, was not able to secure the presidential nomination at the next election. However, it is to his lasting credit that the country successfully passed through its second case of presidential succession.

The succession of Fillmore left a vacancy in the vice-presidency

---

* He resigned after a month and was replaced by Alexander H. H. Stuart.

for the fourth time in less than fifty years. The Senate promptly filled the post of President pro tempore on July 11, 1850, electing a Democrat, William R. King of Alabama. From the time of Taylor's death on July 9 to King's election, the only available successor in case of a vacancy in the presidency was Howell Cobb of Georgia, Democratic Speaker of the House, who was then in his fourth term as a congressman but, at the age of thirty-four, not quite old enough to be President.

Presiding over the Senate was no new chore for King, as he had served in that position from 1836 to 1841, at a time when the office of President pro tempore "was of more than usual importance while the inefficient Richard Mentor Johnson occupied the Vice-Presidency."[10] King was considered "the great parliamentarian of the Senate" and, because of his extended service and advanced age, was called the "Father of the United States Senate."

The 1852 Democratic Convention nominated forty-eight-year-old Franklin Pierce of New Hampshire for President on the forty-ninth ballot. Pierce had not been a major contender for the nomination, but when none of the leading candidates (James Buchanan, Lewis Cass and Stephen Douglas) was able to obtain the necessary two-thirds vote of the Convention, he became the second "dark horse" in American history to win the presidential nomination. In order to satisfy the supporters of Buchanan, the vice-presidential nomination was given to King, who had been an ardent champion of Buchanan's cause. King, then in his sixty-seventh year, thus realized "an ambition of long standing."[11] His nomination, however, was "more a personal tribute than a political triumph, for King had an incurable disease which made it nearly certain that he would not survive another administration."[12]

In the election of 1852, Pierce and King carried all but four of the thirty-one states. They defeated the Whig candidates, General Winfield Scott of New Jersey and William Alexander Graham of North Carolina. But King was never actually to serve as Vice-President. After the election, he continued to serve as President pro tempore until he resigned on December 20, 1852, in order to travel to Cuba because of his health.

As Inauguration Day, 1853 approached, it became evident that King would not be able to return to the United States in order to be sworn in as Vice-President. On February 24, 1853, Senator Andrew P. Butler of South Carolina introduced a bill authorizing William L.

Sharkey, United States Consul at Havana, to administer the oath to King. The bill was unanimously passed on March 2 and, on March 24, 1853, King became the first and only Vice-President of the United States to take the oath on foreign soil. The oath was administered to King, who had to be assisted to stand, on the Ariadne estate, near Matanzas, Cuba, in the presence of some fifteen persons.[13]

King's health continued to deteriorate and he decided to return to the United States for his last days. He arrived at his home in Alabama on April 17 and the following day he died of tuberculosis at his plantation in Cahawba, Dallas County, Alabama. By proclamation dated April 20, 1853, President Pierce ordered appropriate military and naval honors for King and decreed that all "public offices will be closed tomorrow and badges of mourning be placed on the Executive Mansion and all the Executive Departments at Washington." Pierce paid further tribute to the memory of his Vice-President in his first annual message to Congress on December 5, 1853, in which he said, "His loss to the country, under all the circumstances, has been justly regarded as irreparable."[14]

The death of the Vice-President came at a time when President Pierce was not in the best of health, being troubled by malaria. Consequently, time and again during the next few months speculation was aroused as to the chances of David R. Atchison of Missouri, President pro tempore and a leading exponent of southern interests in the Senate, succeeding to the presidency.* As in the case of Harrison's death, there was confusion as to the status of the President pro tempore. *The Evening Post* felt it necessary to declare in its edition of April 22, 1853 that:

The death of the late Vice-President of the United States creates a vacancy in that office for which there is no authority at present existing in any quarter to fill. The statement current in the morning prints that Senator Atchison of Missouri, the present President of the Senate, is or

---

* Atchison remained President pro tempore until December 4, 1853, when Lewis Cass of Michigan was chosen. On the following day, Cass was replaced by Jesse D. Bright of Indiana. As the House had not assembled, there was no Speaker at the time of King's death. Linn Boyd of Kentucky, a Democrat, was elected on December 5, 1853. During the period of the vacancy in the vice-presidency, Charles E. Stuart of Michigan and James M. Mason of Virginia also served as President pro tempore and Nathaniel P. Banks of Massachusetts as Speaker.

can be Vice-President *ex officio,* is a mistake. The Constitution of the United States has made no provision for supplying a vacancy in the Vice-Presidency in the place of that officer.

The *Post* was doubtless correct, since the Constitution made no provision for filling a vacancy in the vice-presidency. The Act of 1792, moreover, provided only for vacancies occurring in both the offices of President and Vice-President.

King's death gave rise to one of the first attempts to amend the 1792 succession law. Several bills were introduced in Congress to amend the law.[15] On June 26, 1856, the Senate adopted a resolution directing its Committee on the Judiciary to examine the law of succession and determine whether the provisions were constitutional, proper and adequate, or whether further legislation was necessary.[16] The Committee thoroughly examined the subject and concluded that the law of 1792 was constitutional both as to the President pro tempore and Speaker and as to its special election feature.* Recognizing that there might be periods when there was no President pro tempore or Speaker, it recommended that the line of succession after the Speaker be added to so as to include the Chief Justice (provided he had not participated in the impeachment trial of the President) and then the justices of the Supreme Court according to the date of their commissions.[17] It specified in its recommendation that no justice be permitted to act if he were under impeachment or if he did not have the constitutional qualifications for President. The Committee objected to a Cabinet line of succession on the grounds that in a case where the President was impeached, the Cabinet members might be involved in a plot with him, and that it was questionable whether they could be regarded as "officers" when the President's authority had ceased. In it deliberations the Judiciary Committee overlooked the question of de-

---

* The Committee thought that if a special election occurred, the persons selected to fill the vacancies in the offices of President and Vice-President would serve for a full four-year term. It noted that Congress had no power to fill a vacancy occurring in the vice-presidency. Despite the debates at the Constitutional Convention and the adoption of language clearly intended to allow for a special presidential election in the event of a double vacancy (see pp. 46–47, 55), questions arose immediately after the passage of the 1792 law as to whether its special election feature was constitutional (see p. 60, ‡). The precise meaning of the words "until another President shall be elected" has been debated ever since by constitutional authorities. It has been maintained that they do not permit a special election.

106

vising a procedure for filling a vacancy in the vice-presidency despite the fact that, because of King's death, the office was to be vacant for nearly four years. It was not until the inauguration, on March 4, 1857, of James Buchanan's Vice-President, John C. Breckinridge (who, at the age of thirty-six years, was the youngest man ever to hold the vice-presidency) that the vacancy was filled. No significant development occurred in the vice-presidency during Buchanan's administration.

Under Abraham Lincoln, however, the Vice-President was to become an influential figure in the administration. Elected with Lincoln in 1860 as his Vice-President was a fifty-one-year-old United States Senator from Maine—Hannibal Hamlin. Hamlin had served several terms in both Houses of Congress and was Governor of Maine for a brief period in 1856 before resigning to return to the Senate. He had been a member of the Democratic Party, but had withdrawn in 1856 because he could not accept the party's position on slavery. Since Lincoln was from the West and had Whig antecedents, Hamlin's eastern orientation and past Democratic affiliations made him an ideal running mate. It is said that Hamlin accepted the nomination reluctantly because he regarded his Senate post as more influential than the vice-presidency.[18]

Shortly after Hamlin became Vice-President-elect, Lincoln wrote him a letter asking him to come to Chicago to discuss Cabinet appointments and federal patronage. At this meeting, Lincoln said: "Mr. Hamlin, I desire to say to you that I shall accept, and shall always be willing to accept, in the very best spirit, any advice that you, the Vice-President, may give me."[19] This policy represented a drastic departure from that of the past where communication between Presidents and Vice-Presidents was, as has been noted, almost nonexistent. The relationship thus established was a friendly one. Lincoln communicated frequently with Hamlin. He respected Hamlin's judgment and relied on his advice: "Indeed, it is a fact which may be stated in passing that Mr. Hamlin never asked the great President to perform any act which he did not perform."[20]

The election of 1864 returned Lincoln to the presidency and with him a new Vice-President. Hamlin failed to obtain renomination, in part because of the need, for the sake of national unity, of a Democrat on the ticket who had opposed secession and stood by the Union during the Civil War. Andrew Johnson of Tennessee was the logical choice. He had successively been a state legislator, United

107

States Representative, Governor, United States Senator and Military Governor. In all, he had served for twenty-eight years in public life. When Tennessee seceded from the Union in 1861, Johnson's principles would not permit him to acquiesce. He was the only southern Senator who refused to secede with his state.

In December of 1860, Johnson had made an impassioned speech for unity in the Senate, saying of President-elect Lincoln: "I voted against him; I spoke against him; I spent my money to defeat him; but still I love my country; I love the Constitution; I intend to insist upon its guarantees."[21]

As Military Governor of Tennessee, to which position he had been appointed by Lincoln, and as a supporter of the Union, Johnson had been the most prominent of the War Democrats. When the Union wing of the Democratic Party joined the Republicans in 1864 to form the National Union Party, he was selected on the fourth ballot to run with Lincoln.

The inauguration of President Lincoln and Vice-President Johnson in 1865 came at a time when the Civil War was almost at an end and when the responsibilities of the presidency were indeed great. How to restore the seceded states to the Union was the major question of the day. Forty-one days after the inauguration, President Lincoln was dead, the victim of an assassin.*

In the autumn of 1864, John Wilkes Booth, an actor and Confederate sympathizer, had conceived a plot to kidnap Lincoln and turn him over to the Confederate authorities in Richmond. He was able to persuade several others who sympathized with the South to join the conspiracy. By March, 1865, there were seven in all— Booth, Samuel Bland Arnold, Michael O'Laughlin, John H. Surratt, George E. Atzerodt, David Herold, and Lewis Thornton Powell.

The kidnap attempt was scheduled for March 17, when Lincoln was expected to attend a theatrical performance at an army hospital encampment. The conspirators met and waited, armed, for Lincoln to appear but he never came, and the plan failed. The conspirators separated and the plan was dropped, at least temporarily.

By April 2, when Richmond fell, Arnold, O'Laughlin and Surratt had left Washington and notified Booth that they no longer

---

* It is to be noted that before his inauguration in 1861, a plot to assassinate Lincoln in Baltimore had been foiled by Allan Pinkerton, a detective who guarded him.

wanted to be a part of the plan. But Powell, Atzerodt and Herold were willing to try again.[22]

On April 14, five days after Lee surrendered to Grant, the stars and stripes were once again raised over Fort Sumter. It was a day of great celebration. Booth, however, was greatly shaken at the turn of events. Early that day he noted in his diary. "[O]ur cause being almost lost, something decisive & great must be done."[23]

In keeping with the festive spirit of the day, Lincoln had made plans to attend a play at Ford's theatre that night with Mrs. Lincoln and two guests. The day began with a Cabinet meeting, at which the President told about a peculiar dream in which he seemed to be floating in a vessel of water and moving toward some indefinite shore. It was the same dream, said Lincoln, that he had frequently just before something important happened. He said he thought it meant there would soon be good news from Sherman.

After lunch Lincoln worked in his office for a while and saw several callers. Then he and Mrs. Lincoln went for a carriage ride. When the President returned to the White House he conferred with some visitors and then had dinner, after which he paid a business call on Secretary of War Stanton. He returned to the White House and spoke to a few more visitors before leaving for the play.

The presidential party did not arrive at Ford's Theatre until after the play had begun. Accompanying the President as his sole guard that night was one of four Washington policemen assigned to the President. This particular man had a record which indicated that he was not one of the most conscientious of the guards. When the President's party entered the theatre the play ceased temporarily as the band played "Hail to the Chief," and the party made its way to the reserved box amid loud applause and cheers. As President and Mrs. Lincoln and their guests settled down in their box, the play was resumed. Lincoln seemed to enjoy the play and the frequent ad-libbed references to him. Meanwhile, the guard had left his post outside the door of the box to find a seat.

During the day, Booth had been busy making preparations to assassinate the President. An hour before the play began he met with Powell, Atzerodt and Herold at Powell's boarding house near Ford's Theatre to discuss the plan. Booth was to kill Lincoln. Atzerodt was to go to Kirkwood House, where Vice-President Johnson lived and where Atzerodt had already taken a room, and kill Johnson. Powell was to kill Secretary of State Seward at his home, where he was confined to bed due to injuries received in a recent accident. Herold was to guide Powell out of Washington after Seward had been killed.

At a little after ten o'clock, Booth entered the theatre. He walked up some stairs to the dress circle which led to the President's box. Slowly making his way through the crowd, he quietly entered the vestibule outside the box and barred the door behind him. Then he slipped unnoticed into the President's box and, placing his pistol close to the back of the President's head, fired one shot. Major Rathbone, one of the President's two guests, quickly jumped to his feet and, seeing Booth attempted to seize him. Booth had a knife, however, and stabbed Rathbone in the arm. Then shouting "Sic semper tyrannis," he leaped from the box to the stage, breaking a bone in his leg as he landed, and ran out a rear exit to an alley where his horse was waiting. Before anyone could overtake him, he had disappeared.

Meanwhile, Powell had gone to Seward's residence under the pretext of delivering medicine, and when Seward's son, Frederick, refused to admit him, forced his way in by beating young Seward over the head with a gun. He then ran upstairs to the elder Seward's room and stabbed him several times in the face and neck. As the male army nurse attending Seward tried to intervene, he too was stabbed several times. Before leaving, Powell also attacked another of Seward's sons and a messenger who had arrived on the scene. Atzerodt, on the other hand, after a few drinks, had decided not to kill the Vice-President and fled to Maryland.*

After Lincoln had been shot, he was carried, unconscious, to the nearby home of William Petersen. Lincoln's family and governmental officials quickly assembled at the house. Leonard J. Farwell, Inspector of Inventions at the Patent Office and a former Governor of Wisconsin, who was in Ford's Theater at the time of the shooting, ran to the nearby Kirkwood House to tell Johnson that Lincoln had been shot and to arrange to have the Vice-President protected. Others soon arrived at Kirkwood House with conflicting accounts of what had happened. Johnson asked Farwell to go to both Lin-

---

* The conspirators all paid for their actions. Powell was arrested on April 17, Atzerodt on April 20, and Herold on April 26. Booth refused to surrender when trapped by United States troops at a tobacco farm in Virginia, and was shot to death. Powell, Atzerodt and Herold were tried by a military commission and hanged. Arnold and O'Laughlin were sentenced to prison.

coln and the Secretary of State and find out what actually had happened. Shortly thereafter, Farwell returned with the information that Lincoln was unconscious and near death, and that an attempt had been made to murder Seward in his home. It had failed, but Seward had been badly stabbed and his son Frederick, the Assistant Secretary of State, had also been seriously wounded. Upon receiving this news, Johnson hurriedly left his residence and, traveling several blocks on foot through crowded streets, went to the room where Lincoln lay dying. He stayed there for a while and then returned to his room at the Kirkwood House.

Lincoln expired at 7:22 A.M. on Saturday, April 15. "Now he belongs to the ages," Secretary of War Edwin M. Stanton is reported to have said at that moment.[24] James A. Garfield, then a member of the House of Representatives, on learning of Lincoln's death, spoke from a balcony to a crowd of hysterical people on Wall Street, saying: "Fellow citizens: God reigns, and the Government at Washington still lives."[25]

On the morning of Lincoln's death, the Cabinet—Secretary of the Treasury Hugh McCulloch, Secretary of War Edwin M. Stanton, Secretary of the Navy Gideon Welles, Postmaster General William Dennison, Secretary of the Interior John P. Usher and Attorney General James Speed—gave Johnson official notification of the death. They addressed him as "Vice-President of the United States" but said:

By the death of President Lincoln the office of President has devolved, under the Constitution, upon you. The emergency of the Government demands that you should immediately qualify, according to the requirements of the Constitution, and enter upon the duties of President of the United States.[26]

At 10:00 A.M., on April 15, in a parlor at the Kirkwood House, Chief Justice Salmon Portland Chase of the Supreme Court administered the presidential oath of office to the fifty-seven-year-old Johnson. Those present included the members of the Cabinet, except for Welles and Seward, and several friends of Johnson. After taking the oath, Johnson proceeded to deliver a brief address, which was later criticized for its failure to mention Lincoln by name and for the frequent recurrence of the pronoun "I". The address, in part, went as follows:

111

I must be permitted to say that I have been almost overwhelmed by the announcement of the sad event which has so recently occurred. I feel incompetent to perform duties so important and responsible as those which have been so unexpectedly thrown upon me. As to an indication of any policy which may be pursued by me in the administration of the Government, I have to say that that must be left for development as the Administration progresses. . . . The only assurance I can now give of the future is reference to the past. The course which I have taken in the past in connection with this rebellion must be regarded as a guaranty of the future. . . . In conclusion, gentlemen, let me say that I want your encouragement and countenance. I shall ask and rely upon you and others in carrying the Government through its present perils.[27]

The public mourning and grief which followed Lincoln's death was unparalleled in the history of the young nation. Many regarded the late President as a martyr. Newspapers were filled with stories about this man who was so soon to become a legend. Funeral services for the assassinated President were held in the East Room of the White House on April 19. His body was then moved to the rotunda of the Capitol, and on April 21 began the journey to Springfield. The funeral train did not reach its destination until May 3, having stopped at principal cities along the 1600-mile route. On May 4, Lincoln was buried in Oak Ridge Cemetery in Springfield.

Shortly after taking the oath, Johnson notified Mrs. Lincoln that she could remain at the White House as long as she wished. She was to remain for several weeks. In the interim, Representative Sam Hooper lent Johnson his home at the corner of H and Fifteenth Streets. Johnson used a room in the Treasury Building for his office.

President Andrew Johnson entered upon his duties under the most difficult circumstances. To him fell the task of restoring the southern states to the Union. Congress was not then in session and would not be for seven and one-half months. One of Johnson's first decisions was to retain Lincoln's Cabinet.* He then began to formulate his policies on reconstruction. As his program unfolded, it became evident that his views were similar to those of Lincoln—res-

---

* This proved to be a thorn in his side. Secretary of War Edwin M. Stanton constantly schemed behind his back and most of the others opposed his reconstruction policies. Seward, McCulloch and Welles remained in the Cabinet for the rest of the term. Usher retired on May 15, 1865; Speed and Dennison in July, 1866. Stanton was suspended on August 12, 1867, reinstated on January 13, 1868, and removed on May 26, 1868.

toration of the South peacefully and without severe punishment. On May 29, 1865, he issued a proclamation of amnesty whereby all southerners (with certain exceptions) who would take a loyalty oath would be pardoned. He appointed provisional governors for the southern staes, who were charged with setting up new governments and arranging for elections of representatives to Congress.

Unfortunately, Johnson's reconstruction policies met with rigid opposition when Congress assembled in December, 1865. Congress was controlled by Radical Republicans who were intent on punishing the South. These Radicals were led by Representative Thaddeus Stevens of Pennsylvania and Senator Charles Sumner of Massachusetts. They refused admission to the elected representatives of the southern states and proceeded to pass measures which were extremely harsh on the South. Johnson vetoed these measures, but most of them were promptly passed over his veto.

Johnson's struggle with the Congress reached a climax on February 24, 1868, when the House of Representatives impeached him by a vote of 126 to 47.* The principal charge against him was that he had violated the Tenure of Office Act which had been passed by the Radical Congress. The Act forbade the President to remove, without the Senate's consent, any official confirmed by the Senate. Johnson had disregarded this attempt to downgrade the presidency by trying to dismiss Secretary of War Edwin M. Stanton, without the Senate's consent.

The Senate organized itself to try Johnson on Thursday, March 5, 1868. Salmon P. Chase, Chief Justice of the United States Supreme Court, was to preside at the trial. The President was represented by a group of lawyers including Benjamin R. Curtis, an ex-Justice of the Supreme Court, and William M. Evarts, the dean of the New York Bar. Associate Justice Samuel Nelson of the Supreme Court administered the following oath to the Chief Justice:

I do solemnly swear that in all things appertaining to the trial of the

---

* There was some discussion prior to Johnson's impeachment as to whether he should be impeached as President or Vice-President. Some in the House of Representatives contended that he was not President but rather Vice-President acting as President and therefore should be impeached as Vice-President. Cong. Globe, 40 Cong., 2d Sess. (1868), pp. 319–21. The House decided to impeach him as President. One argument advanced at the time was that if he had become President, it had to be for a full four-year term. Dewitt, *The Impeachment and Trial of Andrew Johnson* (New York, 1903), p. 411.

impeachment of Andrew Johnson, President of the United States, now pending, I will do impartial justice according to the Constitution and laws. So help me God.

Chief Justice Chase then administered the oath to the members of the Senate present. One of those Senators was Benjamin F. Wade, a Radical Republican from Ohio. As President pro tempore, Wade would succeed Johnson if he were convicted.* Senator Thomas A. Hendricks of Indiana objected to Wade's being sworn in. He said that since the Constitution did not allow the Vice-President to participate when the President is on trial, the same should hold true of the would-be successor in this case.[28] In rebuttal, it was argued that Ohio would be deprived of its equal vote in the matter. After some discussion, Hendricks withdrew his objection and Wade thereupon took the oath. When the vote was taken to remove Johnson, Wade voted "guilty."

The trial began on March 13, 1868. Two-thirds, or thirty-six of the fifty-four members, were necessary to convict. Acquittal required nineteen votes. On May 16, the Senate voted thirty-five to nineteen on one of the charges.[29] The same vote prevailed on two other charges submitted for resolution. Thus, the first President to be impeached survived removal by only one vote.†

In 1868, Johnson's hopes for the Democratic presidential nomination failed to materialize. Governor Horatio Seymour of New York was nominated for President and Francis P. Blair, Jr., of Missouri for Vice-President. The Democrats, however, lost to the

---

* Wade was elected President pro tempore on March 2, 1867. Upon Lincoln's assassination, Lafayette S. Foster, a fifty-nine-year-old Senator from Connecticut, was President pro tempore, having been elected at a special session on March 7, 1865. He continued to serve as such until Wade was elected. At the time of Johnson's succession, moreover, there was no Speaker, since the new Congress had not assembled in the first of its regular sessions. On December 4, 1865, Schuyler Colfax was elected to this position.

† Several of the Senators who voted for Johnson knowingly did so at the expense of their careers—e.g., Senators Edmund G. Ross of Kansas, William P. Fessenden of Maine, Joseph O. Fowler of Tennessee, James W. Grimes of Iowa, John B. Henderson of Missouri, Lyman Trumbull of Illinois, and Peter G. Van Winkle of West Virginia. None was ever again to hold elective office.

After the impeachment episode, Johnson recommended changing the line of succession to the members of the Cabinet thus preventing Congress from using the impeachment power to place one of its members in the presidency. Congress, however, failed to give the subject any consideration.

Republican ticket of General Ulysses S. Grant of Illinois and Schuyler Colfax of Indiana.

Grant's first administration passed without the occurrence of any national tragedy, but his second administration was to find death once again visited upon one of the nation's two highest officers. On November 22, 1875, his second Vice-President, Henry Wilson of Massachusetts, died in office at the age of sixty-three, twelve days after having suffered a paralytic stroke.

Wilson, or the "Natick Cobbler" as he was sometimes called, had risen from a background of hard work to the United States Senate in which he had served for almost eighteen years. The story is told of Wilson's financial circumstances at the time of his becoming Vice-President. On the evening before the inauguration, Wilson called upon a friend, saying: "[C]an you lend me a hundred dollars? I have not got money enough to be inaugurated on." The friend quickly wrote out a check for the amount and after Wilson had left, remarked to a companion who witnessed the scene: "There is an incident worth remembering—such a one as could never have occurred in any country but our own."[30]

The vice-presidency, Wilson found, was less influential and challenging than his Senate post. He found that it afforded him an excellent opportunity to complete his work, *History of the Rise and Fall of the Slave Power in America.*[31] Sixty-one years old at the time of his inauguration on March 4, 1873, Wilson suffered the first of three paralytic strokes within that year. As a result, he was not able to preside over the Senate with the same constancy as had his immediate predecessor, Schuyler Colfax. During one of Wilson's recuperative periods, a rather poignant incident occurred. A friend called at the place where he was staying and asked the servant to see him. The servant replied that she had never heard of a "Mr. Wilson." Upon further questioning, she stated that "there is an invalid stopping here; but I don't know who he is, and he is out today." Later, she was shocked to learn that the person upon whom she had been waiting for several weeks was the Vice-President of the United States.[32]

When death came to Wilson, a widower, at 7:30 A.M. on Monday, November 22, 1875, he was alone in the quiet of the Vice-President's Room in the Capitol (where he had been taken when afflicted) with one person in attendance. Upon Wilson's death, President Grant issued orders that "appropriate . . . honors be rendered to the memory of one whose virtues and services will long be borne in recollection by a grateful nation."

As in the case of other vacancies in the vice-presidency, Wilson's death caused no concern that there would be a vacancy in the office for sixteen months. The *New York Herald* of November 23, 1875, noted that as President pro tempore, Senator Thomas W. Ferry* of Michigan "would act as President in case the present incumbent of the office should die before the expiration of his term. . . ." In an editorial on the following day, the *New York Herald* viewed Ferry's possible succession as cause for alarm: "According to his record he [Ferry] is a fanatical inflationist. . . . If President Grant should suddenly be taken away Thomas W. Ferry, of Michigan, would be his successor. The country has reason to shudder at the possibility. . . . [I]f Mr. Ferry is still an inflationist it would be inexcusable for the Senate to retain him in his present position, when only a single life stands between so dangerous a man and the Presidency of the United States."†

---

* Ferry had been elected President pro tempore when Wilson vacated the chair before the last session of the Senate had adjourned in March, 1875. See p. 83, §.

† There was no Speaker at the time. When Congress convened in December, Michael C. Kerr of Indiana, a Democrat, was chosen Speaker.

9

First Case of Presidential Inability

[U]nquestionably, he is unable to discharge the general "powers and duties" of the executive office. The Government is practically without a head. . . .

The New York Times
August 11, 1881

Grant's successor in the White House was Rutherford B. Hayes of Ohio. Hayes' running mate was William A. Wheeler of New York. The election of 1876 remains one of the most controversial in American history. Samuel J. Tilden of New York won a plurality of the popular vote and one short of a majority in the electoral college. Some electoral votes were in doubt. A Republican-controlled Senate and a Democratic-controlled House could not agree on how they were to be counted. A bipartisan Electoral Commission was formed by Congress to resolve the controversy. Its membership consisted of five Senators, five Representatives and five Supreme Court Justices. Three Senators and two Representatives were Republicans, while two Senators and three Representatives were Democrats. Two Justices were Republicans and two Justices were Democrats. The four selected a fifth Justice, who was a Republican. Thus, the Commission consisted of eight Republicans and seven Democrats. Hayes, the Republican candidate, became President by a strict party vote of eight to seven. The outcome was not known until Friday, March 2, 1877, three days before the inauguration.*

---

* Since March 4, 1877 fell on a Sunday, Hayes, at the urging of President

117

In 1880, Hayes declined to run for a second term, and the Republican Party selected as its standard-bearer forty-eight-year-old Senator James A. Garfield of Ohio, who had been a member of the 1876 Electoral Commission and the Republican floor leader in the House of Representatives during Hayes' administration. Chester A. Arthur of New York, a confidant of Senator Roscoe Conkling who ran the New York Republican political machine, was endorsed for Vice-President. Garfield and Arthur won nearly fifty-eight percent of the electoral votes as against the forty-two percent received by the Democratic candidates, Winfield Scott Hancock of Pennsylvania and William Hayden English of Indiana.

On the morning of July 2, 1881, a short four months after his inauguration, President James A. Garfield prepared to leave Washington, D.C., for a two-week tour of New England. Included in the itinerary was a visit to his alma mater, Williams College in Williamstown, Massachusetts, for the commencement exercises. He left the White House at about 9:00 A.M., accompanied by Secretary of State James G. Blaine. They drove to the Washington depot of the Baltimore and Potomac Railroad where they were to meet other members of the Cabinet and proceed to New York and New England. As Garfield walked through the depot arm in arm with Blaine, he was shot from behind. The President fell to the floor, bleeding. Two shots had hit him—one grazing his arm and the other lodging in his back. The assassin was immediately captured as he ran from the scene and was identified as Charles J. Guiteau, a disappointed office-seeker. Upon being taken into custody by a police officer, Guiteau said: "I did it and will go to jail for it. I am a Stalwart, and Arthur will be President."[1]

The following letter, addressed "To the White House," was found in Guiteau's pocket: "The President's tragic death was a sad necessity, but it will unite the Republican party and save the Republic. . . . I had no ill-will toward the President. His death was a political necessity."[2]

Also found on Guiteau's person was a letter addressed to Arthur, informing him of the "assassination" and of his succession to the presidency. Guiteau made the following recommendations for Cabinet appointments: Coulsburg for Secretary of State, Levi P.

Grant and Secretary of State Hamilton Fish, took the oath of office privately in the White House on March 3. He took it publicly on Monday.

Morton for Secretary of Treasury, Emory A. Storrs for Attorney General, and John A. Logan for Secretary of War. Postmaster General Thomas L. James should remain where he was, said Guiteau, and it was optional whether any changes be made in the departments of Navy and Interior.

Garfield was taken to an office on the second floor of the station house and was examined by several physicians who had been summoned. After about an hour they decided to remove him to the White House. Although his condition was described as "critical," his mind remained clear. In the afternoon he greeted, with a warm and cheerful manner, members of the Cabinet and friends who called. While at the depot, concerned about the effect of the news on his wife who was just recovering from a serious illness, Garfield had dictated to his secretary, Colonel Rockwell, the following message to her at Elberon, New Jersey, where she awaited him:

Mrs. Garfield, Elberton, N.J.:

The President wishes me to say to you from him that he has been seriously hurt—how seriously he cannot yet say. He is himself and hopes you will come to him soon. He sends his love to you.

A. F. Rockwell[3]

When she arrived shortly before seven o'clock, she was left alone with him, and they conversed for about fifteen minutes.

In the late afternoon, the President had begun to lose strength and as night approached there was little hope that he would survive much longer. Evidence of internal hemorrhage had been discovered. "There is no hope for him," Dr. D. W. Bliss said. "He will probably not live three hours; he may die in half an hour." But late that night Garfield rallied and his cheerful manner returned. Having been informed by Dr. Bliss, his close friend and chief physician, that he had one chance of life, and only one, he smilingly replied: "We will take that one chance, Doctor, and make good use of it."[4] By the following morning, although it was recognized that his condition was still critical, there was new hope that he would recover.

As the news of the shooting was relayed across the country, a wave of shock and horror passed over the people. "The astonishment following the startling announcement deepened into unbelief, and the people seemed paralyzed with the horror of the moment."[5]

119

The sympathy of the nation had been stirred and, almost without exception, men of one political creed joined those of another in the anxious vigil for further news. Said *The New York Times*: "[T]he indignation and condemnation against the assassin and his crime were freely uttered. Men knew no politics in such discussion—Democrats and Republicans were all men, and, for once at least, united in a common belief and sentiment."[6] Although there was at first a suspicion that Guiteau was part of a conspiracy, this notion was quickly dispelled when it became clear that he had acted alone and had had no assistance. People could not believe that any sane person would want to kill Garfield. However, the possibility of Vice-President Chester A. Arthur's succeeding to the presidency was viewed with some alarm.

Arthur had been selected for the Republican vice-presidential nomination in the usual manner. He belonged to the Stalwart wing of the Republican Party and had supported Ulysses S. Grant in his effort to obtain the presidential nomination for a third term. When various anti-Grant factions were able to unite and defeat Grant by nominating Garfield on the thirty-sixth ballot, it was decided that the vice-presidential nomination should be given to a "Grant man" in order not to lose the votes of that faction of the party. Arthur was thereupon nominated.

During the weeks immediately preceding the shooting of Garfield, Arthur had become involved in a struggle between Garfield and the two New York Senators, Roscoe Conkling and Thomas C. Platt, over patronage. This struggle had resulted in the two Senators' resigning. Arthur had openly sided with Garfield's opponents and, as a result, had been widely criticized. When Garfield was shot in the name of Arthur and the Stalwarts, Arthur's popularity was further diminished. Although no one seriously believed that he or any other Stalwarts were involved in the shooting, it was nonetheless said that they were the ones who stood to gain from Garfield's death. The *Charleston News and Courier* stated that:

[T]hey [the Stalwarts] were the bitter foes of the President, and what the country will not forget is that the deed is done in their name, and that they and their followers will derive place and power from the President's death.[7]

Arthur found himself in a very uncomfortable position. He is reported to have said to Marshall Jewell of Connecticut on July 4 that: "This is dreadful. Gov. Jewell, the Presidency would not be a very bad thing if a man were nominated for it and elected to it, but to receive it in this manner, at the hands of an assassin is a very different thing. If Garfield has got to die, God knows I would gladly exchange places with him at this moment."[8]

Arthur had first been informed of the alarming events on the morning of July 2 when he alighted from a Hudson River boat in New York City with ex-Senator Conkling. On receiving the report, the Vice-President was stunned into speechlessness. He hurried to his home at 123 Lexington Avenue, stopping at the Fifth Avenue Hotel on the way. When asked if he would go to Washington, Arthur said he probably would not "until officially notified of the President's death."[9] At his home, he received the following messages from Secretary of State Blaine by telegraph:[10]

Washington, July 2, 1881.

The Hon. Chester A. Arthur, Vice-President of the
United States, No. 123 Lexington Avenue:

The President of the United States was shot this morning by an assassin named Charles Guiteau. The weapon was a large-sized revolver. The President had just reached the Baltimore and Potomac station at about 9.20, intending, with a portion of his Cabinet, to leave on the limited express for New York. I rode in the carriage with him from the Executive Mansion, and was walking by his side when he was shot. The assassin was immediately arrested, and the President was conveyed to a private room in the station building and surgical aid at once summoned. He has now, at 10.20, been removed to the Executive Mansion. The surgeons are in consultation. They regard his wounds as very serious, but not necessarily fatal. I will keep you advised of his condition. His vigorous health gives strong hopes of his recovery. He has not lost consciousness for a moment.　　　　　　　　　　　　James G. Blaine,
Secretary of State.

Washington, July 2, 1881.

Hon. Chester A. Arthur, Vice-President United States,
No. 123 Lexington Avenue:

At this hour, 1 o'clock P.M., the President's symptoms are not regarded as unfavorable, but no definite assurance can be given until after the probing of the wound at 3 o'clock. There is strong ground for hope, and at the same time the greatest anxiety as to the final results.
James G. Blaine,
Secretary of State.

Executive Mansion,
Washington, July 2, 1881.

The Hon. Chester A. Arthur, Vice-President
United States, No. 123 Lexington Avenue:

At this hour, 3.30, the symptoms of the President are not favorable. Anxiety deepens.
James G. Blaine,
Secretary of State.

Washington, July 2, 1881.

The Hon. Chester A. Arthur, Vice-President:

At this hour, 6 o'clock, the condition of the President is very alarming. He is losing his strength, and the worst may be apprehended.
James G. Blaine,
Secretary of State.

Executive Mansion, Washington, July 2, 1881.

The Hon. Chester A. Arthur, Vice-President, New York:

Mrs. Garfield has just arrived, at 6.45 o'clock. The President was able to recognize and converse with her, but, in the judgment of his physicians, he is rapidly sinking.
James G. Blaine,
Secretary of State.

In reply to Secretary Blaine, Arthur sent the following:

New York, July 2, 1881.

Hon. James G. Blaine, Secretary of State, Washington, D.C.:

Your telegram, with its deplorable narrative, did not reach me promptly, owing to my absence. I am profoundly shocked at the dreadful news. The hopes you express relieve somewhat the horror of the first announcement. I await further intelligence with the greatest anxiety. Express to the President and those about him my great grief and sympathy, in which the whole American people will join.
C. A. Arthur.

New York, July 2, 1881.

The Hon. James G. Blaine, Secretary of State, Washington, D.C.

Your 6:45 telegram is very distressing. I still hope for more favorable tidings, and ask you to keep me advised. Please do not fail to express to Mrs. Garfield my deepest sympathy.
C. A. Arthur

122

Later that night, Arthur decided to go to Washington by mid-night train. He arrived early in the morning of July 3, accompanied by his friend Senator John P. Jones of Nevada. They went immediately to Jones' residence on Capitol Hill. During the day Arthur refused all requests for interviews but was visited by Post-master General Thomas L. James and Attorney General Wayne MacVeagh. That night he went to the White House where he spoke with Mrs. Garfield. He was anxious to see the President, but it was impossible, as the doctors' orders were that only "attendants and persons whose presence was necessary" could see him.[11] However, he saw the members of the Cabinet and some foreign ministers who were assembled in the Cabinet room of the White House. When he

was ushered to the office where the Cabinet were waiting, he paused at the threshold, expecting an invitation to enter. No one moved to greet him; for a moment, all stared in silent hostility. Arthur, in confusion, was on the point of withdrawing when another visitor, who had not seen him, looked up from a far corner, came forward cordially, offered his hand, and drew him into the room. The others then came up to receive him.[12]

It was agreed that Arthur should remain in Washington until the President's condition had improved. He stayed until July 13, during which time he remained at Senator Jones' home and was frequently visited there by members of the Cabinet. He was never able to meet and speak with Garfield.

Meanwhile, the attention of the nation was focused on his every move. His conduct, however, was beyond criticism and some of the fear of his succeeding to the presidency was beginning to be allayed. The Washington correspondent of *The New York Times* wrote on July 4:

To tell the truth, Mr. Arthur has suffered severely in mind since receiving the news of the President's shooting . . . . Many of the statements which have been made about him the Times's correspondent has good reason for believing to be untrue. His demeanor while in this city has been very carefully watched. As the possible President, his actions have been made the subject of very general scrutiny, and those who have observed him most closely are loudest in their praises of his conduct.[13]

For the next eleven weeks, Garfield remained confined to his bed. Bulletins were released daily, keeping the people informed as to his condition. The Secretary of State kept Europe apprised through the American Minister in London. During the first three weeks

Garfield seemed to make almost steady progress toward recovery. On July 18, the newspapers announced that a day of national thanksgiving for his recovery was being planned. Then, on July 23, he had a relapse. Twice that day he was seized with severe chills which left him exhausted. The doctors made an incision in a pus sac in his back and he seemed to improve.

For the next two weeks Garfield again made good progress. The newspapers of August 3 said that the previous day had been the "best day yet." Then, on August 7, he had another relapse. A new incision was made in his back and, again, he seemed to improve. On August 12, the newspapers carried the reassuring news that the maximum degree of debility had been reached. But, on August 13, a new alarm was sounded. The President's high fever was causing great anxiety. By August 15 his condition was described as very low. He was extremely weak, and his pulse was very high—a sign that he was becoming exhausted. To make matters worse, his stomach would not retain food. Through the next two weeks one complication followed upon another. Hope alternated with despair and days of physical strength and mental alertness inevitably gave way to days of extreme weakness and moments of mental aberration. The parotid gland became inflamed, possibly because of blood poisoning. An incision was made in it, with little noticeable effect.

It was at this time that Garfield asked to be taken from the White House. The doctors, however, refused because of his critical condition. On the 27th and 28th of August, when almost all hope had been abandoned, Garfield began to improve. By September 2 the doctors had agreed to permit him to be moved to the shore at Long Branch, New Jersey, in the hope that the change of air might be helpful. Preparations were made. Railroad tracks were laid from the depot in Long Branch to the Francklyn Cottage at Elberon which was made ready for the invalid.

On the morning of September 6 Garfield was taken from the White House for the trip to Elberon which was reached safely in the early afternoon. "As he was carried out of the White House, those watching were shocked by the change that had come over the great, strong man who had been the President of the United States."[14] The next day the President was low again and the doctors had some second thoughts about the wisdom of their decision. On September 8, there was a marked improvement and hopes were once again raised. A few good days followed until September 11 when the development of respiratory difficulties coupled with a rise in pulse, temperature and respiration sent hopes for Garfield's recovery plunging. In the next few days there seemed to be some improvement. On the 13th and 14th he was allowed to sit up in a reclining chair from which he could view the ocean through a window. On the 15th the doctors admitted that he was suffering from blood poisoning. Then, on September 16, Garfield had another relapse, with a return of the high fever and hallucinations. On the next day a half-hour rigor was followed by a low temperature and chills. The following day he suffered another rigor which left him extremely weak. The next night at approximately 10:35 P.M., after complaining of a sudden pain in his chest, President James A. Garfield was dead.

An autopsy showed that the immediate cause of Garfield's death was rupture of the peritoneum caused by hemorrhage from the mesenteric artery in the chest. It also disclosed that what the doctors had thought was the path of the bullet was actually a channel formed by the burrowing of pus. The bullet had, unknown to them, become encysted in the muscles of Garfield's back so as to cause no trouble, but several abscesses had formed. It was these which had caused the blood poisoning.[15] The doctors had done the best they could with the means that were at their disposal, but under the circumstances, the President could not have survived.

In the eighty days during which he was disabled, President Garfield performed almost no executive functions. At the outset of his inability the doctors had announced that his one chance of survival lay in "being kept perfectly quiet." On the evening of July 2 they had ordered that no one was to enter the President's room except Mrs. Garfield and attendants.

As the President gained strength, he began to take an interest in the affairs of state. During the night of Wednesday, July 6, for example, he awakened and remarked to his attendant that he would have liked to have had a Cabinet meeting that day. (Wednesday was the day the Cabinet usually met.) On the next day, he expressed a wish to discuss the business of the executive departments, but Dr. Bliss forbade it. Said Dr. Bliss: "I told him that he must dismiss that subject from his mind until he was fully recovered. He said that it was on his mind and he had to let it off; but he obeyed me as implicitly as a schoolboy would obey his teacher, and he has said hardly anything since."[16]

125

On July 21, Garfield asked to see the members of his Cabinet, none of whom he had seen since the day of the shooting. Again, the doctors forbade it. If he continued to improve, they said, he could see the Cabinet members in a few days. That night, however, Secretary of State James G. Blaine was permitted to visit him for about ten minutes. This was the first time since July 2 that anyone outside of Garfield's family and attendants had gained entry to his room. As July came to an end, Mrs. Garfield was permitted to read the newspapers to the President on a daily basis.

On August 1, Dr. Bliss announced that Garfield would be able to sit up within two or three weeks and sign urgent papers within ten days. "He could do so now, for that matter," said the doctor, "but we hardly feel justified in permitting it. We are very particular about keeping his mind as far removed as possible from everything appertaining to public affairs."[17] As a result of Garfield's inactivity, the prosecution of post office swindlers, the filling of a vacancy on the Supreme Court, certain matters involving foreign relations and various other executive problems were neglected.

On August 10, President Garfield performed the one and only official act of his illness. Despite a high pulse, he "appended his signature to a paper relating to an extradition case of a forger pending between this country and the Dominion of Canada. The President signed his name without any special effort, and the signature shows very little evidence of nervousness."*[18] The next day he wrote his mother a letter in which he stated: "Don't be disturbed by conflicting reports about my condition. It is true I am weak and on my back, but I am gaining every day, and need only time and patience to bring me through."[19]

After the move to Long Branch, Dr. Bliss granted the President's request to see members of his Cabinet. On September 9, Attorney General Wayne MacVeagh was permitted to visit Garfield for a few minutes. He had been instructed not to talk business. On the following day, Secretary of Treasury William Windom saw the President. Two days later, Secretary of Navy William H. Hunt and Postmaster General Thomas L. James visited him, and on Septem-

---

*"[I]t is no performance of his official functions," said the August 15, 1881 issue of *The New York Times,* "to set his name, even 'with a firm, clear hand,' to a document brought to him by the Secretary of State. So far as consideration of the subject involved or approval of the document is concerned, it is the act of the Secretary, not of the President."

126

ber 14, Secretary of War Robert Todd Lincoln did so. Lincoln, the son of President Lincoln, was the last Cabinet member to see Garfield alive for, after September 16, the President became successively worse until his death on September 19.

Throughout the eighty days, the Cabinet members remained close at hand. During the first few days they kept an almost constant vigil at the White House. Then, on July 8, when the President appeared to be on the road to recovery, they resumed their usual places in their respective departments. Thereafter, although they spent most of their time at work in their departments, they continued to visit the White House for a few hours each day. They conferred regularly with the doctors and kept Arthur informed of significant developments on the President's condition. Secretary of State Blaine continued to keep Europe apprised through periodic telegrams to Minister Lowell in London.

Toward the end of August when the President's condition was critical, the Cabinet spent long hours at the White House, often staying until almost midnight. It was at this time that they began to consider the possibility of asking Vice-President Arthur to assume the executive duties. On August 27, Postmaster General James was sent to New York "as the special envoy of the Cabinet to communicate certain of their decisions to Gen. Arthur concerning the advisability of summoning him to Washington."[20] At the meeting, Arthur indicated that he had no wish to go to Washington to assume presidential authority. By September 1 the advisability of this course was being widely debated in the newspapers and by September 3 the Cabinet had decided against the move, at least for the time being. Arthur's feelings were undoubtedly a factor in the decision.

When the President was moved to Long Branch, the Cabinet took up lodgings nearby. On September 12 some of them left Long Branch for vacations in the White Mountains of New Hampshire. Four days later they were summoned back to Long Branch. When Garfield died on September 19, all but two members of the Cabinet were in Long Branch. Blaine and Lincoln were en route from Boston.

From the time that he had returned to New York on July 13, Arthur had remained in seclusion, refusing all interviews. He was aware that he was in a very delicate position and that he was being closely watched. On the occasion of Garfield's first relapse it was reported that Arthur "will remain in the City [New York] unless requested by Secretary Blaine to go to Washington. This is understood by Mr. Blaine."[21] When, in mid-August, the President's condition became critical, the newspapers said that Arthur was "indisposed" and remained confined to his residence.[22] As hopes for the President's recovery alternately waxed and waned through the latter part of August, Arthur continued to remain secluded.

The possibility of Garfield's death and Arthur's succession to the presidency received much attention at this time. Arthur himself was not unaware of the possibility, and he discussed it with his intimates, particularly with reference to where and by whom the oath should be administered when and if the time should come. *The New York Times* of August 17 observed that "a friend of Gen. Arthur said last night that the Vice-President was averse to going to Washington at this time, as though to sit in waiting for President Garfield's death and eager to assume the vacant office. . . ."

On August 26, when the newspapers reported that there was "very little hope left," Arthur's movements were again recorded. The *Times* listed his visitors that day and reported that "Gen. Arthur said, a little before midnight, that he had not received any dispatches other than the official bulletins from the White House, and that he had no intention of going to Washington last night." Arthur's general demeanor was such as to elicit from the *Times* the comment that:

Such impending fear as there might have been early in July of the dangers to the common weal from the President's sudden taking off has passed away. If his legal successor has not disarmed criticism, he has at least done nothing to sharpen it. . . . A change of Executive eight weeks ago would have been felt as one of the most violent of the jars to which the institutions of the United States have been subjected. A change to-day would be effected merely amid a certain silent and watchful expectancy. . . .[23]

Late on the night of September 19, Arthur received the following message from Long Branch, signed by Secretary of Treasury William Windom, Secretary of Navy William H. Hunt, Postmaster General Thomas L. James, Attorney General Wayne MacVeagh, and Secretary of Interior Samuel J. Kirkwood:

It becomes our painful duty to inform you of the death of President

Garfield, and to advise you to take the oath of office as President of the United States, without delay. If it concurs with your judgment, we will be very glad if you will come here on the earliest train tomorrow morning.[24]

When this telegram arrived, Arthur was in the library of his home with a few friends. He decided to take the presidential oath at once, and accordingly, Judge John R. Brady of the New York Supreme Court was summoned. At approximately 2:15 A.M. on the morning of July 20, Brady administered the oath to Arthur in the parlor of 123 Lexington Avenue in the presence of a number of friends. Included among these were Elihu Root, Dr. Pierre C. Van Wyck, Stephen B. French, Daniel G. Rollins, Arthur's son, Alan, and Judge Charles Donohue, who had been summoned in case Brady should be unavailable.

Later that day Arthur, having waited for Secretaries Blaine and Lincoln to arrive in New York from Boston, proceeded to Long Branch. There, he paid his respects to the dead President, called on Mrs. Garfield, and had his first formal meeting with the Cabinet. Then he returned to his home in New York. The next morning he returned to Long Branch for funeral services and joined the funeral party to accompany the late President's body back to Washington.

In Washington, after consulting Secretary of State Blaine and Attorney General MacVeagh, Arthur decided to repeat the presidential oath before Chief Justice Morrison R. Waite of the Supreme Court in order that there would be a federal record of it. At noon on September 22, 1881, he took the oath before the Chief Justice in the Vice-President's room at the Capitol. Present at the private ceremony were the members of the Cabinet, Senators, Representatives, and several other prominent persons, including ex-Presidents Grant and Hayes, General Sherman, and Associate Justices of the Supreme Court John M. Harlan and Stanley Matthews.

Upon taking the oath, Arthur delivered a brief inaugural address. He said:

For the fourth time in the history of the Republic its Chief Magistrate has been removed by death. All hearts are filled with grief and horror at the hideous crime which has darkened our land, and the memory of the murdered President, his protracted sufferings, his unyielding fortitude, the example and achievement of his life and the pathos of his death will forever illumine the pages of our history. For the fourth time, the officer elected by the people and ordained by the Constitution

129

to fill a vacancy so created is called to assume the Executive Chair. The wisdom of our fathers, foreseeing even the most dire possibilities, made sure that the Government should never be imperiled because of the uncertainty of human life. Men may die, but the fabric of our free institutions remains unshaken. No higher or more assuring proof could exist of the strength and permanence of popular government than the fact that, though the chosen of the people be struck down, his constitutional successor is peacefully installed without shock or strain, except the sorrow which mourns the bereavement. All the noble aspirations of my lamented predecessor . . . will be garnered in the hearts of the people; and it will be my earnest endeavor to profit, and to see that the nation shall profit, by his example and experience. . . . Summoned to these high duties and responsibilities and profoundly conscious of their magnitude and gravity, I assume the trust imposed by the Constitution, relying for aid on divine guidance and the virtue, patriotism, and intelligence of the American people.[25]

Those who had witnessed the inauguration then tendered their congratulations and withdrew. The Cabinet remained and when all others had left, "the room was closed" and Arthur held his second formal Cabinet meeting. At this meeting all of the Cabinet members submitted their resignations in writing. Arthur, however, promptly requested them to remain for the present.*

On September 22, President Arthur performed his first official act when he issued a proclamation appointing September 26, the day of burial, as a day of national mourning. The following day, September 23, he issued a proclamation calling the Senate into special session on October 10, 1881 for the purpose of electing a President pro tempore. Shockingly, there was then no available successor to the presidency, and Congress was not in session.†

---

* As it developed, in October, 1881, Secretary of Treasury Windom resigned to run for the Senate; in November, Attorney General MacVeagh resigned due to lack of sympathy with Arthur's wing of the Republican Party; in December, Secretary of State Blaine and Postmaster General James resigned; and in early 1882, Secretary of Navy Hunt and Secretary of Interior Kirkwood did so. Secretary of War Lincoln was the only member of Garfield's Cabinet to remain with Arthur for the rest of the term.

† Arthur apparently had prepared for the eventuality of his death before October 10 by writing a secret proclamation summoning an immediate special session of the Senate to elect a President pro tempore. The proclamation was placed in a sealed envelope addressed to the President in Washington. Thus, should anything have happened to him, a method would have existed for choosing a successor. See *The New York Times,* November 21, 1886; Howe, *Chester A. Arthur* (New York, 1957), p. 154.

When the Senate had met in special session the previous March, Arthur had presided and, consequently, no President pro tempore had been chosen.

There were two reasons why the Senate failed to elect a President pro tempore at its special session. First, the Senate was equally divided for a time and Arthur's casting vote was required. Then, when the two Republican New York Senators resigned (Conkling and Platt), the Democrats had a majority. Rather than allow them to elect a Democratic President pro tempore, Arthur had retained his seat. Since the new House of Representatives would not convene until December, there was no Speaker. This incredible state of affairs had caused considerable concern during the eighty days Garfield lay dying. The concern had been temporarily heightened when it was rumored that Arthur was of Canadian birth and thus would not be eligible to succeed to the presidency should Garfield die.*

With the approach of October 10, the day on which the special session of the Senate would begin, there was much criticism of the succession act of 1792. This was because, as Senate procedures were examined, it became apparent that a Democrat would be elected President pro tempore since, on the Senate's convening, the Democrats would have a majority of three Senators. Although three Republican Senators had been chosen—two to fill vacancies caused by resignation and one to fill a vacancy caused by death—it was the practice for the President pro tempore to be elected before new Senators were sworn so that he could administer the oath to them. Republicans insisted that it would be unpatriotic for the Democrats to take advantage of this opportunity to elect a Democrat as the possible successor to Arthur. Democrats maintained that they had every right to elect a Democratic President pro tempore. Editorials denounced the act of 1792 for placing in the line of succession "officers" who might not be of the same party as the President.[26]

When the Senate convened on October 10, the Republicans submitted a resolution to permit the new Senators to be sworn before the election of a President pro tempore. They cited a case in which this had been done (i.e., March 4, 1853). The resolution,

---

* This report was refuted by an investigation conducted by the *New York Sun* which was published the day after Arthur took the presidential oath.

however, was defeated and the Senate proceeded to elect Thomas F. Bayard of Delaware, a Democrat, as President pro tempore. The Senate then adjourned. The following day the three new Republican Senators were sworn in. On October 12 the Republicans, who now had exactly the same number of Senators as the Democrats, proposed David Davis of Illinois, an Independent, for President pro tempore. The following day Davis was elected and Bayard unseated.*

The next matter of business for Arthur was that of appointments. As vacancies occurred in the Cabinet and other offices, Stalwarts were appointed to fill them. However, these were not purely patronage appointments for Arthur sought to act according to his own judgment regarding the country's best interests. Many had expected him to appoint ex-Senator Roscoe Conkling, Secretary of State. Instead, Arthur replaced Blaine with ex-Senator Frederick T. Frelinghuysen of New Jersey. Step by step, Arthur put the lie to the argument, which had been advanced in some quarters, that he would be a Conkling puppet. By December, 1881, it was generally agreed that he had made a good start. "[A]ll his acts and utterances as President," declared *The New York Times,* "have tended to deepen that respect [earned during Garfield's illness] into esteem and confidence."[27]

Prior to his accession to the presidency, Arthur had been viewed as a machine politician, and it was expected that under him the spoils system would flourish. This was an empty fear. Arthur soon embraced Garfield's policy of civil service reform and, on January 6, 1883, he signed the Pendleton Civil Service Act. In addition to civil service reform, Arthur sought and obtained legislation to prevent future postal frauds. His concern about national defense led to needed appropriations for the United States Navy. Fairly considered, Arthur proved to be an honest and conscientious President.

In 1884 Arthur sought the Republican presidential nomination but it went to former Secretary of State James G. Blaine. Upon retiring from the presidency, Arthur resumed his law practice in New York City.

---

* Warren Keifer of Ohio, a Republican, was chosen Speaker on December 5, 1881. It is interesting to note that later in the term, when George F. Edmunds of Vermont was President pro tempore, he worked out of the Vice-President's office in the Capitol and used letterheads printed "Office of the Vice President."

Discussion of Presidential Inability

During and after Garfield's inability there was much discussion of the question of presidential inability. Several aspects of the subject received considerable attention at the time. First, what is meant by inability? Is it limited to mental incapacity? Is there such a thing as a temporary inability? Second, if the Vice-President were to assume the functions of the chief executive, what would be his status and tenure? Finally, who, under the Constitution is authorized to determine whether inability exists? Widespread variation in the opinions of "experts" on all of these questions revealed itself.

According to Professor Theodore W. Dwight of Columbia Law School, one of the leading constitutional authorities of the day, inability was limited to mental incapacity.[28] "There can be no disability that the President can be conscious of," said former Senator William W. Eaton of Connecticut. "It must be a disability, as, for example, if he were insane, which is patent to everybody except himself."[29] The more general view was expressed in the *New York Herald,* as follows: "The word 'inability' . . . means an inability of any kind . . . of the body or mind . . . temporary or permanent, . . . [which] disables . . . [the President] from discharging the powers and duties of his office."[30] The *New York Daily Tribune* said that inability means a "permanent loss of power."[31] "I do not think the framers of the Constitution meant . . . a temporary illness, however severe. . . ," stated Senator George F. Hoar of Massachusetts.[32] Former Senator Lyman Trumbull of Illinois argued that inability must be of such a nature that its existence is known to all and there must be an urgent need for executive action which would make it patent to all that the Vice-President should act.[33] Similarly, Judge Thomas M. Cooley of Michigan urged that no mere temporary inability was contemplated but that the Constitution required the inability to be of such kind and duration as to make it essential that a substitute act.[34]

A not inconsiderable body of opinion was to the effect that if the Vice-President assumed presidential authority, he would become President for the remainder of the term. Senator Charles W. Jones of Florida was of the opinion that in a case of inability, the office of President devolves on the Vice-President for the rest of the term and the elected President is therefore dispossessed. He argued that the framers of the Constitution had deliberately substituted the word "devolve" for "exercise" and had intended the so-called special election clause "until another President be elected" as a limitation on the tenure of an officer appointed by Congress but not on the Vice-President, who was elected for a period of four years.[35] Professor Dwight and Senator Hoar agreed that the Vice-President becomes President for the remainder of the President's term in a case of presidential inability as well as in a case of death. The Washington *Sunday Gazette* declared that "the Constitution provides, in distinct and mandatory enactment, that the Vice-President shall 'become' President in the event of 'death, removal, resignation, or disability of the President.' It does not say he shall 'act' as President. . . ."[36] Abram J. Dittenhoeffer, a noted lawyer, advanced this proposition:

I start with this conclusion:—That whenever the Vice President gets lawfully into the Presidency the President gets lawfully out of it. There cannot be two lawful Presidents at the same time. . . . Mark, no limit to the time for which these powers and duties "shall devolve" is fixed. It is just as absolute and limitless as if the language were:—In case of the removal of the President from office, or of his death, resignation, or inability to discharge the powers and duties of said office, the Vice President shall become President. . . . And when the President gets lawfully out there is no way in which he can get in again.[37]

The predominant view was that in a case of presidential inability, the Vice-President acts temporarily until the President recovers. Among those who expressed themselves accordingly were Augustus Schoonmaker, a former attorney general of New York, General Benjamin F. Butler of Massachusetts, Henry E. Davis, a New York lawyer, Senator James B. Beck of Kentucky, Samuel B. Maxey of Texas, ex-Senators Eaton and Trumbull, General T. L. Clingman of North Carolina, *The New York Times,* and the *New York Herald.*

As for who could declare a President disabled, many held the view that Congress had such authority under its power to make all laws necessary and proper for carrying out the provisions of the Constitution. Thus, Augustus Schoonmaker argued that Congress could, under this clause, "provide . . . some mode of proceeding by which the inability of a President may be formally pronounced."[38] In accord were Senator Charles W. Jones, Professor Dwight, ex-Judge Samuel Shellabarger, General Clingman, *The New York*

Times and the *New York Herald*. Judge Cooley said that Congress is the only tribunal for deciding when inability exists and it should act in each case individually. In contrast to Cooley's view was that of the *New York Daily Tribune,* which said that Congress can provide by law what constitutes inability but that Congress could not "excercise any judicial power, or declare of itself that an inability exists."[39]

General Butler and Henry E. Davis persuasively argued that as the Vice-President was charged with acting as President in a case of presidential inability, it was his sole duty to determine when the President was disabled. Ex-Senator Eaton said that if the President "is suffering from disability, such as is clearly evident . . . , the Vice-President . . . must assume the functions of the office. . . ."[40] If a real inability existed, said Senator Trumbull, the people would demand that the Vice-President take over.[41] Some thought that Congress had authority to deal with the matter but, in the absence of any legislation, it was the responsibility of the Vice-President to decide when to act as President.* Included in this group were Congressmen George D. Robeson of New Jersey, Benjamin H. Brewster of Pennsylvania, later Attorney General of the United States under President Grover Cleveland, Judge Shellabarger, Governor John D. Long of Massachusetts, and A. Schoonmaker. Senator Augustus H. Garland of Massachusetts stated that the Constitution left the question of presidential inability to the President and Vice-President.[42] Governor William D. Bloxham of Florida suggested that the Vice-President should act only if requested to do so by the Cabinet or President.[43]

Because of the overwhelming disagreement on these questions, it is not surprising that the Garfield Cabinet, after due consideration, considered it best to do nothing. In their discussions, the Cabinet unanimously agreed that it was desirable for Vice-President Arthur to assume the executive responsibilities. In pondering how this could be done, they decided to recommend to the President that he invite Arthur to act in his place.[44] After consulting various authorities, however, it became evident that it was not clear whether, if the President consented and Arthur assumed the execu-

---

* Vehemently opposed to the Vice-President's so deciding were Senators Jones and Hoar, and the *New York Tribune*. Hoar said the idea that the Vice-President alone has the responsibility to decide when to act is utterly impracticable and "fraught with the greatest perils."

tive powers, the President would be able to resume his powers and duties when he recovered.*

The Cabinet consulted but received little help from the standard works on the Constitution. Henry Flanders, in his *An Exposition on the Constitution,* wrote that the Vice-President succeeds to the presidential office in all cases but "when he succeeds to the office upon the inability of the President, he discharges its power and duties only so long as such inability continues."[45] In his monumental treatise, Supreme Court Justice Joseph Story noted that when the Vice-President succeeds to the office of President, it is for the remainder of the term.[46] However, it was accepted that Story referred only to a permanent vacancy. Kent's *Commentaries on American Law* asserted that the Vice-President is supposed to act for the rest of the term except when "the President is enabled to reassume the office. . . ."[47]

The Cabinet had no precedent by which to be guided, except for the situation which had occurred in England under King George III. The facts of that situation, which undoubtedly were known to the Cabinet, are these:[48]

King George III went insane in November, 1788. His son, the Prince of Wales, was first in line of succession. He asserted his right to act as Regent during the King's inability and was supported by the Whig Party, the party of opposition in Parliament. William Pitt, the twenty-nine-year-old Prime Minister, would not submit to this view. After the King's physicians had been examined before the Privy Council and their testimony submitted to Parliament,† a Regency Plan was drawn up by Pitt. It placed certain restrictions on the Regent. The Whigs objected to the Plan on the ground that the Prince of Wales had the right to become Regent independently of Parliament's approval. Charles J. Fox, the Whig leader, argued that the powers of the regency were the Prince's by right "as if the

---

* It is reported that within the Cabinet itself, Secretaries Blaine, Hunt and Lincoln were of the opinion that the Vice-President could act as President while the inability lasted, while Attorney General MacVeagh, Postmaster General James and Secretaries Windom and Kirkwood believed that if Arthur assumed the executive duties he would become President for the remainder of the term and thus supersede Garfield.

† They agreed that the King was disabled but differed about the matter of recovery. Some said that it might take two years or more for him to recover. Others said that it might take only six weeks or two months.

Majesty had suffered a natural demise." Pitt said that the Prince had no more right to take over than any other man in the Kingdom. To hold otherwise was treason to the Constitution.

The debate continued for several weeks. Finally, on February 12, 1789, the House of Commons passed the Regency Bill with the restrictions and sent it to the House of Lords. A few days later an official bulletin announcing the King's recovery was issued and the bill never became law.

In October, 1810, the King again went mad and, this time, it was apparent to all. On February 6, 1811, a Regency Bill, with restrictions, became law with the King's assent, although he noted an objection to being deprived of his office. The regency was to last for a year as it was expected that the King would recover. Instead, he became worse, and in February, 1812, the restrictions were removed and the Prince became an unrestricted Regent. He served in that capacity until his father's death on January 29, 1820.

This case was, if anything, troublesome to the Garfield Cabinet because Parliamentary approval was necessary.* In their case, Congress was not in session and would not meet until December, 1881.

When the Garfield Cabinet proposed their plan to Arthur, he was extremely reluctant to accept it. The matter of presenting it to Garfield was indeed delicate. The Cabinet hesitated to broach the subject when he was very weak, although they believed he would gladly consent.†

---

* This case was examined several years later in Bavaria when King Louis II became insane. Since the business of government had come to an almost complete standstill, the ministers of state took it upon themselves to request a panel of doctors to examine the King. They gained entry to the King's quarters on the pretext that they were lawyers, and then reported to the ministers that he was, indeed, disabled. Thereupon, the ministers proclaimed the King disabled and had him placed under restraint. Prince Luitpold, the King's uncle, assumed the regency, which lasted less than a week. On June 13, 1886, the King was drowned, together with his doctor. Gerard, *The Romance of Ludwig II of Bavaria* (New York, 1899), pp. 257–90; Richter, *The Mad Monarch* (Chicago, 1954), pp. 250–80.

† The Cabinet, it should be noted, did not escape criticism during the inability for assuming many executive functions. As the *Times* noted in its issue of August 11, 1881: "The Government is practically without a head, and is conducted by the Cabinet—a body unknown to the Constitution, and having only an advisory character in its collective capacity, its individual members being the heads of executive departments and subordinates of the President. We

On September 3, the Cabinet reviewed the wide variety of opinions and the reluctance of Arthur, himself, to be a party to anything that might be construed as usurpation. They decided that it would be unfair to advise Garfield to invite Arthur to act in his place without presenting to him for his consideration all the questions involved and the possible consequences. In view of Garfield's weak state at the time, they refused to raise the matter just then. The opportunity they sought never presented itself for, in just over two weeks from that day the President was dead. "Nothing more, it appears, was done with respect to presidential 'inability.' Arthur awaited Garfield's death with deep apprehension and, as long as the President lived, would probably have never taken over his functions until Congress had set up some procedure possessing general support."[49]

Owing largely to his own experiences, Arthur expressed deep concern over the inability problem in his messages to Congress in 1881, 1882, and again in 1883. No more complete statement of this manifold problem can be found than that given by Arthur in his special message of December 6, 1881:

Is the inability limited in its nature to long-continued intellectual incapacity, or has it a broader import?

What must be its extent and duration?

How must its existence be established?

Has the President whose inability is the subject of inquiry any voice in determining whether or not it exists, or is the decision of that momentous and delicate question confided to the Vice-President, or is it contemplated by the Constitution that Congress should provide by law precisely what should constitute inability, and how and by what tribunal or authority it should be ascertained?

If the inability proves to be temporary in nature, and during its continuance the Vice-President lawfully exercises the functions of the Executive, by what tenure does he hold his office?

Does he continue as President for the remainder of the four years' term?

Or would the elected President, if his inability should cease in the interval, be empowered to resume his office?

---

almost might say that the Secretary of State, instead of the Vice-President is 'acting as President.' This certainly was not contemplated by the Constitution."

And if, having such lawful authority, he should exercise it, would the Vice-President be thereupon empowered to resume his powers and duties as such?[50]

Congress, however, declined to take any action on the problem.

10

The Succession Law of 1886

The present condition of the law relating to the succession to the Presidency . . . is such as to require immediate amendment.

GROVER CLEVELAND

The election of 1884 brought to the presidency and vice-presidency, respectively, two former governors—Grover Cleveland of New York and Thomas Andrews Hendricks of Indiana. Hendricks reached the vice-presidency after many years of public service in which he had been a Representative and a Senator. In 1868, he had been a contender for the presidential nomination of the Democratic Party. When Horace Greeley, the Democratic nominee for President, died on November 29, 1872, three weeks after the election but before the meeting of the electoral college, Hendricks received forty-two of the sixty-two electoral votes won by his party.* In 1876, he was the vice-presidential candidate on the ticket headed by Samuel Jones Tilden. In 1880 and again in 1884, he was a contender for the presidential nomination of his party. In the latter in-

---

* This is the only time in history when a presidential candidate died between the election and the convening of the electoral college. In the election, Greeley and his running mate, Benjamin Gratz Brown, won 2,834,079 popular votes (six states) as against Grant's and Wilson's 3,597,070 (twenty-nine states). The electoral votes of the six states carried by Greeley and Brown were cast for Hendricks (forty-two votes or four states), Brown (eighteen votes of two states), Charles Jones Jenkins of Illinois (two votes), and Daniel Davids of Illinois (one vote). Greeley received three votes but, by resolution of the House, they were not counted. See p. 274.

stance, Cleveland succeeded in obtaining the nomination, while Hendricks was given the vice-presidential nomination in order to give the ticket geographic representation and unify the party.

At the time of his nomination, Hendricks, then sixty-four, was physically weak. In the fall of 1880, he had had his first indication of oncoming paralysis and, in 1882, he had become lame. On November 25, 1885, less than nine months after his inauguration, he died suddenly at his home in Indianapolis, probably of a stroke.[1]

Hendricks' death came at a particularly inauspicious time, since there was neither a President pro tempore nor a Speaker. At the special session of the Senate in March, 1885, Hendricks had presided and, as in the case of Arthur, had not stepped down before the expiration of the session so that a President pro tempore could be chosen.

Because no one was available to act as President should Cleveland die, many prominent persons, including friends of the late Vice-President and Mrs. Hendricks, herself, urged Cleveland not to attend Hendricks' funeral in Indiana. The reason for this was "not that there would be more than the ordinary danger involved in the proposed journey, but that the emergency is such that it is his duty to the country to avoid every possible risk of accident to his life and health until Congress meets and a presidential succession provided."[2] In deciding not to attend, Cleveland said:

I am now reminded by some of the best and most patriotic and thoughtful of our citizens that the real and solemn duties of my office are at the national capital, and that in the present peculiar and delicate situation I ought not to take even the remote chance of accident incident to travel to gratify a sentiment so general and characteristic as that involved in this subject.[3]

The sudden death of Vice-President Hendricks startled leaders of both parties. Not only was there no available successor to the President at the time but, since the Republicans had a majority in the Senate, it was likely that a Republican would be elected as President pro tempore when the Senate convened. The Forty-Ninth Congress met in December, 1885, and on December 7, the Republican majority in the Senate elected as President pro tempore a Republican, sixty-two-year-old John Sherman of Ohio. The Democratic-controlled House, on the other hand, elected as Speaker a Democrat, fifty-year-old John G. Carlisle of Kentucky.

The deaths of Garfield and Hendricks, both occurring at times when there was no President pro tempore or Speaker, generated considerable discussion of the succession law of 1792.

One defect of the law had become apparent almost immediately upon the shooting of Garfield. On July 7, 1881, a few days after the attack, the *New York Herald* commented: "Should . . . [Garfield die] there would be no one left to succeed the President. . . . [T]he provision for succession to the Presidency is inadequate to meet emergencies heretofore deemed wholly improbable. . . ."

When Garfield died in September, 1881, another defect in the law became apparent. Noted *The New York Times* on September 21, 1881:

[I]f the Senate is called together in "extra" session for the purpose of electing a presiding officer, another evil consequence of the constitutional provision may be revealed. The reasons are sufficiently obvious why the person in order of succession to the Presidency . . . should not be of the party hostile to that which elected the President. . . . The possibilities of the case forcibly illustrate the defective character of the existing provisions in regard to the succession.

When the Forty-Seventh Congress convened in December, 1881, the succession law came under immediate discussion.

Senators James B. Beck of Kentucky and Samuel B. Maxey of Texas introduced resolutions directing the Senate Committee on the Judiciary to examine the law of 1792 to discover whether it was constitutional and adequate, and whether any further legislation was necessary.[4] Senators Augustus H. Garland of Arkansas and George F. Hoar of Massachusetts submitted bills to change the line of succession from the President pro tempore and Speaker to the Cabinet.*[5] A Cabinet line of succession promptly received favorable comment: 'With the succession lodged in the Cabinet Ministers," the *Herald* commented, "there could be no danger of an interregnum for want of the designated person, and each of these officers would be in full harmony with the President and thoroughly conversant with the policy and aims of his administration."[6]

The Beck and Maxey resolutions, together with the Garland

---

* Garland's bill included only the Secretaries of State, Treasury and War, while Hoar's suggested the whole Cabinet in this order: Secretary of State, Secretary of Treasury, Secretary of War, Attorney General, Postmaster General, Secretary of Navy and Secretary of Interior.

and Hoar bills, were referred to the Senate Committee on the Judiciary, which subsequently recommended a proposal along the lines of the Hoar bill. This proposal was debated in the Senate in the years 1882 and 1883, and was finally adopted by the Senate, with certain amendments.[7] No action, however, was taken by the House.

When the Forty-Eighth Congress convened in December, 1883, Senator Hoar reintroduced his bill and the Senate passed it and forwarded it to the House.[8] But again the House declined to act. The death of Vice-President Hendricks reopened discussion of the succession law. *The New York Herald* of November 30, 1885, urging reconsideration of the Hoar bill, said:

The plan of vesting the succession in the Cabinet seems to be the most acceptable solution yet advanced of the problem with which Congress now has to deal. It remedies two very grave defects in the existing law, namely, those which render possible, first, a failure in the line of succession, and, second, a political transfer of the administration.

In his first message to the Forty-Ninth Congress on December 8, 1885, President Grover Cleveland also advocated a change of the succession law, saying:

The present condition of the law relating to the succession to the Presidency . . . is such as to require immediate amendment. This subject has repeatedly been considered by Congress, but no result has been reached. The recent lamentable death of the Vice President and vacancies at the same time in all other offices the incumbents of which might immediately exercise the functions of the Presidential office, have caused public anxiety and a just demand that a recurrence of such a condition of affairs should not be permitted.[9]

Senator Hoar reintroduced his bill, with some modifications, and it was passed by the Senate on December 17, 1885 and forwarded to the House.[10] There, the bill was favorably reported and passed. It became law on January 19, 1886, with President Cleveland's signature.[11]

The Act of 1886 substituted the Cabinet officers, in the order originally proposed by Senator Hoar, for the President pro tempore and Speaker in the line of succession. It provided that in case of the removal, death, resignation or inability of both the President and Vice-President, such officer would "act as President until the disability of the President or Vice-President is removed or a President shall be elected." If Congress were not then in session or due to meet within twenty days, the officer was to call a special session, giving no less than twenty days' notice.* The Act also provided that for a member of the Cabinet to act as President, he had to have been appointed by and with the advice and consent of the Senate and be eligible to the office of President and not under impeachment.

During the Congressional discussions between the years 1881 and 1886, numerous objections to the law of 1792 had been advanced. In addition to the two already noted was the further objection that the President pro tempore and Speaker were not "officers" of the United States, as intended by the succession clause. It was urged, especially by Senators Hoar, Maxey, Beck and Garland, that they were merely officers of their respective Houses or States.[12] The view of James Madison was cited in support of this position that they were not officers of the United States,† as was the classic *Blount* case.[13] There, Senator William Blount of Tennessee had been impeached by the House of Representatives in 1797 for having conspired, while territorial governor of Tennessee, to transfer New Orleans and neighboring lands to Great Britain by means of a joint expedition of Englishmen and Creek and Cherokee Indians. When he was tried in the Senate, Jared A. Ingersoll and A. J. Dallas, who represented him, pleaded lack of jurisdiction on the grounds that a Senator was not a civil officer and therefore not subject to impeachment.‡ It was also argued that even if he had been an officer, he was one no longer, since he had been expelled by the Senate. The Senate dismissed the case, giving no reason for its decision.

Also said to support this position were parts of the Constitution which distinguished "officer" from President pro tempore and Speaker or member of Congress, or obviously excluded a President pro tempore or a Speaker or member of Congress from the scope of the term "officer."§[14] An officer under the succession provision, it

---

* The reason for this is explained at p. 146.

† See p. 61.

‡ Article II, Section 4 of the Constitution provides: "The President, Vice President and all civil officers of the United States, shall be removed from Office on Impeachment for, and Conviction of, Treason, Bribery, or other high Crimes and Misdemeanors."

§ Senator Maxey argued that under the language of the Constitution the President pro tempore was not even an officer of the Senate, since Article I, Section 3, Clause 5 provides: "The Senate shall chuse their other Officers, and also a President pro tempore. . . ."

was argued, was an officer of the United States, a permanent officer (whose office is not vacant for long periods of time), one who receives his commission from the President.

The law of 1792 was not clear as to whether the President pro tempore or Speaker had to resign as a Congressman before he could act as President. If he were to resign, the law, some thought, would be objectionable on legal grounds, since the function of acting as President must be attached to an existing office.

Senator Hoar distinguished: "[T]he Presidency is annexed by law to an office. It is not a person holding an office at the time succeeding to the Presidency, but it is an officer continuing in that office who is to perform as an annex or incident merely to another office the great duties of the Presidency itself."[15] Thus, if the President pro tempore or Speaker resigned, he would have no office to which the function of acting as President could be attached. If he did not resign, there would be a violation of the principle of separation of powers, because he would be a Congressman and the presiding officer of his House as well as acting President. Further, while acting as President, his tenure could be ended by the will of his respective House or by the loss of his legislative seat at the polls.

On policy grounds, it was felt that a Cabinet line of succession was far preferable to a legislative line. With the Cabinet, there would be no doubt regarding their status as officers. Moreover, there would be continuity of administration and policy. The Secretary of State, it was stressed, was generally better qualified for the presidency than either the President pro tempore or Speaker. Senator Hoar defined "President pro tempore":

[He is] a person never selected by anybody with reference to his special capacity, either of opinion or intellectual quality, for the discharge of executive duties. He is a Senator, a senior, a legislator, a debater, and selected from this body for his capacity for presiding over and regulating the debates of a parliamentary body.[16]

It was emphasized that, although many Secretaries of State had become President, the same was not true of Presidents pro tempore or Speakers.*

---

* Six Secretaries of State had become President—Thomas Jefferson, James Madison, James Monroe, John Q. Adams, Martin Van Buren and James Buchanan. John Tyler was the only president pro tempore to become president and James K. Polk the only Speaker.

Opposition to a Cabinet line of succession centered on the points that the 1792 law was written by the Founding Fathers and that the President would have the power to appoint his potential successor, which would be contrary to the elective principle of our democracy. Representative William McKinley of Ohio, later President of the United States, was one of those who felt that the law of 1792 should remain in effect.

During the debates, the special election feature of the 1792 Act was criticized on the grounds that it was unwise and unconstitutional. It was stated that a special election would disrupt the orderly processes of government which contemplated regular elections. Yet, the special election words of the Constitution ("until . . . a President shall be elected") were inserted in the 1886 Act. The probable intention of the provision in the 1886 Act for calling Congress into session was to let Congress decide whether or not to have a special presidential election under the circumstances. It seems to have been assumed during the debates that if there were such an election, the new President would have to serve for a full four-year term on the theory that this is the only term referred to in the Constitution for a President.[17] However, some were of the opinion that the Act, as written, did not give Congress any special election authority.[18]

Writing several years later for the *Harvard Law Review* about this special election feature of the Act, Charles S. Hamlin stated:

The Act of 1886, therefore, leaves the question of the constitutionality and expediency of a special election absolutely unsettled. The acting President, under the law, must call Congress together, and that body will then decide whether it deems a special election desirable and incidentally constitutional. If it decides in the affirmative, it will frame an act which may speedily oust the acting President from office. Such an act the acting President can veto, and if vetoed, the usual two-thirds vote will be necessary to overcome the veto. Even a death-blow might be administered by a pocket veto.[19]

The Act of 1886 was to remain the law of the land for the next sixty-one years.

11

The Concealed Inability

[The] crisis would have been changed into a national disaster had the actual facts [of the operation] become known. . . .

W. W. KEEN

President Grover Cleveland ran for re-election in 1888, with Allen G. Thurman, a former Ohio Senator, as his running mate. Although Cleveland and Thurman obtained a plurality of the popular votes, Benjamin Harrison of Indiana and Levi P. Morton of New York received a majority of the electoral votes and won the election. Four years later, Cleveland and Adlai E. Stevenson, a former Illinois Congressman, succeeded in defeating the Republican candidates, Harrison and Whitelaw Reid, editor of the *New York Tribune*.*

Shortly after Cleveland took the oath of office on March 4, 1893, a financial panic enveloped the country. Among its causes were a farm depression, a business decline abroad, and the depletion of the Treasury's gold reserve. As a result, over fifty railroads went into bankruptcy, hundreds of banks closed their doors, thousands of businesses shut down, and millions of people were thrown out of work. Cleveland felt that a primary cause of the depression was the Sherman Silver Purchase Act of 1890, under which more than one hundred and fifty million dollars worth of silver was added to the

---

* Because he was elected President for non-consecutive terms, Cleveland is considered by most authorities the twenty-second and twenty-fourth President of the United States.

147

nation's currency at a time when the rest of the world was returning to the gold standard. Accordingly, on June 30, 1893, Cleveland issued a call for a special session of Congress to meet on August 7 for the purpose of repealing the Sherman Act.

The repeal of the Sherman Act was opposed by those who would benefit from the continued use of silver, and it was generally felt that only Cleveland's leadership could bring about the repeal. As Allan Nevins put it:

The whole strength of the assault upon the Sherman silver-purchase clauses lay, as everyone realized, in the grim determination of Cleveland's purpose. His weight of character could force enough members of the party into line, and nothing else could. . . . [I]f any accident suddenly removed him from the scene, all would be lost, for the Vice President, Adlai E. Stevenson, would infallibly bring the nation to the silver standard.[1]

On the night that he issued his call for a special session, Cleveland boarded the *Oneida,* a yacht belonging to his friend, Commodore E. C. Benedict, in New York City. After five days of cruising in Long Island Sound, he left the yacht at his summer home, Gray Gables, on Buzzards Bay, Massachusetts. On July 17, he once again boarded the yacht and, after a few more days of cruising, returned to Gray Gables, where he remained until August 5. On that day, he left for Washington, D.C. and on August 7, he addressed the special session of Congress, urging repeal of the Sherman Act. On August 11, he returned to Gray Gables. On August 28, the House of Representatives passed the repeal by a vote of more than two to one, and sent it to the Senate for action.

On August 29, the Philadelphia *Press* published a letter from its New York correspondent, "Holland" (E. J. Edwards), giving the details of an alleged operation recently undergone by Cleveland. On the same day, the *Commercial and Financial Chronicle* declared in an editorial that "Cleveland is about all that stands between the country and absolute disaster. . . ." The next day found Cleveland in Washington. Less than a week later he opened the First Pan-American Medical Congress in Washington, at which time it was observed that his voice was "even clearer and more resonant" than at his inauguration.[2] The story which had been published in the *Press* was sensational and alarming. According to the report, a serious operation had been performed on Cleveland on July 1, aboard the *Oneida,* by Dr. Joseph D. Bryant of New York. The names of several other doctors in attendance were also listed. The operation, said Edwards, had consisted in the removal of a few teeth and a large part of the left upper jawbone.

This story precipitated a tremendous furor. Many newspapers asserted there had been no operation at all. Others held that Cleveland simply had some teeth extracted. Doctor Bryant, members of Cleveland's Cabinet, and other government officials either refused to confirm or denied the report. The editor of the Philadelphia *Public Ledger,* L. Clarke Davis, a close friend of the President, issued a statement in which he said the only basis for the story was a toothache. President Cleveland, himself, seemed to belie the whole account. He went about his normal duties, making public appearances and speeches. There was no evidence of any change in his facial structure, his speech, or his general health. Eventually the clamor died, with the general feeling that the story had been a fake.

Twenty-four years later, the *Saturday Evening Post* published a detailed account, written by Dr. W. W. Keen, one of the participating surgeons, setting out what actually had occurred on the *Oneida.*[3] Doctor Keen stated that the story published in the Philadelphia *Press* had been "substantially correct, even in most of the details." According to Keen, an "ulcer" had been discovered on June 18, 1893, by Dr. R. M. O'Reilly, the official medical attendant assigned to officers of the government, when Cleveland complained to him of a rough spot on the roof of his mouth. O'Reilly removed a fragment and had it examined by the pathologist at the Army Medical Museum, who reported that it was malignant. Thereupon, O'Reilly advised Cleveland to consult his friend and medical attendant, Doctor Bryant. Bryant confirmed the diagnosis and ordered an immediate operation.

In view of the critical state of the country's financial affairs and the possible effect on the public of the revelation that he had cancer, Cleveland insisted the operation be performed at such a time and place as would insure complete secrecy. He chose Benedict's yacht on July 1. The doctors predicted that he would be sufficiently recovered to be in Washington by August 7.

Bryant contacted Keen and together they made arrangements for the operation on the yacht. A dentist, Dr. Ferdinand Hasbrouck, was asked to assist by administering the nitrous oxide.* On June 30 Cleveland issued his special session call and that night all concerned boarded the *Oneida,* docked at Pier A on the East River in New York City. Among those who went aboard were Secretary of War Daniel S. Lamont, Doctors Bryant, Keen, O'Reilly, Hasbrouck, John F. Erdmann, an assisting surgeon, and E. G. Janeway, who was to observe the President's pulse and general condition.†

Doctors Keen and Janeway examined Cleveland on the morning of July 1. It was decided that, in view of the possible danger of anesthetic to a man of Cleveland's age (fifty-six) and corpulence, ether would be used only if necessary in the last stages of the operation. Nitrous oxide would be used in the earlier stages. As the *Oneida* proceeded up the East River on July 1, the operation was begun. In addition to the doctors, the only other person present at the operation was a steward, who was there to run errands. The ship's crew had been told that the President was to have two badly ulcerated teeth removed and that the unusual precautions were necessary to prevent blood poisoning.

The operation consisted in the removal of two teeth on the upper left side and the entire rear portion of the left upper jaw as far as the floor of the orbital cavity (eye socket), together with a portion of the soft palate. No external incision was made. The entire operation was performed from within the mouth, and took less than one hour.

By July 3, the President was "up and about." In the evening of July 5, he walked from the yacht to his house, Gray Gables. On a subsequent examination of Cleveland's mouth, Doctor Bryant feared that some of the malignant tissue had not been removed. Thus, on July 17 the *Oneida,* with Doctors Bryant, Keen, Erdmann and Janeway aboard, picked the President up at Gray Gables and, as the yacht cruised, a second operation was performed to remove the suspicious tissue and to cauterize the entire surface. Two days later, the President was again up and about. By September 1, Bryant recorded that Cleveland's mouth was completely healed.

After the first operation and while the President was recuperating at Gray Gables, Dr. Kasson C. Gibson of New York had fitted him with an artificial jaw of vulcanized rubber. With this in place,

---

* The leak to the press in late August has been attributed to Hasbrouck. Nevins, *Grover Cleveland* (New York, 1962), p. 533 & n.1.

† The other members of the Cabinet and Vice-President Adlai E. Stevenson apparently were kept totally ignorant of the operation.

Cleveland's speech seemed unaltered. Without it, his speech was "wholly unintelligible, resembling the worst imaginable case of cleft palate."[4] This device, together with the absence of a scar and the normal appearance of the eye, made it possible to conceal the true facts. Doctor Erdmann later said that during this period he "did more lying than in all the rest of his life put together."[5]

According to Keen, this "was by far the most responsible operation in which I ever took part" because "on it hung the life not only of a human being and an illustrious ruler but the destiny of a nation. The instant decision of Mr. Cleveland himself," said Keen, "concurred in by his professional advisers and such friends as Secretary Lamont and Commodore Benedict, to keep the operation a profound secret was wise, and one may say imperative. What the consequences would have been had it become known at once we can only surmise, and shudder!"[6]

12

Succession: 1897—1912

Don't any of you realize that there's only one life be-tween this madman and the White House?

MARK HANNA

When William McKinley took the oath of office on Thursday, March 4, 1897, as the twenty-fifth President of the United States, there was little indication that the vice-presidency was to undergo any significant change. The election of 1896 had brought to the vice-presidency in the person of Garret Augustus Hobart a highly popular New Jersey figure. Hobart had been both speaker of the state assembly and president of the state senate. He won the vice-presidential nomination largely because he was from New Jersey and had been instrumental in some significant Republican victories there. Hobart had not sought the nomination. As he said in a letter to his wife before receiving it: "[W]hen I realize all that it means in work, worry, and loss of home and bliss, I am overcome, so over-come I am simply miserable."[1] Yet, the Republican selection proved to be a good one. Hobart's appealing personality, his clear stand on the currency questions then facing the country, and his general forthrightness contributed greatly to the Republican victory against William Jennings Bryan and Adlai E. Stevenson.

At the time of his inauguration as Vice-President, Hobart barely knew McKinley, but in the course of a short time a relationship de-veloped between them which rivals any that existed before or since. Although, in keeping with the nineteenth-century tradition, Ho-bart was never made a member of the Cabinet, he was almost daily

152

called upnn by the President for his advice and opinions.[2] Hobart's residence at 21 Lafayette Square, a short distance from the White House, facilitated frequent contact between the two. Their relationship was so close that it was not unusual for the newspapers to refer to Hobart as the "Assistant President." McKinley recognized Hobart's position as the second officer during the dispute between Hobart and the British Ambassador, Sir Julian Pauncefote. The Ambassador insisted that his position at receptions was immediately after the President, citing the practice which had existed under Cleveland. McKinley rejected this claim and asserted that the second place at receptions was for the Vice-President of the United States.[3]   Although Hobart was never noted for his forensic ability, his manner of presiding over the Senate won for him the unqualified respect and admiration of that body. He presided with such ability that Senator Henry Cabot Lodge of Massachusetts declared that he "fulfilled carefully and thoroughly every duty of the place. He abandoned once for all the bad habit which had grown up, of submitting nearly every question of order to the Senate, and ruled promptly on all these points, as every presiding officer ought to do."[4]

The increased prestige and dignity which Hobart had brought to the vice-presidency came to an abrupt end. Long hours of work and a weak heart caused him to collapse in the spring of 1899 and he never completely recovered. He died in his sleep at his home in Paterson, New Jersey, on the morning of November 21, 1899, at the age of fifty-five. Present at the time of his death were Mrs. Hobart, his son and only surviving child, Garret Augustus, Jr., his secretary, his doctor, and his nurse. His death was a tremendous shock to the President who had relied so heavily on his Vice-President.*

The eulogies which followed recognized what Hobart had done for the vice-presidency. Senator Lodge of Massachusetts expressed his feelings in these words:

He restored the Vice-Presidency to its proper positon and lifted it up before the people to the dignity and importance which it merits . . . merely by the manner in which he filled it and performed its duties. Quietly, firmly, and with perfect tact he asserted the dignity of his high position, never going too far and always far enough. Without knowing exactly why, people suddenly came to realize there that was a Vice-Presi-

---

* As a result of Hobart's death, Secretary of State John Hay became next in line to the presidency.

dent of the United States, that he held the second position in the Government. . . .[5]

Senator John W. Daniel of Virginia stated: "Nothing that happened in this hall escaped the eye of his alert attention. . . . [O]ur late [Vice-] President [was] the model presiding officer of a deliberative assembly."[6] "Hobart made the office of Vice-President," said Lodge, "what the framers of the Constitution intended it to be."

McKinley's renomination as the Republican standard bearer in the election of 1900 was certain. The selection of the vice-presidential candidate was the only real subject of interest and excitement. The nomination would probably have gone to Elihu Root, then Secretary of War, if he had wanted it, but he had announced several months prior to the Convention that he would not seek it. Soon after Root's declaration, the name of Theodore Roosevelt, the forty-one-year-old governor of New York and the hero of San Juan Hill during the Spanish-American War, was put forth. But his preference was to secure a second term as Governor of New York, since, as he put it, he "greatly disliked the office of Vice-President."[7] This sentiment had been indicated during the previous year in a letter to Senator Henry Cabot Lodge in which Roosevelt had said:

The Vice-Presidency is a most honorable office, but for a young man there is not much to do. It is infinitely better than many other positions, but it hardly seems to me as good as being Governor of this State, which is a pretty important State. . . . If I am Vice-President I am "planted" for four years. Here I can turn around.[8]

In order to quell the sentiment for him as the vice-presidential candidate, Roosevelt issued a statement saying: "It is proper for me to state definitely that under no circumstances could I, or would I, accept the nomination for the Vice-Presidency. . . ."[9]

Other possible nominees were then considered—John D. Long of Massachusetts, Secretary of Navy; Cornelius N. Bliss, ex-Secretary of the Interior under McKinley; Timothy L. Woodruff, New York's Lieutenant Governor; and Senators William B. Allison and Jonathan P. Dolliver of Iowa and Charles W. Fairbanks of Indiana. The lack of unanimity was all the Eastern political bosses needed. As Governor of New York, Roosevelt had done a good deal of reforming which had brought him into conflict with large corporations and insurance companies. Senator Thomas C. Platt, the political boss of New York State, who was fearful of Roosevelt's threat to his political machine, decided to join forces with Senator Matthew S. Quay of Pennsylvania to put Roosevelt on the vice-presidential "shelf" lest he ruin the party organization.[10]

The more Roosevelt expressed his lack of interest in the vice-presidency, the more popular he became for the position. The major opposition to his nomination came from the Republican National Committee, in particular Senator Mark Hanna of Ohio, the national chairman. Hanna is reported to have said on one occasion, in reference to a possible Roosevelt nomination, "Don't any of you realize that there's only one life between this madman and the White House?"[11] Two days before the Convention opened, Senator Charles Dick, Secretary of the Republican National Committee, asked McKinley to stop the Roosevelt boom. McKinley, who was not as receptive to a Roosevelt candidacy as to others, replied through his Secretary, George B. Cortelyou, as follows:

The President has no choice for Vice-President. Any of the distinguished names suggested would be satisfactory to him. The choice of the convention will be his choice; he has no advice to give. The convention is the lawfully constituted body to make nominations, and instead of giving advice he awaits its advice, confident now as always that it will act wisely and for the highest interest of the country and of the party.[12]

The advice of the Convention was unanimous, except for Roosevelt himself. He was nominated on the first ballot.

During the campaign which followed, Roosevelt "crisscrossed the country so thoroughly that by the time the campaign ended, the New York *Times* estimated that he had covered 21,209 miles and addressed a total of 3,000,000 people—perhaps a record for the era that preceded TV, radio, or even platform amplifiers."[13] McKinley left most of the campaigning to Roosevelt, regarding it below a President's dignity to engage in partisan politics on his own behalf. In the election, McKinley was re-elected and Roosevelt became the twenty-fifth Vice-President of the United States. Less than seven months after his inauguration, Roosevelt became the fifth Vice-President to succeed to the presidency upon the death of the incumbent.

On September 5, 1901, President McKinley journeyed to Buffalo, New York, to deliver a major speech at the Pan-American Exposition on the need for cooperation with other countries. The address was delivered before a throng of at least 50,000. On the following day McKinley held a public reception in the Temple of Music, one of the public buildings at the exposition. Before leaving for Buffalo, McKinley had been cautioned to be careful while attending the Exposition but it was inconceivable to him that anyone might want to kill him.[14]

The public reception commenced at 4:00 P.M. on Friday, September 6, and it was scheduled to last for only ten minutes. Rows of soldiers and policemen were stationed near the President. In the immediate vicinity were four Buffalo detectives, four soldiers and three Secret Service agents. Two Secret Service agents were only three feet from McKinley. At approximately 4:07 P.M., as the President reached out to shake the hand of a young man in the line, two shots pierced the air. Leon F. Czolgosz, an anarchist who held no particular grudge against the President, had shot him in the abdomen. The assassin was quickly subdued.* McKinley, who was conscious, was rushed to the emergency hospital at the Exposition grounds. As he was being carried into the building, he remarked to Cortelyou, "It must have been some poor misguided fellow."

An operation to remove the bullet was immediately decided upon and at 5:20 P.M. the President was given ether. It was discovered that the bullet had passed through the stomach. The wounds were bathed and the holes made by the bullet repaired. However, the operation was only partially successful, since the doctors could not locate the bullet itself. That evening, while still under the effects of ether, McKinley was removed to the home of John G. Milburn, President of the Exposition. The house was converted to a semi-hospital. A telegraph system was set up nearby to keep the country apprised of all developments.

Within minutes after McKinley had been shot, the Associated Press wires were busy sending the news to all parts of the country. The immediate reaction of the people was "stunned horror."[15] The Cabinet, members of the Congress and close friends of McKinley quickly departed for Buffalo. Vice-President Roosevelt was then vacationing in Vermont on an island in Lake Champlain. Upon being notified of the attempted assassination, all he could say was "My God!" After the shock had subsided, he stated: "I am so inexpressibly grieved, shocked and horrified that I can say nothing."[16]

---

* Within fifty-three days, Czolgosz was tried, convicted and executed.

Saturday, September 7, found the pages of the country's news-papers filled with stories about the wounded President. Messages of inquiry and sympathy began to come in from all parts of the world. The Vice-President and the Cabinet, with the exception of Secre-tary of State John M. Hay and Secretary of Navy John D. Long, had assembled in Buffalo. The President was fully conscious. No com-plications had set in. Optimism was reflected in the September 7 medical bulletin issued by Cortelyou. It read: "The President passed a fairly comfortable night and no serious symptoms have de-veloped."[17] The belief that McKinley would recover grew stronger with each passing hour. The bulletins on Monday, September 9, said that his condition was "more and more satisfactory." On Tues-day, they spoke of "the most comfortable night since the attempt on his life." Wednesday's were even more encouraging—"the Presi-dent continues to gain."

By Tuesday, September 10, President McKinley had improved to such extent that the Vice-President, the members of the Cabinet, and others were told that there was no need to remain in Buffalo. So they dispersed. Said Roosevelt: "The President's condition seemed to be improving, and after a day or two we were told that he was practically out of danger. I then joined my family, who were in the Adirondacks, near the foot of Mount Tahawus."[18]

By Thursday, however, the President's condition ceased to im-prove. His fever rose and general infection set in. By the afternoon of Friday, September 13, the news was released that "the President is sinking." The Cabinet and others again converged on Buffalo. Vice-President Roosevelt, however, was difficult to locate. Few knew that he was vacationing in the Adirondacks and when a mes-senger arrived late Friday afternoon at the place where Roosevelt was staying, he had to journey many miles into the forest before he could find the Vice-President. He brought this telegram from Sec-retary of War Elihu Root: "The President appears to be dying and members of the Cabinet in Buffalo think you should lose no time in coming."[19] Roosevelt promptly set out for Buffalo. He traveled all Friday night and through the early hours of Saturday morning by wagon to North Creek, some forty or fifty miles away, arriving at dawn. There, where he was to take a train to Buffalo, he was notified by his secretary, William Loeb, that the President had died at about 2:00 A.M.[20]

Upon arriving in Buffalo at 1:30 P.M. on Saturday, Roosevelt met

Secretary of War Root who stated: "Mr. Vice-President, I have been requested on behalf of the Cabinet of the late President—at least those who are present in Buffalo, all except two—to request that for reasons of weight affecting the affairs of Government you should proceed to take the constitutional oath of President of the United States."[21] Roosevelt replied: "I shall take the oath at once in accordance with your request. . . ."[22]

At approximately 3:32 P.M. at the residence of Ansley Wilcox, 641 Delaware Avenue, Buffalo, New York, the oath was administered by Judge John R. Hazel of the United States District Court. In attendance were representatives of the press, close friends of Roosevelt and all the members of the Cabinet except Secretary of State Hay and Secretary of Treasury Lyman J. Gage. The new President, who was then only forty-two years old, delivered an address, in which he said:

I will show the people at once that the administration of the Government will not falter, in spite of the terrible national blow. . . . I wish to say that it shall be my aim to continue, absolutely unbroken, the policy of President McKinley for the peace, prosperity, and the honor of our beloved country.[23]

In reviewing this period in his life, Roosevelt said in his autobiography that :

I at once announced that I would continue unchanged McKinley's policies . . . , and I asked all the members of the Cabinet to stay. There were no changes made among them save as changes were made among their successors whom I myself appointed. I continued Mr. McKinley's policies, changing and developing them and adding new policies only as the questions before the public changed and as the needs of the public developed.[24]

In a letter to Senator Lodge, Roosevelt remarked that "it is a dreadful thing to come into the Presidency this way; but it would be a far worse thing to be morbid about it. Here is the task and I have got to do it to the best of my ability; and that is all there is about it. . . ."[25]

After taking the oath, Roosevelt went to Washington where he held his first Cabinet meeting. He asked the members of McKinley's Cabinet to stay on and help him carry out McKinley's program.* In the three and one-half years during which he occupied the presidency as McKinley's successor, Roosevelt was able to render remarkable leadership. He embarked on a program of social reform which he referred to as the "square deal." He recommended the "organization of labor into trade unions" and the enactment of laws to secure for the laboring class "a larger measure of social and industrial justice." His intervention on behalf of the miners in the coal strike of 1902 to force arbitration was a significant step in this program. He actively worked at regulating business trusts and in so doing, became known as a "trust buster." Under his leadership the Reclamation Act of 1902 was passed providing for the reclamation and irrigation of dry western lands, the Department of Commerce and Labor was established in 1903, and in the same year a treaty was signed by the United States for the construction of the Panama Canal. In the field of foreign relations, he enunciated the famous "Roosevelt Corollary" of the Monroe Doctrine in 1904 and his policy, "speak softly and carry a big stick," did much to enhance American prestige abroad.

Roosevelt proved to be a colorful and forceful figure—a man who understood and dominated his era. So effective was his leadership that the Republican Party nominated him for President by acclamation at its 1904 national convention. Senator Charles W. Fairbanks of Indiana was endorsed for the vice-presidency. Roosevelt was re-elected by over two and one-half million votes, the largest majority any President had received up to that time.

In 1908, Roosevelt decided not to run for what would be considered a third term, thus adhering to the precedent set by his predecessors. He supported the candidacy of William Howard Taft, his Secretary of War. Representative James Schoolcraft Sherman of New York was suggested by Congressional leaders as a possible running mate for Taft (as were Senators Albert J. Beveridge of Indiana and Jonathan P. Dolliver of Iowa). It was felt that Sherman, as a conservative, would balance the ticket. Taft was not delighted with the prospect, and wrote Roosevelt before the Republican Conven-

---

* Secretary of Treasury Lyman J. Gage, Secretary of Navy John D. Long and Postmaster General Charles E. Smith resigned in 1902; Attorney General Philander C. Knox and Secretary of War Elihu Root resigned in 1904; and Secretary of State John M. Hay, Secretary of Interior Ethan A. Hitchcock and Secretary of Agriculture James Wilson remained for the rest of the term.

tion met, saying of Sherman that "he ought to be eliminated" as a vice-presidential possibility.[26] In a letter to Charles Nagel before the Convention, Taft stated: "I am a great deal troubled about . . . [the selection of a vice-presidential candidate]. My own preference would be to have a man west of the Mississippi, like Senator Dolliver of Iowa, or some western senator who has shown himself conservative and at the same time represents the progressive movement."[27] W. R. Nelson, publisher of the *Kansas City Star,* telegraphed to Taft the day after the Republican Convention opened in Chicago: "Sherman would be a sinker in our section. What about Beveridge?"[28] Beveridge, however, was not interested in the nomination, because of disagreement with the Republican platform and because "he had no intention of wasting his own great talents in so obscure an office."[29] Sherman was subsequently nominated.

In the election of 1908 Taft and Sherman defeated the Democratic ticket of William Jennings Bryan of Nebraska and John Worth Kern of Indiana. As Vice-President, Sherman often came into conflict with Taft on matters of New York politics and was instrumental in widening the breach between Taft and Roosevelt. However, in 1912, the Republican Party renominated Taft and Sherman. They were pitted against Theodore Roosevelt and Senator Hiram Warren Johnson of California (Progressive Party) and Governors Woodrow Wilson of New Jersey and Thomas R. Marshall of Indiana (Democratic Party). The election of 1912 was marred by a near assassination of a presidential candidate and the death of a Vice-President who was also a vice-presidential nominee.

On October 14, 1912, as Theodore Roosevelt was leaving the Hotel Gilpatrick in Milwaukee, on his way to deliver a speech, John N. Schrank, a thirty-six-year-old ex-tavern keeper, shot him in the chest.* Roosevelt's life was spared because most of the momentum of the bullet was spent on the folded manuscript of his speech and the metal case for his eyeglasses which were in his breast pocket. Since the wound was not serious, Roosevelt went on to deliver his speech before receiving medical attention. Of this incident Roosevelt later said: "I did not care a rap for being shot. It is a trade risk which every prominent public man ought to accept as a matter of

---

* Schrank reportedly shot Roosevelt because of a dream in which McKinley had instructed him to prevent Roosevelt, McKinley's murderer according to the dream, from becoming President. Schrank was subsequently declared insane and spent the rest of his life in mental institutions.

course. For eleven years, I have been prepared any day to be shot. . . ."[30]

On October 30, six days before the election, Vice-President Sherman, who had been seriously ill even before the convention, died. His death came at a time when the Republican Party could ill afford to have its strength further diminished. It undoubtedly caused some confusion in the minds of the voters and may have been a factor in Taft's failure to win re-election.

The Republican Party was not unprepared for such an eventuality. The convention of 1912, in recognition of Sherman's physical condition, had passed for the first time in its history, a resolution to provide the means for filling a vacancy occurring in the national ticket. The national committee of the party was given the authority either to fill the vacancy itself or to call a national convention to do so. In this case, the committee decided to fill the vacancy itself but was unable to meet for this purpose until after the election. As a result, Sherman's name appeared on the ballot and 3,483,922 popular votes were cast for a vice-presidential candidate who was dead. When the Republican National Committee met shortly after the election, Nicholas Murray Butler, President of Columbia University in New York City, was designated to receive the eight electoral votes which would have been cast for Sherman. The victors in the election, however, were the Democrats, Wilson and Marshall.

13

The Wilson Inability

I studied every paper, sent from the different Secretaries or Senators. . . . I, myself, never made a single decision regarding the disposition of public affairs. The only decision that was mine was what was important and what was not, and . . . when to present matters to my husband.

EDITH BOLLING WILSON

Woodrow Wilson and Thomas R. Marshall served two successive terms together as President and Vice-President. Marshall had been selected according to the usual practice. He "was the greatest possible contrast to the President in every way besides geographically and so had been nominated in 1912 and again in 1916 to balance the ticket."[1] In 1912, Marshall's name had been one of those placed in nomination for the presidency. When a deadlock occurred between Champ Clark of Missouri, the Speaker of the House of Representatives and the leading candidate for the nomination, and Woodrow Wilson, William F. McCombs, Wilson's manager, promised the vice-presidential nomination to Marshall if the Indiana delegation were released in favor of Wilson. Indiana switched from Marshall to Wilson on the twenty-eighth ballot, which helped to make possible Wilson's victory over Clark on the forty-sixth ballot. Wilson apparently had not been informed of the promise. His personal preference was Representative Oscar W. Underwood of Alabama, the House Democratic Majority Leader. Underwood refused to be considered. Albert S. Burlson, one of Wilson's managers, told

162

Wilson that the convention favored Marshall, whereupon Wilson reportedly said: "But Burlson, he is a small-calibre man."[2] Burlson pointed out that Marshall was a good politician and came from the right section of the country.* Wilson finally submitted, and Marshall was nominated on the second ballot.

Marshall entered the vice-presidency with no illusions of grandeur. At his inauguration, he said that he thought he was entitled to make a few remarks since he was "about to enter upon a four-year period of silence."[3] He soon discovered how insignificant the vice-presidency could be. As he later said: "So far as any actual power in the affairs of government is concerned, this epithet ["His Superfluous Excellency"] hurled at the first vice-president expressed the truth."†[4]

Marshall had little, if any, influence in the Wilson administration. "I soon ascertained that I was of no importance to the administration beyond the duty of being loyal to it and ready, at any time, to act as a sort of pinch hitter; that is, when everybody else on the team had failed, I was to be given a chance."[5] He was known for his folksy sense of humor and enlivened the task of presiding in the Senate by interrupting its debates with humorous asides and occasional jokes. One such aside whispered to a clerk during a Senate debate endured. That is: "What this country needs is a really good five-cent cigar."

Since Marshall had no source of income other than his $12,000 annual salary, he sought to augment this amount by lecturing. In the course of his travels, taking advantage of the fact that few people recognized him, he told tall tales about himself or led people on in their derogatory remarks about the Vice-President. He expressed his philosophy as follows: "[W]hen a man finds himself in a position in which he believes that people are likely to crack fun at him, he has chosen the better part if he beats them to the fun making."[6]

---

* Before becoming Governor of Indiana in 1909, Marshall had practiced law in Columbia City for over thirty years and had acquired a reputation as an effective and witty speaker.

† Woodrow Wilson, himself, had early expressed himself on the vice-presidency in these words: "The chief embarrassment in discussing this office is, that in explaining how little there is to be said about it one has evidently said all there is to say." Wilson, *Congressional Government* (Boston, 1898, 13th ed.), pp. 240–41.

At one time he is said to have remarked, "The Vice President is like a man in a cataleptic state; he cannot speak; he cannot move; he suffers no pain; and yet he is perfectly conscious of everything that is going on about him."[7] Once when he was in Denver, he noticed a policeman following him around. Asked what he was doing, the officer replied that he was guarding Marshall's person. Said Marshall: "Your labor is in vain. Nobody was ever crazy enough to shoot at a vice-president. If you will go away and find somebody to shoot at me, I'll go down in history as being the first vice-president who ever attracted enough attention even to have a crank shoot at him."[8]

Thomas R. Marshall was to become an actor in a situation which remains to this day clouded in mystery—the Wilson inability. This case of presidential inability occurred during one of the most turbulent periods of American history.

On November 11, 1918, the Armistice ending World War I was signed. That Wilson played a major part in bringing Germany to submission was acknowledged. His appeal for justice, fairness and peace had reached the minds and hearts of the world and his idealistic Fourteen Points had won wide acclaim at home and abroad. He was at the summit of his career.

After the Armistice was signed, President Wilson decided he would go to Europe to see that the peace treaty included his ideals of justice and his plan for a League of Nations. This decision met with some criticism. Some said that it was unconstitutional for a President of the United States to leave the country. Never before had it been done. Notwithstanding, on December 4, 1918, Wilson set sail for Europe.* There he succeeded in obtaining general acceptance of his plan for a League of Nations. He returned to the United

---

* Prior to his departure, Wilson asked Marshall to preside over the Cabinet during his absence. No Vice-President up to that time had ever done so. Marshall presided for the first time on December 10, 1918, at which meeting he said: "I am here and am acting in obedience to a request preferred by the President upon the eve of his departure and also at your request. . . . I am not undertaking to exercise any official duty or function. I shall preside in an unofficial and informal way over your meetings out of deference to your desires and those of the President." *The New York Times,* December 11, 1918, p. 14. Marshall presided over several meetings during Wilson's absence and when Wilson returned in February, 1919, Marshall was invited to attend a meeting "as a special mark of courtesy for his presiding over the meetings during President Wilson's absence." *The New York Times,* Feb. 26, 1919, pp. 1–2.

States in February, with the hope of winning American approval. In March he again left for Paris to continue negotiations on the Peace Treaty.

By April 1, 1919 the strain of the past months began to tell on Wilson. On April 3 he was sick with a fever. The illness was diagnosed as influenza although there was talk of a slight stroke.[9] Some believe he may have suffered slight strokes even before this which had impaired his judgment. In any event, when Wilson was up and around again his face twitched. There was comment that his judgment was not the same. The Treaty of Versailles was signed on June 28, and Wilson then returned to the United States.

Upon his return to Washington, Wilson was confronted with the greatest challenge of his career. The Republican-controlled Congress, led by Senator Henry Cabot Lodge of Massachusetts, denounced the treaty and set out to defeat it. Wilson decided that its only chance of passage lay in his making a trip across the country to win the support of the people. Not yet recovered from the toll in exhaustion and nervousness which the struggle in Paris had taken and still affected by the facial twitch, Wilson nonetheless refused to let his health deter him. Mrs. Wilson, Cary T. Grayson, his close friend and physician, and Joseph Tumulty, his Secretary, tried to dissuade him from his intended course. Tumulty says that his attempt met with this answer:

I know that I am at the end of my tether, but my friends on the Hill say that the trip is necessary to save the Treaty, and I am willing to make whatever personal sacrifice is required, for if the Treaty should be defeated, God only knows what would happen to the world as a result of it. In the presence of the great tragedy which now faces the world, no decent man can count his own personal fortunes in the reckoning. Even though, in my condition, it might mean the giving up of my life, I will gladly make the sacrifice to save the Treaty.[10]

On the evening of September 3, 1919, President and Mrs. Wilson, Dr. Grayson and Tumulty left the White House for Union Station where the presidential train was waiting. The itinerary called for visits to every state west of the Mississippi except four. The trip would take twenty-seven days with twenty-six major stops and an average of more than one major speech and at least ten minor speeches a day. The first major speech was in Columbus, Ohio.

Others were delivered in Indianapolis, St. Louis, Kansas City, Des Moines, Omaha, Sioux Falls, St. Paul, Bismarck, Billings, Helena, Coeur D'Alene, Spokane, Tacoma, Seattle, Portland, San Francisco, Los Angeles, Reno, Salt Lake City, Cheyenne and Denver.

Almost immediately from the start of the trip, Wilson began to have severe headaches. At each stop there was great clamor— bands, drums, sirens, noisemakers, shouting, clapping, and so on. The President had to strain to make himself heard, as amplifiers were then unknown. The weather was hot and his asthma gave him trouble. He was forced to sleep sitting up in an easy chair, and dictated sitting with his forehead resting on the back of a chair. It progressively became more difficult for him to sleep. He lost his appetite, and his voice became hoarse.

On September 25, 1919, after Wilson had delivered a speech in Denver, his headache was so bad that he said he would cut short his speech at Pueblo. But, although his voice was not strong, this Pueblo speech turned out to be one of the longest and most moving of his speeches. At one point during the speech he faltered and several persons in his retinue thought he was about to collapse. About 11:30 that night, as the presidential train was heading toward Kansas, the President knocked on the door of Mrs. Wilson's compartment and asked her to call Grayson, because his headache was so bad that he could not sleep. Grayson was unable to relieve the pain. The night passed.

When morning came, Wilson insisted on preparing for his speech at Wichita. Grayson sought out Tumulty to ask his help in persuading the President that he should not do it. When they arrived at Wilson's compartment, they found him fully dressed and seated. One side of his face had fallen and he was having difficulty talking. With tears running down his face, he expressed bewilderment—such a thing had never happened before. He said, however, that he would proceed with his speech. When he tried to move, it became obvious to the onlookers that his left side was paralyzed.

Wilson's tour was promptly canceled and the presidential train ordered to return to Washington. A statement was shortly released to the press that Wilson had "suffered a complete nervous breakdown." During the two-day trip back to Washington, Wilson regained the use of his left arm and leg. Meanwhile, the country had been informed in vague terms that Wilson was sick. Grayson continued to issue bulletins—"strain . . . has brought on a serious reaction in his digestive organs"; "condition is due to overwork"; "trouble dates back to an attack of influenza last April . . . from which he has never entirely recovered"; "activities . . . have over-taxed his strength"; "suffering from nervous exhaustion"; "condition is not alarming"; "necessary . . . that he have rest and quiet for a considerable time"; "no material change"; "headaches and nervousness"; "about the same."

The presidential train arrived in Washington on September 28 and Wilson walked to his car. On his arrival at the White House some members of the staff were struck by the drastic change in his appearance.[11] They were told that the President had suffered a collapse and no further details were given. That afternoon, Wilson went for a drive. He did so again the following day and on Tuesday, September 30, he attended to some pressing executive matters. Although he had regained the use of his left arm and leg during these days, Wilson still had headaches and trouble sleeping.

On the morning of October 2, Mrs. Wilson went to the President's room and found that his left hand was again paralyzed. He asked her to help him into the bathroom where she left him while she went to call Dr. Grayson. When she returned, she found the President unconscious on the floor. Grayson arrived and together they moved the President to his bed. Grayson then sent for five doctors—Dr. Francis X. Dercum of Philadelphia, a neurologist, Rear Admiral E. R. Stitt, head of the naval medical school, Captain John B. Dennis, director of the naval dispensary in Washington, Dr. Sterling Ruffin, a Washington physician, and Dr. George De Schweinitz, of Philadelphia, an eye specialist—for consultation. That night Dr. Grayson issued the following medical bulletin: "The President is a very sick man. His condition is less favorable today and he has remained in bed throughout the day."[12]

Almost from the time that Grayson issued this bulletin, rumors began to circulate that the President's true condition was much worse than indicated. Day after day, the illness continued to be referred to vaguely as a nervous breakdown and the rumors multiplied. *The New York Times* of October 7 observed that "all sorts of rumors have been running the gamut of gossip in the capital regarding the exact nature of the President's illness." "One of the most insistent reports," said the *Times,* "has had it that the President's real trouble has been a slight abscess of the brain. . . . Another very persistent report has had it that the President had suffered from a slight cerebral leakage or hemorrhage. . . ."[13] All of these rumors were denied by Grayson.*

After a week of vague bulletins, agitation arose for a complete statement of the facts. The New York *World* carried an editorial in which it decried the fact that "from the beginning of his illness until the present moment not a word has come from the sick chamber that could be regarded as frankly enlightening."[14] The influential *World* declared that "the incapacity of the President from any cause is of vital interest. . . . Above every consideration of sympathy is the right of the people to be informed as to his actual condition." The *New York Tribune* said on October 9: "The President's health is a matter of public concern. The people have a right to know. For ten days there has been secrecy, and . . . it is time to abandon it."

On the following day, *The New York Herald* took up the cry: "The World . . . is right in saying that the health of the President . . . is a matter of public concern and that it is the right of the people to be informed as to his actual condition."

Then, on October 12, the newspapers of the country published a letter from Senator George Moses of New Hampshire to a constituent. In the letter Moses said:

The President is a very sick man. He suffered some kind of a cerebral lesion . . . and one of the readily discernible results is a slight facial paralysis. . . . [H]e is absolutely unable to undergo any experience which requires concentration of mind. . . . Of course, he may get well— that is, he may live, but if he does he will not be any material force or factor in anything.[15]

The Moses letter gave renewed vigor to the speculation regarding the President's "real condition." It increased the insistence that the exact nature of the President's illness be disclosed. When confronted with the letter, Dr. Grayson refused to comment. Said he: "Senator Moses must have information that I do not possess."[16] Upon being asked whether the President had suffered a cerebral lesion or hemorrhage, Grayson said he would not comment on rumors. Rather he would stand on his medical bulletins. The news-

---

* One rumor that passed through Washington was that Wilson had become insane and was being kept a prisoner in the White House. People noted bars on the White House windows and pictured behind them a raving maniac. Overlooked was the fact that the bars had been installed by Theodore Roosevelt to protect the windows from his ball-playing children.

papers promptly pointed out that in none of the more than thirty bulletins issued had there been any technical statement of the illness more definite than "nervous exhaustion," nor had there been any reference to pulse, temperature, or blood pressure. For the most part, the twice-daily bulletins had consisted of no more than two brief sentences.

On October 13, the day after the Moses letter appeared, *The Providence Journal* printed the following information which, it said, it had received from "a high governmental official":

President Wilson is suffering from a very dangerous cerebral hemorrhage. . . . There is partial physical paralysis and . . . Mr. Wilson has suffered several periods of aphasia, although . . . these have been less frequent in the past three days. . . . [E]ven if the President should show signs of improvement . . . any mental strain to which he would be subjected by the attempt to take up public matters would mean an immediate recurrence of the earlier symptoms and a more dangerous condition than at present exists. . . . [T]here is no possibility that Mr. Wilson would be able to perform the functions of his office either in the immediate or the remote future. . . .

In his noon bulletin of October 13, Doctor Grayson did not deny the brain lesion rumor as had been expected. The "demand to know" was thereby intensified. Vague medical bulletins continued to be issued until October 30, and thereafter none at all was issued. The rumors and the doubts persisted month after month. Finally, on February 11, 1920, the *Baltimore Sun* carried a copyrighted dispatch from its Washington correspondent, giving the text of an interview with Dr. Hugh H. Young of Johns Hopkins, a gland specialist who had been called in when Wilson developed a prostatic obstruction on October 14. Said Dr. Young:

As you know, in October last we diagnosed the President's illness as cerebral thrombosis [clot in a blood vessel] which affected his left arm and leg, but at no time was his brain power or the extreme vigor and lucidity of his mental processes in the slightest degree abated. This condition has from the very first shown a steady, unwavering tendency toward resolution and complete absorption. . . . The President walks sturdily now, without assistance and without fatigue. And he uses the still slightly impaired arm more and more every day.

As to his mental vigor, it is simply prodigious. . . . The public documents which the President has written and signed in the past months and his public study and comment on the questions of the day are, of course, known to all. It is, however, perhaps not so well known that the President is taking a progressively greater part in the daily work of the executive offices, and that he is now able without fatigue to devote several hours every day to official business.

This interview apparently was not authorized by Doctor Grayson because, when he was questioned about it, he declined to comment. Young's interview was "the first admission by one of the President's physicians publicly made that the President in October had suffered from a cerebral congestion, with resultant paralysis of the left side."[17]

Not everyone, however, had been kept in the dark as to the President's true condition. A few were told, but in the strictest confidence. Tumulty knew. He told Secretary of State Robert Lansing on October 3, and Secretary of Treasury David F. Houston on October 4.[18] Dr. Grayson told Secretary of Navy Josephus Daniels on October 5.[19] The rest of the Cabinet apparently were never officially informed. In an interview published on October 14, 1919, Attorney General A. Mitchell Palmer stated that he knew no more than what he read in the newspapers.[20] This was certainly true of Vice-President Marshall. It is reported that he asked Houston for the real facts on October 5. He complained bitterly about his being kept in the dark and said that it would be a tragedy for him and the people if he had to assume the powers and duties of the presidency under the circumstances. Since Houston had received the facts in confidence, he was unable to comply with the Vice-President's request.[21] As a result, Marshall had to rely upon what he read in the newspapers and what he received secondhand from others.

After Wilson was rendered disabled, it became urgent that some direction be given the government. On October 3, Secretary of State Lansing called on Tumulty to suggest that Vice-President Marshall be requested to act in Wilson's place. Lansing read the succession provision to Tumulty, who replied: "Mr. Lansing, the Constitution is not a dead letter with the White House. I have read the Constitution and do not find myself in need of any tutoring at your hands of the provision which you have just read." Tumulty then asked who should certify the President's inability, to which Lansing replied that it would have to be either Doctor Grayson or Tumulty himself. Thereupon, Tumulty declared: "You may rest assured that while Woodrow Wilson is lying in the White House on the broad of his back I will not be a party to ousting him. He has been too kind, too loyal, and too wonderful to me to receive such treatment at my hands."[22] As Tumulty was speaking, Doctor Grayson appeared, and Tumulty added: "And I am sure that Doctor Grayson will never certify to his disability. Will you, Grayson?" Grayson said he would not. Tumulty then remarked that if anyone else tried to declare Wilson disabled, he and Grayson would repudiate it. In closing, Tumulty informed Lansing that if Wilson knew of this episode, he would take decisive measures. Lansing then issued a call for a Cabinet meeting to be held on Monday, October 6.

At the Cabinet meeting, Lansing again brought up the question of presidential inability. Two of the Cabinet members present, Houston and Daniels, have recorded the incident. According to Daniels, Lansing said that important matters needed attention, and that if the President would not be able to attend to the public business, they ought to consider what steps to take. Lansing asked whether the Vice-President should be called upon. He thought so. He then read the "inability" provision of the Constitution, noting that the provision is not clear as to what constitutes "inability" and who is to decide it.[23] According to Houston, someone then suggested that the Cabinet consult Grayson before any further discussion took place. Grayson was quickly summoned.

While the Cabinet awaited Grayson, they "talked informally about the legal situation. There were no pressing matters requiring the President's decision and signature, and, therefore, there was no need for haste."[24] Grayson and Tumulty arrived together. When asked about the President's condition, Grayson replied that it had improved, but he could not say when he would be out of danger. Grayson added that the scales might tip either way so that Wilson should be disturbed as little as possible. "He told us," said Houston, "that the President's mind was very clear, but that he was suffering from a nervous breakdown, from indigestion and a depleted system."[25] Grayson refused to be more specific, and remarked that Wilson wanted to know by what authority the Cabinet was meeting, since he had issued no call. Wilson was, Grayson said, irritated when he heard that a meeting was taking place. Lansing suggested that Grayson tell him that they met to learn about the President's condition, to express their sympathy, and to discuss departmental matters that needed attention.[26]

Following the Cabinet meeting, Tumulty issued a statement that inter-departmental affairs had been considered and that Doctor

Grayson had advised the group that only urgent matters should be brought to Wilson's attention. Added Tumulty: "The state of business in the departments is such that there is little requiring the President's immediate consideration." In answer to a question about whether the Cabinet had considered the question of Marshall's acting as President, Tumulty said that there was no foundation for such a report.[27]

When it was announced on October 11 that Wilson would not be able to leave his bed "for an extended period," the subject of presidential inability took on great importance, and all the uncertainty which had confounded the nation when Garfield lay disabled recurred. Who could declare a President disabled? Some authorities said the Cabinet; others the Congress; and still others the Supreme Court. What would be the status of the Vice-President should he assume presidential responsibilities? Many constitutional lawyers said that he would take over for the remainder of the term regardless of whether Wilson recovered sooner. Said the *Tribune* on October 16: "President Wilson's present illness, threatening a degree of inability as yet undetermined, is strikingly differentiated from President Garfield's by the fact that Congress is at present occupied with business of the most vital character—part of it executive—and that the functions of the Executive cannot be suspended without causing the greatest inconvenience and confusion." "Apart from all personal considerations," said the *Herald,* "the government of the country must be carried on."[28]

Despite the demand for action on the inability problem, none was forthcoming.* It remained for the government to manage as best it could without its leader. From this vacuum arose a "family household junta, composed of Mrs. Wilson, Doctor-Rear Admiral Grayson, his physician, and his secretary, Joseph Patrick Tumulty."[29] It was decided that the President "must remain constantly in bed and divorce his mind from his executive duties," and that he was to have no visitors except his immediate family. All contact with him had to be made through notes, forwarded to either Mrs. Wilson, Grayson or Tumulty.

---

* The Republican leaders refused to do anything for fear that the Republican Party would be criticized for taking advantage of the illness of a Democratic President. At the time, it should be noted, the Republicans had forty-nine Senators and 240 Representatives against the Democrats' forty-seven Senators and 190 Representatives.

In the months which followed, the White House was literally flooded with notes to the President. Most of them went unanswered. Sometimes answers were written in the margins of the original note in Mrs. Wilson's handwriting, signed almost illegibly by the President. Other times answers were given orally by Mrs. Wilson in a conference held with the party seeking to communicate with the President. In her *Memoir,* Mrs. Wilson said that she made no decisions except as to what matters were important enough to go to the President. "Woodrow Wilson was first my beloved husband whose life I was trying to save, fighting with my back to the wall— after that he was the President of the United States."[30] She also noted that, after learning that the President would have to be isolated from difficult problems for an extended period, she suggested to Dr. Dercum the possibility of Wilson's resigning. Dercum, she said, replied that this would be bad for the country and would remove Wilson's main incentive to recovery. He felt that the matter could be avoided if she would act as a filter, deciding what matters should be seen by the President.*

It is not surprising, however, that questions arose over whether Wilson was actually in touch with what was going on. For instance, when certain notes were received in the Senate on October 4, supposedly from Wilson, the clerks thought that the signature had been forged. After much discussion, however, they decided that it must be Wilson's although it had changed greatly. According to Colonel Edward M. House, Lansing was of the opinion that "the President is [not] writing any of the papers purporting to come from him. Lansing himself wrote the Thanksgiving Proclamation, and it came back unchanged with the President's signature . . . on the top instead of at the end. The signature was almost illegible."[31] The White House statement of October, 1919, regarding a threatened strike by coal miners was actually drafted by Tumulty, then revised by the Cabinet and signed by Wilson. Wilson's message to Congress in December, 1919, was written by his stenographer from notes made available by the Cabinet.[32]

In the fall and winter of 1919–1920, very few persons obtained access to President Wilson. Among his first visitors were the King,

---

* Some are of the opinion that President and Mrs. Wilson rejected any thought of resignation. McKinley, *Woodrow Wilson* (New York, 1957), p. 269.

Queen and Prince of Belgium. They saw him on October 30 and reported that he had a "white beard." The Prince of Wales saw him on November 3. The new British Ambassador, Viscount Grey, was not so fortunate. His travelling companion, Major Charles Kennedy Craufurd-Stuart, was *persona non grata* with Mrs. Wilson so that neither was given permission to see Wilson. Attorney General A. Mitchell Palmer and Secretary of War Newton D. Baker are known each to have visited Wilson on one occasion. Senator Gilbert Hitchcock of Nebraska, the Democratic minority leader and the chief administration spokesman on the Peace Treaty and the League of Nations, met with Wilson on three occasions prior to December 5. When relations with Mexico reached a crisis, Senator Albert B. Fall of New Mexico, who doubted the President's sanity and believed that Mrs. Wilson was running the government, was appointed to head a subcommittee of the Senate Foreign Relations Committee to elicit Wilson's views on Mexico. He and Senator Hitchcock were granted permission to confer with the President. The actual purpose of the visit was "to ascertain the truth or falsity of the many rumors that . . . [he] was in no physical or mental condition to attend to important public business. . . ."[33] They saw Wilson on December 4 and found him remarkably up-to-date on the Mexican situation. William Allen White, in his biography of Wilson, describes the meeting as follows: "[T]hey had from Wilson thirty minutes of the gayest, blithest, sanest talk they had heard in months."[34] The President, however, was seldom capable of such vitality.

Although all throughout this period there had been repeated assurances that Wilson's mind was clear, some had privately received contrary reports. As late as the spring of 1920, Dr. Grayson is reported to have said:

No matter what others may tell you, no matter what you may read about the President being on the road to recovery, I tell you that he is permanently ill physically, is gradually weakening mentally and can't recover. . . . At times the President . . . seems to show a slight improvement, is in good spirits for several days, transacts business with Tumulty—and then suffers a relapse, or . . . becomes very morose. . . . [H]e is definitely becoming more feeble.[35]

The unavailability of President Wilson forced the Cabinet to do what it could under the circumstances. The decision at the meeting of October 6 not to ask Vice-President Thomas R. Marshall to act as President was, in effect, a decision to attempt to carry on the government themselves. On October 15, the *New York Tribune* carried these headlines: "Cabinet Takes Up Duties; President Will Not Be Superseded; White House Advisers Are To Handle Only Pressing Domestic Questions Pending His Recovery." On the same day the *Times* noted that "the handling of the affairs of the executive branch of the Government, so far as can be ascertained . . . is now in the hands of the Cabinet."

Yet, there were many matters the Cabinet could not handle. It could not sign bills into law, make presidential appointments, or answer important letters sent to Wilson. It could not accept amendments to the Versailles Treaty which would assure some kind of United States participation in the League of Nations. Nor could it guide the country back to its normal condition from a state of wartime discipline. This was the job of a President or a legitimate acting President. Consequently, only the most urgent of matters were attended to. Because of the absence of presidential leadership, the League of Nations was defeated in the Congress, numerous governmental vacancies went unfilled, some twenty-eight bills became law by default of any action,* foreign diplomats were unable to submit their credentials to the President as required and, in many other respects, the operation of government was suspended.

During this critical period in American history, the Vice-President of the United States stood on the sidelines. His only executive function was that of entertaining the Belgian monarchs who were visiting the United States. Since Wilson was unable to perform this function, the White House "unofficially requested" Marshall to act as the President's representative. Although there was much talk that he should take over at the head of the government, he would not hear of it. There was the constitutional problem that if he did so, Wilson might be permanently ousted as President.† And, there was

---

* When Congress is in session, the failure of the President to act on a bill within ten days of its presentation to him results in its becoming law. Failure to act within ten days when Congress is not in session constitutes a pocket veto.

† Marshall was not unaware of the constitutional problems involved, for during the fall of 1918 it was suggested that he act as President during Wilson's absence from the United States. He refused to do so, largely because of the constitutional ambiguities. He said that he was not sure what he would do in the event of a congressional resolution that he act, but he would act, he said, if a court of proper jurisdiction so decreed. Swisher, *American Consti-*

Mrs. Wilson. According to *Times* pundit Arthur Krock, Marshall told him that: "I am not going to get myself entangled with Mrs. Wilson. No politician ever exposes himself to the hatred of a woman, particularly if she's the wife of the President of the United States."[36] Marshall would act only if there were "a Congressional resolution approved in writing by Cary Grayson and the First Lady."[37]

Lansing took the initiative which Marshall would not. In the period between October, 1919 and February, 1920, the Cabinet met unofficially on at least twenty-one different occasions, largely under Lansing's direction. The purpose of these meetings was to discuss and take action on various problems of government and to recommend action to the President on others. For this initiative, Lansing received this unexpected letter from President Wilson on February 7, 1920:

My dear Mr. Secretary:

Is it true, as I have been told, that during my illness you have frequently called the heads of the executive departments of the Government into conference. . . ?

Under our constitutional law and practice, as developed hitherto, no one but the President has the right to summon the heads of the executive departments into conference. . . .

Lansing replied, on February 9, as follows:

My Dear Mr. President:

It is true that frequently during your illness I requested the heads of the executive departments of the Government to meet for informal conference.

Shortly after you were taken ill in October, certain members of the Cabinet, of which I was one, felt that, in view of the fact that we were denied communication with you, it was wise for us to confer informally together on interdepartmental matters and on matters as to which action could not be postponed until your medical advisers permitted you to pass upon them. Accordingly, I, as the ranking member, requested the members of the Cabinet to assemble for such informal conference, and in view of the mutual benefit derived the practice was continued.

I can assure you that it never for a moment entered my mind that I was acting unconstitutionally or contrary to your wishes, and there cer-

---

tutional Development (Boston, 1943), pp. 666–67. Former President Taft said at the time that the Constitution provided for an acting President where the "public exigency" required it, so that Marshall could act in the domestic sphere if need be while Wilson was in Paris. 57 Cong. Rec. 119–20 (1918).

tainly was no intention on my part to assume powers and exercise functions which under the Constitution are exclusively confided to the President.

Wilson responded on February 11 with this letter:

My Dear Mr. Secretary:

I am very much disappointed by your letter. . . . I find nothing in your letter which justifies your assumption of Presidential authority in such a matter.

. . . I have to remind you, Mr. Secretary, that no action could be taken without me by the Cabinet, and therefore there could have been no disadvantage in awaiting action with regard to matters concerning which action could not have been taken without me. . . .

. . . I must say that it would relieve me if you would give your present office up and afford me an opportunity to select some one whose mind would more willingly go along with mine.

Lansing tendered his resignation in a letter of February 12, in which he stated that:

. . . I cannot permit to pass unchallenged the imputation that in calling into informal conference the heads of the executive departments I sought to usurp your presidential authority. I had no such intention, no such thought. . . . I believe that the conferences were held for the best interests of your administration and of the republic, and that belief was shared by others whom I consulted. I further believe that the conferences were proper and necessary, in the circumstances, and that I would have been derelict in my duty if I had failed to act as I did.[38]

Lansing's "resignation" was accepted the following day and it resulted in widespread condemnation and disapproval of the President's action. Many said that the entire episode showed that Wilson was still very sick and that his judgment was far from what one would expect of a President. Some went so far as to say that his action indicated that he was insane. Others, however, doubted that Wilson had written the letters.

It was pointed out that Wilson had known all along that Cabinet meetings were taking place and had made no attempt to stop them. It was recalled that, at the time of the first meeting, he had asked Grayson to find out why the Cabinet was meeting, and an answer had been sent to him. In addition, he should have received numerous notes regarding matters discussed at these meetings. Supposedly, he had approved actions taken at these meetings. On one occasion, moreover, Attorney General Palmer had visited Wilson to discuss a matter brought up at one of the meetings.

In answer to Wilson's claim that the meetings were unconstitutional, some authorities of the day noted that nowhere in the Constitution is there any mention of the Cabinet or Cabinet meetings.* Therefore, no one has "constitutional" authority to call Cabinet members together. It was facetiously argued that according to Wilson's line of reasoning, any Cabinet members caught talking together should be discharged. It was further said that there were two precedents for the meetings—the case of Garfield, when his Cabinet assembled regularly and informally during his inability; and the case of Taft, when his Cabinet met several times at the call of Secretary of State Knox during his absence from Washington.

It was widely believed that the reason given for Lansing's discharge was entirely inadequate and improper. No reason need have been given, but since one had been advanced it should have been a satisfactory one. Wilson's growing lack of confidence in Lansing, a widely known fact, would have been sufficient. But to dismiss him for calling Cabinet meetings was something else entirely. As *The Sun And The New York Herald* said on February 15, 1920:

[W]hat shocks the nation . . . is . . . [Mr. Wilson's] attitude . . . that, even under the circumstances of the President's utter and prolonged incapacity to perform his public duties, the public interest counts for nothing.

Mr. Wilson was incapacitated for weeks; yet when the administration of government had to continue to operate somehow . . . he challenges the authority of anybody but himself to keep it so going. He denies the duty, not to mention the right, of any Cabinet officer to assemble the others . . . to serve or to save this nation.

Many felt that the reason given for the discharge was a cover for some other reason. There was much speculation as to what that reason might be. It seems to have been Wilson's suspicion that Lansing was plotting to oust him. Most likely, Wilson had learned of Lansing's suggestion that the Vice-President be called upon to take over. Wilson is reported to have said to Tumulty upon the dismis-

---

* Article II, Section 2 simply provides that: "The President . . . may require the Opinion, in writing, of the principal Officer in each of the executive Departments, upon any Subject relating to the Duties of their respective Offices. . . ."

sal: "Tumulty, it is never the wrong time to spike disloyalty. When Lansing sought to oust me, I was upon my back, I am on my feet now and I will not have disloyalty about me."[39]

One result of Lansing's dismissal was a surge of discussion of the subject of presidential inability. Concern was expressed that a precedent whereby the Cabinet could not meet without the President would be dangerous, since the government might come to an absolute standstill in any future case of presidential inability. Several "inability" proposals were almost immediately introduced in Congress. On February 18, 1920, Representatives Simeon D. Fess of Ohio and John J. Rogers of Massachusetts introduced proposals to empower the Supreme Court to declare a president disabled when authorized to do so by resolution of Congress*[40] On the following day Representative Martin B. Madden of Illinois introduced a bill under which the Secretary of State would be authorized to convene the Cabinet to inquire into a President's ability to discharge his powers and duties whenever the President had been unable to discharge them for six consecutive weeks.[41] A majority of the Cabinet could then declare the President disabled. These proposals were sent to the House Judiciary Committee.[42] Hearings were held but no action was ever taken.†

On April 13, 1920, Wilson held his first Cabinet meeting since his stroke in October. Secretary of Navy Houston recorded that meeting in these words:

The President looked old, worn and haggard. It was enough to make one weep to look at him. One of his arms was useless. In repose, his face looked very much as usual, but, when he tried to speak, there were marked evidences of his trouble. His jaw tended to drop on one side, or seemed to do so. His voice was very weak and strained. . . . He put up a brave front and spent several minutes cracking jokes. Then there was a brief silence. It appeared that he would not take the initiative. Someone brought up the railroad situation for discussion. The President seemed at first to have some difficulty in fixing his mind on what we were discussing. Doctor Grayson looked in the door several

---

* The Fess proposal was in the form of a constitutional amendment, while Rogers' looked toward a statute. Under the Rogers proposal, a resolution of either House would suffice to permit the Supreme Court to act.

† One of the most perplexing questions discussed at these hearings concerned the status of the Vice-President, should he act in a case of inability—i.e., does he act for the rest of the term? No agreement was reached.

179

times, as if to warn us not to prolong the discussion unduly for fear of wearying the President. The discussion dragged on for more than an hour. Finally, Mrs. Wilson came in, looking rather disturbed, and suggested that we had better go.[43]

Wilson gradually became more active in the affairs of government but he never did fully recover. This period of presidential inability came to an end with the inauguration of Warren G. Harding as President on March 4, 1921.

14

Succession: 1921—1933

I thought I could swing it.

CALVIN COOLIDGE

The Wilson inability, the defeat of the League of Nations, and the war in Europe made the American people receptive to the Republican campaign theme for 1920—"A Return to Normalcy." The Republican ticket of Warren Gamaliel Harding of Ohio and Calvin Coolidge of Massachusetts received over sixty percent of the popular vote and defeated the Democratic ticket of Governor James M. Cox of Ohio and Franklin Delano Roosevelt of New York. The electoral vote was 404 to 127.

In Calvin Coolidge, the Republicans had chosen an unusually quiet person who was noted for his dry wit and Yankee twang. Coolidge had obtained the vice-presidential nomination largely on his own merits. In his second term as Governor of Massachusetts, he had achieved national recognition. During the course of the Boston police strike of September, 1919, he made the classic statement: "There is no right to strike against the public safety by anybody, anywhere, any time."

At the Republican Convention of 1920, the Massachusetts delegation actively sponsored Coolidge for the presidential nomination. The nomination, however, was easily won by Senator Warren G. Harding. The name of Coolidge was then placed in nomination for Vice-President. Frank W. Stearns, Coolidge's main supporter, is reported to have urged Coolidge not to accept the nomination because he "might be shelved politically" and because the "idle life might kill him.[1]" Despite the views of Stearns, Coolidge accepted the nomination when endorsed by a landslide on the first ballot, disregarding the wishes of the group responsible for Harding's nomination.

During the ensuing campaign, Senator Harding indicated that, if elected, he would like to give Coolidge added responsibilities, stating that:

The sort of government I have in mind ought to take advantage of the capacity and experience of a man like Governor Coolidge by bringing him into the councils. It would be a fine thing, and I don't see why it hasn't been done long ago. Governor Coolidge is an eminent American and has had experience as an executive and should be helpful. I think the Vice-President can be a most effective agency in keeping the executive officers in touch with the legislative branch of the Government.[2]

The Democratic vice-presidential candidate of 1920, thirty-eight-year-old Franklin D. Roosevelt, reportedly asked Cox to permit him to sit in the Cabinet if they were elected.* In an article for the *Saturday Evening Post* in October, 1920, Roosevelt suggested that the Vice-President could be used to study and report on problems which concerned more than one executive department, and also as liaison to Congress.

Upon the occasion of his election as Vice-President, Coolidge received the following congratulatory message from the incumbent Vice-President, Thomas R. Marshall: "Please accept my sincere sympathy." Partly because of the attention given the vice-presidency during the campaign, the office was to attain greater prestige under Harding than it had under Wilson. Shortly after the election, Harding notified Coolidge that he should expect "to play a full part in the coming administration." On December 17, 1920, Coolidge conferred with Harding at Harding's residence in Marion, Ohio. At that meeting Coolidge was consulted on certain administration appointments and policies, and he agreed to serve as an ex officio member of the Cabinet.[3]

During Harding's tenure as President, Coolidge sat with the

---

* It is interesting to note that prior to his nomination, Roosevelt had never met Cox. Following the practice of balancing the ticket, Roosevelt's identification with the Wilson administration (as Assistant Secretary of Navy) made him a desirable running mate for Cox, who was never in sympathy with the policies of Wilson.

Cabinet at its meetings on Tuesdays and Fridays. His place, however, was not near the President, as would be suitable for the second officer of the land, but at the end of the table next to the Secretary of Labor, then the lowest ranking Cabinet member in terms of seniority. It is said that Coolidge "was a wonderful listener. And when asked for his opinions gave them with a crisp Yankee vigor that was like a breeze from his native Vermont mountains. He never intruded his views unless asked for them."[4]

Although he had had no prior experience in Congress, Coolidge did not, as had many of his predecessors, find his job of presiding over the Senate difficult or boring. As he said in his *Autobiography:*

Presiding over the Senate was fascinating to me. . . . It may seem that debate is endless, but there is scarcely a time when it is not informing, and, after all, the power to compel due consideration is the distinguishing mark of a deliberative body. . . . I was entertained and instructed by the debates. However it may appear in the country, no one can become familiar with the inside workings of the Senate without gaining a great respect for it. The country is safe in its hands.[5]

Coolidge was regular in his attendance, but at times he would delegate his duty of presiding to other Senators. Democrats and Republicans alike were the recipients of these delegations. When they occurred, it was not unusual for Coolidge to disappear into his office behind the Senate Chamber to work on his mail and speeches.* One of his biographers says that the vice-presidency gave him the "leisure to read, to observe, to reflect, and to reach conclusions."[6]

When Congress recessed in the summer of 1923, Coolidge left Washington for his father's home in Plymouth, Vermont. While he was vacationing there, President Harding was on a speech-making tour of the western states which had taken him to Alaska and then to Seattle. Since June 20 he had made about eighty-five public speeches, more than two a day. The fifty-seven-year-old President grew weary during his tour and on July 27, in Seattle, became ill, faltering several times while delivering a speech. Surgeon General

---

* An unsuccessful attempt was made in Congress in 1922 to get Coolidge an official residence—the John B. Henderson house. Mrs. Harding was one of those against the idea, saying: "I just couldn't have people like those Coolidges living in that beautiful house." Fuess, *Calvin Coolidge* (Boston, 1940), p. 299 and n. 10.

Charles E. Sawyer, one of three doctors with Harding on the tour, diagnosed the illness as acute indigestion caused by eating crabmeat. Since Harding had eaten no crabmeat, this diagnosis later became the basis for stories that Harding had been poisoned by his wife. Actually, what appeared to be indigestion was probably a dilation of the heart. Harding was known to have been suffering from heart trouble.*

Despite his illness, Harding refused to cancel the remainder of his tour. He continued on to San Francisco. When he arrived there on July 29 he was very ill, and the newspapers so indicated. He was promptly confined to his quarters at the Palace Hotel. A medical statement was issued that bronchial pneumonia had developed. For a while President Harding seemed to be getting better. On Wednesday, August 1, Doctor Sawyer announced that the crisis had been passed. On August 2 a medical bulletin read: "While recovery will inevitably take some little time, we are more confident than heretofore as to the outcome of his illness." *The New York Times* carried these headlines: "Harding Gains; Wants to Return Soon; He Rallies From a Slight Indigestion; Jests With Doctors; Reads Newspapers." "There is every indication," noted the *Times,* "that he ultimately will recover his health and strength. It may as well be understood by the country, however, that Mr. Harding will be an invalid for a considerable period, during which he will be unable to attend actively to important public business."

The reports of August 2 were unduly optimistic. That evening at about 7:30 P.M. President Warren Harding suddenly shuddered and lost consciousness while his wife was reading to him from an article of which he was the subject entitled "A Calm View of a Calm Man."[7] Mrs. Harding summoned Doctors Boone and Sawyer to the President's bedside. There was nothing they or anyone else could do —the President was dead. Death was probably due to a cerebral thrombosis, but since Mrs. Harding would not permit an autopsy, the exact cause of death remains undetermined.[8] The official bulletin released by the doctors stated:

---

* Dr. Joel T. Boone of the Navy is said to have disagreed with the diagnosis, telling a few members of the Harding party that the illness was due to a cardiac condition, not indigestion. Adams, *Incredible Era* (Boston, 1939), p. 374. In the fall of 1922 Dr. Emmanuel Libman, who saw the President at a dinner party, remarked that Harding was suffering from a coronary ailment and would probably not live more than six months. *Ibid.,* p. 333.

The President died instantaneously and without warning and while conversing with members of his family at 7:30 P.M. Death was apparently due to some brain evolvement, probably an apoplexy.

During the day he had been free from discomfort and there was every justification for anticipating a prompt recovery.

C. E. Sawyer, M.D.
Ray Lyman Wilbur, M.D.
C. M. Cooper, M.D.
J. T. Boone, M.D.
Hubert Work, M.D.

August 2, 1923, 7:35 P.M[9]

Harding died at 10:30 P.M., Vermont time, as the fifty-one-year-old Vice-President, Calvin Coolidge, slept. George B. Christian, Jr., Harding's secretary, immediately issued this telegram to Coolidge: "The President died instantly and without warning and while conversing with members of his family at 7:30 P.M. His physicians report that death was apparently due to some brain embolism, probably an apoplexy." This message was received in Bridgewater, the nearest station to Plymouth, Vermont, and carried by automobile some ten miles to the Coolidge homestead at the southern end of the Green Mountains. It was then after midnight. John C. Coolidge, seventy-eight-year-old father of the man who had gone to sleep as Vice-President, was awakened and given the news.* He quickly awakened his son and handed him the telegram, addressing him as President. Coolidge read the message, hurriedly washed and dressed, and then knelt in prayer before going downstairs.

One of Coolidge's first acts after coming downstairs was to dictate a message of condolence to Mrs. Harding. He then issued the following statement:

Reports have reached me, which I fear are correct, that President Harding is gone. The world has lost a great and good man. I mourn his loss. He was my Chief and friend.

It will be my purpose to carry out the policies which he has begun for the service of the American people and for meeting their responsibilities wherever they may arise.

For this purpose I shall seek the cooperation of all those who have

---

* Among those first on the scene were W. A. Perkins, the station attendant at Bridgewater, Erwin C. Geisser, Coolidge's stenographer, John N. McInerny, his chauffeur, and William H. Crawford, a newspaperman who had scheduled an interview with Coolidge for the next day.

been associated with the President during his term of office. Those who have given their efforts to assist him I wish to remain in office that they may assist me. I have faith that God will direct the destinies of our nation.

It is my intention to remain here until I can obtain the correct form for the oath of office, which will be administered to me by my father, who is a notary public, if that will meet the necessary requirement. I expect to leave for Washington during the day.[10]

After receiving a telegram from Attorney General Harry M. Daugherty urging that he do so as quickly as possible, Coolidge decided that he would take the presidential oath. He later said that it was not clear to him that he was required to take the oath at all in view of the vice-presidential oath which covered the possibility of his succeeding to the presidency.[11]

Before taking the oath, Coolidge spoke with several people on the telephone in a store across the road. (His father's telephone could be used only for local calls.) One of those to whom Coolidge spoke was Secretary of State Charles E. Hughes—one of the two Cabinet members then in Washington; the other was Postmaster General Harry S. New.* Hughes advised him as to the form of the presidential oath and suggested that he come to Washington as early as possible.

And so it was that at 2:47 A.M. Colonel John C. Coolidge, a notary public and magistrate of the State of Vermont, administered the presidential oath to his son in a small parlor before an "old-fashioned kerosene lamp." Those assembled included Mrs. Coolidge, Congressman Porter H. Dale, L. L. Lane, President of the New England Division of the Railway Mail Association, Captain Daniel D. Barney of Springfield, Vermont, Herbert P. Thompson, Commander of the Springfield Post of the American Legion, Joseph H. Fountain, editor of the *Springfield Reporter,* Crawford, Geisser and McInerny. Coolidge added to the prescribed oath the words, "So help me God," and, after taking the oath, retired for the night.

President Coolidge departed for Washington in the morning and

---

* Attorney General Harry M. Daugherty, Secretary of Interior Hubert Work, Secretary of Agriculture Henry C. Wallace and Secretary of Commerce Herbert Hoover were in San Francisco; Secretary of Labor James T. Davis was in England; and Secretary of Treasury Andrew W. Mellon was in France. Secretary of War John W. Weeks was vacationing in New Hampshire and Secretary of Navy Edwin Denby was also in New Hampshire.

arrived that night. He was greeted by Hughes and New who rode with him to his quarters at the New Willard Hotel, from which he would direct as Chief Executive for the time being. Mrs. Harding was told that she could remain in the White House as long as she wished.

Quietly Coolidge took hold of the reins of government in a calm fashion. He announced that he would have nothing to say about his policies until after Harding's funeral, and he delayed calling a Cabinet meeting until that time. He later remarked, when asked what his first thoughts were upon becoming President, that he thought he "could swing it."

Coolidge attended Harding's funeral in Marion, Ohio, on August 10, and held his first Cabinet meeting on August 14.* He moved into the White House on August 21. That same day the presidential oath was secretly administered to him, for a second time, by Justice Adolph A. Hoehling of the Supreme Court of the District of Columbia. This cured a controversy as to whether a notary of a state could administer an oath of office to other than an official of his state. That controversy had led to an examination of the law by James M. Beck, Solicitor General of the United States. He had concluded that the oath was not valid and so informed Daugherty, who agreed and had advised Coolidge. The oath was administered in private in order to avoid alarming the country.[12]

In interviews and statements Coolidge informed the country that he would continue Harding's policies. His succession came at a time when Congress was not in session and would not convene until December, 1923. Europe was then in chaos, the Philippines in political ferment, and a coal strike imminent. Looming even larger on the horizon was the matter of the governmental scandals which were just beginning to be revealed. Coolidge turned his attention to all these matters and handled them in such a manner that he won the respect and admiration of the American people.

At the Republican National Convention of 1924, Coolidge was nominated for the presidency on the first ballot without opposition. Former Governor Frank Lowden of Illinois was nominated for the vice-presidency, but he declined the nomination. Charles G. Dawes,

---

* Three members of Harding's Cabinet—Daugherty, Denby and Wallace —resigned in 1924. Two—Hughes and Weeks—resigned in 1925. Two— Work and Hoover—resigned in 1928. Three—Mellon, New and Davis— remained through Coolidge's entire administration.

a retired general, banker and a former director of the budget, was then nominated. In the election of 1924, Coolidge and Dawes received almost twice as many popular votes as did their Democratic opponents, John W. Davis of West Virginia and Charles W. Bryan of Nebraska.

After his election, Coolidge was anxious to have Dawes sit in his Cabinet. He felt that it was important because the Vice-President "might become President and ought to be informed on the policies of the administration. He will not learn all of them. . . . But he will hear much and learn how to find out more if it ever becomes necessary."[13] His experience in the Cabinet, said Coolidge, "was of supreme value" when he became President. Dawes, however, was of a different mind, believing it to be politically and constitutionally unwise for the Vice-President to sit in the Cabinet. As Dawes noted in an interview:

Long before I had any thought that I would have an individual interest in the question, I said the plan of having the Vice-President sit with the Cabinet was unwise. The Cabinet and those who sit with it always do so at the discretion and inclination of the President. Our Constitution so intended it. The relationship is confidential and the selection of a confident belongs to him who would be injured by the abuse of confidence, however unintentional. No precedent should be established which creates a different and arbitrary method of selection. Should I sit in the Cabinet meetings, the precedent might prove injurious to the country. With it fixed, some future President might face the embarrassing alternative of inviting one whom he regarded as unsuitable into his private conferences, or affronting him in the public eye by denying him what had been generally considered his right.[14]

Dawes' tenure as Vice-President was not notable for achievement. He not only refused to attend Cabinet meetings but he alienated the Senate from the very beginning when, in his inaugural address, he lectured them on the necessity for changing the Senate's rules and on the Vice-President's duties. The Senate did not appreciate this attempt and made life miserable for him. Dawes soon acquiesced and silently served out his term.

Coolidge surprised the country in 1927 when he announced that he would not seek re-election. Thus, in 1928, the Republicans turned to Herbert Hoover and nominated him for President and Senator Charles Curtis of Kansas for Vice-President. Again victory came to the Republican Party. Hoover and Curtis won forty of the forty-eight states, defeating Governor Alfred E. Smith of New York and Senator Joseph T. Robinson of Arkansas.

Under Hoover, one noticeable development occurred in the vice-presidency. Curtis was invited to and did sit with the Cabinet, a precedent that has been continued ever since. The Hoover-Curtis team ran for re-election in 1932 but lost by an electoral vote of 472 (42 states) to 59 (6 states) to the Democratic ticket of Governor Franklin Delano Roosevelt of New York and Speaker of the House John Nance Garner of Texas.

15

The Roosevelt-Truman Years

...I felt like the moon, the stars, and all the planets had fallen on me.

HARRY S. TRUMAN

The subject of presidential succession unexpectedly came into the public consciousness shortly before Roosevelt's inauguration. On the evening of February 15, 1933, after a cruise aboard a yacht owned by Vincent Astor, Roosevelt landed in Miami to deliver a brief speech. He traveled by car to Bayfront Park, where, sitting on top of the rear seat of his automobile, he spoke informally into a small portable microphone. Just as he slid down into the seat five shots rang out. None of them hit Roosevelt but Mayor Anton Cermak of Chicago was mortally wounded by one bullet and four other persons also were wounded. The shots were fired by a young bricklayer, Giuseppe Zangara, who later said that he had planned to kill President Herbert Hoover but had decided on President-elect Franklin Roosevelt when he learned that he was in town. Roosevelt was spared, Cermak died on March 6 and Zangara was electrocuted on March 20, 1933.

Coincidentally, just nine days before the shooting, Secretary of State Henry L. Stimson had certified that the Twentieth Amendment had become a part of the Constitution. Thus, if anything had happened to Roosevelt, the provisions regarding Presidents-elect would have been applicable. The amendment provides that where a President-elect dies before the time fixed for his term to begin, the Vice-President-elect becomes President. Where the President-elect fails to qualify, the Vice-President-elect acts as President until a President qualifies.* Hence, John N. Garner would have become President on Inauguration Day if Roosevelt had been assassinated.

After taking office, President Roosevelt set out to increase the importance of the vice-presidency. Garner was invited to sit with the Cabinet and, from the start, a good working relationship grew up between the President and Garner. As a former Speaker of the House, Garner was highly regarded in the Congress, so that he was able to use his influence in that body to push various New Deal programs. Garner's concept of the vice-presidency made him reluctant to grant interviews or make public speeches. He preferred to remain silent on matters of policy and appointments unless asked by Roosevelt for advice. According to Bascom Timmons, his biographer, Garner could be very much to the point when his advice was sought, but he would first ask: "Do you want it with the bark on or off, Cap'n?"[1] In 1936, the Democratic Party enthusiastically endorsed Roosevelt and Garner for another four years. They won by a landslide (in excess of eleven million popular votes and an electoral vote of 523 to 8, winning every state except Maine and Vermont) over Governor Alfred M. Landon of Kansas and Frank Knox of Illinois, publisher of the Chicago *Daily News*.

During the course of their second term together the Roosevelt-Garner relationship deteriorated somewhat. When Roosevelt sought to impose his Court-packing scheme on the Congress, Garner deliberately absented himself from the Senate when it was voted upon rather than support it. As Roosevelt's term drew to a close, Garner identified himself with the wing of the party which sought to deny Roosevelt a third term, and he became a candidate for the presidential nomination. This, of course, estranged him from the President

---

* Moreover, the amendment gives Congress the power to provide for the case where neither a President-elect nor a Vice-President-elect has qualified. In such case Congress can declare "who shall then act as President, or the manner in which one who is to act shall be selected, and such person shall act accordingly until a President or Vice President shall have qualified." The amendment also made these fundamental changes: the terms of President and Vice-President would end at noon on January 20, the terms of Senators and Representatives would end at noon on January 3 and the terms of their successors would then begin, and the Congress would assemble at least once a year, such meeting to begin at noon on January 3 ("unless they shall by law appoint a different day").

and, as it seemed likely that Roosevelt would be renominated, made it next to impossible for him to become the first Vice-President to hold the office for more than two terms.*

When the Democratic Convention of 1940 nominated Roosevelt, he gave the nod to his Secretary of Agriculture, Henry A. Wallace, for the vice-presidency. Wallace, aged fifty-one, was a brilliant but controversial liberal, considered by some to be an impractical dreamer. He received the nomination after President and Mrs. Roosevelt expressed their preference for him and after the President threatened to decline the presidential nomination unless Wallace was nominated for Vice-President.

Roosevelt and Wallace defeated Wendell L. Willkie of Indiana and Senator Charles McNary of Oregon by about five million popular votes and an electoral vote of 449 to 82.† As it turned out, Roosevelt and Wallace shared a warm relationship and Wallace became one of the most effective Vice-Presidents in history up to that time. In addition to sitting as a regular member of the Cabinet, he became the first Vice-President to head some executive agencies and to represent the President on goodwill and diplomatic tours around the world.

This new dimension of the vice-presidency came into existence even before Wallace's inauguration. When Vice-President-elect he was Roosevelt's Ambassador Extraordinary and Plenipotentiary to attend the inauguration of General Avila Camacho as President of Mexico in December, 1940. Several months after he became Vice-President, Wallace was appointed chairman of an Economic Defense Board, which was set up under Roosevelt's direction to review international affairs. The Board later became the Board of Economic Warfare, with Wallace as chairman. However, owing to a feud between Secretary of Commerce Jesse Jones and Wallace, it was abolished in July, 1943, and replaced by the Office of Economic Warfare, on which Wallace was neither chairman nor a

---

* Only five Vice-Presidents before him had been elected for two terms— Adams, Clinton, Tompkins, Calhoun and Marshall. Of these, Clinton and Tompkins died and Calhoun resigned before completing their second terms.

† It is to be noted that the Republican candidates both died before Roosevelt completed his third term. McNary died on February 25, 1944 and Willkie on October 8, 1944. Willkie's Secretary of State would have served as President from October 8, 1944 to January 20, 1945.

member. During this period Wallace also served as chairman of the Supply Priorities and Allocations Board.

A significant expansion in the Vice-President's role occurred in 1943 and 1944. In March, 1943, President Roosevelt asked Wallace to undertake a goodwill tour to Bolivia, Chile, Colombia, Costa Rica, Ecuador and Panama. Wallace complied with the request and spent forty days in South America. Upon his return to the United States in April, 1943, he gave an extended oral report to Roosevelt regarding his impressions and experiences. In the following year, Roosevelt asked Wallace to fly to eastern Asia over the North-to-the-Orient route to visit New Siberia and proceed from there to China, carrying important messages to Generalissimo Chiang Kai Shek.

Wallace's main weakness as a Vice-President was his inability to get along with the Congress. Since he had no prior legislative experience, he was not held in high esteem by that body. His refusal to court the politicians also hurt him politically. These were undoubtedly elements in Roosevelt's concurring in the decision to drop him as his running mate in 1944.

At the Democratic National Convention of 1944, the main point of interest centered on the vice-presidential nomination. After Roosevelt announced that he would seek re-election, no other candidates for the presidency were seriously considered and Roosevelt was subsequently nominated on the first ballot.

Roosevelt's first choice for a running mate was the incumbent, Henry Wallace. But the party leaders disapproved of Wallace, believing that he would be a liability in the hard race anticipated against Governor Thomas E. Dewey of New York. (Roosevelt defeated Dewey by about three and one half million popular votes out of forty-seven and one-half million cast. This was the closest margin in his four contests.) Also, "there was little doubt in the minds of the party bosses that Roosevelt would not live to complete his fourth term, and a powerful group . . . was determined that Henry Wallace would never be President of the United States."[2] Notwithstanding, Wallace was able to obtain from Roosevelt a promise to support his candidacy. Thus, on July 14, a week before the convention opened, Roosevelt wrote a letter to Senator Samuel D. Jackson of Indiana, chairman of the Democratic National Convention, saying that if he were a delegate, he would vote for Wallace. However, he went on to say that he did not wish to dictate to the convention. Robert E. Hannegan, chairman of the Democratic National Committee, sought a letter backing Senator Harry S. Truman of Missouri. Although Roosevelt recognized that Truman had made a good reputation for himself as a Senator and was liberal in his thinking, his personal choice was Supreme Court Justice William O. Douglas if he could not have Wallace. Therefore, when Roosevelt did write the letter requested by Hannegan, he said that he would be glad to run with either Douglas or Truman (naming them in that order). Hannegan was not satisfied. He asked Roosevelt to change the letter so that Truman's name preceded Douglas' on the grounds that Truman "was the stronger candidate and that the convention would go for whomever the President named first."[3] Roosevelt agreed to the change and gave Hannegan the letter he sought.

Truman's choice for Vice-President was not himself but James F. Byrnes. Byrnes, who had left the Supreme Court to become the head of the Office of Economic Stabilization, was eliminated from Roosevelt's list of possibilities as being too conservative and opposed by labor. Truman was not interested in the nomination. He, as well as others, was aware that Roosevelt might not survive another term. Edwin Pauley, treasurer of the Democratic National Committee, is reported to have said before the convention that "you are not nominating a Vice-President of the United States, but a President."[4] Truman reportedly said to a friend: "Do you [know] . . . what happened to most Vice-Presidents who succeeded to the Presidency? Usually they were ridiculed in office, had their hearts broken, lost any vestige of respect they had had before. I don't want that to happen to me."[5]

Despite his reluctance, Truman agreed to run for the vice-presidency after hearing Roosevelt say to Hannegan over the phone: "Well, tell him if he wants to break up the Democratic party in the middle of a war, that's his responsibility."[6] Hannegan thereupon released Roosevelt's letter, and the Convention nominated Truman.

Roosevelt entered his fourth term in the sixty-third year of his life. His health had badly deteriorated.* There is considerable mys-

---

* While on vacation at Campobello Island in August, 1921, Roosevelt had been severely stricken by poliomyelitis which left him paralyzed in his arms, back and legs. Through dogged determination and constant exercise he

tery surrounding the true state of his health in the last years of his life. There are indications that he was not completely frank with his family or his doctors. It also appears that the doctors were not completely frank with either the President's family or the public. It is alleged that Roosevelt suffered the first of a series of small strokes in 1938.[7] Following the Teheran Conference late in 1943 "a definite physical change was obvious to everyone. . . ."[8] His changed appearance gave rise to numerous rumors. One friend said that he thought Teheran was "the turning point of . . . [Roosevelt's] physical career."[9] Some say that Roosevelt suffered a stroke in December, 1943, after Teheran. An ambassador who saw him at Cairo after the Teheran Conference was "dumbfounded" at his aged appearance and shakiness. It is reported that beginning January, 1944, the "White House Circle" became increasingly worried about his health and "tried to build a kind of protective screen around him."[10] This concern led to the President's being induced to submit to a thorough medical checkup at Bethesda Naval Hospital on March 26, 1944. "Here a group of Navy doctors most distinctly did not like what they saw. . . . The result was that the President was told in the sternest terms that he must rest, rest, rest."[11] It is not clear what the doctors had found. That they were worried is attested to by the fact that "he was forbidden to fly at high altitudes, and . . . Dr. Bruenn [a heart specialist] saw him every day."[12]

During the campaign of 1944 there were frequent claims that Roosevelt was in poor health and unable to continue as President. These criticisms were effectively countered with increased campaigning by Roosevelt and the issuance of medical reports testifying to his good health.* But there could be no effective denial that the World War, domestic problems and the campaign of 1944 had left their mark.

At Roosevelt's fourth inauguration on January 20, 1945, there was much concern about his appearance. Roosevelt's son, James, recounts how badly his father shook during the address. Later, when

---

regained the use of his hands and the paralysis left his back. However, he was never able to walk again without assistance. Despite this handicap he proved that he could be an able President.

* In a letter to the author, dated Nov. 12, 1963, former Vice-President Henry A. Wallace stated: "Curiously enough, I gave this problem "The President's inability to discharge his office," no thought while I was vice-President."

they were alone together, the President suffered some extremely severe pains but he nonetheless continued his activities as if nothing had happened.[13] When President Roosevelt left the United States in February, 1945, for the fateful Yalta Conference, it seems clear that he was a sick man. Many at the Conference were shocked by his appearance. Secretary of State Edward R. Stettinius, however, insists that the President's mind was clear.[14] Upon his return to the United States, there was considerable discussion as to how he had changed. Vice-President Truman met him a week after his return and recorded his reaction as follows: "I . . . was shocked by his appearance. His eyes were sunken. His magnificent smile was missing from his careworn face. He seemed a spent man. I had a hollow feeling within me, for I saw that the journey to Yalta must have been a terrible ordeal."[15]

When President Roosevelt addressed Congress in person on March 1, 1945 to report on the Yalta Conference, he delivered his speech from a sitting position and seemed to have some difficulty with his enunciation.* It was plain to all that he was a tired man. On March 29, Roosevelt left for a rest at Warm Springs, Georgia. He apparently was not concerned about his health since neither his wife nor personal physician, Admiral Ross T. McIntire, accompanied him.

At Warm Springs, Roosevelt continued to perform the duties of the presidency. Among other things, he worked on an agenda for the San Francisco Conference scheduled for April 25, wrote a speech to be delivered at a Jefferson Day dinner on April 13, communicated with Winston Churchill regarding Poland, conferred with Secretary of Treasury Henry Morgenthau, signed official documents, and read his mail. There was little indication that death was near.

Then, shortly before lunch on Thursday, April 12, while Mrs. Elizabeth Schoumatoff painted his portrait, President Roosevelt fell over in his chair, murmuring "I have a terrific headache." Two servants carried the unconscious President to a nearby bedroom and Dr. Howard G. Bruenn, who, for a year, had been assigned to the President, was called to the room. He administered artificial respiration and other emergency measures. But it was to no avail. At about

---

* There is reason to believe that during this period Roosevelt suffered from temporary cerebral aphasia and labial difficulties. Gunther, *Roosevelt in Retrospect* (New York, 1950), p. 374.

3:35 P.M., the President died. He had completed less than three months of his fourth term. The cause of death was a cerebral hemorrhage.

No autopsy was held, and the body did not lie exposed in state. The cause of the death was obvious, and the family saw no reason why, in wartime, the funeral ceremonies should be sumptuous or prolonged. As a result stupid rumors began to circulate, some of which are still heard today—that FDR had shot himself, that he had been shot, that he had fallen off a cliff, and even that he didn't die, but had been packed off to a sanitarium as a mental cripple. To deny stories as childish as these is hardly necessary.[16]

News of the President's death was immediately sent to the White House, where Stephen T. Early, Roosevelt's press secretary, Dr. McIntire, Jonathan Daniels, another press secretary, and Anna Rosenberg, his labor adviser, received the news. Early promptly contacted Mrs. Roosevelt, who was then at the Sulgrave Club in Washington, and asked her to return to the White House.

At about 5:00 P.M., Vice-President Truman was notified by Speaker Sam Rayburn that Early had tried to reach him by phone and that he wanted Truman to call the White House. The Vice-President did so and was asked to come over as quickly as possible. Thinking that President Roosevelt had returned to Washington and wanted to speak with him privately, Truman hurried to the White House. He arrived around 5:25, and went to Mrs. Roosevelt's study. What ensued Truman describes as follows:

I . . . was immediately . . . ushered into Mrs. Roosevelt's study. Mrs. Roosevelt herself, together with Colonel John and Mrs. Anna Roosevelt Boettiger and Mr. Early, were in the room as I entered, and I knew at once that something unusual had taken place. Mrs. Roosevelt seemed calm in her characteristic, graceful dignity. She stepped forward and placed her arm gently about my shoulder.

"Harry," she said quietly, "the President is dead."

For a moment I could not bring myself to speak. . . .

"Is there anything I can do for you?" I asked at last. . . .

"Is there anything *we* can do for *you*?" she asked. "For you are the one in trouble now."

. . . The overwhelming fact that faced me was hard to grasp. I had been afraid for many weeks that something might happen to this great leader, but now that the worst had happened I was unprepared for it. I did not allow myself to think about it after I became Vice-President.

But I had done a lot of thinking about it at the Chicago convention. I recall wondering whether President Roosevelt himself had had any inkling of his own condition. The only indication I had ever had that he knew he was none too well was when he talked to me just before I set out on my campaign trip for the vice-presidency in the fall of 1944. He asked me how I was going to travel, and I told him that I intended to cover the country by airplane.

"Don't do that, please," he told me. "Go by train. It is necessary that you take care of yourself."[17]

Less than two hours after Truman had received the news of Roosevelt's death, Chief Justice Harlan Fiske Stone administered the presidential oath of office to him in the Cabinet room of the White House. Among those present were Mrs. Truman, Margaret Truman, nine members of the Cabinet,* members of Roosevelt's White House staff, Speaker Sam Rayburn, House majority leader John W. McCormack, House minority leader Joseph W. Martin, Fleet Admiral Leahy, and General Philip B. Fleming. After everyone had left except the Cabinet, Truman held his first Cabinet meeting.

At the start of the Cabinet meeting President Truman informed Early that the San Francisco Conference regarding a United Nations would meet as scheduled—the first decision made by the new President. "It was of supreme importance that we build an organization to help keep the future peace of the world."[18] Early left to tell the press of the decision and Truman spoke to the Cabinet, as follows:

I told them briefly, as I had already told some of them individually, that I would be pleased if all of them would remain in their posts. It was my intention, I said, to continue both the foreign and the domestic policies of the Roosevelt administration. I made it clear, however, that I would be President in my own right and that I would assume full responsibility for such decisions as had to be made. I told them that I hoped they would not hesitate to give me their advice—that I would be glad to listen to them. I left them in no doubt that they could differ with me if they felt it necessary, but that all final policy decisions would be mine. I added that once such decisions had been made I expected them to support me. When there is a change in administration, there are bound to be some changes in the Cabinet, but I knew how necessary it was for me to keep an open mind on all the members of the Cabinet until we had had an opportunity to work together. Their experience with

---

* The tenth member, Postmaster General Frank C. Walker, was ill.

President Roosevelt and their knowledge were necessary to me in this crisis.[19]

"From my reading of American History," said Truman, "I knew there was no cut-and-dried answer to the questions of what obligations a President by inheritance had in regard to the program of his predecessor—especially a program on which a great President had recently been re-elected for the fourth time. I always fully supported the Roosevelt program—both international and domestic—but I knew that certain major administrative weaknesses existed. . . ."[20] "[O]n that first day," Truman recounts in his *Memoirs*, "I knew that I would eventually have to make changes, both in the Cabinet and in administrative policy."*[21]

After the Cabinet meeting, President Truman conferred with Secretary of War Henry L. Stimson, who informed him of the Manhattan Project—the development of the atom bomb, which had been kept secret not only from the Congress but from the Vice-President of the United States. The day ended with the new President's issuing a statement of support for the San Francisco Conference and declining to hold a press conference. At some point that evening he found time to tell Mrs. Roosevelt that she should remain in the White House as long as necessary.†

Truman's succession to the presidency came at a critical juncture in American history. The death of Roosevelt had a profound effect on the nation and the Allied leaders. Grief and shock were the immediate responses to the death of a man who had occupied the presidency longer than any other President. The reins of government had fallen into the hands of a person who had spoken with the President less than ten times since his nomination for the Vice-Presidency. "In my eighty-two days as Vice-President," said Truman, "only a few Cabinet meetings were held, for the President was

---

* Of Roosevelt's Cabinet, seven members resigned in 1945—Secretary of State Edward R. Stettinius, Jr., Secretary of the Treasury Henry Morgenthau, Jr., Secretary of War Henry L. Stimson, Attorney General Francis Biddle, Postmaster General Frank C. Walker, Secretary of Agriculture Claude R. Wickard, and Secretary of Labor Frances Perkins; one resigned in 1946—Secretary of the Interior Harold L. Ickes; one resigned in 1947—Secretary of Commerce, Henry A. Wallace; and one remained for Truman's entire administration—Secretary of the Navy James V. Forrestal.

† On April 16 Truman moved from his apartment on Connecticut Avenue to Blair House, across Pennsylvania Avenue from the White House. He remained there until May 7 when he moved into the White House.

abroad the greater part of the time or at Warm Springs."[22] Yet, it was now Truman's lot to end the War and lead the nation through the postwar period. Over three years and nine months in the presidency lay before him.

Truman proved equal to the challenge. On the morning of April 13, he met with leading members of the military and Cabinet, receiving reports on the state of world affairs. That afternoon, he met with the legislative leaders, and in the days which followed, he did his best to become acquainted with the major problems facing the nation. He addressed a joint session of the Congress on April 16.* The San Francisco Conference commenced as scheduled on April 25, and from it flowered the United Nations. On May 8, 1945, Germany surrendered and on August 14, after Truman had ordered American flyers to drop the atomic bomb on Japan, Japan surrendered. President Truman met the crisis of the postwar period with equal success, the Truman Doctrine and Marshall Plan standing out as major examples.

During the early days of his succession, Truman had occasion to reflect on the office of Vice-President. He states in his *Memoirs* that:

I was beginning to realize how little the Founding Fathers had been able to anticipate the preparations necessary for a man to become President so suddenly. It is a mighty leap from the vice-presidency to the presidency when one is forced to make it without warning.

Under the present system a Vice-President cannot equip himself to become President merely by virtue of being second in rank. Ideally, he should be equipped for the presidency at the time he is elected as Vice-President. The voters, instead of considering a vice-presidential candidate as a sort of appendage to the presidency, should select him as a spare Chief Executive. As such he should be kept fully informed of all the major business transacted by the President.

. . . [W]hen I became Vice-President, I was familiar with the incongruities and inadequacies of that office.

*   *   *   *

_____

* One of the memorable events of that day occurred when Truman began his speech to Congress without any introduction. Speaker Rayburn, who was sitting nearby, interrupted him to whisper: "Just a minute, Harry. Let me introduce you." Although Rayburn spoke softly, the microphones had been turned on so that he was heard all over the chamber and the country via the radios. Rayburn "straightened up" and announced: "The President of the United States."

I could now appreciate how Tyler had felt on finding himself suddenly catapulted into the nation's highest office. It takes some time for a man to adjust himself to such an overwhelming responsibility. . . .

No Vice-President is ever properly prepared to take over the presidency because of the nature of our presidential, or executive, office. The President is the man who decides every major domestic policy, and he is the man who makes foreign policy and negotiates treaties. In doing these things it would be very difficult for him to take the second man in the government . . . completely into his confidence. The President, by necessity, builds his own staff, and the Vice-President remains an outsider, no matter how friendly the two may be. There are many reasons for this, but an important one is the fact that both the President and Vice-President are, or should be, astute politicians, and neither can take the other completely into his confidence.

*   *   *   *

. . . [V]ery few Vice-Presidents have been in complete agreement with the policies of the Presidents with whom they have served. The fact that both the President and the Vice-President are nominated and elected makes for a formal relationship despite appearances between the two.[23]

Truman's handling of the government brought him the presidential nomination at the 1948 Democratic Convention. Supreme Court Justice William O. Douglas was Truman's first choice for Vice-President. When Douglas declined, Truman expressed his preference for the popular Senator Alben W. Barkley of Kentucky, who was chosen. In the 1948 election, Truman and Barkley, the apparent underdogs, won a surprising victory over Governors Thomas Dewey of New York and Earl Warren of California. The popular vote margin was in excess of two million.

The relationship that existed between Truman and his Vice-President was presaged at the inaugural ball, when Truman said: "I don't think this country ever had a President and Vice President who were more congenial or whose adherence to the principles of the Democratic party was so much in parallel."[24]

Of his tenure as Vice-President, Barkley said:

With President Truman's active concurrence . . . I became a working Vice-President. From his own experience Truman knew how little opportunity had been given in the past for Vice-Presidents . . . to acquaint themselves with the job they might have to take over, and he wisely set out to rectify this situation. He had me attend his Cabinet meetings, and, with his approval, Congress passed an act making the Vice President a member of the National Security Council.

I suppose I traveled, mostly by air, more than any Vice President had up to that time, making speeches in all parts of the country. Many of these speeches were of semi-official nature, for I often represented the President. . . .*[25]

Barkley's long experience as a legislator—seven terms in the House and four in the Senate—made him an effective spokesman for the administration in Congress. Truman later said of Barkley that he "was in a class by himself. He had the complete confidence of both the President and the Senate. He had been a majority leader longer than any other senator in the history of the Senate [1937–1947]. He and I were personally very close, and he was in complete agreement with the policies and platform of the 1948 convention."[26]

Barkley, who was affectionately referred to as the "Veep," enjoyed his job of presiding over the Senate, although he says he "came to sympathize with Vice President Dawes's feeling of frustration, as I often itched to get back into the fray of debate."[27] Barkley was at times amused by occurrences in the Senate Chamber. On one occasion, a Senator "hotly addressed the chair and objected to the conduct of . . . [another Senator who] actually had dared to 'yawn' while . . . [the first Senator] was speaking." Says Barkley, "I considered the objection, then solemnly ruled, 'The yawn of the Senator . . . will be stricken from the record.' "[28]

On one occasion during his vice-presidency, Barkley was made readily aware of the adage that "the Vice-President is only one heartbeat from the Presidency." On November 1, 1950, when President Truman was living in Blair House while extensive repairs were being made on the White House, two Puerto Rican nationalists, Oscar Collazo and Griselio Torresola, attempted to rush the house and kill President Truman. One Secret Service guard was killed in the ensuing struggle and two others were wounded. Torresola was killed and Collazo was captured.

* Congress' decision in 1949 to make the Vice-President a statutory member of the National Security Council, the country's highest body dealing with national security matters, added yet another dimension to the vice-presidency. No longer would a Vice-President succeeding to the presidency upon the death of the incumbent be ignorant of important matters of policy. In his role as a member of the Council, Barkley took part in the decision to defend South Korea. At meetings of the National Security Council and Cabinet, Barkley did not hesitate to express his opinions and make suggestions.

As the 1952 Democratic Convention approached, there was much speculation as to whether President Truman would run for re-election. Although he was not prevented from doing so by the recently passed Twenty-Second Amendment,* Truman announced at a Jefferson-Jackson Day dinner in Washington on March 29, 1952, that he would not be a candidate. This threw the door open to a number of possibilities—Senators Estes Kefauver of Tennessee, Richard Russell of Georgia, and Robert S. Kerr of Oklahoma, W. Averell Harriman of New York, Governor Adlai E. Stevenson of Illinois, and Vice-President Barkley. In July, 1952, after Kefauver had won impressively in the primaries and Stevenson had indicated his lack of interest in the nomination, President Truman expressed privately his support for his seventy-four-year-old Vice-President. On the day before the convention, Barkley's hopes were crushed when he was informed that labor could not support him because of his age. Although Barkley had intended to balance the ticket with a young running mate such as Representative Franklin D. Roosevelt, Jr., or Governor G. Mennen Williams of Michigan, the position of labor upset him so that he withdrew from the race. The Convention went on to nominate Governor Stevenson for the presidency and Senator John Sparkman of Alabama for the vice-presidency.† Perhaps the most moving moment of the convention came on Wednesday, July 23, when Barkley appeared to deliver an extemporaneous talk. In a spontaneous outburst, he received a thirty-minute ovation upon making his appearance and, after his address he was applauded for another forty-five minutes.‡

---

* The amendment, which was proposed in 1947 and ratified in 1951, provides that no person shall be elected to the office of President more than twice. Where a person holds the office of President or acts as President for more than two years of a term to which another is elected, he cannot be elected to the office more than once. Truman was excepted from the coverage of the amendment by the proviso in the amendment that "this Article shall not apply to any person holding the office of President when this Article was proposed by the Congress."

† Sparkman was Stevenson's choice, and he was agreed on at a meeting attended by Stevenson, Truman, Rayburn and a few other party leaders. Truman rejected any thought of giving the nomination to Senator Kefauver.

‡ Barkley was re-elected to the Senate in 1954 and died on April 30, 1956, just under nine months before the expiration of the presidential term to which he had aspired.

16

The Succession Law of 1947

*[I]t was my feeling that any man who stepped into
the presidency should have at least some office to
which he had been elected by a vote of the people.*

HARRY S. TRUMAN

After the succession of Vice-President Truman to the presidency
on April 12, 1945, criticism of the succession law of 1886 manifested itself. In a speech at Hazelton, Pennsylvania, on May 9, 1945,
former Postmaster General James A. Farley called attention to the
fact that under the Succession Act of 1886 President Truman was in
a position to appoint the person who would succeed him in case of
his death. This, Farley said, was undemocratic and the law should
be changed.[1]

Another object of criticism was the then Secretary of State, forty-
four-year-old Edward R. Stettinius, Jr., who was first in the line of
succession. Many members of the Congress felt that he had not had
sufficient governmental experience to act as President should anything happen to President Truman. Stettinius had not had any clear-
cut political affiliation. He had been a successful steel executive before entering the government, in 1939, as chairman of Roosevelt's
War Resources Board. He became Lend-Lease Administrator in
1941, Under Secretary of State in 1943, and Secretary of State in
1944. On June 27 he resigned his position. Until a new Secretary of
State was appointed, Secretary of Treasury Henry Morgenthau, Jr.
was first in line. On July 3, former Senator James F. Byrnes, whose
experience included service in both Houses of Congress, on the

Supreme Court, and in the Cabinet, was appointed Secretary of State. His appointment was generally accepted as a good one but there was some concern about the fact that he was then sixty-eight years of age and not in the best of health.

In a special message to Congress on June 19, 1945, President Truman declared:

[B]y reason of the tragic death of the late President, it now lies within my power to nominate the person who would be my immediate successor in the event of my own death or inability to act.

I do not believe that in a democracy this power should rest with the Chief Executive.

Insofar as possible, the office of the President should be filled by an elective officer. There is no officer in our system of government, besides the President and Vice-President, who has been elected by all the voters of the country.

The Speaker of the House of Representatives, who is elected in his own district, is also elected to be the presiding officer of the House by a vote of all the Representatives of all the people of the Country. As a result, I believe that the Speaker is the official in the Federal Government whose selection, next to that of the President and Vice-President, can be most accurately said to stem from the people themselves.[2]

In placing the Speaker* ahead of the President pro tempore, President Truman stated that the members of the House are closer to the people than those of the Senate since they are elected every two years, whereas Senators are elected every six years. Thus, the Speaker would have a more recent mandate than a President pro tempore. Under Truman's recommendation, if a Speaker or President pro tempore were called upon to act as President, he would have to relinquish his seat in Congress. If no Speaker or President pro tempore were available, the first-named Cabinet officer available would act as President until there was either a Speaker or President pro tempore who could so act. No one would be qualified to act as President if he did not possess the constitutional qualifications for President. Truman further recommended that whoever succeeds after the Vice-President should serve only until the next Congressional election at which time there would be an election of a President and Vice-President. The reaction to Truman's proposal was at first enthusiastic but later its constitutionality was questioned.

---

* At that time the Speaker was Sam Rayburn of Texas, one of the country's most able public servants.

On June 25, 1945, Representative Hatton W. Sumners of Texas introduced a bill embodying the President's recommendations, adding the Speaker and President pro tempore, respectively, before the Cabinet in the line of succession.[3] It provided that if a vacancy occurred more than ninety days before the next Congressional election, presidential electors would be chosen at that election and the President chosen by them would hold office only for the remainder of the term. The Sumners bill was reported favorably by the House Committee on the Judiciary which merely stated, without thoroughly examining the question, that it was constitutional. The bill was debated briefly in the House on June 29.

In the House debates, the question of constitutionality was largely ignored. Most of the arguments in favor of the bill centered around the point that it would be more democratic. The Speaker, it was argued, is an elected official who repeatedly has been elected to Congress and then selected for the speakership by the representatives of the people. He usually, the argument proceeded, has had long experience in government and, if called upon to act as President, would be able to get along with the Congress.[4]

The fact that the first succession law (which placed legislative officers in the line of succession) was passed by the Second Congress which, presumably, understood the intent of the Constitution, the long acquiescence in the Act of 1792, the Supreme Court's decision in *Lamar* v. *United States,** and parts of the Constitution itself† were referred to in support of the contention that a law placing the Speaker and the President pro tempore in the line of succession would be constitutional.

Representatives John W. Gwynne of Iowa, Charles E. Hancock of New York and Raymond S. Springer of Indiana argued that the Speaker and President pro tempore were not officers under the succession clause.[5] The special election feature of the bill was attacked

---

* In that case, the Supreme Court held that a member of the House of Representatives was an officer of the government within the meaning of a penal statute making it a crime for one to impersonate an officer of the government. 241 U.S. 103 (1916).

† The late Estes Kefauver argued that U.S. Const., Art I, §2, cl. 5, which provides that "the House of Representatives shall chuse their Speaker and *other* Officers ∨ . . . ," shows that the Speaker is an officer. 91 Cong. Rec. 7008–28 (1945).

by Representative John M. Robsion of Kentucky. He stated that it would require conforming changes in the state election laws and even in some state constitutions and, further, that it would be bad policy as it would cause instability in the executive by allowing for four Presidents within one term.*[6] He was joined by Representatives Estes Kefauver of Tennessee, Mike Monroney of Oklahoma and Chauncey W. Reed of Illinois. Monroney pointed out that a national election always causes disunity and division and that a time when the country had been upset by the loss of both its President and Vice-President would be a time when unity would be most needed. Thus, he thought there should be no special election and the Speaker should serve for the remainder of the term. He went on to say that if a special election law were passed at a time when a Speaker or President pro tempore was acting as President, it could be vetoed by that person.

Reed argued that a special election provision would be "impractical . . . cumbersome . . . expensive and of doubtful constitutionality."[7] The provision was finally eliminated from the bill.

As amended, the Sumners bill passed the House on June 29, 1945, by a vote of 167 to 32 and was forwarded to the Senate, where it became pigeonholed in committee, probably because of doubts about its constitutionality.

In the 1946 Congressional elections the Republican Party won a majority in both Houses of Congress. President Truman, however, still asked Congress for action on his succession recommendations, despite the fact that their enactment would place the Republican Speaker, Joseph W. Martin of Massachusetts, in the line of succession. Finally, in June, 1947, the Senate gave serious thought to a bill (similar to that of Sumners) which had been introduced several months before by Senator Kenneth S. Wherry of Nebraska. Unlike the Sumners bill, it contained no special election provision and it expressly required the Speaker and President pro tempore to resign from Congress before they could act as President.[8]

In the Senate debates, Senator Carl A. Hatch of New Mexico argued at length that the Speaker and President pro tempore were not officers, that if an officer resigns his office he cannot act as Pres-

---

* Namely, the elected President, the Vice-President who succeeded, the Speaker and the new President.

ident, that it would violate the principle of separation of powers for a member of Congress to act as President, and that a Speaker or President pro tempore is not elected on the basis of his qualifications for the presidency.[9] Some felt that the Wherry bill represented piecemeal legislation, and that it should be given further consideration in committee.[10]

Objection was directed at the provision that the Speaker and President pro tempore would have to resign their offices and membership in Congress before they could act as President in a case of inability, even if it were to be for only a day. This provision, it was felt, was unfair and would make these officials reluctant to act in a case of presidential inability.

An amendment which would place the President pro tempore ahead of the Speaker was proposed by Senator Richard B. Russell of Georgia. It was narrowly defeated, largely because of Senator Arthur Vandenberg of Michigan, the then President pro tempore, who argued that the Speaker was "the officer reflecting the largest measure of popular and representative expression at the instant moment of his succession."[11] The vote was 55 to 31. A proposed amendment by Senator Brien McMahon of Connecticut regarding a provision for a special election was defeated, as was an amendment by Senator Alexander Wiley of Wisconsin to add the highest-ranking military or naval officers to the line of succession after the Cabinet heads.[12]

The arguments for and against the Wherry bill were similar to those for and against the Sumners proposal. The constitutional question again was largely ignored. The bill was finally put to a vote on June 27, 1947, and it passed by a vote of 50 to 35. Thirty-five Democrats opposed it, while forty-seven Republicans and three Democrats favored it.*[13] After only short debate it passed the House on July 10 by a vote of 365 to 11 (ten Democrats and one Republican opposed it) and became law on July 18, with President Truman's signature.

The 1947 law includes all of President Truman's recommendations except a special election. It provides that "if, by reason of

---

* Among those voting for it were Representatives Lyndon B. Johnson of Texas and John W. MCormack of Massachusetts. Appendix C contains the text of the law.

death, resignation, removal from office, inability, or failure to qualify, there is neither a President nor Vice President to discharge the powers and duties of the office of President then the Speaker . . . shall, upon his resignation as Speaker and as Representative in Congress, act as President." If there is no Speaker at the time, then the President pro tempore shall act as President, upon his resignation as President pro tempore and as Senator. However, if the Speaker, while acting as President, dies, is removed, becomes disabled, or resigns, and a new Speaker has been appointed, the new Speaker, not the President pro tempore, then acts as President. Although the act itself is not entirely clear on this point, the legislative history is.[14] If either the Speaker or President pro tempore acts, he does so until the end of the presidential term except in cases of failure to qualify or inability, in which cases he acts until a President or Vice-President qualifies or recovers from an inability.* (If the President pro tempore acts, he cannot be replaced by a new Speaker.)

If there should be no Speaker or President pro tempore at the time of an emergency, the line of succession then runs to the highest on the following list who is not under a disability to discharge the powers and duties of the President: Secretary of State, Secretary of Treasury, Secretary of Defense,† Attorney General, Postmaster General, Secretary of Interior, Secretary of Agriculture, Secretary of Commerce, Secretary of Labor. The Act provides that to be eligible the Cabinet officers must have been appointed by and with the advice and consent of the Senate, and must not be under impeachment at the time of succession. A Cabinet officer automatically resigns his departmental position upon taking the presidential oath of office. He acts as President for the rest of the term or until a President, Vice-President, Speaker or President pro tempore is available. Thus, a Secretary of Treasury who acts as President cannot be superseded by a Secretary of State but he can be by either a Speaker or President pro tempore. The 1947 law makes it clear that no one may act as President who does not have the constitutional

---

* The Act is not explicit as to whether the Speaker and President pro tempore are required to take the presidential oath. However, this was intended.

† This official was not added to the line of succession until the passage of the National Security Act of 1947, which eliminated the posts of Secretary of Army and Secretary of Navy. The Secretary of Health, Education and Welfare has never been added to the line of succession.

requirements for the presidency. The law further provides that any-one who acts as President is paid at the rate then applicable to the President.

This law has never been applied but it stands as the nation's security against the possibility of a vacancy occurring in both the pres-idency and vice-presidency at the same time.

17

The Eisenhower Years

*. . . [I]n each of these three instances there was
some gap that could have been significant—in which
I was a disabled individual from the standpoint of
carrying out the emergency duties pertaining to the
office—I was fortunate that no crisis arose.*

DWIGHT D. EISENHOWER

The Republican National Convention of 1952 nominated for
the presidency and vice-presidency General Dwight D. Eisenhower
and Senator Richard M. Nixon of California, respectively. How
Nixon was selected is explained by the former President in his recent
memoirs, as follows: Nixon's was the first of five names on a list of
those persons whom Eisenhower considered qualified and available
for the position. The others were Congressmen Charles Halleck
and Walter Judd and Governors Dan Thornton and Arthur Langlie.
The names on the list were read to a small committee of advisors—
and Nixon was approved. Says Eisenhower:

My reasons for placing Nixon's name on this list and at its head were
my own. First, through reports of qualified observers I believed that his
political philosophy generally coincided with my own. Next, I realized
that before the election took place I would have attained the age of
sixty-two. I thought we should take the opportunity to select a vice-
presidential candidate who was young, vigorous, ready to learn, and of
good reputation.[1]

In November, Eisenhower and Nixon defeated the Democratic candidates, Stevenson and Sparkman, by a margin of six and one-half million popular votes and an electoral vote of 442 to 89.

Eisenhower and Nixon won by an even larger margin in 1956 against Stevenson and Senator Estes Kefauver—over nine and one half million popular votes and an electoral vote of 457 to 73.

Shortly after having been nominated in 1952, Eisenhower related to Nixon how Truman had been unaware of major administration policies on his succession. Said Eisenhower: "It is vitally important that this never happen again. During my administration, if we are elected, I shall make sure that you participate in all the meetings where policy is developed."[2] It was Eisenhower's conviction that the Vice-President should be trained and prepared so as to be able to "take over the presidency smoothly and efficiently should the need arise."

Under Eisenhower the vice-presidency soared to new heights and "for the first time, . . . began to take on some semblance of a true 'second office.' "[3] From the start President Eisenhower regarded Nixon as a vital member of his team. Nixon not only was a statutory member of the National Security Council and a regular participant in Cabinet meetings, but he was also asked to preside over meetings of these bodies in the President's absence. In this capacity Nixon presided over nineteen meetings of the Cabinet and twenty-six meetings of the National Security Council during his eight years as Vice-President.

As a former legislator, Nixon proved to be an excellent liaison for the administration in the Congress. Eisenhower, whose background was strictly military, often relied on the advice of his Vice-President in political matters. Nixon attended the weekly meetings of the legislative leaders but he seldom presided over the Senate.* He states:

If during my two terms as Vice-President the duties in the Senate were the only ones I performed, then I would agree . . . that the vice-presidency is indeed the dullest office I can imagine. For I voted only eight times to break ties—an average of one a year. As for presiding over the Senate, this duty generally took only a half hour to an hour of my time in a normal 14-hour day when the legislature was in session.[4]

---

* *U.S. News & World Rep.*, June 26, 1953, p. 71, quoted Nixon as saying that he spent less than ten percent of his time in this role.

Nixon found his executive assignments far more interesting and challenging than his legislative functions. According to his concept of the vice-presidency, to serve the President was primary. Consequently, he spent over ninety percent of his time on various presidential assignments. As the President's personal representative, he visited over fifty-four countries of the world, including countries in Central and South America, the Far East, the Middle East, Europe, and Africa. Each of the Vice-President's tours brought him into contact with world leaders and gave him a keen insight into world problems.

In addition to this role, Nixon was given other executive responsibilities. He became a leading spokesman for administration views. He was appointed chairman of the President's Commission on Government Contracts, which was charged with eliminating discrimination in employment on federal contracts, and chairman of the Cabinet Committee on Price Stability, whose task was to examine economic trends and make recommendations to prevent inflation. Not infrequently, Vice-President Nixon performed some of the President's ceremonial functions, such as representing the President at state dinners for visiting dignitaries, attending various social gatherings as the President's representative, and making presentations of awards at official ceremonies.

On three different occasions during his vice-presidency, Nixon came face to face with the perplexing problem of presidential inability and learned first hand how difficult the position of a Vice-President can be in such situations.

On August 14, 1955, President Eisenhower left Washington for a vacation in Denver, Colorado. On September 23, after returning from a four-day fishing trip in the Rocky Mountains at Fraser, Colorado, he played twenty-seven holes of golf at Cherry Hills Country Club in Denver. While playing, he experienced some uneasiness in his stomach which he attributed to indigestion. He went to bed early that night and awoke around 1:30 A.M with a severe chest pain.

I . . . thought immediately of my after-luncheon distress the previous noon. My wife heard me stirring about and asked whether I wanted anything. I replied that I was looking for the milk of magnesia again. Apparently she decided from the tone of my voice that something was seriously wrong; she got up at once to turn on the light to look at me.

Then she urged me to lie down and promptly called the White House physician, General Snyder. She thought I was quite sick.[5]

Major General Howard McC. Snyder arrived shortly before 3:00 A.M. and gave the President some injections, one of which was morphine. Eisenhower went back to sleep. Snyder remained with him throughout the night, and in the morning he called the Denver White House at Lowry Air Force Base to report that the President was ill. Acting White House Press Secretary Murray Snyder received the news and held an 8:00 A.M. press conference, at which he made the public announcement that President Eisenhower had suffered " 'a digestive upset' during the night." This was repeated at press conferences held at 9:30 A.M. and 12:15 P.M. At the latter conference Murray Snyder stated that he had talked with Dr. Snyder. "He tells me," said the press secretary, "that the President is resting. He said that this indigestion is not serious and he says that it is the same type of indigestion that many people have had."[6]

In the meantime, Dr. Snyder had called Fitzsimons General Hospital nearby to request electrocardiograph equipment. Physicians from the hospital arrived at about 12:30 and an electrocardiogram was taken. It confirmed Dr. Snyder's initial diagnosis that the President had suffered a coronary thrombosis. The doctors decided that Eisenhower should be removed to the hospital. Shortly after 2:00 P.M., he was helped into a car and taken to the hospital where he was immediately placed under oxygen.

Murray Snyder was informed of the heart attack and broke the news at a hurriedly called press conference at about 2:40 P.M. He stated: "The President has just had a mild coronary thrombosis. He has just been driven to Fitzsimons General Hospital. He was taken to the hospital in his own car and walked from the house to the car. . . ."* This news was repeated, in substance, at 3:05 P.M. At about 3:45 P.M., Snyder read the following bulletin: "General Snyder in-

---

* In a report to the White House, Dr. Snyder later gave the following reasons for the twelve-hour delay before the public was informed of the President's condition: ". . . I wished the President to benefit from the rest and quiet induced by the sedation, incident to combatting the initial manifestations. This decision also spared him, his wife and mother-in-law emotional upset upon too precipitant announcement of such serious import. This action, I believe, limited the heart damage to a minimum and enabled us to confirm the diagnosis by cardiogram and make an unhurried transference from home to hospital." Nixon, *Six Crises* (Garden City, 1962), pp. 137–38.

forms me that the President had a mild indigestion yesterday evening. He had the first symptoms of an occlusion, or thrombosis, at 2:45 A.M. Upon completion of his diagnosis, the General decided to move the President to the hospital where he could be given better treatment. The General says the President has been comfortable since the initial pain [and] that the prognosis is good."[7]

In a news conference at 10:18 P.M. that evening, one of the reporters noted that, although the bulletin of 2:40 P.M had described the heart attack as "mild" and that of 3:45 P.M. had said the prognosis was "good," these adjectives had been dropped. Murray Snyder could offer no explanation except that further prognosis would have to await the arrival of Dr. Thomas W. Mattingly, chief of cardiology at Walter Reed Hospital. A call had also gone out to Dr. Paul Dudley White, a noted Boston heart specialist.

Mattingly arrived late on the night of September 24, and Dr. White the following afternoon, Sunday. Upon his arrival, White immediately went into consultation with General Snyder, Drs. Mattingly, Byron Pollock, head of the heart clinic at Fitzsimons, and George M. Powell and Martin E. Griffin, both of the Fitzsimons staff. White House Press Secretary James Hagerty, who had arrived in Denver with Mattingly, issued a statement at 4:12 P.M., Sunday, signed by Drs. Snyder, Pollock, Mattingly and White. It said that President Eisenhower "has had a moderate attack of coronary thrombosis without complications. His present condition is satisfactory." In answer to a question regarding the meaning of "moderate," Dr. White said that he would define it as meaning neither "mild" nor "serious."[8]

Dr. White gave the President a thorough examination on Monday, September 26, and reported at a news conference later in the day that Eisenhower "has had an average attack" and that his chances for recovery were "reasonably good." He said that the President would have to have complete rest for about a month but that, barring complications, the President would be well enough to resume some of his duties within two weeks. Complications, he said, might well set in during the first two weeks. Only time could tell. In giving this press conference and expressing himself in a frank manner, White was carrying out President Eisenhower's wish that the public be told the "whole truth." Says Eisenhower: "I had been one of those who during President Wilson's long illness wondered why the public was kept so much in the dark about his real condition, and thought that the nation had a right to know exactly the status of the President's health."[9]

The news that President Eisenhower had suffered a heart attack stunned the nation. Fortunately, it came at a time when Congress was not in session, the programs for 1956 were in their early stages, and no emergencies existed in either the foreign or domestic spheres. Yet, thousands of ordinary affairs of government had to continue somehow without the President.

After Murray Snyder had been told of the heart attack on the morning of September 24, and before he made any announcement to the public, he called James C. Hagerty, who had just arrived in Washington from a vacation. Hagerty advised Snyder that the public should be fully informed of the facts and that no details should be withheld. Hagerty then called Vice-President Richard M. Nixon, who was at his home. It was shortly after 5:00 P.M., E.D.S.T. Nixon had read in the newspapers that the President was not feeling well, but had thought nothing of it. Upon learning of the heart attack, the stunned Vice-President exclaimed, "Oh, my God!" Hagerty said that the press would be informed shortly and that he was leaving for Denver.* "Let me know," said Hagerty, "where you can be reached at all times." Deputy Assistant to the President, Major General Wilton B. Persons and Secretary of State John Foster Dulles were also informed of the heart attack. They, assisted by several others, notified the rest of the Cabinet and other government leaders.

In the evening of Saturday, September 24, at a time when the extent of Eisenhower's illness was unknown, Vice-President Nixon, General Persons, and Acting Attorney General William P. Rogers met at Rogers' home in Maryland.† They discussed the situation, and spoke by phone with Dulles and Secretary of Treasury George M. Humphrey, and reached a consensus that the administration of the government should be continued by the Cabinet and the White

* Hagerty arrived in Denver late in the evening. Dr. Snyder informed him that Eisenhower had said: "Tell Jim to take over and make the decisions —and handle the story." Some interpreted these words as meaning to act as President. Hagerty says—and this seems to be the fact—that they meant to discharge his duties as press secretary.

† Persons was the senior White House staff member as presidential assistant Sherman Adams was then on vacation in Scotland. Similarly, Attorney General Herbert Brownell was on vacation in Spain. Adams arrived in the capital on the morning of September 26. Brownell arrived on September 27.

House staff. Other officials were then called, and they were in agreement with this plan. On the following day, Nixon announced that "the President's well-defined policies and Government business would be carried out without delay."[10] Similar statements were echoed by other members of the Cabinet. In order to be consistent with this approach, Secretary of State Dulles, Secretary of Agriculture Ezra Taft Benson, Secretary of Treasury Humphrey, and Secretary of Commerce Sinclair Weeks left the United States later that day for previously scheduled talks in Canada regarding economic and trade matters. Sunday night, Nixon, Persons and Rogers met at Rogers' home for a second time. Nixon expressed the opinion that a Cabinet meeting should be called for Friday, September 30, but no final decision was reached. On Monday, September 26, Vice-President Nixon, after a three-hour luncheon conference with Rogers, Adams, and Persons, and after having consulted the members of the Cabinet, announced that the Cabinet would meet on Friday, September 30. This meeting, it was felt, would demonstrate that the government of the United States was functioning in an orderly manner.

In the first days after the heart attack the question of delegating presidential authority received some consideration. Hagerty reported on Sunday evening, September 25, that the Attorney General's office had been asked for an opinion "on the legality of delegating President Eisenhower's authority while he is in the hospital unable to handle any official duties."[11] No such request actually seems to have been made of the Attorney General. After the luncheon meeting on September 26, Rogers said: "[I]t may not be necessary to make any formal delegation of powers." On the following day, September 27, he ordered a study of the problem of delegating a President's non-constitutional functions to subordinates by executive order. On the same day, Attorney General Herbert Brownell, after a luncheon in the office of the Secretary of Treasury with Nixon, Persons, Adams, Rogers and Humphrey, stated that there were "sufficient legal arrangements to carry on 'the day-to-day operations of the government.'" "I don't know that it will be necessary," he said, "'to deliver a legal opinion' as requested by the Summer White House in Denver."[12] None was ever delivered.

On Wednesday, September 28, Nixon signed some non-legal ceremonial papers on Eisenhower's behalf. On Thursday, September 29, the National Security Council met, as scheduled before the heart attack, and Nixon presided in the President's absence. This meeting was attended by about twenty-three members of the administration. Among the matters discussed was the manner by which the government should be continued. Nixon said that all government action taken should be within the framework of previously established policies of President Eisenhower. The Council decided "that those actions in the Council's field which customarily are taken only after discussion with the President should now, during his illness, be reviewed in the N.S.C. in lieu of or as preliminary to discussions with the President."[13] It was further decided, subject to Cabinet approval, that Sherman Adams should go to Denver as liaison and administrative assistant to Eisenhower* and that General Persons should remain in charge of the White House office of the President and send to Adams papers requiring the President's examination.

On the following day, September 30, the Cabinet met for the first time since the illness and, again, the Vice-President presided in the President's absence. Secretary of State Dulles reported on the world situation. Attention then was turned to the question of an interim government. Brownell read a statement, drafted at the request of the National Security Council, regarding Adams' going to Denver as a liaison officer. According to Adams, Nixon objected to the proposal on the ground that Adams should remain in charge of the White House.[14] Dulles, however, was firmly for Adams' going to Denver. He argued that it was preferable to have one person act as an official spokesman for the President so that various people outside the government could not purport to do so.† Dulles believed that there could be no better spokesman than Adams, as he was closely identified with the administration. Dulles' arguments were then seconded by Nixon. The following procedure was approved:

(1) On actions which Cabinet members would normally take without consulting either the Cabinet or the President, there would be no change in procedure from the normal.

---

* Up to this time, Hagerty, who was in Denver, was the official spokesman for Eisenhower.

† Dulles referred to the Wilson situation and the apprehensions which had been created by the Cabinet meetings, for which his uncle, Lansing, had been fired. To guard against this, he said, Adams should go to Denver.

(2) Questions which would normally be brought before the Cabinet for discussion before decision should continue to be discussed there.

(3) *Decisions* which would require consultation with . . . [the President] should go first to the Cabinet or the National Security Council for thorough discussion and possible recommendation and then go to Denver for . . . [his] consideration.

(4) The proper channel for submission to . . . [the President] of matters requiring presidential decisions should be to General Persons in the White House and then through Governor Adams to . . . [the President] in Denver.[15]

It was agreed at the meeting that the government would continue to function under the general policy directives previously given by President Eisenhower. New policies, said Nixon, could be set only by the President. The meeting ended with Dulles complimenting Nixon for the manner in which he had acted during the preceding week. Following the meeting, Murray Snyder released a statement which said, in part:

After full discussion of pending matters, it was concluded that there are no obstacles to the orderly and uninterrupted conduct of the foreign and domestic affairs of the nation during the period of rest ordered by the President's physicians.

Governor Sherman Adams, the Assistant to the President, will leave for Denver today and will be available there, in consultation with the President's physicians, whenever it may later become appropriate to present any matters to the President.

The policies and programs of the administration as determined and approved by the President are well established along definite lines and are well known. Coordination of the activities of the several departments of the government within the framework of these policies will be continued by full co-operation among the responsible officers of these departments so that the functions of the government will be carried forward in an effective manner during the absence of the President.[16]

Sherman Adams arrived in Denver on the next day, October 1, and informed Eisenhower that meetings of the NSC and Cabinet had taken place and that the Vice-President had presided. Several days later Eisenhower received a full record of the Cabinet meeting, and approved the minutes. Inspired by what he "had read of President Wilson's illness" in reference to Wilson's becoming incensed when he learned that Cabinet meetings had been called by Lansing, Eisenhower sent out an order "to the effect that all regularly scheduled meetings of the Cabinet and National Security Council should be held under the chairmanship of the Vice President."[17] On October 3, he sent Nixon the following "request."*: "I hope you will continue to have meetings of the National Security Council and of the Cabinet over which you will preside in accordance with procedures which you have followed at my request in the past during my absence from Washington."[18]

During the first few days after his heart attack Eisenhower was kept under an oxygen tent. He says that "the doctors kept [him] . . . practically incommunicado for almost a week before they let any of [his] . . . staff come in and see [him] . . . with particular problems."[19] On September 30, the day on which the Cabinet met, he performed his first official act, that of signing lists of foreign officer appointments. In the next few weeks, the Cabinet met regularly and was presided over by Vice-President Nixon. The President was represented at the meetings by Sherman Adams, who flew in from Denver for that purpose and returned to report the happenings to the President.

It would be inaccurate to say that the government functioned perfectly under this arrangement. The President's hand, says former Secretary of Agriculture Ezra Taft Benson, was "keenly" missed. Adds Benson:

[I]t had seemed to me that Nixon deferred too much to Sherman Adams; sometimes you wondered whether Sherman or Dick was running the meeting. On the one hand most major policy matters were held over until later. But there also was a spreading tendency for Cabinet officials to go ahead on their own—on things that before the heart attack would have been checked out with the President.[20]

According to Adams, all "were well aware that a national or international emergency could have arisen during the President's illness to make this unofficial government by 'community of understanding' entirely inadequate."[21]

President Eisenhower began to have visitors during the second and third weeks after the heart attack. He saw Adams almost daily, often more than once a day, beginning October 1. Nixon visited him

---

* It was a request, says Eisenhower, because "the Vice President, not being technically in the Executive branch of government, was not subject to presidential orders. . . ."

on October 8,* and together they discussed a plan by which Adams would bring Eisenhower all matters requiring action and members of the Cabinet and White House staff could visit him at appointed times to discuss their problems. Accordingly, Dulles visited him on October 11 to discuss a Foreign Minister's meeting scheduled for Geneva later that month. During the next few weeks, Eisenhower was visited by every member of the Cabinet, Admiral Radford, the chairman of the Joint Chiefs of Staff, several presidential special consultants, President Castillo Armas of Guatemala, and many personal friends. "During those same weeks I was able to take on an increased work load and to give fuller attention to the detailed problems of government. In all, I saw sixty-six official visitors between October 1 and my departure from the hospital in early November."[22]

Eisenhower was allowed to walk on October 25, and was discharged from the hospital on November 11. He returned to Washington for a brief period and then, on November 14, departed for Gettysburg, Pennsylvania. On November 22, at his Camp David retreat in the Catoctin Mountains of Maryland, he met with his Cabinet for the first time since the illness, chiefly to discuss the 1956 legislative and budgetary programs. At the meeting, some members "were openly astonished by the President's fast recovery." Shortly thereafter, in early December, a second meeting was held.

The President finally returned to Washington during the week of January 16, after convalescing in Georgia and Florida. "And so," says Adams, "this interlude of sickness and uncertainty came to an end. But it left us uncomfortably aware of the Constitution's failure to provide for the direction of the government by an acting President when the President is temporarily disabled and unable to perform his functions."[23] As Vice-President Nixon noted:

[The committee system] worked during the period of President Eisenhower's heart attack mainly because . . . there were no serious international crises at the time. But had there been a serious international crisis requiring Presidential decisions, then . . . the committee system might not have worked.[24]

Nixon's position throughout this critical period was precarious, to say the least. His "crisis was how to walk on eggs and not break

---

* Arthur and Marshall, it will be recalled, were never permitted to visit Garfield and Wilson, respectively, while the Presidents were disabled.

them." No matter which way he turned he was subject to criticism—either for doing too much or too little.*

I had to move ahead, realizing that any misstep could bring disaster. [A]side from the President, I was the only person in government elected by all the people; they had a right to expect leadership, if it were needed, rather than a vacuum. But any move on my part which could be interpreted, even incorrectly, as an attempt to usurp the powers of the presidency would disrupt the Eisenhower team, cause dissension in the nation, and disturb the President and his family.[25]

Consequently, Nixon was careful during the early weeks to meet with Cabinet officials, individually as much as possible, in their own offices. When in the White House, he used a conference room instead of the President's office. At Cabinet meetings, he occupied his chair across from the President's rather than the President's chair. All in all, it can be said that Vice-President Nixon exercised good initiative, making it possible for a small group to carry out the Eisenhower policies.

The Eisenhower heart attack, however, underscored the seriousness of the problem of presidential inability. It is reported that he asked himself these questions right after his heart attack: "If . . . [he] had been unable to talk or to think clearly, what would have happened if a massive air attack had been directed against the United States at that time? Who would have had the undisputed authority to assume leadership in the absence of the President?"[26] And, recently, in speaking of this period, Eisenhower stated:

. . . I was not required to make any immediate operational decisions involving the use of the armed forces of the United States. Certainly, had there been an emergency such as the detection of incoming enemy bombers, on which I would have had to make a rapid decision regarding the use of United States retaliatory might, there could have been no question, *after* the first forty-eight hours of my heart attack, of my capacity to act according to my own judgment. *However,* had a situation arisen such as occurred in 1958 in which I eventually sent troops ashore in Lebanon, the concentration, the weighing of the pros and cons, and the final determination would have represented a burden, during the

---

* Said the late Senator Styles Bridges of New Hampshire: "You are the constitutional second-in-command and you ought to assume the leadership. Don't let the White House clique take command." Nixon, *Six Crises* (Garden City, 1962), p. 149.

first week of my illness, which the doctors would likely have found unacceptable for a new cardiac patient to bear. As it was, with a period of rest, I was able to keep my mind clear, to talk to members of the government on matters of long-range interest, and to experience a satisfactory recovery (Italics added).[27]

The President's fast recovery and speculation over the 1956 presidential candidates took the steam out of the inability problem. But on two other occasions during the Eisenhower administration, the problem was forcibly revived.

On the night of June 7, 1956, not nine months after his heart attack, President Eisenhower attended a dinner of the White House News Photographers Association. After the dinner he returned to the White House and went to bed at about 11:00 P.M. At 12:45 A.M., June 8, Mrs. Eisenhower called Dr. Snyder stating that the President had stomach cramps. Dr. Snyder advised her to administer milk of magnesia. At 1:20 A.M. she called again telling him that the President was still in distress. Dr. Snyder immediately left for the White House and arrived at about 2:00 A.M. He stayed with the President.

At 7:15 A.M., Press Secretary James Hagerty was told that the President was ill and he informed Vice-President Nixon. At 8:50 A.M., Hagerty made the following announcement in the press room: "The President had an upset stomach and headache this morning. We have postponed his schedule for the day. . . . There is nothing wrong with his heart."

On further questioning Hagerty said: "This is just a stomach ache!"

Shortly after noon Hagerty made another announcement: "The President had an attack of ileitis [inflammation of the ileum, a portion of the small intestine]. As a precautionary measure, he is being taken to Walter Reed Hospital this afternoon."[28]

On the afternoon of June 8, at about 1:25 P.M., Eisenhower was taken on a stretcher from the White House to Walter Reed Hospital. A later medical bulletin noted that there was a "partial obstruction" of the small intestine. During the afternoon attempts were made to relieve the obstruction by medication. These attempts proved futile and it was decided that an operation would be necessary.

At 2:15 A.M., June 9, while the nation slept, Hagerty made the following announcement to the press: "[S]ince . . . the . . . obstruction . . . has persisted, an exploratory operation is necessary. This operation will be undertaken immediately . . . to find the cause of the obstruction and to relieve that cause."

The operation was begun at 2:59 A.M. and lasted one hour and fifty-three minutes. It was performed by a group of four surgeons consisting of Major General Leonard Dudley Heaton, the commanding officer at Walter Reed Hospital, Dr. Isidor S. Ravdin of the University of Pennsylvania Medical School, Dr. Robert T. Gants, chief of the Department of Surgery, and Dr. Max D. Smith, assistant chief of surgery at the hospital.

After the conclusion of the operation Press Secretary Hagerty announced: "The operation was concluded at 4:52 A.M. The operation was successful. The President . . . left the operating table in excellent condition."

The obstruction, which was described as non-malignant, had been removed and the President's condition was described as "very satisfactory" on the afternoon of June 9. At a press conference Dr. Heaton stated:

We look for a rapid and complete recovery. . . . During the coming week he should be able to sign official papers and carry on those functions of the Government which are necessary. We should like to establish here that his cardiac condition had no relationship to this present illness. We do not expect his heart in any way to affect his convalescence. . . . I want you to know that there was nothing suggesting a malignant disease found at operation.[29]

Because the speculation was renewed about whether or not the President would seek re-nomination at the Republican National Convention that summer, Dr. Ravdin saw fit to add: "I see no reason why the President should not make a complete recovery and go ahead and carry on his normal activities."

The physicians at the press conference agreed that the President should be able to resume full official duties within four to six weeks. They said he should spend fifteen days in the hospital but he would be able to see members of his staff and sign official papers by June 11.

The day after the operation, the President began walking and a few days later he began performing official acts. It was not, however, until late in July that he was back in full swing. This was signified by his trip to Panama on July 21 to attend a meeting of American Presidents. On August 1 Dr. Snyder pronounced the

President "in fine shape" and on August 27 he said he was "completely recovered." On October 29 a panel of doctors said his health was "excellent."

While at Walter Reed Hospital, President Eisenhower told those around him that he would resign if another illness should occur. He was profoundly disturbed about the operation and its significance to the nation. Says Nixon: "On several occasions afterwards, he pointed out to me that for the two hours he was under anesthesia the country was without a Chief Executive, the armed forces without a Commander-in-Chief. In the event of a national emergency during those two hours, who would have had the undisputed authority to act for a completely disabled President?"[30]

Seventeen and one-half months later, on November 25, 1957, another crisis struck. On that morning Eisenhower went to the Washington National Airport to welcome King Mohammed V of Morocco who arrived at noon. When he returned to the White House, he said he felt a chill and was put to bed by Dr. Snyder. He arose in the afternoon and started to dictate to his secretary, Ann Whitman, but his words became jumbled and he was unable to express himself. The President returned to his quarters and Dr. Snyder was called. He ordered Eisenhower to bed.

Adams called Nixon and explained to him what had happened. A dinner was scheduled that night for the King. It was clear that the President could not attend. Hence the question: Should Vice-President Nixon act in his place? Adams, staff secretary Andrew Goodpaster, Mrs. Eisenhower and Dr. Snyder met to discuss the question.

While we were talking, the President walked casually into the room. He was wearing a long robe over his pajamas and his feet were in bedroom slippers. He smiled at us, as if to let us know that nothing was wrong with him.

He started to say something, "I suppose you are dis—" but he stammered, hesitated and then struggled on with the rest of the sentence: ". . . talking about the dinner tonight."

We saw that he was trying to talk about the plans for the evening but he was frustrated and getting angry at his inability to form words.

"There's nothing the matter with me!" he said finally with effort. "I am perfectly all right!"[31]

Attempts were made to dissuade the President from going to the dinner. He left the room, saying, "If I cannot attend to my duties, I

225

am simply going to give up this job. Now that is all there is to it."
Adams subsequently told Nixon: "This is a terribly, terribly difficult
thing to handle. You may be President in the next twenty-four
hours."[32] The nation was informed at 6:20 P.M. that the President
had suffered a chill and would be unable to attend the dinner or deliver a nationwide television speech the following night. Mrs. Eisenhower and Vice-President and Mrs. Nixon attended the dinner in
his place.

At 2:58 P.M. on the following day, November 26, a medical report by Doctors Snyder and Heaton was submitted to the press. It
revealed that an examination of the President that morning had confirmed an original diagnosis made the preceding day that "the President suffered an occlusion of a small branch of the middle cerebral
artery on the left side." The report continued, saying:

It cannot be determined at this time whether the condition present is
one of a small clot or a vascular spasm. All findings indicate no brain
hemorrhage. . . . Although the present condition is mild and is expected
to be transitory in nature, it will require a period of rest and substantially
decreased activity estimated at several weeks. Hospitalization will not
be necessary. . . . [T]he outlook for complete recovery within a reasonable period of time is excellent.[33]

Later that day, at 6:15 P.M., the White House issued a second bulletin:

The President has had an occlusion of a small branch of a cerebral vessel which has produced a slight difficulty in speaking. There is no evidence of a cerebral hemorrhage or any serious lesion of the cerebral
vessels. The difficulty in speaking has improved . . . and is now manifested only by a hesitancy in saying certain difficult words. Reading,
writing and reasoning powers are not affected. The President's physical
strength is normal, and he is allowed to be up and about his home. . . .
He is alert, his spirits are good, and he discussed with interest and
clarity recent events. The present disability is mild and transitory in
nature. . . . [T]he original recommendation for rest and decrease in
physical activity should be followed.

The state of world affairs at the time was not encouraging. It was,
says Nixon, "the worst time possible, short of outright war, for the
President to be incapacitated." The Russians had just launched
their first Sputnik and the nation's military and scientific programs
were under critical review. An important NATO meeting was sched-

226

uled for December 16, at which Eisenhower's attendance was essential. Considerable work had to be done on the administration's 1958 legislative program.

On the day following Eisenhower's speech impairment, Adams asked Nixon and Brownell to meet with him and Persons to discuss "the President's competency."[34] Also that day, it was decided that Vice-President Nixon would attend the NATO meeting. Fortunately, the medical news of the President's condition was favorable —he had suffered a "mild stroke" which affected only his ability to speak. It was unknown, however, whether other strokes might follow. None did, and almost from the start President Eisenhower regained his health. He was up on the day following the stroke, performed some government work on the next day, and on the next— Thanksgiving—he accompanied Mrs. Eisenhower to church services. On Friday, November 29, he went by car to Gettysburg for the weekend. By December 2 he was back at work and by December 3 the White House was back on its normal routine. Two weeks later President Eisenhower left Washington for the NATO meeting in Paris.

These illnesses so emphasized the critical nature of the inability problem to the President that in 1956 he asked the Department of Justice to study the problem and recommend a solution. On February 8, 1957, the entire matter came up for review at a Cabinet meeting. Attorney General Herbert Brownell informed the group that his staff could not reach a conclusion on the procedure that should be followed if the President were unable to declare his own inability. Brownell and Adams favored the Vice-President's making the determination, checked by the Cabinet. Eisenhower expressed a preference for a commission consisting of the Chief Justice and some medical persons. A President, asserted Eisenhower, should be able to declare his own inability and its termination. He also believed that the 1947 succession law should be revised in favor of a Cabinet line of succession. Brownell and Nixon pointed out that an attempt to change the line of succession would cause a political controversy in which the important problem of presidential inability might be lost sight of. Accordingly, it was decided to push an inability amendment along the lines favored by Brownell.[35]

A meeting of the legislative leaders was held on March 29, 1957, at which opposition to the amendment manifested itself. Speaker Sam Rayburn said that the public would be suspicious of any attempt by Eisenhower to turn over the government to another. Senator William Knowland of California, the Republican leader in the Senate, felt that a President's competency should be decided by a committee having congressional representation. "There being no unanimity and little enthusiasm among the Republican leaders, and strong opposition from Rayburn, it was apparent that the proposal would not get far and it didn't."[36]

Another attempt was made to get Congress to take action on the problem following Eisenhower's speech impairment. It, too, met with failure. According to Nixon, "the reason was purely political and obvious. The Democratic congressional leaders would not approve any plan which might put Richard Nixon in the White House before the 1960 election."[37]

While Congress manifested reluctance to solve this critical problem, Eisenhower went to work on an agreement to cover possible future cases of his inability. He showed it to Nixon and Rogers in early February, 1958. They approved it, with minor suggestions, and it was embodied in a letter, copies of which were sent to Nixon, Rogers and Dulles. The letter agreement was made public on March 3, 1958, and provided as follows:

The President and the Vice President have agreed that the following procedures are in accord with the purposes and provisions of Article 2, Section 1, of the Constitution, dealing with Presidential inability. They believe that these procedures, which are intended to apply to themselves only, are in no sense outside or contrary to the Constitution but are consistent with its present provisions and implement its clear intent.

(1) In the event of inability the President would—if possible—so inform the Vice President, and the Vice President would serve as Acting President, exercising the powers and duties of the office until the inability had ended.

(2) In the event of an inability which would prevent the President from so communicating with the Vice President, the Vice President, after such consultation as seems to him appropriate under the circumstances, would decide upon the devolution of the powers and duties of the Office and would serve as Acting President until the inability had ended.

(3) The President, in either event, would determine when the inability had ended and at that time would resume the full exercise of the powers and duties of the Office.[38]

This agreement represented the first act of real significance in meeting the inability problem.* It was later adopted by President John F. Kennedy and Vice-President Lyndon B. Johnson in August, 1961, and by President Lyndon B. Johnson and Speaker John W. McCormack in December, 1963 and by President Lyndon B. Johnson and Vice-President Hubert H. Humphrey in January, 1965.†

---

* For the view that it did not solve the problem, see p. 246.

† It seems that President Johnson's agreement was originally an oral one (*The New York Times,* December 6, 1963, p. 1) and was later put in writing (*The New York Times,* March 16, 1964, p. 18.). The oral nature of his agreement with Humphrey received some criticism. *The New York Times,* January 28, 1965, pp. 13, 28.

18

The Johnson Vice-Presidency

*I think I am equipped for the job. Lyndon Johnson
is the only other man I can think of with the equipment for the job of President.*

JOHN F. KENNEDY

When it came time for the Republican Party to select its 1960 presidential candidate, Vice-President Richard M. Nixon was the overwhelming choice. United States Ambassador to the United Nations Henry Cabot Lodge was Nixon's choice for Vice-President. This was, says Nixon,

not because he was from the East and I was from the West, nor because on some domestic issues his views were more liberal than mine, but because on the all-important issue of foreign policy we were in basic agreement. I felt that his experience in the Senate and at the United Nations qualified him to lead the Free World in the event that responsibility should come to him.[1]

The year 1960, however, was a Democratic year—Senator John F. Kennedy of Massachusetts and Senate Majority Leader Lyndon B. Johnson of Texas were elected to the nation's highest offices. Johnson had been Kennedy's chief adversary at the Democratic Convention several months before. After John Kennedy received his party's endorsement for the presidency, the question of his running mate was given a good deal of attention. Senators Henry M. Jackson of Washington and Stuart Symington of Missouri were thought to be the leading candidates. But Kennedy's choice was

Lyndon B. Johnson. Speaker Sam Rayburn, a close friend of Johnson, was of the opinion that the vice-presidency was no place for a person of Johnson's energy and ability, and so advised Johnson. Other Johnson intimates agreed. Despite this, Johnson said that he would run. "Power," he remarked, "is where power goes." On his return to Washington, Johnson drafted a form letter which set out his reasons for accepting the nomination.

Dear Friend:

You are a little bit disappointed at the way the convention turned out, and so, I think was everyone. For no man can go into a political convention and come out with everything he wants. For my own part, I feel strongly that no man ever fulfills an obligation by turning his back on a duty to which he is called. I neither sought nor solicited the Vice-Presidency, but when the invitation to join Senator Kennedy on the ticket came, I had the choice of turning tail and abandoning any opportunity for Texas and the South to have a voice in the carrying out of national policy or repaying the confidence of the Democrats from all over the country who voted for me for President.

His experience of twenty-two years in the Congress, his Southern background, and his recognized ability made him an excellent choice. Unquestionably, his presence on the ticket was a factor in the Democratic victory of 1960.

The enlarged role of the Vice-President under President Eisenhower was expanded even more under President Kennedy. As Vice-President, Johnson was sent as a personal representative of the President to over thirty countries—Germany, Vietnam, India, Pakistan, France, Belgium, Norway and Sweden, to name a few. "These were not good-will missions or the cornerstone-laying sort of thing," said William S. White. "They were vital trips in which Johnson went for broader purposes than to estimate and to report on nearly all the foreign crises which arose in the almost three years of his vice-presidency. Kennedy gave his Vice-President wide powers to negotiate and to act on behalf of the United States."[2] In addition to these journeys abroad, Johnson traveled to forty-three states of the United States.

Johnson, like Nixon before him, became an informed, consulted and working member of the executive machinery. He was made chairman of the National Aeronautics Space Council, of the President's Committee on Equal Employment Opportunity, and of the Advisory Council of the Peace Corps. He was also a statutory member of the National Security Council and attended meetings of the Cabinet and the weekly conferences which President Kennedy had with the congressional leaders. He was frequently consulted by the President on political matters and few major decisions, if any, were reached without Johnson being consulted. When important decisions had to be made concerning Berlin, Cuba, Laos and Vietnam, President Kennedy took into consideration the views of his Vice-President.

James Reston of *The New York Times* gave this picture of Johnson as Vice-President:

When he was Vice President, he had to discipline his energies. He had a limited catalogue of duties, limited for a man of his expansive nature. He stayed within the bounds of his assignment, seldom talked up in Cabinet meetings or the National Security Council unless requested to do so, and, in keeping with his sense of political loyalty, never differed with President Kennedy in the presence of anyone else.[3]

Little did the nation realize how well equipped and prepared for the presidency was its Vice-President until the untimely death of its President. The manner in which Johnson picked up the reins of government, upon succeeding to the presidency, was a tribute to Kennedy, to himself, and to that office created by our Founding Fathers as an afterthought.

It is no wonder that in the months following his succession, Johnson emphasized the principle that a Vice-President must be selected on the basis of his qualifications for the presidency. At a news conference on April 23, he said that, in selecting a Vice-President, his main criterion would be: Who would serve "the best interest of the country and who would make the best President of the United States in the event he were called upon to be President."[4] On Thursday, July 30, 1964, he said that the Vice-President should be

a person that is equipped to handle the duties of the Vice Presidency, and of the Presidency, if that awesome responsibility should ever fall upon him. I think he should be a man that is well received in all the states of the Union among all of our people. I would like to see a man that is experienced in foreign relations and domestic affairs. I would like for him to be a man of the people who felt a compassionate concern for their welfare and who enjoyed public service and was dedicated to it. . . . I would like him to be one who would work cooperatively with the Congress and with the Cabinet and with the President. . . . He ought to be available to do anything the Chief Executive wants him to do and he ought to be competent to do it.[5]

Later that day President Johnson made the unprecedented announcement that he thought it "inadvisable" for him to recommend "any member of my Cabinet or any of those who meet regularly with the Cabinet."

As the 1964 Democratic National Convention approached, the main subject of interest was the vice-presidential nomination. President Johnson, whose nomination for the presidency was a certainty, consulted thousands of persons from every walk of life before making up his mind about a running mate. Then, on the evening of August 26, after having been nominated for the presidency, Johnson made an historic visit to the convention to announce his choice of Senator Hubert H. Humphrey of Minnesota. Humphrey, a close friend of the President ever since they started in the Senate together in 1949, was thereupon enthusiastically endorsed as Johnson's running mate. The ensuing campaign found the vice-presidential nominee campaigning perhaps longer and harder than any other vice-presidential candidate in history. As the new Vice-President of the United States, Humphrey awaits a role at the completion of which he may be proclaimed the most effective Vice-President in history. This remains entirely with President Johnson, who has described a role for Humphrey which approximates that of a "Deputy President."* A new dimension to the vice-presidency is, indeed, in the offing.

---

* One of President Johnson's first acts in this connection was to designate Vice-President Humphrey to coordinate the government's various civil rights programs. During the 1960 campaign, former Vice-President Nixon had said that, if elected, he would make his Vice-President responsible for coordinating all agencies dealing with international affairs.

III. IMPROVING THE SYSTEM

19

Presidential Inability

*Fifty years ago the country could afford to "muddle
along" until the disabled President got well or died.
But today . . . there could be a critical period when
"no finger is on the trigger" because of the illness of
the Chief Executive.*

RICHARD M. NIXON

For 176 years the problem of presidential inability plagued the nation. Then, after the death of President Kennedy, a consensus on
how to solve the problem was reached at a conference convened by
the American Bar Association. The background of, the work at and
the aftermath of the conference are described below.

The problem was created, as noted, because the Constitution did
not clearly provide that the Vice-President could act as President
during a period of inability without becoming President for the rest
of the term, and because it did not define inability, nor indicate who
may decide whether an inability has occurred or ended. The problem was complicated by the fact that eight Vice-Presidents had succeeded to the "office" of President upon the death of the incumbent
and that the Constitution said "the Same" shall devolve on the
Vice-President in all cases—removal, death, resignation and inability. Thus, if a Vice-President were to act as President during a
period of presidential inability, it could be persuasively argued that,
following these precedents, he became President for the rest of the
term regardless of whether the President recovered in the meantime.

Former President Harry S. Truman said that this is the way it should be, since otherwise "it would make the Presidential office up for sale and that's not the way it ought to be."[1]

Congressional attempts to meet the problem occurred, as seen, during the Garfield and Wilson inabilities. From 1920 to 1946, Congress paid no attention to the problem despite occasional remarks by some of its members that it must and should do something about the problem. On March 14, 1946 the Senate passed a resolution introduced by Senators Theodore F. Green of Rhode Island and H. Alexander Smith of New Jersey with a view to setting up a joint Congressional committee to examine all the problems surrounding succession to the presidency, including presidential inability.[2] The House failed to act on the resolution and the matter died. In subsequent Congresses similar attempts were made, to no avail.

The Eisenhower Period

Shortly before President Eisenhower's heart attack in September, 1955, Representative Emanuel Celler of New York, chairman of the House Judiciary Committee, ordered the Committee's staff to undertake a preliminary study of the inability problem. In November of 1955, during the course of this study, the staff prepared and distributed to various jurists, political scientists and public officials, a questionnaire comprised of eleven fundamental questions.[3] Among these were: "What was intended by the term 'inability' as used in . . . the Constitution?" "Shall a definition be enacted into law?" "Who shall initiate the question of the President's inability to discharge the powers and duties of his office?" "Once raised, who shall make the determination of inability?" "If temporary, who raises the question that the disability has ceased to exist?" "Once raised, who shall make the determination of cessation?" "In the event of a finding of temporary disability, does the Vice-President succeed to the powers and duties of the office or to the office itself?" "Does Congress have the authority to enact legislation to resolve any and all of these questions, or will a constitutional amendment or amendments be necessary?"

Seventeen replies to this questionnaire were included in a committee print of January 31, 1956.[4] The replies were analyzed, and six proposals were put into legislative drafts, two in the form of statutes and the others in the form of constitutional amendments.

These proposals varied as to how a President's inability might be determined. Two proposals gave a decisive role to the Vice-President; two, to the Cabinet; one, to the Supreme Court; and one to a panel of medical specialists appointed by the Chief Justice. All of the proposals permitted the President to declare his own inability and four provided that he could declare the end of his inability, whether or not he had made the initial determination of inability.

The Eisenhower heart attack prompted the Judiciary Committee to set up a special subcommittee to study the problem. It consisted of Representative Celler, as chairman, and Representatives Thomas J. Lane of Massachusetts, Kenneth B. Keating of New York, William M. McCulloch of Ohio, and Francis E. Walter of Pennsylvania. This subcommittee held hearings on April 11 and 12, 1956, and took testimony from eleven persons (six of whom had previously replied to the questionnaire). Four other persons submitted replies to the questionnaire.[5] In all, the Committee had obtained the views of twenty-six distinguished authorities.[6]

Following these hearings, the subcommittee met several times in executive session to discuss the problem. Unfortunately, it could recommend no final solution. It met again on April 1, 1957 to listen to the testimony of Attorney General Herbert Brownell, whose staff had studied the problem for over a year.[7] The Attorney General offered, on behalf of the Eisenhower administration, a proposed constitutional amendment whereby when the President declared his inability in writing the Vice-President would thereupon discharge the powers and duties of the office. If the President should fail or be unable to declare his own inability, the Vice-President, "if satisfied of the President's inability, and upon approval in writing of a majority of the heads of executive departments who are members of the President's Cabinet," would act as President. The President would resume his powers and duties upon his written declaration of recovery. Under the administration's approach, the question of a President's inability could be raised by either the Vice-President or a majority of the Cabinet.

Kenneth B. Keating observed that the administration's approach would allow the Vice-President to declare the President disabled, and the President to declare immediately that he was able, and the Vice-President then to declare him disabled again. In reply, Brownell stated that in declaring a President disabled the Vice-President could

239

not act without the approval of the Cabinet and would not do so unless he were sure his decision would be approved by public opinion and that the people would not want to obstruct the President from readily resuming his powers and duties when he considered himself able. Should there be, however, a disagreement between the President and Vice-President, he said, impeachment would lie as a remedy against whichever one was wrongfully attempting to exercise the powers of the presidency.

Celler's subcommittee, in addition to considering Brownell's proposal, also examined the approach of its chairman. Celler personally recommended that the President could declare himself disabled, or the Vice-President could do so by announcement to Congress. In either case, the President could declare the end of the inability. Keating's plan differed from those of Celler and Brownell. He suggested a ten-member Inability Commission consisting of the Vice-President (or, if none, the person next in the line of succession), who would have no vote, the Chief Justice of the Supreme Court, the Senior Associate Justice of the Court, the Speaker and Minority Leader of the House, the majority and minority leaders of the Senate, the Secretaries of State and Treasury and the Attorney General. Seven members would constitute a quorum and the concurrence of six would be necessary for any determination.

On May 16, 1957, the subcommittee reported to the parent committee, without making any recommendation. While the House Judiciary Committee was reviewing the matter, former President Harry S. Truman set forth a proposal of his own in a copyrighted article for *The New York Times*.[8] He suggested a commission of seven, consisting of the Vice-President, the Chief Justice of the Supreme Court, the Speaker of the House, and the majority and minority leaders of the House and Senate. Truman's commission would be empowered to select a group of medical authorities from the top medical schools in the country. If the medical group found the President "truly incapacitated," the commission would so inform Congress. If Congress agreed by a two-thirds vote of its membership, the Vice-President would become President for the remainder of the term.

The full Judiciary Committee was also unable to reach agreement and the matter came to an end in the House. While the House grappled with the problem, little was done in the Senate. Proposed legislation on the problem was introduced in 1956 but no hearings were held.* In December, 1957, after President Eisenhower had suffered his third illness and after he had renewed his efforts to stir congressional action, Senator Estes Kefauver of Tennessee, chairman of the Subcommittee on Constitutional Amendments of the Senate Judiciary Committee, announced that his subcommittee would hold hearings in 1958.

Kefauver's subcommittee held hearings on January 24 and February 11, 14, 18 and 28, 1958. Nine experts were heard and many others submitted their views in the form of memoranda and letters.[9] Attorney General William P. Rogers testified and endorsed, with one modification, the proposal presented by Brownell.

After Brownell had testified, much concern had developed over the possibility of a President's disagreeing with a Vice-President's determination of inability. An insane President, it was said, probably would disagree with such a determination and would thereby insist on and succeed in, continuing to discharge his powers and duties. Brownell's suggestion that impeachment would be an available remedy was generally not acceptable. It was pointed out that impeachment is a long and complicated process, that there are periods when Congress is not in session, that the Vice-President has no power to convene it, that once removed by impeachment, the President could not regain his office, and that it was doubtful that a President could be impeached for an inability.

Rogers suggested a provision whereby the Vice-President, with the approval of a majority of the Cabinet, could bring before Congress any disagreement he had with the President and Congress would decide the matter. If a majority of the House voted that the President was disabled and the Senate concurred by a two-thirds vote, the Vice-President would then discharge the powers and duties of the President until a majority of both Houses decided that the inability had ended or until the end of the term.

After the completion of these hearings, members of the Senate Judiciary Committee introduced a proposal which was substantially the same as the modified administration approach.[10] It was approved by the subcommittee and reported to the full Commit-

---

* On February 20, 1956, however, the Senate passed a resolution introduced in January by Senator Green, calling for a joint Congressional Committee to study all matters relating to succession and emphasizing the necessity for acting on presidential inability. The House failed to pass the resolution. S. Cong. Res. 65, 84th Cong., 2d Sess. (1956).

tee on March 12. Several months later Congress adjourned without acting on the proposal. It was reintroduced by Senator Kefauver in January, 1959, reported favorably by the subcommittee on Constitutional Amendments on May 11, 1959, and discussed by the parent Committee on July 20. When Congress adjourned in the summer of 1960, it was still on the Committee's agenda.

The Senate hearings, like the House hearings, resulted in no action on the problem of presidential inability, but the hearings were not entirely without effect. During the course of the hearings certain things had become clear. It was generally agreed that any solution to the problem of presidential inability must provide: (1) that whenever the Vice-President succeeds in cases of death, resignation and removal, he becomes President for the remainder of the term, and (2) that in cases of inability, the Vice-President merely acts as President for the duration of the President's inability.

Many of those who expressed themselves on the problem were of the opinion that a constitutional amendment was necessary for any real solution. Many felt that the President should be able to declare his own inability and that no definition of inability should be enacted into law. Professor Joseph E. Kallenbach of the University of Michigan expressed the feeling of many when he said that " 'inability,' in the constitutional sense, has reference to a mental or physical condition or any other condition, which prevents the actual exercise of the powers and duties of the office of President as the public interest and necessities require."[11]

Why did Congress fail to solve this problem after the most concerted effort in history? General disagreement had manifested itself on the procedure for determining the existence and termination of an inability. Numerous proposals were advanced, giving the decisive role variously to the Vice-President, the Cabinet, the Congress, the Supreme Court, an Inability Commission, and to combinations of these. Each proposal had its adherents and critics. None was able to muster enough support for passage.

The Kennedy Period

With the election of John F. Kennedy, the problem of presidential inability receded from general congressional and public consciousness. Only a few members of the Congress continued to press for action. The administration seemed not much concerned about the whole matter. In early 1963, Senators Kefauver and Keating, having decided to put their previous proposals aside, joined in sponsoring a resolution which, by constitutional amendment, would clarify the Constitution on the status of the Vice-President in a case of inability and empower Congress to legislate on the problem of inability. Said Keating:

... Senator Kefauver and I ... agreed that if anything was going to be done, all of the detailed procedures which had been productive of delay and controversy had best be scrapped for the time being in favor of merely authorizing Congress in a constitutional amendment to deal with particular methods by ordinary legislation. This, we agreed, would later allow Congress to pick and choose the best from among all the proposals without suffering the handicap of having to rally a two-thirds majority in each House to do it.*[12]

In an effort to revive interest in the problem, Senator Kefauver commenced hearings of his subcommittee on June 11, 1963, stating at the outset that: "We are very fortunate that this country now has a young, vigorous and obviously healthy President. This will allow us to explore these problems in detail without any implication that the present holder of that high office is not in good health." The Senator added: "The essence of statesmanship is to act in advance to eliminate situations of potential danger, . . . [We should] take advantage of our present good fortune to prepare now for the possible crises of the future."[13]

At the hearings, testimony was taken from seven witnesses, including the then Deputy Attorney General, Nicholas deB. Katzenbach, who spoke on behalf of the administration and indicated its support of S. J. Res. 35. Shortly thereafter, on June 25, 1963, the Subcommittee on Constitutional Amendments favorably reported S. J. Res. 35 to the full Committee, but the sudden death of Senator Kefauver in August brought the progress of the movement virtually to a stop. The Kennedy tragedy revived it once again, former Senator Keating noting, "as distasteful as it is to entertain the

---

* This resolution (S.J. Res. 35) initially had been proposed by a special subcommittee of the New York State Bar Association consisting of Martin Taylor, as chairman, Arthur Dean and Elihu Root. The proposal was subsequently endorsed by the New York State Bar Association in 1957, by the American Bar Association in 1960 and again in 1962, and by the Association of the Bar of the City of New York in 1962.

thought, a matter of inches spelled the difference between the painless death of John F. Kennedy and the possibility of his permanent incapacity to exercise the duties of the highest office of the land."[14]

The Johnson Period

Following President Kennedy's death, a flurry of proposals descended on Congress dealing with the inability problem, as well as with the vice-presidential vacancy. Senator Birch Bayh of Indiana, Kefauver's young successor as chairman of the Subcommittee on Constitutional Amendments, announced in December, 1963, that his subcommittee would hold hearings on these problems in early 1964. Senator Bayh, together with several other Senators, introduced a proposal (S.J. Res. 139) containing provisions on inability, the vice-presidential vacancy, and the line of succession beyond the vice-presidency. The inability provisions were essentially the same as those embodied in the revised Eisenhower administration approach, as endorsed by Kefauver's Committee in 1958 and 1959.[15]

Meanwhile, the internal machinery of the most powerful lawyer's group in the country—the American Bar Association—was operating to assist the Congress. President Walter E. Craig of the American Bar Association sent out special invitations to twelve lawyers familiar with the inability problem, inviting them to attend a Conference on Presidential Inability and Succession at the Mayflower Hotel in Washington, D.C., January 20 and 21, 1964. The attending lawyers were former Attorney General Herbert Brownell; Professor Paul A. Freund of the Harvard Law School, one of the nation's foremost authorities on the Constitution; Jonathan C. Gibson of Chicago, chairman of the Committee on Jurisprudence and Law Reform of the American Bar Association; Richard Hansen of Nebraska, author of *The Year We Had No President;* Professor James C. Kirby, Jr., of Vanderbilt University, former chief counsel to the Subcommittee on Constitutional Amendments; former Deputy Attorney General Ross L. Malone; Dean Charles B. Nutting of the George Washington Law Center; Lewis F. Powell, Jr., then President-elect and now President of the American Bar Association; Martin Taylor of New York, Chairman of the Committee on Federal Constitution of the New York State Bar Association; Edward L. Wright of Arkansas, Chairman of the House of Delegates (governing body) of the American Bar Association, and the author. Representatives from the offices of Senator

Bayh, Everett Dirksen, and Jacob K. Javits sat with the group, which spent two long days of intensive study on the inability problem, considering its every aspect.* Brownell later said that the conferees "differed widely in their views just as individual Senators probably do. But they all agreed that the dire necessities of promptly solving the problems outweighed their individual preferences."

From this Conference emerged a consensus that the Constitution should be amended to provide:

(1) In the event of the inability of the President, the powers and duties, but not the office, shall devolve upon the Vice-President or person next in line of succession for the duration of the inability of the President or until expiration of his term of office;

(2) in the event of the death, resignation or removal of the President, the Vice-President or the person next in line of succession shall succeed to the office for the unexpired term;

(3) the inability of the President may be established by declaration in writing of the President. In the event that the President does not make known his inability, it may be established by action of the Vice-President or person next in line of succession with the concurrence of a majority of the Cabinet or by action of such other body as the Congress may by law provide;

(4) the ability of the President to resume the powers and duties of his office shall be established by his declaration in writing. In the event that the Vice-President and a majority of the Cabinet or such other body as Congress may by law provide shall not concur in the declaration of the President, the continuing disability of the President may then be determined by the vote of two-thirds of the elected members of each House of the Congress; and

(5) when a vacancy occurs in the office of the Vice-President the President shall nominate a person who, upon approval by a majority of the elected† members of Congress meeting in joint session, shall then become Vice-President for the unexpired term.

The process of reasoning by which the panel arrived at this consensus is as interesting as it is informative.

---

* Senators Bayh, Keating and Hruska, Representatives Celler and Wyman, and Deputy Attorney General Katzenbach gave the group the benefit of their thinking during the two days.

† This word inadvertently was placed in the statement of the consensus. It was in no way intended that members of Congress appointed to fill vacancies were to be deprived of their votes.

The first subject discussed at the Conference was the effect of agreements between Presidents and Vice-Presidents on the inability problem. It was pointed out that, while such agreements were useful, they could not be considered as a permanent solution. First, an agreement would not be effective if one or both of the parties should decide to break it. As former Vice-President Nixon has said:

[I]t would not be effective in the event you happen to have a President and Vice President who didn't get along. . . . The President might not want to write a letter. If he had written one, he might tear it up. Let's suppose, for example, that the President became disabled and that the Vice President decided that he should step in and assume the duties of the Presidency, but . . . a member of the President's family held a Cabinet position or some other high post and didn't believe that the President was so disabled. . . . You'd have a constitutional crisis there of great magnitude. . . .[16]

Another objection to a letter agreement as a permanent solution was the fact that it could not have the force of law. No mere agreement could solve the constitutional problem created by the Tyler precedent—should the Vice-President permanently replace the President in cases of inability, as in cases of death?

The panel came to the conclusion that a permanent solution to the problem of presidential inability required a constitutional amendment. The group recognized, however, that there was a respectable body of opinion which held that Congress had the power to legislate on the problem under either the succession provision or the Necessary and Proper Clause of the Constitution.* The succession provision, some members felt, gave Congress only one power: the power to establish a line of succession beyond the vice-presidency. The legal maxim, *inclusio unius, exclusio alterius* (i.e., the inclusion of one means the exclusion of all others), was referred to as being applicable. That is, since the Constitution specified this one power, all others were excluded. At least one member of the panel believed that the Constitution empowered Congress to declare the inability of anyone in the statutory line of succession who acted as President. This is because the Constitution allowed Congress to declare who may act when there is neither a President nor Vice-President. Incidental to this power, it was argued, was the power to determine his inability.

---

* See pp. 134–35.

246

As for the Necessary and Proper Clause, some members of the ABA panel thought that, since the Constitution did not *specifically* give Congress or any department or officer the power to declare a President disabled, Congress could have no power under this clause. If the Vice-President now had the power to declare a President disabled, as most authorities held,* no statute could constitutionally take it away. The general feeling was that Congress' power in inability situations was in such doubt that if a mere legislative solution were adopted, it would be subject to constitutional challenge in the courts, which would come very likely at a time of inability. Prudence, it was stressed, required a constitutional amendment.

Points (1) and (2) above were agreed upon without any debate. It was considered essential that the ambiguous wording of the succession clause which prevented Vice-Presidents Arthur and Marshall from acting as President be eliminated—that it be made indisputably clear that the Vice-President only acts as President in a case of inability.† Point (2) was inserted in order to give express recognition to the precedent that a Vice-President becomes President when there is a vacancy in the presidential office due to death, resignation or removal.

The most difficult subject presented for resolution and upon which the panel spent the greater part of its time was the method for declaring a President disabled. There was no objection to allowing a President to declare his own inability. It was considered unlikely that a President would ever use this as a pretense for shirking his duties but if he did, he would be subject to impeachment. The crux of the problem was how to declare a President disabled when he could not or would not do so himself.

One possibility was to let the Supreme Court decide whether the President was disabled. This was rejected largely because of the

---

* Benjamin Butler was one of the first proponents of this view. During the Garfield inability he argued that "when the Constitution imposes a duty on an officer, to be done by him, he must be the sole judge when and how to do that duty. . . ." "Symposium—Presidential Inability," 133 *North American Review* 435 (November, 1881).

† Former President Truman believes that the Vice-President should become President for the remainder of the term in a case of inability. He bases this on the ground that the Vice-President would be encouraged to exercise the President's powers and duties to the fullest extent without fear of reprisal after the President recovers.

principle of separation of powers. It was argued that to give the Court such a power would upset the balance of power among the three branches of government by making the Executive subject to the Judiciary. It was also noted that an inability decision might have to be made swiftly whereas the Court's processes are time-consuming. If the Court had to decide the question of the President's inability the whole matter might take on the appearance of a public trial at which the President would insist on being represented by counsel. This could bring the Court and presidency into disrepute. Moreover, if the Court reached a decision by a split vote, the acceptability of the decision would be greatly impaired.

The Conference also considered the general attitude of the Court itself, which was set forth by Chief Justice Earl Warren in a letter of January 20, 1958 to former Senator Keating:

It has been the belief of all of us that because of the separation of powers in our Government, the nature of the judicial process, the possibility of a controversy of this character coming to the Court, and the danger of disqualification which might result in a lack of a quorum, it would be inadvisable for any member of the Court to serve on such a Commission.[17]

Its partisan nature, its size, and the principle of separation of powers ruled Congress out as the body for declaring a President disabled. The possibility of an unruly Congress, such as the Congress President Andrew Johnson had to face, wrongly exercising the power to work its will on the President was mentioned.

Giving the Vice-President the decisive role had some advocates at this Washington Conference. It was urged that the Constitution gave the Vice-President such a role, and that if the ambiguities of the succession provision had been eliminated prior to 1881 and 1919, Vice-Presidents Arthur and Marshall would not have been so reluctant to act as President. It was pointed out that the inability problem arose because of the fear that if a Vice-President acted as President, he would, by virtue of the Tyler precedent, become President for the remainder of the term regardless of whether the elected President recovered. It was further argued that if the succession provision were clarified so as to provide that the Vice-President only acts as President in a case of inability, the President would be encouraged to make a determination of his own inability in such cases as where he is actually very ill or about to undergo an operation, without fear of losing his office. It would also encourage the Vice-President to act swiftly and without hesitation in cases where the President is clearly unable to make the determination of inability (e.g., where he is in a coma, kidnapped or a prisoner).

The arguments for the Vice-President's deciding by himself failed to prevail partly because of the type of situation dramatized in *The Caine Mutiny,* which was referred to by one of the conferees. It will be recalled how much difficulty Executive Officer Stephen Maryk had in telling Captain Philip F. Queeg that he was disabled and that he (Maryk) was taking over pursuant to certain Naval Regulations.*[18]

For a critical period there was doubt as to who would prevail in the dispute. The executive officer finally did but he was later tried for his act (and was acquitted). The point of this argument was that a Vice-President would be on precarious ground in a case where a President had become insane, refused to declare himself disabled, or disagreed with the decision of the Vice-President. In such a case, it was said, the Vice-President would be too reluctant to act or, if he did act, he might be labelled a usurper.

Although it was agreed that the Vice-President should not be given the sole responsibility for declaring a President disabled, it was nonetheless felt that he should be included in the decision-making process, particularly since he is the only other nationally-elected official and since he is the one who will have to act as President.

Turning from the Vice-President, the American Bar Association panel explored the possibility of setting up an inability commission. One member said that a commission of purely medical personnel would be undesirable because a determination of whether inability exists is more than a medical question. Evidence as to the medical facts of a particular situation would, of course, be highly relevant. Also relevant, however, would be the actual need for an acting President at the time. This would involve a consideration of the state of foreign and domestic affairs. In these areas, medical peo-

---

* One of those Regulations (Article 185) provided that the next in command, if unable to refer the matter to an appropriate higher authority, could take over if "thoroughly convinced that the conclusion to relieve his commanding officer is one which a reasonable, prudent, and experienced officer would regard as a necessary consequence from the facts thus determined to exist."

ple are not best qualified to pass judgment. Although the ABA panel did not look favorably upon the idea of recommending a medical commission, it was observed that whatever body was decided upon would be expected to gather the medical facts, consulting the President's physicians and others.

A preference was expressed by some at the Conference for a commission of members of the Executive and Legislative Branches of the government. One prominent member of the panel said that he had initially leaned toward such a solution when the matter first came up during the Eisenhower years but rejected it after hearing these arguments: An inability decision might have to be made quickly, and a political commission of the two branches would have difficulty in meeting this requirement, particularly if both political parties were represented on the commission. A commission of the two branches would not harmonize with the principle of separation of powers, and it might well make a determination of inability by a split vote,* with possibly disastrous consequences to the country.

The type of commission which appealed most to the panel was one within the executive branch as it would be in keeping with the fundamental principle of separation of powers. One member suggested that the President be required to appoint a commission after taking office.† This was objected to on the ground that the President might not appoint anyone or, if he did, he could remove the members at will.

Most members of the panel thought that a commission of the heads of the executive departments (popularly known as the Cabinet) would be the best body.‡ A number of reasons were advanced:

---

* A ready example of this is what occurred in the election of 1876. See p. 117.

† A suggestion then current was that the President appoint members of the Cabinet, the Supreme Court, the House and the Senate to an inability commission to hold office at his pleasure. Hofstadter & Dinnes, "Presidential Inability: A Constitutional Amendment is Needed Now," 50 *American Bar Association Journal* 59 (January, 1964).

‡ Although the Constitution is silent on the matter of a President's Cabinet, each President has had a Cabinet, composed of the heads of the executive departments, of which there are now ten. In recent years others than the heads of the executive departments, such as the Budget Director and the United States Representative to the United Nations, have been invited to attend Cabinet meetings. Since the composition of the Cabinet is at the com-

They are close to the President, would likely be aware of the existence of an inability and would be in a position to know if the state of executive affairs was such that the Vice-President should act. The Cabinet's involvement would be consistent with the principle of separation of powers, and the public would have confidence in its decision. Another factor favoring the Cabinet was the feeling that it could act faster, and with greater unanimity, than any other body. Thus, when Garfield lay dying, the Cabinet met and unanimously agreed that Arthur should act as President. However, its lack of constitutional authority and the possibility that Arthur might permanently replace Garfield prevented it from asking Arthur to act. There is little doubt that if the Wilson Cabinet had had the authority, it would have unanimously agreed that Vice-President Marshall should act as President. These historical examples serve also to show that, though close to the President, the Cabinet would not let their allegiance to him obstruct their duty in a time of real inability.

Having arrived at a consensus that the Cabinet was the best body and, as previously indicated, that the Vice-President should have a part in the decision, the ABA panel recommended that a President's inability be determined by the Vice-President (or whoever might be first in the line of succession) and a majority of the Cabinet.

The next question taken up was how to determine the end of an inability. Several conferees expressed the opinion that the President should be allowed to resume his powers and duties upon his own declaration of recovery. If he announced his recovery when he was still disabled and thus acted irresponsibly, it was said he would be subject to impeachment. In support of this approach, it was argued that if the status of the Vice-President in a case of inability were clarified, it would be unlikely that the President would announce his recovery prematurely. But this question persisted: What if the President were insane and announced his recovery one minute after he had been declared disabled? If there were no quick-operating check on him, a major crisis would then confront the country. In answer, it was noted that the United States has never had an in-

---

plete discretion of the President, most congressional proposals use the expression "heads of the executive departments instead of "Cabinet" in order to be perfectly clear on the point.

sane President and that there is practically nothing that could be done to meet a case where a President suddenly became insane and pulled the "nuclear trigger."

There emerged, however, a consensus that there should be a built-in check for the extraordinary case where a President recklessly seeks to resume his powers and duties. The check, it was concluded, should be weighted as heavily in favor of the elected President as possible, inasmuch as the people would require it. Thus evolved this check: The President could declare the end of his inability, but if the Vice-President and a majority of the Cabinet disagreed with this declaration, the disagreement would be submitted to Congress for resolution.* The two Houses would meet separately and it would take a two-thirds vote of each House to prevent the President from resuming his powers and duties. Until Congress decided the issue, the Vice-President would act as President so that the office of President would not be filled by one whose capacity was seriously in doubt. To permit the President to act in this interim period would defeat the very purpose for having such a check—to cover that extraordinary case. It was pointed out that Congress, if it were politically opposed to the President, might delay (even engage in a filibuster) in deciding the issue. It was answered that the American people would see to it that Congress acted promptly.

An important question at this ABA Conference was whether the method of determining a President's inability should be included in a constitutional amendment. One member of the panel persistently argued that no method should be included in an amendment but that the amendment should simply give Congress the power to legislate on the subject. To include the method, he argued, would be contrary to the Constitution, which contains only general principles. It would freeze something into the Constitution which could not be changed (except by constitutional amendment) should it become advisable to do so at a later date. And, he added, the inclusion of a method would make it difficult for the amendment to obtain ratification by the necessary three-fourths of the states,

---

* The impeachment provision of the Constitution was used as an analogy. There, a majority vote of the House is required to impeach a President and a two-thirds vote of those present (provided there is a quorum) in the Senate is required to remove him.

since each state would examine the method in detail and, if it disagreed with all or part of it, would refuse to endorse it.*

A host of arguments was advanced to support the inclusion of the method. It was emphasized that the Constitution is specific in its provisions relating to the presidency—how a President is elected and how he may be removed. Consequently, since a determination of inability would deprive a President of his prerogatives—at least temporarily—the method of determining the same should be no less specific. Merely to give Congress a broad power to adopt and readopt methods by legislation, some felt, would be a flagrant violation of the principle of separation of powers, under which certain powers were separately distributed among the legislative, executive and judicial branches and made subject to specified checks and balances. Some members of the panel were of the opinion that the inclusion of a specific method would avoid the uncertainty and probable delay involved in leaving the problem for action by the Congress in the future. The time to solve the problem, it was underscored, was now, while there was general interest in it.

After careful consideration, the panel concluded that the method should be included in any amendment. To meet the objection that such an amendment would be extremely inflexible, it was suggested that it contain language by which Congress could change, by statute, the prescribed method. Thus, if unforeseeable circumstances and contingencies developed, Congress could provide for a presidential commission, or a group of selected Cabinet members, or any other body to determine a President's inability.† Whatever it proposed would, of course, be subject to presidential veto. The sug-

---

* A frequent objection to a constitutional amendment is that it would take too long to be enacted by the necessary three-fourths of the states. The record shows that the lengths of time from proposal to ratification of the twenty-four amendments were as follows: 1–10: 26 mos.; 11: 11 mos.; 12: 6 mos.; 3: 10 mos.; 14: 25 mos.; 15: 11 mos.; 16: 43 mos.; 17: 11 mos.; 18: 13 mos.; 19: 14½ mos.; 20: 11 mos.; 21: 9½ mos.; 22: 47 mos.; 23: 9½ mos.; 24: 16 mos.

† Although the wording of the consensus released by the American Bar Association (see Appendix D) would permit Congress to eliminate, by legislation, both the Vice-President and the Cabinet as the persons empowered to declare a President disabled, this author believes that the intention of the panel was merely to give Congress the power to provide for a different body to function with the Vice-President.

gested language ("such other body as Congress may by law provide") was adopted despite some feeling that the inability problem should be removed entirely from the political arena.*

The consensus which emerged from this Washington Conference was immediately released to the press.† It was endorsed by the American Bar Association on February 17, 1964, and formally presented to the Subcommittee on Constitutional Amendments on February 24, by the President and President-elect of the American Bar Association.

At the Congressional hearings held during the months of January, February and March, 1964, a number of witnesses expressed their support for the ABA consensus. Former President Eisenhower indicated his basic agreement with the proposal in a letter to Senator Birch Bayh, dated March 2, 1964. He said: "Many systems have been proposed but each seems to be so cumbersome in character as to preclude prompt action in emergency. My personal conclusion is that the matter should be left strictly to the two individuals concerned, the President and the Vice-President, subject possibly to a concurring majority opinion of the President's Cabinet."[19] Eisenhower felt that if there were a disagreement between the President and the Vice-President, the issue should be referred to a commission consisting of the three ranking Cabinet officials, the Speaker and minority leader of the House, the President pro tempore and minority leader of the Senate, and four medical persons recognized by the American Medical Association (and selected by the Cabinet). The findings of this commission could, Eisenhower said, then be submitted to Congress for approval.

Former Vice-President Nixon and Professor Ruth Silva, one of the country's foremost authorities on presidential succession and inability, were also in substantial agreement with the ABA inability provisions. Professor Silva, however, thought it unnecessary to make provision for a disagreement situation. She said that the possibility of a disagreement was remote but that, in any case, the "two-thirds vote" was a "sufficiently heavy majority to protect the integrity of the office" of President. Silva further stated that Congress should

---

* The author has long felt that because of the principle of separation of powers, Congress should have no decisive role in this matter.

† The consensus was issued in the form of a statement of substantive principles and not in the form of a proposed constitutional amendment. See Appendix D.

be given no power to change the Cabinet as the body to function with the Vice-President.[20]

Senator Roman L. Hruska of Nebraska, testifying in support of his own proposal, urged that the determination of a President's inability should be left to the Executive. In his opinion the Cabinet was the best possible body and should be specified as the body in the amendment. Instead of giving Congress carte blanche authority to designate a body other than the Cabinet, Senator Hruska would provide that Congress could designate another body "within the Executive Branch."

Views not in agreement with the ABA consensus were, however, expressed at the hearings. Professors Clinton Rossiter of Cornell University and Richard Neustadt of Columbia University suggested a joint resolution by Congress endorsing the President–Vice-President agreement approach. They regarded a constitutional amendment as being unnecessary. Former Senator Keating and Martin Taylor of New York were of the opinion that a constitutional amendment along the lines of S.J. Res. 35 should be adopted. Sidney Hyman, a noted author of books on the presidency, believed that the Vice-President should have the power to declare a President disabled in the event of a great emergency. This, he said, might require a constitutional amendment. Professor James McGregor Burns of Williams College spoke in favor of a constitutional amendment allowing Congress to establish an inability commission composed of the Chief Justice, two ranking Cabinet members, the Speaker and the President pro tempore. Each member would have the power to appoint a doctor to gather the facts. Francis Biddle, Attorney General of the United States under Franklin Roosevelt, recommended a commission of three Cabinet officials. It would be empowered to declare an inability temporary or permanent. If permanent, its finding would have to be approved by Congress.

Almost all of the witnesses who testified and those who sent their views to Bayh's committee expressed concern about this glaring gap in our system and emphasized the necessity for its early elimination. Said Senator Bayh: "Our obligation to deal with the question of Presidential inability is crystal clear. Here we have a constitutional gap—a blind spot, if you will. We must fill this gap if we are to protect our Nation from the possibility of floundering in the sea of public confusion and uncertainty."[21]

The Senate hearings ended on March 5. On May 27, 1964, the

Subcommittee on Constitutional Amendments favorably reported to the Judiciary Committee a revised S. J. Res. 139 with provisions only on inability and the vice-presidential vacancy. The inability provisions of the original proposal were revised to conform with the consensus of the American Bar Association Conference, with the exception that no mention was made in the new proposal as to how a President's inability was to be determined when there was no Vice-President. Apparently, the Subcommittee viewed this as an unlikely contingency if its provisions on the vice-presidential vacancy were adopted.* The proposal also did not attempt to cover the case of a vice-presidential inability, occurring either at the same time as the President's or at a different time.

On August 4, 1964, the revised S.J. Res. 139 was unanimously approved by the Senate Judiciary Committee. On Monday, September 28, 1964, the Senate passed the proposal by voice vote.[22] Since there were less than a dozen Senators on the floor at the time of the vote, Senator John Stennis of Mississippi moved the following day to reconsider the vote. Senator Stennis supported the proposal but felt that it would set a dangerous precedent to have a proposed constitutional amendment approved by voice vote and without a sufficient number of legislators present.† A roll call was taken, and the sixty-five Senators present all voted in favor of the Bayh Plan. This unique achievement represented the first time in history that a House of Congress passed a proposal to deal with presidential inability. Although Congress adjourned without the House of Representatives taking any action, the progress made during 1964 is leading Congress to solve this critical problem once and for all.‡

The Bayh proposal is in substantial agreement with the views of

---

* This aspect is discussed at p. 263.

† The Constitution requires two-thirds of both Houses to propose a constitutional amendment. This means two-thirds of those present provided there is a quorum (a majority of each house). In practice, unless an objection of lack of quorum is raised, votes are taken on the basis of those present, whether constituting a quorum or not. It is not unusual for bills to pass a House with only a handful present.

‡ S.J. Res. 139 was reintroduced by Senator Birch Bayh and over seventy other Senators in January, 1965, as S.J. Res. 1. It was also introduced in the House of Representatives by Representative Emanuel Celler as H.J. Res. 1. President Johnson's special message to Congress on January 28, 1965 (see *The New York Times,* January 29, 1965, p. 14), in which he specifically endorsed and urged prompt action on this proposal, all but assures the speedy

the Eisenhower administration and with the proposal approved by the Senate Judiciary Committee in 1958 and 1959. It has the overwhelming support of the legal profession in America and many responsible citizens' groups as well. Walter Lippmann has said of it that it is "a great deal better than an endless search . . . for the absolutely perfect solution . . . which will never be found, and . . . is not necessary."[23] The great merit of the proposal is that it is complete in itself, it is practical and it is consistent with the principle of separation of powers. It gives the decisive role to those in whom the people presumably would have most confidence. It involves only persons who have been elected by the people or approved by their representatives, and it embodies checks on all concerned—the President, the Vice-President and the Cabinet. Since it would be embodied in a constitutional amendment, there would be no question about its constitutionality.

---

passage of it for submission to the state legislatures for ratification as the Twenty-Fifth Amendment to the Constitution. An important step in this direction was the unanimous decision of the Subcommittee on Constitutional Amendments on February 1, 1965, to Report S.J. Res. 1 favorably to the full committee.

20

Vice-Presidential Vacancy

> *[W]hatever tragedy may befall our national leaders,
> the Nation must continue in stability, functioning to
> preserve a society in which freedom may prosper. . . .
> [T]he best way to assure this is to make certain that
> the Nation always has a Vice President as well as
> a President.*

BIRCH BAYH

For more than thirty-seven years—over twenty percent of its history—this nation has been without a Vice-President. Although eight Vice-Presidents have succeeded to the presidency upon the death of the incumbent, seven Vice-Presidents have died in office and one has resigned, no procedure has ever been provided whereby a vacancy in the vice-presidency could be filled when it occurs.

The succession of Lyndon B. Johnson to the presidency, leaving a vacancy in the vice-presidency for almost fourteen months, brought this deficiency into sharp focus.* Unusual agreement manifested itself at the 1964 Senate hearings on the need for a Vice-President at all times. "It is significant," said Senator Bayh, "that every measure placed before this committee since President Kennedy's assassination agrees on one vital point—that we shall have a Vice-President."†[1] Witness after witness at the 1964 hearings com-

---

* Among other things, it was a factor in President Johnson's decision not to go abroad during this period. *The New York Times,* March 27, 1964.

† The need for a Vice-President at all times was also underscored in the replies to a questionnaire which then Senator Humphrey had circulated,

mented that today the Vice-President is the official best able to succeed to the presidency, since he has the best opportunity for first-hand knowledge of and experience in the various facets of the executive machinery. Neither the Speaker nor the Secretary of State, it was pointed out, is selected on the basis of his qualifications for the presidency, and neither is as well positioned as the Vice-President to prepare himself for the possibility of serving as President.

At a press conference held at the White House on the evening of March 15, 1964, President Johnson, without expressing a preference for any specific proposal, stated that Congress ought to set up some mechanism by which the office could be kept filled at all times. He said that it was "important" that something should be done but doubted that Congress would make any "realistic progress" in 1964.[2]

The question of how to fill the vacancy prompted a number of suggestions. One was that there be a special election. This was objected to on the ground that it would disrupt the normal government processes and would come at a time when a national official had died and when the country would not be receptive to the activities incident to a political campaign. Moreover, a special election could bring a person of another party into the vice-presidency.

Former President Truman and former Vice-President Nixon recommended that the last electoral college be convened. It is important, said Nixon, that the new Vice-President "come from the elective raheer than the appointive process."[3] Nixon observed that a majority of the membership of the college will always be the same as that of the President's own party. In criticism of the electoral-college proposal, it was noted that the members of the college are not chosen to exercise a considered judgment but rather to carry out the will of the voters of the respective states. Since the college would have no mandate from the voters, said Professor Ruth Silva, "it would be a step away from democratic control, not a step toward it" to give the college a role in this area.[4] Others pointed to the fact that Congress for many years has been studying plans to abolish the college altogether. Senator Bayh noted that the electors are generally "unknown quantities" and that, therefore, the people would be hesitant about having them decide on the "confirmation

shortly after President Kennedy's death, seeking the opinions of leading scholars on succession. *The New York Times,* February 16, 1965, p. 48.

of a Vice-President of the United States."[5] Another objection registered against convening the last electoral college was that many of its members might have died in the meantime so that there would be a delay in filling those vacancies.

Former Senator Kenneth B. Keating of New York made the suggestion of providing for the election of a President and two Vice-Presidents every four years.[6] One Vice-President would be an Executive Vice-President, who would be first in the line of succession and ready to undertake assignments for the President. The other would be a Legislative Vice-President and as such would be second in line and President of the Senate. Keating remarked that his two Vice-Presidents would be selected from among the most competent people in the party, that most Senators, Representatives and Governors would, indeed, be only too interested in either position, and that the Legislative Vice-President would be no less busy than the Vice-President is now. The great advantage of this arrangement, said Keating, was that both Vice-Presidents would be of the President's party and elected by the people.

Nixon voiced perhaps the strongest objection to the Keating proposal and others like it, when he said that by dividing "the already limited functions of the office, we would be downgrading the vice presidency at a time when it is imperative that we add to its prestige and importance."[7] Others remarked that having two Vice-Presidents might result in neither Vice-President being as adequately prepared as were Vice-Presidents Nixon and Johnson to assume the powers and duties of the presidency in cases of emergency. A further objection is that one or both Vice-Presidents might be selected to "balance the ticket," regardless of whether they were able to work harmoniously with each other or the President."*

---

* The *New York Herald* made these interesting observations in its issue of December 26, 1881: "There is . . . [an] ingenious proposition to elect at least three Vice Presidents every four years. . . . The . . . scheme strikes us as extremely dexterous. In every national convention there is a large number of gentlemen who, failing to obtain the first place on the ticket, are only too glad to accept the second. It is a cause of vexation and political heartburning that only one can be chosen. Why not satisfy all parties and make as many Vice Presidents as there are members of the Convention? In this way all interests and factions might be harmonized. For this and other equally weighty reasons it is to be hoped the three Vice Presidential proposition will be adopted with an amendment that the number shall be increased to three hundred."

260

Yet another proposal for filling the vacancy was to give Congress the power to select the new Vice-President. It would have the advantage of selection by the representatives of the people without incurring the disadvantages incident to a special popular election. Senator Jacob K. Javits of New York was one of the leading advocates of this proposal. When it was pointed out that the proposal would permit Congress to designate a Vice-President of a different party from that of the President and would give it a new and unprecedented power in the selection of potential Presidents, Javits modified his proposal to give the President an absolute veto.

Many felt that the best way to handle the vice-presidential vacancy problem was to give the President the power to nominate a person, whose name would then be submitted to Congress for approval. The merits of this approach, it was urged, were several: The presidential candidate now selects his running mate so that it would be consistent with present practice. As the people must give their stamp of approval to the presidential and vice-presidential candidates in order for them to be elected, so, too, here their representatives in Congress would have to give their approval to the President's nominee before he could become the new Vice-President. This method would also insure that the President would have a Vice-President of compatible temperament and views—one who would be able to work with him. After all, it is argued, the effectiveness of a Vice President depends completely on his ability to get along with the President.

Critics of the above proposal said that Congress would have the passive role of merely rubber-stamping the President's nominee. Hence, some suggested that the President submit to Congress a list of names (between three and five) from which one would be chosen as Vice-President. Against this proposal were the important objections that the President might not get the person with whom he could best work, and that no one person might be able to obtain the necessary number of votes for selection.

Those inclined toward a presidential nomination approach differed as to whether the name or names should be submitted to one or both Houses of Congress. Some said the Senate was preferable, since it could be assembled more quickly than the House of Representatives and since it has the Constitutional role of confirming presidential nominations, such as ambassadors, the heads of the executive departments, and Supreme Court justices. Also, it was noted that under the Constitution it is the Senate which chooses the Vice-President when no candidate receives a majority of the electoral votes. Others preferred the House on the ground that it was the more representative of the two Houses. A greater number favored participation by both Houses because it would distinguish the selection of a Vice-President from other presidential appointments. It was observed that, together, the two Houses approximate the composition of the electoral college. Among the adherents of joint participation there was a difference of opinion as to whether the Houses should meet separately or jointly. If they met separately, it was argued, there could be considerable delay in the confirmation process and either House could prevent any action at all. If they met jointly, on the other hand, the delay would be minimized and a majority of those present would be in a position to approve the President's choice. However, it was stated that if every member had an equal vote in the joint session, the voice of the House would be over four times greater than that of the Senate. Action by a joint session, moreover, would require the adoption of a new set of Congressional rules, since there are no established rules of procedure regarding such sessions.*

While most proposals for filling a vacancy in the vice-presidency contemplated a constitutional amendment, some did not. Governor Nelson A. Rockefeller of New York expressed a preference for a statutory office of First Secretary. The First Secretary would be appointed by the President, by and with the advice and consent of the Senate, and would be a member of the Cabinet and National Security Council and would assist the President in the areas of national security and internal affairs. Said the Governor: "An individual with the knowledge and experience gained from this position would be well suited to succeed to the Presidency in the absence of a Vice-President. He would provide the essential continuity of Government in our international relations and leadership of the machinery of Government."[8]

Senator Eugene J. McCarthy of Minnesota proposed the creation, by statute, of an office of Deputy President to be filled within thirty days after a vacancy had occurred in the vice-presidency. The President would appoint, subject to Senate confirmation, a person

---

* Joint sessions are now held to count the electoral vote, to receive messages delivered by the President, and to hold formal ceremonies.

from among the members of Congress, the Justices of the Supreme Court, and the Governors of the states. The Deputy President would be placed first in the line of succession. According to Senator McCarthy, "the choice of the Deputy President would be made under politically realistic conditions. A weakness of our previous succession laws has been that the designated successor often attained the position for reasons and considerations quite apart from the possibility of succession."*[9]

After studying the various proposals, the Bayh Committee adopted the following: "Whenever there is a vacancy in the office of Vice President, the President shall nominate a Vice President who shall take office upon confirmation by a majority vote of both Houses of Congress." The proposal, which calls for the Houses to meet separately, is directed at two sets of contingencies: (1) when the Vice-President succeeds to the presidency upon the President's death, resignation or removal; and (2) when the Vice-President dies, resigns, or is removed.

This provision was part of the inability proposal approved by the Senate in September, 1964, and is now awaiting Congressional action prior to submission to the state legislatures.

---

* The Rockefeller and McCarthy proposals are constitutionally sound. This is because Congress has the power to create an office of First Secretary or Deputy President under the Necessary and Proper Clause of the Constitution, and the power to invest the occupant with a place in the line of succession under the succession provision. But Congress could not, by statute, give such an officer the power to preside over the Senate (this is the exclusive duty of the Vice President or, in his absence, the President pro tempore). And, the method of filling the office is limited: appointment by the President, by and with the advice and consent of the Senate, as in the case of any other executive appointment.

21

Line of Succession

*The essence of statesmanship is to act in advance to
eliminate situations of potential danger. . . .*

ESTES KEFAUVER

President Kennedy's death generated renewed discussion and
criticism of the 1947 succession law. Some of the discussion, unfortunately, was more concerned with the persons who were in the
line of succession than with what would be the best kind of law.
Speaker John W. McCormack of Massachusetts, who in his early
seventies was the immediate successor to President Johnson for
more than a year, and President pro tempore Carl Hayden of Ari-
zona, who in his late eighties was next in line, were objects of biting
criticism. The ability of both to act as President should it become
necessary was seriously questioned, and it was suggested that they
resign their positions so that persons more suitable to be in the line
of succession could replace them.

This type of criticism aside, it has been frequently said that the
1947 law is impractical, since the Speaker and President pro tempore are not chosen on the basis of their qualifications for the presidency and since it allows a person of a political party different from
that of the President and Vice-President to take over after them. It
has also been said that they are not officers within the meaning of
the succession provision and, even if they are, Congress has no
power to authorize them to act after they have resigned from their
respective offices—which the present law requires that they do pre-

264

paratory to acting as President. As a result of these observations there has grown up considerable demand for a change in the succession law.

Since President Kennedy's death, the lines for and against the 1947 law have been clearly drawn. Former President Truman continues to favor it. "The Speaker of the House," says Truman, "has usually been a member of the House for a good, long time before he's ever elected Speaker, and when he's elected Speaker, he comes more nearly being elected by the country at large than any other public servant in the federal government and, of course, that's the reason I placed him next to the Vice President in the succession. . . ."[1] President Lyndon B. Johnson, who voted for the 1947 law when he was a Representative, says that it is a "very good law."[2] Speaker McCormack's attitude is summed up as follows: "I supported the 1947 Act recommended by former President Harry S. Truman and I still support it."[3] The members of Congress, he says, "are pretty much wedded to it." Former Senator Keating has stated that: "I don't like the succession to the regular members of the Cabinet because. . . . One, they are not elected officials. Second, they are very apt to be specialists in their field."[4]

Former President Eisenhower is foremost in the group which opposes the 1947 law. Says he:

[I]f you have a line of succession which, right after the Vice-President, brings in two of the legislative group, you can have a very, very bad situation arise . . . in a period of crisis. For six years of my administration, of course, I had a Congress that was controlled by the Democrats, so right behind Mr. Nixon in the line of succession stood, under the present law, Mr. Rayburn, the Speaker of the House. . . . [M]y immediate predecessor . . . had . . . the same experience I did in reverse. He had Mr. Martin. . . . [W]hen there was no Vice-President, you would have had different parties taking over suddenly . . . [in] the Executive department. . . . You can't change it overnight and get it working effectively. I believe that if the electorate says that such-and-such a party should have the White House for four years, it ought to have the White House for four years.[5]

In expressing a preference for the old Cabinet line of succession, Eisenhower observed that ". . . if the Presidency went to a member of the Cabinet, then if that man had more than one year to serve his Presidency, I think there might be called a special election and

. . . let the people decide this thing."[6] The weight of popular opinion, if gauged from the newspapers, would also seem to favor a change to the Cabinet line of succession.

There is little likelihood that Congress will change the line of succession within the foreseeable future. The recent criticisms of the Speaker and President pro tempore have placed the whole matter so squarely in the political realm that Congress has not yet even examined the succession statute. To do so, it is felt, would be a great insult to the presiding officers of both Houses. This attitude, understandable as it may be, is unwise and dangerous, for there are aspects of the 1947 statute which require consideration. It is true that the urgency of examining the line of succession would be lessened if a procedure for filling the vice-presidential vacancy were adopted. But the possibility of simultaneous vacancies in the presidency and vice-presidency, and the ever present threat of a nuclear war make it essential that there be no imperfections in the country's presidential succession law.

Whether the Speaker and President pro tempore should be removed from the line of succession in favor of immediate succession after the Vice-President by the heads of the executive departments involves questions of both policy and law.

From the standpoint of policy, there seems to be little justification for having the Speaker and President pro tempore in the line of succession. The fact is that the experience of Speakers and Presidents pro tempore is almost strictly legislative in nature and they arrive at their positions of leadership after many years of service in Congress so that they are usually well on in years. The argument that the present line of succession is more in keeping with the American tradition than the Cabinet line of the 1886 law is of doubtful validity. For over 155 years of our existence the immediate successor after the Vice-President was not an official elected by the people. From 1792 to 1886, the President pro tempore was a person indirectly elected to the Senate, as Senators during this period were elected, not directly by the people, but by the state legislatures. From 1886 to 1947, the Secretary of State, an appointed official, was the immediate successor. Even the present law puts the Cabinet in the line of succession after the President pro tempore.

The policy question should not, of course, be resolved on the basis of how many Speakers or Secretaries of State were later elected President. If this were the criterion, however, the Cabinet line of succession would seem preferable as six Secretaries of State (Jefferson, Madison, Monroe, J. Q. Adams, Van Buren and Buchanan) and only one Speaker (Polk) have been elected to the presidency. Yet, some excellent Speakers have been: Vice-Presidents (John N. Garner and Schuyler Colfax), Secretaries of State (James G. Blaine and Henry Clay), Secretaries of Treasury (Howell Cobb and John J. Carlisle), Secretaries of War (John Bell), and nominated for the presidency (Blaine, Clay and Bell), and vice-presidency (Polk). One can hardly deny the general executive competency of the men who have been Secretaries of State—e.g., John Marshall, Daniel Webster, John C. Calhoun, William H. Seward, John Hay, Elihu Root, William Jennings Bryan, Robert Lansing, Charles E. Hughes, Henry L. Stimson, Cordell Hull, James F. Byrnes, George C. Marshall, and John Foster Dulles.

The answer to the policy question, it seems, is to have a line of succession that will insure continuity of policy and administration in a time of crisis. This cannot be insured when legislative officers are in the line of succession. History shows that the possibility of having a President and Vice President of one party and a Congress dominated by another is by no means remote. For about eight of the thirty-seven years during which the vice-presidency has been vacant, the person next in line was of the opposite party. This was the case for a substantial part of the time when Tyler, Fillmore and Truman were serving out the terms for which others had been elected. Although there was neither a President pro tempore nor Speaker when Arthur succeeded to the presidency and when Vice-President Hendricks died in office, the President's party was not in control of the Senate in either case. During Eisenhower's entire second term Congress was controlled by the Democrats. Former Presidents Taft, Wilson and Hoover were confronted with a Congress controlled in one or both Houses by the opposite party.

Surely, a leader of a political party other than that of the President is not in a position to insure such continuity as is a Secretary of State or other Cabinet member. A Cabinet officer normally would be of the same party as the President, of similar views, and of sufficient knowledge of his predecessor's programs to maintain continuity.

From the legal standpoint, there is reason to believe that the present law is unconstitutional on several grounds. First, there is a serious question as to whether the Speaker or President pro tempore is an officer of the United States.* Professor Ruth C. Silva, who has studied this aspect in detail, states that "the Constitution does not contemplate the presiding legislative officers as officers of the United States" (as is required by the succession clause), and that this view is "supported by all the commentators."[7]

A second area of legal difficulty concerns the requirement that the Speaker and President pro tempore resign their positions and seats in Congress in order to act as President. It is argued that Congress can only attach the powers and duties of the presidency to an existing office which the occupant continues to occupy while acting as President.† In rebuttal, it has been contended that the Constitution merely requires the successor to be an officer of the United States at the time he begins to act as President. Hence, if the officer resigns at the time he takes the presidential oath, this requirement is satisfied. The flaw in this position is that the Constitution specifically provides that the officer shall act as President "until the Disability be removed, or a President shall be elected," implying that he is to remain an officer. On the other hand, if the Speaker and President pro tempore retained their legislative positions and seats, there would seem to be a violation of the principle of separation of powers.‡

A third legal objection to the 1947 law involves its so-called bumping provision—that is, where a Cabinet officer acts as President, he may be superseded by a Speaker or President pro tempore. It is pointed out that the Constitution provides that the officer appointed by Congress shall act "until the Disability be removed, or a President shall be elected." The officer should not be replaced except by the President or Vice-President whose disability had

---

* The Twentieth Amendment avoids the officer problem in giving Congress the power to provide for the situation where neither President-elect nor Vice-President-elect have qualified by Inauguration Day. It states that Congress may declare what "person" shall then act as President. See p. 191n.

† See pp. 61–62, 145.

‡ To be noted here is that, after succeeding to the presidency, Johnson extended an invitation to Speaker McCormack to sit in on sessions of the National Security Council and "other key decision-making meetings" not "inconsistent with his legislative responsibilities." *The New York Times,* December 4, 1963, p. 24. His status as a member of Congress precluded him from receiving a Cabinet invitation. Then Presidential Press Secretary Pierre Salinger explained that the Cabinet "might be deciding on a foreign aid request which he as a member of Congress might have to vote on later. . . ."

ended or by a newly-elected President. Practical considerations which militate against this type of provision are that the presidency could be occupied by four different persons within a short period of time, and that the Cabinet officer temporarily serving as President would be considerably straitjacketed in exercising presidential power.

Most of the legal problems raised by the 1947 Act would not exist with a Cabinet line of succession. Cabinet officers are officers of the United States and if they retained their offices while acting as President, there would not be any separation of powers problem. A deputy could supervise the work of the department whose head might be serving as President. At the very least, Congress owes it to the American people to consider these legal problems and eliminate them.

22

Other Areas

Perhaps our present system is as good as can be achieved, but we should study it . . . to make sure.

A. S. MIKE MONRONEY

One area in which improvement may be needed is that concerning what happens if a presidential or vice-presidential candidate should die before election day or after election day but before January 20, Inauguration Day. The importance of this neglected subject was underscored when the life of the 1964 Republican presidential candidate, Barry Goldwater, was threatened during the campaign.

About certain aspects of this matter there is no question. If the incumbent President died or became disabled before the end of his term on January 20, the existing law on succession would be operative until the end of the term. If the President-elect died between January 6—when the electoral votes are counted—and Inauguration Day, the Vice-President-elect would become President on January 20 under section 3 of the Twentieth Amendment.* If the Vice-President-elect also had died before Inauguration Day, the present succession law, which provides for the possibility of there being

---

* It provides: "If, at the time fixed for the beginning of the term of the President, the President-elect shall have died, the Vice President-elect shall become President. If a President shall not have been chosen before the time fixed for the beginning of his term, or if the President-elect shall have failed to qualify, then the Vice President-elect shall act as President until a President shall have qualified; and the Congress may by law provide for the case wherein neither a President-elect not a Vice President-elect shall have qualified. . . ."

neither a President nor a Vice-President, would apply. However, the constitutionality of this provision in the 1947 law is not free from doubt. The Twentieth Amendment does not provide for the case where both the President-elect and Vice-President-elect have *died* before Inauguration Day and the succession provision of Article II, Section 1 only gives Congress the power to establish a line of succession to cover the cases where both a President and Vice-President have died, resigned, been removed, or become disabled. Hence, if the constitutional term of the President and Vice-President expires at noon on January 20 and the President-elect and Vice-President-elect have both died by that time, it would seem that Congress is without power to provide for the case, as the deaths of the President-elect and Vice-President-elect are not those of a President and Vice-President.* On the other hand it might be successfully argued that "failure to qualify" covers a number of possibilities, including death, so that Congress does have the power to so provide.

The death of a presidential or vice-presidential candidate before election day is not covered by law. Both national political parties, however, have adopted procedures to cover such an eventuality. The Democratic Party has a procedure under which the 108-member Democratic National Committee would assemble to fill the vacancy. The representatives of each state, territory, and district would have the same number of votes as their state, territory, or district had at the original nominating convention. The Republican Party has the same procedure, with an option given to the Republican National Committee to call a new convention.† Neither Party has ever had occasion to use its procedure with respect to a presidential nominee. The Republican Party procedure was used, however, in a situation involving the death of a vice-presidential nominee.‡ It is probable that if a presidential nominee died before the

---

* Section 3 of the Twentieth Amendment was inserted largely because of the belief that the succession provision gave Congress no power with respect to the death or failure to qualify of a President-elect or Vice-President-elect, or both. H. R. Rep. No. 345, 72nd Cong., 1st Sess. (1932).

† The procedure of the Democratic Party is provided for in that party's rules, while that of the Republican Party depends on a resolution being adopted at each national convention. Appendices F and G set forth in full the existing procedure of each party.

‡ This was when vice-presidential nominee James Sherman died in 1912. See p. 161. When Benjamin Fitzpatrick of Alabama who was nominated for

election, the vice-presidential nominee would be selected to fill the vacancy and some other person would be chosen as his running mate.* But there is no guarantee that this would be the case. While both national committees are similarly authorized to deal with a case of disability of a candidate, there are no definite procedures for declaring a candidate disabled.

The question, what would happen if a candidate died after the election, involves a brief consideration of the electoral college process. When the people cast their votes on election day, they do not vote directly for a presidential candidate but choose between slates of presidential electors. Each slate consists of persons nominated prior to the election by either state conventions of the political parties, or the state committees of the political parties, or state primaries, or the presidential nominee (Pennsylvania), or the governor upon the recommendation of the state executive committees of the political parties (Florida). In most of the states the names of the electors do not appear on the ballots, although it is usually understood that a slate is pledged to a particular candidate. The slate which wins the most popular votes in the state receives all the electoral votes of that state. (This is the same as the number of Senators and Representatives.) Nowhere in the Constitution is there any requirement that an elector vote in accordance with the voting in the national election in his state. Thus in 1956 W. F. Turner of Alabama voted for Judge Walter E. Jones for President instead of Adlai E. Stevenson and, in 1960 Henry D. Irwin of Oklahoma, a Republican elector, voted for Democratic Senator Harry F. Byrd of Virginia rather than Richard M. Nixon. Also in 1960, unpledged Democratic electors in Alabama voted for Senator Byrd notwithstanding the fact that John F. Kennedy carried the popular vote in that state.

If a presidential or vice-presidential candidate died after the election but before the electors of the respective states met in their state capitals on the first Monday after the second Wednesday in December to cast their votes,† the electors would be even more free to vote

---

Vice-President in 1860 declined the nomination after the convention had adjourned, the Democratic National Committee filled the vacancy, selecting Herschel V. Johnson of Georgia by unanimous vote.

* If it happened immediately before election day, Congress could change the date of the election.

† Congress has the power to change this date.

for anyone they pleased. Since the procedure adopted by each national political party would cover this contingency, a new candidate could be nominated by the appropriate national committee. This nomination, it seems likely, would be honored by the electors so that if they would have voted for the dead candidate, they would probably now vote for the new nominee. If the presidential nominee had died, the people would likely insist that the vice-presidential nominee be chosen to fill the vacancy and another chosen to fill his position. There are no precedents, however, by which the country can be guided in this area.*

The area of greatest uncertainty, it is frequently said, is the time between the meeting of the electoral college and January 6, when the electoral votes are opened, announced and counted before a joint session of Congress. The death of a presidential candidate in this period would raise the question as to whether votes for a dead man could be counted. Some argue that the votes could not be counted so that if the dead man were the winner and his votes were deducted from the total, no one would have a majority and the election would fall into the House of Representatives, each state having one vote. Others believe that Congress could reconvene the electoral college so that the electors could change their votes. Still others say that Congress could make the vice-presidential winner the President-elect.[1]†

It is suggested that the correct approach is that the dead man, if the winner, could be declared President-elect and, under the Twentieth Amendment, the Vice-President-elect would become President on January 20. The Twelfth Amendment provides that:

The Electors shall . . . name in their ballots the person voted for as President, and in distinct ballots the person voted for as Vice-President, and they shall make distinct lists of all persons voted for as President, and of all persons voted for as Vice-President, and of the number of votes for each, which lists they shall sign and certify, and transmit sealed to the seat of the government of the United States, directed to the President of the Senate;—The President of the Senate shall, in the presence of the Senate and House of Representatives, open all the

---

* See p. 140n., dealing with the situation surrounding Horace Greeley's death after his unsuccessful race for the presidency in 1872.

† Some of those who argue along these lines believe that Senate confirmation of the House's action in selecting a President in this case would be desirable to prevent a successful attack on the results.

certificates and the votes shall then be counted;—The person having the greatest number of votes for President, shall be the President, if such number be a majority of the whole number of Electors appointed. . . .

This amendment gives Congress no choice but to count all ballots provided the "person" voted for was alive at the time they were cast. Congress has no discretion in the matter.

This view is partly supported by what happened in 1873 when Congress was proceeding to count three votes cast for Horace Greeley, who had died after the election but before the electoral college met. The question was raised as to whether the votes could be counted. Senator George F. Hoar of Massachusetts and others argued that Greeley, having died, was not a person within the meaning of the Constitution at the time the votes were cast. Consequently, the votes were void. The Senate, however, concluded that they could be counted but the House of Representatives, by a vote of 101 to 99 (with 40 members absent) said that they could not. The lack of a concurrence of both Houses resulted in the votes not being counted.[2] The decisive fact in the House was that Greeley was not alive when the votes had been cast and, therefore, was not a person within the meaning of the Constitution at that time.

It would seem to follow that so long as a person is alive at the time the electoral votes are cast, then his votes must be counted and, if they be a majority, he becomes the President-elect, whether he is dead or alive. The same line of reasoning would support the argument that a person could be declared Vice-President-elect even if he had died between the casting of the electoral votes and the counting of them. There being no provision at present to fill a vice-presidential vacancy, the office would remain vacant.

Another area of uncertainty is, what would happen if an election for President fell into the House of Representatives because no candidate had received a majority of the electoral votes. Under the Twelfth Amendment, the House is to choose a President from the persons having the highest numbers, not exceeding three, of votes for President. If one of those persons died before the House voted, there would be no procedure for filling the vacancy.* The same problem would exist if the election of a Vice-President fell into the Senate and one of the persons having the two highest numbers of

---

* The dead candidate, of course, would not be a person within the meaning of the Constitution at the time the House voted.

274

votes died. Although neither of these problems has ever been solved, Congress has the power to resolve them under Section 4 of the Twentieth Amendment.* Perhaps Congress would permit the national committee of the party affected by the death to recommend a substitute. The matter obviously needs to be examined.

Adding to the Line of Succession

It is suggested that, aside from the recommendations made in the preceding chapter, the line of succession could be improved by increasing its length. It is conceivable that, since all of those persons who are presently in the line of succession spend much time in Washington, D.C., the whole line could be wiped out in a nuclear attack on that city. Hence, in view of this possibility, it would be advisable for Congress to give some consideration to extending the line of succession to persons in widely separated parts of the country. One possibility might be to include the governors of the states in the order of size according to population at the last census. Another possibility would be to include members of the Armed Forces such as the Joint Chiefs of Staff. This would have the advantage of providing military organization at a time of disaster, but the former proposal would be more democratic since the persons involved would be elected officials. There are, undoubtedly, numerous other ways of covering the possibility of a disaster resulting from a nuclear attack. In view of the times, it would be unwise for Congress to continue to leave this area unexplored.

The Vice-Presidency

While the vice-presidency has finally emerged as a vital part of the governmental structure, it is still not above improvement. The practice of selecting vice-presidential candidates on the basis of political considerations rather than their qualifications for the presidency persists, despite some recent exceptions to the rule. From time to time various suggestions have been made with a view to insuring

---

* This section provides: "The Congress may by law provide for the case of the death of any of the persons from whom the House of Representatives may choose a President whenever the right of choice shall have devolved upon them, and for the case of the death of any of the persons from whom the Senate may choose a Vice-President whenever the right of choice shall have devolved upon them."

that the nation's second office be filled with a person of presidential timber.

The subcommittee on Constitutional Amendments of the Senate Judiciary Committee has given much attention to proposals for selection of presidential and vice-presidential candidates on the basis of nationwide primaries. Former President Truman expressed the opinion that nationwide primaries would be an expensive proposition and would therefore deter capable men from seeking these positions. Vice-President Barkley, on the other hand, said that the expense could probably be borne by candidates' committees.[3] Another proposal for placing men of prominence in the vice-presidency is to have the vice-presidential candidate selected before the presidential candidate. This proposal might, it seems, discourage qualified persons from seeking the nomination as they might prefer to wait and try to obtain the presidential nomination. A more serious objection is that it would permit the selection of a candidate whose views and personality might be incompatible with those of the presidential candidate. As former President Eisenhower stated:

[I]t seems obvious to me that unless the man as chosen were acceptable to the presidential nominee, the presidential nominee should immediately step aside, because we have a Government in this day and time when teamwork is so important, where abrupt changes could make so much difference. If a President later is suddenly disabled or killed or dies, it would be fatal, in my opinion, if you had a tense period on, not only to introduce now a man of an entirely different philosophy of government, but he, in turn, would necessarily then get an entirely new Cabinet. I think you would have chaos for a while.[4]

Other suggestions are that a secret ballot be used for nomination of a Vice-President, or that the presidential candidate either indicate several persons whom he would like to have on his ticket and then leave it to the convention to decide among them, or express no preference at all and let the convention decide (as was done in 1956 by Adlai Stevenson).[5] It has also been suggested that slates of presidential and vice-presidential candidates be presented to the convention, or that the vice-presidential candidate be the one who has received the second highest number of votes in the balloting for the presidential nominee. On balance, it would seem that if future presidential candidates employ the principles that President Johnson used in the selection of Vice-President Humphrey, future Vice-

Presidents will be qualified persons. In announcing his recommendation for Vice-President at the 1964 Democratic Convention, Johnson stated:

I have reached . . . [my decision] after consultation with the leaders of the Democratic party in every section of this nation and at every level of our Government.
I have reached it after discussion with outstanding Americans in every area of our national life.
I have reached it after long and prayerful private thought. . . . All of this has had a single guide, to find a man best qualified to assume the office of President of the United States, should that day come.[6]

Another area of possible reform is in the Vice-President's workload. While an enumeration of the President's constitutional and statutory powers and duties would literally fill reams of paper, those of the Vice-President can be briefly catalogued. In addition to being the potential presidential successor and the presiding officer of the Senate,* the Vice-President is a member of the National Security Council, chairman of the National Aeronautics Space Council, and a member of the Board of Directors of the Smithsonian Institution (its presiding officer in the absence of the President). He has the power to nominate a limited number of persons for appointment to the various military service academies, and to administer oaths to executive officials. He is chairman of the Advisory Council of the Peace Corps. He is, by recent custom, a member of the President's Cabinet. As Vice-President, Johnson was chairman of the Advisory Council of the Peace Corps and chairman of the Committee on Equal Employment Opportunity. His salary is $43,000 a year, plus an expense allowance of $10,000 a year. He commands a small staff, is assigned a few Secret Service agents, and has offices in the Capitol, the Senate office building and the executive office building. He may soon have an official residence.[7]

The question of how to make the vice-presidency a full time job has been raised time and again throughout history.[8] As far back as

---

* In his role as President of the Senate, history has shown that the Vice-President seldom presides over the Senate, that Presidents pro tempore seldom preside, and that the job of presiding is frequently given to junior Senators. As presiding officer, the Vice-President's power of appointment to committees is practically negligible, his rulings are subject to appeal to the Senate, he has no right to participate in the debates, and he has no power to decide disputed questions regarding the certificates of the presidential electors.

1789, Fisher Ames suggested that the Vice-President do research work in all phases of the government and then make it available to the administration. In 1868, Representative Thomas Allen Jenckes of Rhode Island proposed the creation of a department of civil service headed by the Vice-President. In 1896, Walter Clark recommended that the Vice-President be made ex-officio head of a new Department of Interstate Commerce, and that he also be made a member of the Cabinet, with authority to preside in the President's absence. In the same year, Theodore Roosevelt suggested that the Vice-President be given, in his role as President of the Senate, a vote on "ordinary occasions," a "voice in the debates" of the Senate, and the power to appoint committees of the Senate. In 1909 Senator Albert J. Beveridge of Indiana, in an article entitled "The Fifth Wheel in Our Government," favored abolition of the office but, if that were not possible, he thought its occupant should be made a member of the Cabinet and be given the power to appoint committees.[9]

In 1920, Franklin D. Roosevelt proposed that the Vice-President should be used as a liaison officer to Congress. Even as the work of the Vice-President increased during the years 1932–1952, there remained those who thought the office should be abolished. In 1947, Lucius Wilmerding, an outstanding constitutional authority, wrote that the reasons for creating the office were frustrated by the Twelfth Amendment and that, therefore, it should be abolished.[10] He added that if the President were to die, be removed, or resign during the first two years of his term, the Secretary of State could act as President until the holding of the mid-term elections, when the vacancy would be filled.

During the 1950s the office of Vice-President received some attention by the Hoover Commission. The Commission, suggesting no change in the office itself, recommended the establishment, by statute, of an administrative Vice-President who would be nominated by the President and confirmed by the Senate. He would serve at the pleasure of the President and his function would be to ease the burden on the President by relieving him of many routine duties. Several authorities opposed this on the ground that it might create a "plural executive." Others said such an office would considerably weaken the constitutional office of Vice-President.

During the 1956 Senate hearings on the Hoover proposal Clark Clifford, an assistant to former President Truman, said that the

Vice-President could truly become the second officer in the government if he were strictly an executive officer.[11] This, he recognized, would require a constitutional amendment but only by becoming a "day-by-day working assistant to the President," said Clifford, would the Vice-President really be prepared for the presidency. The administrative Vice-President proposal faded away when presidential assistant Sherman Adams said in a letter to the then Senator John F. Kennedy, chairman of the committee investigating the proposal, that the experience of the Eisenhower administration had "not brought to light situations requiring the services of an Administrative Vice-President." A more recent suggestion by Herman Finer, author of several books on the presidency, is that the vice-presidency be expanded to include eleven men. The President and Vice-Presidents would be elected together. This expansion, said Finer, would be the best way to achieve efficiency and responsibility in the executive branch.[12]

It is doubtful that there will be any formal changes in the office of Vice-President in the immediate future. It seems more likely that the Vice-President's work and importance will continue to depend almost totally on the President. The nation can little afford to have a Vice-President who is not an informed, consulted and working member of the government, adequately trained to assume the responsibilities of the presidency should the occasion require it. The history of the last few years bodes well for the future of the vice-presidency. President Johnson has, as earlier noted, indicated his desire to increase the role of the Vice-President in Congress and in the affairs of the executive. After their election in November, 1964, Vice-President-elect Humphrey was President Johnson's first official visitor at his ranch in Texas. Shortly thereafter, Humphrey was consulted when policy decisions were being made regarding the activities of the United States in Vietnam. At a press conference of November 28, 1964, Johnson stated that he intended to "engage . . . [Humphrey's] counsel and his years of experience in connection with the budget . . . ," to invite him to act as a liaison between the legislative and executive "in trying to help formulate our program . . . ," and to call upon him often to undertake "particular assignments."[13]

IV. OTHER SYSTEMS

23

Succession in the States

Governments . . . have to keep going in good times and in bad. They therefore need a wide margin of safety.

CALVIN COOLIDGE

The Constitution of every state in the country has a provision on succession to the office of its chief executive—the Governor.* Thirty-eight states have a Lieutenant Governor who stands first in the line of succession. Eight states have a President of the Senate elected by the Senate as the immediate successor to the Governor, and in four states a Secretary of State elected by the people is next in line. Of those states having a Lieutenant Governor, twenty place the President pro tempore of the Senate and the Speaker of the House or Assembly, respectively, next in line; two, the Speaker and President pro tempore; five, the President pro tempore (the Speaker is not included in the line at all); two, the Speaker (the President pro tempore is not included in the line); seven, the Secretary of State (in five the President pro tempore and Speaker are somewhere in the line); one, the Attorney General (followed by the Speaker and President pro tempore). One state has only a Lieutenant Governor in the line. In the eight states where the President of the Senate is the immediate successor, the Speaker is next in line. In two of the

---

* Appendix H contains a chart which shows the alignment of the fifty states on various matters discussed in this chapter.

283

four states where the Secretary of State is first, he is followed by the President of the Senate in one and by the President of the Senate and Speaker, respectively, in both states. In all, thirty-eight states include the President pro tempore (or president) of the Senate and the Speaker in their chain of succession. Seven include one but not both of these officials. In five states neither a President pro tempore (or president) nor Speaker is in the line.

The ever present possibility of nuclear attack has prompted a number of states to extend on their constitutional succession provisions by passing so-called disaster acts. In fact, many states have enacted laws dealing not only with executive but also legislative and judicial succession and changing the seat of government, all designed to meet "an enemy attack of unprecedented destructiveness, which may result in the death or inability to act of a large proportion of the elected officials of the government of the state and the political subdivisions. . . ."[1]

Some of the disaster acts on gubernatorial succession make interesting additions to the constitutional line of succession. Thus, the Florida Disaster Act adds the Superintendent of Public Instruction and the Commissioner of Agriculture to the line of succession. In Kansas, the Chancellor of the University of Kansas and the President of Kansas State University of Agriculture and Applied Science are placed in the line. North Dakota has added former Governors of the state (provided they are not in Congress), starting with the most recent. This is also the case in Virginia and West Virginia. Virginia, moreover, extends the line of succession to the Chief Judge of the Supreme Court of Appeals, and then the Senior Judge of a Court of Record. In Montana, "the chairman of the board of county commissioners of the state's most populous county, as determined by the last preceding official United States census" is placed in the line, and in Oklahoma the members of the state highway commission are given places. The Michigan law requires the Governor, within thirty days of his inauguration, to designate three successors, "taking into consideration the safety factors to be gained by the geographical dispersion of appointments." Nebraska, the only state in the country having a unicameral legislature, has succession running to the chairmen of fourteen legislative committees.

The typical state succession provision lists as contingencies death, resignation, removal, absence from the state, impeachment and inability.* Whenever one of these contingencies occurs, the Lieutenant Governor, Secretary of State, or President of the Senate, as the case may be, takes up the reins of government. In most states he does not become Governor but, retaining his own office, serves as acting Governor for the rest of the term, in cases of death, resignation and removal, or temporarily, in cases of inability, impeachment and absence.†

The operation of the state succession provisions has not been uniform in a number of areas. In some states the mere absence of the Governor from the state devolves the powers and duties of the office upon his successor. In other states the absence must be of some duration and prejudicial to the public interest before the successor can act. Some states require the successor to take the Governor's oath before he can act as Governor. Other states do not. Some states provide that the successor, while acting as Governor, is to be paid at the rate of pay applicable to the Governor. Other states deny him the increase on the ground that succession is one of his duties. In states without any Governor-elect provisions, some provide that if the Governor-elect has not qualified by the time set for the beginning of his term, the incumbent continues as Governor. Others turn the government over to the Lieutenant-Governor-elect. Some states provide for the filling of a vacancy in the office of Lieutenant Governor. Most do not. Some states require a special election when vacancies occur in the offices of both Governor and Lieutenant Governor.

In only a handful of states are the Governor and Lieutenant Governor voted for together—Connecticut, Hawaii, Michigan, New Mexico, New York and North Dakota. It is, therefore, not surprising that Governors are at times reluctant to leave their states. Lieutenant Governor Harry Lee Waterfield of Kentucky pointed this up at a 1964 National Conference of Lieutenant Governors.

In noting that a state's top elective officers were not always so closely in tune, he recalled that a governor of Oklahoma once had been forced to decline to speak in Kentucky "only twenty miles across the border" [sic]

---

* The failure to qualify contingency is frequently found in a separate provision.

† An interesting exception is Oregon where, in *Chadwick* v. *Earhart*, 11 Ore. 389 (1884), the court held that the expression "the same" in the state constitution referred to "the office," so that the Secretary of State became Governor upon the Governor's resignation.

because he did not dare leave his lieutenant governor in command during his absence. The legislature had before it a stack of bills that the governor had vowed to veto and he knew that once his back was turned they would be passed and signed by his elected deputy, a political foe.[2]

The office of Lieutenant Governor has been the object of the same kind of criticism as that directed at the vice-presidency. Various reforms have been considered and appear to be necessary if the office is to become to the state what the vice-presidency has become to the United States.

Gubernatorial Inability

In only a few states are there any definite procedures for determining a Governor's inability. This critical deficiency in the state succession laws has been brought to light more than once.

In 1890, Governor David H. Goodell of New Hampshire became ill and acknowledged that he was unable to discharge the powers and duties of his office. He sought to get David A. Taggart, the President of the Senate, who was next in line, to act in his place, but he was reluctant to act because of the lack of any definite procedure.* He then wrote a letter to Attorney General Daniel Barnard, requesting that he do whatever was necessary to have the President of the Senate assume his power while he was ill, stating: "I am not able to perform the duties of the office, and the public service should not suffer from my inability." The Attorney General filed a petition with the State Supreme Court for an order directing the president of the senate to act. The court held a hearing at which testimony was given that the Governor was sick, that his illness might last a few weeks or months, and that there were several governmental matters requiring immediate attention. The court concluded, seventeen days after the Attorney General had filed his petition, that the President of the Senate should be ordered to serve as Governor during the Governor's inability. He did so, and the Governor later recovered from his illness and resumed his powers and duties, without resorting to the court.[3]

---

* The New Hampshire Constitution provided that the president of the senate exercise the "powers and authorities" of the governor whenever his chair was vacant "by reason of his death, absence from the state, or otherwise."

286

In the course of its opinion the New Hampshire court expressed the view that there might be cases in which the Attorney General would ask for a similar order in the absence of a request by the Governor. The court noted that a determination was not legally required before the President of the Senate could act, but that it would avoid controversy regarding his authority and the validity of his acts.* "The existence of an executive vacancy," said the court, "is a question of law and fact within the judicial jurisdiction. . . . [T]he consideration and decision of such a question may be prospective as well as retrospective."[4]

The difficulty of removing a Governor who refuses to acknowledge his own inability becomes evident upon an examination of what occurred in Illinois in the years between 1938 and 1940.[5] In November, 1938, Governor Henry Horner of Illinois sustained a heart attack and went to Florida to convalesce. During his absence of almost five months, Lieutenant Governor Stelle acted as Governor pursuant to the constitutional provision that the powers and duties of Governor devolve on the Lieutenant Governor when the Governor is absent from the state.† Horner returned in April, 1938, and Stelle stopped serving as Governor.

In the following months Horner spent most of his time at the executive mansion and was seldom seen. Rumors arose that he was incapable of discharging the powers and duties of his office and that his close friends were actually administering the government. Lieutenant Governor Stelle was urged to assume the powers and duties of Governor. It was argued that he had authority to act under the state constitution, since it provided that the powers and duties of Governor devolve upon the Lieutenant Governor in a case of disability. The Lieutenant Governor's position became more difficult when reports were issued from the Governor's mansion to the effect that the Governor was able and was, indeed, performing his duties. The mat-

---

* However, in *Wrede v. Richardson,* 77 Ohio St. 182, 82 N.E. 1072 (1907) the Supreme Court of Ohio noted that "a self-contained lieutenant governor could not be expected to assume the functions of the governor upon his own initiative."

† The succession provision of the Illinois constitution provided that: "In case of the death, conviction on impeachment, failure to qualify, resignation, absence from the state, or other disability of the governor, the powers, duties and emoluments of the office, for the residue of the term, or until the disability shall be removed, shall devolve upon the lieutenant governor."

ter reached a crescendo before the primary election of April, 1940. Suggestions were made that a committee of clergymen and physicians be appointed to examine him, that legal proceedings be instituted to try his right to continue as Governor, and that his salary be withheld in order to force him into court where the issue could be resolved.

Lieutenant Governor Stelle decided to take matters into his own hands. On April 8, 1940, he stated that he was acting Governor. He proclaimed a special session of the General Assembly for the same day as had the Governor two days before on the ground that the Governor was disabled and therefore his call was of no effect. At this point, the Secretary of State, the Attorney General and others supported the Governor and refused to recognize the actions of the Lieutenant Governor.

When the General Assembly met on April 30, each house appointed a committee to inform the Governor that the legislature was in session. Stelle presided at the opening session of the Senate. Since this was a function of the Lieutenant Governor, he thus indicated that he had relinquished his claim to be acting Governor.

Meanwhile, a suit had been commenced by a resident of Chicago against both Horner and Stelle to obtain an order directing the Lieutenant Governor to act as Governor. The Attorney General moved to dismiss the proceeding on the grounds that the petition did not allege facts showing that the Governor was disabled and that the suit was brought in the wrong county. He purported to represent Stelle but the Lieutenant Governor rejected his services and requested the court to decide the question of the Governor's disability. The court, however, agreed with the Attorney General and dismissed the proceeding on the ground that it had no jurisdiction since the Governor was a resident of another county.

This dismal state of affairs continued until October 4, when the Governor's secretary filed a certificate with the Secretary of State, declaring that the Governor was unable to discharge his powers and duties. Two days later Horner was dead.

The case of Governor Earl K. Long of Louisiana is also in point.[6] On May 26, 1959, Long was rebuked for shouting and using profanity at a committee hearing in the Louisiana House of Representatives. Three days later, after a similar outburst, he was ordered to bed by his physicians for an extended rest. He was suffering from "complete physical exhaustion," said his wife. On the following day, with the assistance of Dr. Arthur Long, the Governor's cousin, Mrs. Long drugged the Governor and took him in a plane belonging to the Louisiana National Guard to Texas, where he was placed under psychiatric care at the John Sealy Hospital in Galveston. It was explained that the reason for taking him out of the State was that, under Louisiana law a Governor cannot be committed to a mental hospital against his will while in the state. Said Long's nephew, Senator Russell B. Long, "If he was to be spared the duties of his office while he received the necessary rest and treatment, it was necessary for him to leave the State."[7] Attorney General Jack P. F. Gremillion was quoted as saying that a Louisiana Governor could not be declared mentally incompetent unless he were first impeached and reduced to the status of a private citizen.[8]

On June 2, Judge Hugh Gibson of Texas granted a petition filed by Mrs. Long and Dr. Long requesting that the Governor be ordered held in protective custody. With the petition was filed a statement by Dr. Titus Harris, Chairman of the Department of Neurology and Psychiatry of the Medical College of the University of Texas, saying that the Governor was mentally ill and likely to cause injury to himself or others. Under Texas law the court order would be effective for fourteen days at the end of which a sanity hearing would have to be held to determine whether he could be detained longer.

On June 12, Long applied for a writ of habeas corpus, charging that he had been taken to Sealy Hospital by force. Two days later, he stated that his wife had joined his political associates in a conspiracy to kidnap him. He said that his nephew and the Lieutenant Governor were among those conspiring to put him away, with a view to furthering their own political ambitions. On June 15, the habeas corpus hearing was held, but the decision was postponed for a week. The sanity hearing scheduled for the following day was also postponed.

On June 17, after signing an agreement to submit to treatment in Louisiana, Long was released by court order from the Texas hospital and entered Ochsner Foundation Hospital in New Orleans. The next day he left the hospital and, while heading by car for Baton Rouge, was intercepted by state police. Under the authority of a new court order, they took him to the Southeast Louisiana Hospital (a mental hospital) and committed him. The order, granted at the request of Mrs. Long, was to remain in effect until the hospital superintendent deemed Long well enough to be released. A hospital psychiatrist reported that the Governor was suffering from "paranoid schizophrenia with manic-depressive tendencies."[9]

In the meantime, Lieutenant Governor Lether Frazar, who had assumed Long's powers and duties after Long had been taken to Texas, said that he would not "presume [to continue as acting Governor] while Long is in the State until I have been notified that the Governor is unable to carry out the duties of his office."[10] It made no difference to him that the Governor was in a mental hospital. Attorney General Jack Gremillion delivered an opinion that: "The constitution is very clear that if the Governor is unable to serve for any cause, the Lieutenant Governor acts as Governor ad interim until the disability is removed. The question of Long's inability to serve was answered by the court yesterday when it ordered him to Southeast Louisiana Hospital."*[11]

Despite the opinion, Frazar remained reluctant to take over as acting Governor. Said he: "Never before has a man taken over as Governor when the Governor was in the State. That's what baffles me."[12] The Secretary of State, Wade O. Martin, openly disputed the opinion. Some official body, he said, or Mr. Long, himself, must declare the Governor's inability to act. The difficult question was: What body had the authority to declare the Governor incapacitated? By June 22, the Lieutenant Governor still had not assumed any of the Governor's duties. On June 23, despite urging from some of the Governor's top political aides that he become acting Governor, Frazar was still firm in his refusal "to incur the Governor's wrath by taking control of state affairs."[13]

On June 25, Long filed for a separation from his wife in order to prevent her from attempting to have him recommitted once he obtained his discharge. Then, the following day, with the concurrence of the Lieutenant Governor and the President pro tempore of the

---

* Article V, section 6 of the Louisiana Constitution provides: "In case of vacancy in the office of Governor, the order of succession shall be: first, the Lieutenant Governor. . . . In case of the inability of the Governor to act as such by reason of his absence from the State or for other cause, all the powers and duties of his office shall devolve upon the officers in the order named above, and such officer shall act as Governor ad interim until the inability be removed."

State Senate, he fired the superintendent of the hospital, the director of the state department of hospitals, and the chief of the state police. The hospital superintendent was replaced by a political friend who promptly declared Long "sane." Long was then freed, and the court hearing scheduled for that day to inquire into whether he had been legally committed was dismissed as being academic. The episode thus came to an end. Said *The New York Times* of June 28, 1959:

> The moral of what has been happening in Louisiana in the past few days seems to be that a patient in a mental hospital who wishes to obtain his release should first get himself elected Governor. This procedure was successfully followed by Gov. Earl K. Long, who became . . . a free man by discharging the superintendent of the Southeast Louisiana Hospital. For good measure, he also discharged the director of the state department of hospitals and the head of the state police.
>
> Thus vindicated and cured to the extent that these objectives could be obtained by the exercise of executive authority, the Governor walked out. . . .

On June 29, three physicians stated that Governor Long was now "rational with no intellectual impairment." They said that a lengthy examination begun before his release showed that his "nervous breakdown" had been caused by one or more strokes. This statement, released after approval by the Governor, contradicted the findings of the psychiatrist at Southeast Louisiana Hospital.

Other examples of gubernatorial inability can be cited.* Yet, only a few states have written into their laws provisions to deal with a case of such inability. These are Alabama, Michigan, Mississippi, New Jersey, Nebraska and Oregon.

The Alabama constitution sets forth a procedure by which any

---

* For example, in a 1961 letter of Governor Farris Bryant of Florida to Don H. Sherwood, then Editor-in-Chief of the Nebraska Law Review, a copy of which was sent to the author by James W. Kynes, Attorney General of Florida, it is stated that: "[T]here is no authority set up at this time to determine who shall decide when a Governor is unable to discharge his official duties. A situation arose in Florida during the administration of the Honorable Dan McCarty when due to serious illness he was unable to personally carry out the functions of the Governor's Office and in fact his brother attended to many of these duties for him. Nonetheless, he did continue to hold the position of Governor until his death at which time the President of the Senate succeeded to the Office."

two officers in the line of succession, except the one next in line, who believe the Governor or Acting Governor to be of unsound mind, may petition the State Supreme Court for a determination.*[14] If the court determines that the Governor is of unsound mind, it will enter a decree to that effect, filed in the office of the Secretary of State. The officer next in line then performs the duties of the office until the Governor recovers. If there is a dispute as to whether the Governor has recovered, the State Supreme Court, at the request of any one officer in the line of succession, must "ascertain the truth" and render a decree. In such case the Governor does not resume his powers and duties until the court so decrees.

The new Michigan constitution provides that the inability of the Governor is to be determined by a majority of the Supreme Court on the joint request of the President pro tempore of the Senate and the Speaker of the House of Representatives, both of whom are not in the line of succession.[15] "Such determination shall be final and conclusive." Once an inability is found to exist, the Lieutenant Governor exercises the powers and duties of the office until the Supreme Court determines upon its own initiative that the inability has ended.

In Mississippi, the constitution refers to "protracted illness" as a disability and provides that if there is any doubt as to whether a vacancy has occurred or a disability exists or has ended, the Secretary of State shall submit the question to the State Supreme Court.[16] The court, or a majority thereof, must investigate and render an opinion to the Secretary of State which opinion is "final and conclusive."

A different kind of procedure is to be found in New Jersey. Its constitution provides that the office of Governor shall be deemed vacant if the Governor has been unable to perform his duties for a period of six months "by reason of mental or physical disability."[17] A procedure for determining the existence of a vacancy is prescribed. The State Supreme Court shall decide the matter upon: (1) presentment to it of a concurrent resolution declaring the grounds of vacancy, adopted by two-thirds of the members of both

---

* The line includes, in the order in which they are named, the lieutenant governor, president pro tempore, speaker, attorney general, auditor, secretary of state and treasurer.

houses of the legislature, and (2) notice, a hearing before the court and proof that the vacancy exists.*

Two states—Nebraska[18] and Oregon[19]—because of concern about what would happen in a case of gubernatorial inability, recently established inability boards. Both boards are composed of the Chief Justice of the state's highest court, the dean of the state's medical school, and a leading medical official of the state. Each board is given the responsibility of determining the beginning and ending of an inability. Decisions must be unanimous. Both boards are directed to examine the Governor, but if this is not possible "because of circumstances beyond their control, they shall conduct a secret ballot and by unanimous vote may find that the Governor is temporarily unable. . . ." The Nebraska law provides in addition that the Governor can petition the State Supreme Court to review the board's decision. In the interim, however, his successor would act as Governor.

The constitutions of the remaining states are silent on the question of determining a Governor's inability. A revision of the Florida Constitution of 1957, which failed of adoption, contained a well-thought-out provision on the matter which should be mentioned. Incapacity of the Governor would be determined by the State Supreme Court only after four members of the Governor's cabinet (of which the Lieutenant Governor was not a member) sent a written suggestion to the court. Restoration of capacity would also be determined by the Supreme Court after the docketing of a written suggestion thereof by the Governor himself, the legislature or four members of the cabinet. The revision empowered the Governor to declare his own physical incapacity and in such a case the cessation thereof by filing a certificate with the Secretary of State.

---

* The Alaska constitution provides that if the Governor has been unable to perform his duties as Governor for a period of six months "by reason of mental or physical disability," his office shall be deemed vacant. Although the constitution allows the legislature to provide for disability, no law has yet been passed. The Attorney General of Alaska is presently working on developing a workable and acceptable law. A provision similar to that found in the constitution of Alaska is under consideration by the Constitutional Revision Commission and the legislature of New Mexico.

24

Succession in Foreign Countries

The principal foundation of all states is in good laws. . . .

MACHIAVELLI

About fifty-five percent of the nations of the world give the title "President" to their chief executive. Approximately one half of these nations provide for the direct election of the President, while others provide for his election by an electoral college or appointment by the legislature. In many of the countries where there is a President, he is little more than a figurehead. In some, however, he is an active leader, particularly in Latin America and Africa.

Approximately thirty percent of the nations of the world have a royal personage as chief executive. In these countries the Prime Minister is usually the most powerful figure in the government, which is frequently the case in many systems having titular Presidents. Some nations (e.g., Poland, Soviet Union, Switzerland and Uruguay) give executive authority to a council.

The workings of executive succession in the countries of the world can best be illustrated by an examination of recent events in several of them and by a general treatment of the various succession provisions.*

---

* The constitutional provisions are examined despite the fact that some countries may be under military rule or otherwise not adhering to their constitutions. Since the constitutions generally represent what the framers considered to be ideal, they merit examination.

Succession in Foreign Countries

Great Britain

The nominal head of the government of Great Britain is the Queen and succession is hereditary within the royal family. Executive power is, however, actually in the hands of the Prime Minister and the cabinet. The Prime Minister is the leader of the majority party in the House of Commons. He is nominated by his party for the position and subsequently appointed by the Queen. Cabinet ministers are nominated by the Prime Minister and similarly appointed by the Queen. The Prime Minister is chairman of the cabinet, whose members are almost always members of Parliament and remain so while serving in the cabinet.

In the event a Prime Minister dies in office, there is no provision in law for a substitute to act until a new Prime Minister is appointed.* The cabinet would probably select one of its leaders to act as Prime Minister until the majority party nominated someone for the position. What might happen when a Prime Minister becomes disabled is indicated by what took place in 1963.

On October 8, 1963, Prime Minister Harold Macmillan, after presiding at a three-hour meeting of the cabinet, was rushed to a hospital in London for an operation to relieve a prostatic obstruction. The announcement which made the illness public said that he probably would be away from his duties "for some weeks." As a result, there was much speculation that he might retire. Deputy Prime Minister R. A. Butler, whom Macmillan had named to take charge of the Government ad interim, began to be spoken of as a likely successor.

On October 9, the day before the sixty-nine-year-old Prime Min-

---

* During the Second World War Anthony Eden held the position of deputy prime minister in the all-party coalition government headed by Prime Minister Winston Churchill. In early 1945, prior to the departure of both Churchill and Eden for Yalta, King George VI asked Churchill for his views as to a successor should he and Eden meet death abroad. In a letter of January 28, 1945 to the King, Churchill recommended Sir John Anderson, a dedicated civil servant who, as an independent was not a member of the Conservative Party which held a majority in the House of Commons. Under ordinary circumstances, said Churchill, he would have suggested a Conservative. Under the circumstances then existing, he said, Anderson was the person best qualified to continue the coalition government. Wheeler-Bennett, *John Anderson* (New York, 1962), pp. 315–16.

ister was scheduled to undergo a prostatectomy, the Conservative Party's annual conference opened at Blackpool. General agreement manifested itself that, in view of recent developments, a new leader must be found. But there was no consensus as to who the leader should be.

On October 10, six hours after Macmillan's operation, a letter announcing his decision to retire was read to the Conservative Party conference by the Earl of Home, who was Foreign Secretary and president of the conference. The decision was apparently made in view of the impossibility of carrying "the physical burden of leading the party" due to the necessity of "a considerable period of convalescence."[1] No date was mentioned for the resignation since that would depend on when a successor could be agreed upon.

On October 14, Queen Elizabeth returned from a vacation at Balmoral to await the development of unanimity within the party before seeking the advice of her ministers and others as to whom she should ask to form a new government. On the same day and during the next two, Macmillan held several conferences in his hospital room with the various contenders,* cabinet ministers and party leaders in an effort to settle upon a successor. These consultations were reported to be the most extensive in Conservative Party history. Finally, on October 17, Macmillan decided to recommend the Earl of Home to the Queen as his successor.† He submitted his letter of resignation to the Queen the next day, and she proceeded at once to his bedside to accept the resignation and receive his recommendation. Subsequently, the Queen summoned Lord Home for an audience, at which she requested him to be the next Prime Minister. Home accepted the invitation to attempt to form a government. According to the unwritten British constitution, he thereby became head of the government even though he had not yet been appointed Prime Minister.[2] On October 19, having succeeded in obtaining the support of his party and forming a cabinet, Home accepted appointment as Prime Minister and First Lord of the Treasury. He thus be-

---

* Among these were Butler, Viscount Hailsham, leader of the House of Lords and Minister of Science, Lord Home and Reginald Maudling, Chancellor of the Exchequer.

† Home later recommended to his party that it change its traditional semi-secret method of choosing a party leader in favor of a more democratic method. *The New York Times,* November 30, 1964, p. 4.

came the first peer since 1902 to receive this appointment.* The members of his cabinet were announced on the following day, and among them were all the major contenders for the post of Prime Minister.

Unlike that of a Prime Minister, a case of disability of a sovereign is specifically provided for in the Regency Act of 1937;† a commission, consisting of the spouse of the sovereign, the Lord Chancellor, the speaker of the House of Commons, the Lord Chief Justice of England and the Master of the Rolls, may declare in writing that the sovereign is "by reason of infirmity of mind or body" incapable of performing the royal functions.[3] Any three may so declare but the finding must include evidence furnished by physicians. Until it is declared in like manner that "His Majesty has so far recovered His health as to warrant His resumption of the royal functions . . . ," a Regent shall act in his place. In less serious situations (e.g., absence from the country), the sovereign is permitted to make partial delegations of power to counsellors of state, which include the spouse of the sovereign, if any, and the four persons next in line of succession to the Crown. These delegations may be revoked or varied in like manner.

France

On September 28, 1958, the French people adopted by referendum a constitution which shifted the weight of influence from the National Assembly to a President. General Charles de Gaulle became the first President of the Fifth French Republic. The new constitution prescribed a seven-year-term for the President and empowered him to appoint a premier and a council of ministers. The President was originally elected by the representatives of the people. By a referendum of October, 1962, the method was changed to direct election by the people.

Succession to the presidency of France is provided for in Article 7, which states that if the presidency becomes vacant for any cause whatever, or is impeded in its functioning as declared by the Con-

---

* Although there is no specific constitutional requirement that a British Prime Minister be a member of the House of Commons, tradition requires it. Lord Home subsequently relinquished his peerage and won election to the House of Commons as Alec Douglas-Home.

† This act was prompted by the illnesses of George V in 1928 and 1936.

stitutional Council* to which the matter has been referred by the government, the President of the Senate shall temporarily exercise the powers of President. In case of vacancy or permanent impediment, a special election to fill the office must take place before the expiration of thirty-five days.

Following the death of President Kennedy a great deal of concern was expressed in France over the lack of an office of vice-president. At the time, it was observed that if anything happened to de Gaulle, presidential power would pass to Gaston Monnerville, sixty-six-year-old president of the Senate, who was openly opposed to the de Gaulle regime.[4] De Gaulle was then reported to have considered changing the temporary successor to the president of the National Assembly.

A movement in France to establish an office of vice-president which started prior to the assassination of President Kennedy has gained force since that alarming event. There seems little chance that the proposal will be enacted into law. De Gaulle is reported to be opposed to the idea on the ground that a successor should be chosen in his own right at a new election so that he would have a full seven-year term and a mandate from the people.

The functioning of the French system in a time of presidential inability could be observed in the weeks following April 17, 1964. On that day, de Gaulle, at age seventy-three, underwent surgery for a prostate ailment. The news of this operation came as a tremendous shock to the people since just the previous day he had made an address on radio and television for support of his programs and plans. The operation, of which only a few had been told in advance, took place at 8:00 A.M. and lasted about two hours. De Gaulle remained unconscious into the afternoon. Although rumors of the operation had spread throughout the country during the day, it was not until early evening, as ordered by de Gaulle, that an official announcement was issued by the Elysée Palace:

General de Gaulle, President of the Republic, was operated upon this morning for a disease of the prostate. This operation was decided upon some weeks ago. The following health bulletin is made public: "The

---

* It consists of nine members, three of whom are appointed by the president of the Republic, three by the president of the National Assembly, and three by the president of the Senate. In addition, former presidents of the Republic are to be ex officio members for life. The Council insures the regularity of elections and rules on the constitutionality of laws.

operation took place normally. General de Gaulle's condition is very satisfactory."

Government officials stated that President de Gaulle would remain in the hospital for a week to ten days, and then he would go to his home in Colombey-les-Deux-Eglises for a few weeks' convalescence. Premier Georges Pompidou assumed direction of the government under Article 21 of the Constitution, which provides:

The Premier . . . shall replace, should the occasion arise, the President of the Republic as chairman of the councils and committees. . . . He may, in exceptional instances, replace him as chairman of a meeting of the Council of Ministers by virtue of an explicit delegation. . . .

The tight secrecy surrounding the operation and the optimistic reports as to de Gaulle's recovery apparently were due to a fear that Gaston Monnerville might maintain that de Gaulle was incapacitated and that he should, therefore, take over the government. In order to do so, however, he would have to obtain the approval of a majority of the members of the government.

While de Gaulle remained in the hospital, the medical reports continued to be general and optimistic. Premier Pompidou spoke frequently with him by telephone and on April 21 conferred with him regarding the agenda for a cabinet meeting scheduled for the following day. De Gaulle, as required by the constitution, requested Pompidou to preside at the meeting. On April 22, Pompidou met with the cabinet and explained the reason for the secrecy which had surrounded the operation. "The President thought secrecy necessary, Mr. Pompidou said, to prevent panic and to save the country from distress over his condition."[5] That day a bulletin was issued to the effect that de Gaulle was making a rapid recovery and that, accordingly, daily bulletins would no longer be necessary.

De Gaulle left the hospital on April 30 in what was described as "excellent condition." He returned to his official residence at Elysée Palace where he remained for a week, during which he met with the cabinet. From there he proceeded to his home for several additional weeks of convalescence. In the weeks to follow, as the President gradually became more active in the affairs of government, the period of presidential inability came to an end.

Soviet Union

The governmental framework of the Soviet Union is set out in the constitution of 1936. The highest legislative organ is the Supreme

Soviet, which consists of two houses and meets twice a year. Between sessions, the Presidium of the Supreme Soviet exercises legislative power. Its Chairman is the equivalent of President of the Soviet Union. The post, however, is largely ceremonial. The highest executive organ is the Council of Ministers, which is elected by the Supreme Soviet. The chairman of the Council of Ministers is the Premier of the Soviet Union. Since the Soviet constitution does not provide for concentration of power in a single person, a provision for executive succession is not included.

Real power in the Soviet Union lies not with the government thus described but with the Communist Party, which permeates this government apparatus. The Communist Party elects, at its party Congress,* a central committee (177 members and 155 alternates at present) which is nominally the Party's highest authority. Since it meets only two or three times a year, most of the actual work of the Party is done by the Presidium and Secretariat of the central committee, the actions of which are usually ratified by the central committee. The Presidium consists of ten members and six alternates and is the supreme policy-making board of the party. In effect, it is this body which governs the Soviet Union. The Secretariat is the managing board of the party and executes decisions made by the Presidium. Four of its members are presently members of the Presidium. Historically, the single most powerful figure has been the first secretary (secretary general before 1953) of the Party's Central Committee who is the leading member of the Secretariat and also a member of the Presidium.

There is no law governing succession to the post of first secretary. It is acquired through power and influence in the Party, specifically in the Secretariat and Presidium. It was as first secretary that Khrushchev became the most important figure in the Soviet Union after Stalin's death.† Then, on Thursday, October 15, 1964, the world was stunned by the announcement by *Tass,* the Soviet news

---

* The Congress under Nikita Khrushchev met every three years.

† Stalin died on March 5, 1953, and Georgi Malenkov became both premier and first secretary. He subsequently resigned the latter post and Khrushchev, a member of the secretariat, moved into the position and later ousted Malenkov as premier. In 1957, the presidium sought to remove Khrushchev as first secretary but was thwarted by the central committee, to which Khrushchev had appealed. In March, 1958, Khrushchev became Prime Minister of the Soviet Union.

agency, that the Communist Party had met the day before and had granted Khrushchev's request to be "relieved" of his post as First Secretary "in view of his advanced age [70] and deterioration of his health." It was also announced that the Supreme Soviet had met and relieved him of his post as Premier.[6] The new first secretary, said *Tass,* was fifty-seven-year-old Leonid Ilyich Brezhnev,* and the new Premier was sixty-year-old Aleksei Nikolayevich Kosygin.

The Communist and non-Communist worlds promptly sought to learn the whys and hows of Khrushchev's removal. It was revealed that on September 30, 1964, he had gone to his villa on the Black Sea for a vacation. While he was so vacationing, the Presidium met on October 12 to discuss his fate, and concluded that he must be removed. A select quorum of the Central Committee was hastily convened and it approved the move. Thus, on the evening of October 13, Khrushchev was summoned back to Moscow, where he appeared before the Central Committee. He was openly criticized for numerous political errors and personal misconduct. He attempted to defend himself but it was in vain. The Central Committee voted to remove him as first secretary on October 14 and the Presidium of the Supreme Soviet, with Anastas I. Mikoyan presiding, voted to remove him as Prime Minister on October 15. The Soviet people and the world were then notified of the *fait accompli.*

Despite the succession of Brezhnev to the post of First Secretary by what has been termed a "palace revolution," a cloud of uncertainty as to the permanency of Brezhnev's tenure and the future policies of the Soviet Union remains.

India

Under the constitution adopted on November 26, 1949, India has a parliamentary type of government. The constitutional head of state is the President who is elected for a five-year term. There is also a Vice-President who is elected for the same period. The President is assisted by a Prime Minister and a cabinet, who are appointed by him. As in other parliamentary systems, the Prime Minister is the leader of the majority party in Parliament. The Indian constitution provides for contingencies of death, resignation or re-

---

* In July, 1964, when Brezhnev stepped down as president of the Soviet Union to devote full time to his duties as Khrushchev's deputy in the secretariat, it was said that he was the heir apparent. *New York Herald Tribune,* July 16, 1964, p. 2.

moval of the President. A new election must take place within six months. In the interim the Vice-President acts as President.* The new President is elected to a full five-year term. The constitution further provides that in the event of the President's absence or illness, the Vice-President acts temporarily. Real power in India, however, lies with the Prime Minister, and there are no constitutional provisions to cover his death or disability.

From the time of its independence in August, 1947 through May 27, 1964, India's most powerful governmental figure was Prime Minister Jawaharlal Nehru. When he was suddenly stricken with an inability in January, 1964, a major crisis presented itself to that young nation. On Tuesday, January 7, 1964, Nehru was in Bhubaneswar, India, for the national convention of his Congress Party. It was announced that day that the seventy-four-year-old Prime Minister's doctors "had ordered him to cancel all engagements and take a complete rest because of high blood pressure and general fatigue."[7] On the following day, the medical reports indirectly suggested that Nehru had suffered a paralytic stroke affecting his left side. At about 8:30 that evening, Lal Bahadur Shastri, former Minister of the Interior and a Congress Party leader, told newspapermen that Nehru's blood pressure remained high and that the doctors were "not yet ready to reveal his condition."[8] Two hours later the following medical bulletin was issued:

The Prime Minister has had a restful day. The slight weakness of the left side which was noticed earlier has shown further improvement. His blood pressure has come down to a satisfactory level. He was cheerful and spent a good bit of time reading. He had a good appetite and took his normal meals.

As might be expected, the bulletins released during the next few days were similarly optimistic and made no reference to a stroke. Despite the optimism, it was widely suggested that Nehru should appoint a deputy Prime Minister. Prominent as possibilities for this position were Shastri, Kumaraswami Kamaraj Nadar, newly-elected President of the Congress Party, and Indira Gandhi, Nehru's daughter and the country's leading woman politician.

That Nehru's condition was more serious than reported was in-

---

* The Constitution of India also provides for filling a vacancy in the vice-presidency caused by death, resignation or removal. The new Vice-President serves for a full five-year term.

302

dicated on January 11, with the news that he had asked Gulzarilal Nanda, Minister of Home Affairs and senior member of the cabinet, and T. T. Krishnamachari, Minister of Finance, to administer the government for at least a week. The former would take care of matters relating to domestic affairs and the latter, foreign affairs. This decision was communicated to President Sarvepalli Radhakrishnan who was then recuperating from an eye operation. On January 12, Nehru returned to New Delhi by plane from Bhubaneswar, where he had remained under care at the residence of the Governor of Orissa. Upon his arrival, he was seen by newsmen who reported that he looked weak. On the same day, after a half-hour conference with Nehru, Nanda left New Delhi for Calcutta to study the Hindu-Moslem rioting there. On January 21, 1964, Nehru conferred with Kamaraj for over an hour. It was decided at the meeting that fifty-nine-year-old Lal Bahadur Shastri would be asked to join the cabinet as Minister without Portfolio, or the equivalent of deputy Prime Minister. The announcement was made the following day. On January 26, Nehru made his first public appearance when he attended the annual Republic Day parade. Subsequently, his activity increased and he began to attend sessions of Parliament. Yet, the weakness of his leg and foot was noticeable and it was remarked that he appeared drowsy much of the time.

Despite Nehru's return to limited public activity, feeling began to manifest itself that he should resign. At a March 17 session of Parliament, at which Nehru was present, a Socialist member, Ram Sevak Yadav, rose and stated: "This is not a monarchy. A country with a parliament can go on with an ailing king, but not with an ailing Prime Minister."[9] Yadav was immediately shouted down although there were many who agreed with him. The next few months found Shastri performing many administrative functions of the Prime Minister, without the formal title of deputy Prime Minister. Nehru devoted most of his time during this period to trying to resolve India's controversy with Pakistan over the Kashmir territory.

On Wednesday, May 27, 1964, Nehru awoke with a pain in his shoulders, fell into a coma, and died a few hours later. His death came without his ever having indicated his choice for a successor. In the days following, Gulzarilal Nanda, senior member of the Cabinet, acted as Prime Minister pursuant to appointment by President Sarvepalli Radhakrishnan, while a factionalized Congress Party sought to agree on a successor to Nehru. V. K. Krishna Menon, anti-Western former Indian Ambassador to the United Nations, Morarji Desai, a Hindu traditionalist with rightist views, and Kumaraswami Kamaraj Nadar, President of the Congress Party, each led various factions. Largely because of Kamaraj's support, Lal Bahadur Shastri was, after several days of dispute within the party, chosen leader of the Congress Party and, consequently, Prime Minister. The actual decision was made by a small group and it was unanimously supported by the Congress Party members in parliament.

Just over three weeks later, on June 26, Shastri suffered what was believed to be a mild heart attack. The medical reports, which remained consistently vague, said only that he was suffering from "physical and nervous exhaustion and strain." On July 18, Swaran Singh was named Minister of External Affairs, a position held by the Prime Minister since the country's independence, thus relieving Shastri of these burdens. By July 25, Shastri was back at the helm, faced with momentous food problems. Although India had an able leader once again, the series of events evidenced the need of providing clear-cut provisions for an acting leader in the event of the disability of a Prime Minister.

Italy

Under the Italian constitution of 1947, executive power is given to the President of the Republic, who is elected for a term of seven years by Parliament. The President, in turn, appoints the Prime Minister and members of the council of ministers upon the recommendation of the Prime Minister. Since Italy is a parliamentary democracy, the powers of the Italian President are largely symbolic and ceremonial. However, a strong President can play a large part in the government, particularly in resolving Cabinet crises and exercising behind-the-scenes political influence.

The death or disability of the President is provided for in Article 86 of the Italian constitution:

Should the President prove to be unable to fulfill his duties, these will be carried out by the Speaker of the Senate.

In case of permanent incapacity or death or resignation of the President of the Republic the Speaker of the Chamber of Deputies provides for the election of a new President of the Republic within fifteen days, save for such longer period as is laid down, should the Chambers be dissolved or when their term has less than three months to run."

There are, however, no definite procedures for establishing a permanent disability. The lack of such procedures proved troublesome during 1964.

On August 7, 1964, seventy-three-year-old President Antonio Segni suffered a stroke while at work in his study at the Presidential Palace. The stroke, which left him speechless and partially paralyzed, came at a time when the cabinet, which consisted of Christian Democrats, Left-Wing Socialists and moderate leftists, was badly divided on governmental policies.

Shortly after the stroke, Premier Aldo Moro, together with the cabinet, consulted leading figures in the government, including Senator Cesare Merzagora, the Speaker of the Senate, and Brunetto Bucciarelli Ducci, the Speaker of the Chamber of Deputies. On the basis of a bulletin issued by the President's physicians, they decided that Segni was temporarily disabled. "The medical verdict was that the 'motor and speech disturbances caused by the cerebral vascular lesion remain unchanged' and that 'the President of the republic temporarily is not in condition to fulfill his functions.' "[10] The inability decision was put into effect when Merzagora assumed the duties of the presidency on August 10, despite protests from the Communists that Parliament should first be consulted. During the next several months, the subject of presidential inability was explored by the Italian government.* It was unable to arrive at any conclusion as to the probable duration of the inability. Merzagora therefore continued as acting President until the evening of December 6, 1964, when Segni formally resigned. Present at the signing of the resignation, which took place at the President's official residence, were Segni's physicians. Merzagora, Premier Moro, and others were also there "to take cognizance of his decision."[11] A new election was called and, after a thirteen-day deadlock and twenty-one ballots, Giuseppe Saragat was elected.

Japan

Japan's Constitution, which went into effect in 1947, provides for a Parliament (Diet) consisting of a House of Representatives and a House of Councillors. Executive power is entrusted to a cabinet headed by a Prime Minister, who is elected by the Diet. The

---

* The State Department of the United States made available to the Italian government the results of Congress' examination of the subject.

constitution specifically provides that in the event of a Prime Minister's death, the cabinet is to continue exercising executive power until a new Prime Minister is appointed. The disability of a Prime Minister, however, is not covered.

On September 10, 1964, Premier Hayato Ikeda of Japan entered the hospital with a throat ailment, which was tentatively diagnosed as a "pre-cancerous" tumor. He remained there for the next month and a half, receiving necessary treatment. As a result, considerable feeling developed that, since the public business was being neglected, he should name an acting Premier. However, Ikeda's Liberal-Democratic Party was divided at the time into several factions and if he did so, he would have undoubtedly alienated a large segment of the party. Eisaku Sato, brother of former Premier Nobusuke Kishi and one-time Finance Minister, Aiichiro Fujiyama, former Foreign Minister, and Ichiro Kono, a long-time political leader, were the leading contenders for the post.*

While the feeling in favor of the appointment of an acting Premier raged, Ikeda tried to assure the country through Zenko Suzuki, the Chief Cabinet Secretary, that he was able to handle his normal administrative duties from bed. Yet, various "bedside conferences" had to be cancelled because they interfered with medical treatment. As Ikeda would require prolonged treatment, he decided to announce on Sunday, October 25, that he would soon resign.†

Two weeks of intensive discussion among the leaders of the Liberal-Democratic Party ensued, resulting in the nomination of Sato. Ikeda was notified on November 9 in his hospital room and, due to a special session of the Diet scheduled for later in the morning,‡ had little choice but to acquiesce, though he apparently did so reluctantly. The nomination was thereupon approved by the Diet.

---

* In July, 1964, a combined Sato-Fujiyama challenge for the presidency of the Liberal-Democratic Party came within several votes of being successful, so that Ikeda was not particularly anxious to have either of them as acting Premier.

† Resignation seems to be frequently used as a way of resolving a crisis brought about by disability. Thus, in September, 1920, the immensely popular Paul Deschanel, who had been elected tenth President of the Third French Republic in January 1920, was obliged to resign his post due to a nervous breakdown several months earlier.

‡ The session had been called on November 2 for the specific purpose of electing a successor to Ikeda.

306

Several hours after being elected, the sixty-three-year-old Sato announced that he would retain the entire cabinet, with two exceptions. He named a new Chief Cabinet Secretary and Chief of the Cabinet Legislative Bureau, and pledged his adminstration to a new and stronger leadership for Japan in world affairs.

Other Countries

Most of the constitutions of countries having a President as chief of state provide for temporary (e.g., absence and inability) and permanent (e.g., death or vacancy) situations, without any procedure for establishing inability. They prescribe that in the former the constitutional successor serves until the temporary situation has ended, and in the latter, until a new president is elected, which is often at a special election. Some countries, however, allow the successor to serve for the remainder of the term. Usually, this is where there is an elected Vice-President or Designate whose primary function is to succeed to the first office. Several countries require a new election in case of double vacancies, e.g., Brazil and the Republic of China.

The constitutional successor varies from country to country. For example, in Algeria, the immediate successor is the President of the Assembly; in Argentina, a popularly elected Vice-President; in Burma, a commission of members of the legislature and judiciary; in Chile, a Minister who becomes Vice-President; in Colombia, a Designate previously elected by the Congress; in Costa Rica, one of two popularly elected Vice-Presidents;* in Gabon, a Vice-President appointed by the President; in Guinea, the President's Cabinet; in Iceland, a commission consisting of the Prime Minister, Speaker of Parliament, and Chief Justice of the Supreme Court;† in Ireland, a commission of the Chief Justice of the Supreme Court, the Chairman of the House and the Chairman of the Senate; in Italy, the Speaker of the Senate; in Ivory Coast, a person chosen by the President of the National Assembly; and in Korea, the Prime Minister.

Generally speaking, the constitutions of foreign countries are silent on procedures for declaring a chief of state disabled. Some

---

* Two or more vice-presidents or designates are also provided for by the constitutions of Gabon, Guatemala, Honduras, Panama and Peru.

† This commission so acted in the period between February and June, 1952, following the death of President Sveinn Bjornsson.

constitutions, however, do authorize a body to declare a permanent inability.* A few even have specific procedures.

The constitution of Pakistan lays down an interesting procedure for determining the President's physical or mental incapacity.[12] One-third of all the members of the National Assembly can notify the Speaker of the Assembly in writing that they intend to move a resolution in the Assembly for the removal of the President on grounds of physical or mental incapacity. The writing must set forth the particulars of the alleged incapacity. The Speaker will then transmit the notice to the President, with a request that he submit himself within ten days to an examination by a medical board of five medical practitioners. They are: the most senior medical officers in the civil health service, the medical service of the Army, the health service of East Pakistan, the health service of West Pakistan, and the consultant physician to the Army. The resolution cannot be moved earlier than fourteen days or later than thirty days after notice to the Speaker. If the President has submitted to an examination, the resolution cannot be voted upon until the medical board has had an opportunity to render an opinion. If the President has not submitted himself to an examination before the resolution is moved, it may be voted upon. The President has the right to appear and be represented when the resolution is considered. A vote of three-fourths of the entire Assembly is necessary to remove him from office. If the President has submitted himself to an examination by the medical board and less than one-half of the assembly vote in favor of the removal, the members who noticed the resolution cease to be members of the Assembly. The Pakistan constitution further provides that at any time when the office is vacant or the President is unable to perform his functions because of illness, absence from the country or otherwise, the Speaker of the Assembly shall act as President.

----

* Such a power is given to congress in Ecuador and Peru, to congress subject to supreme court confirmation in Chile, to the senate in Colombia (limited to physical incapacity), to the supreme court in Dahomey, Gabon, Ireland and Mauritania, to the Superior Council of Institutions in Malagasy, and to a council of state (composed of the presiding officer of each house of the legislature and of the president of the council of ministers) in Portugal. The constitution of Nigeria permits the prime minister to declare the President unable, in which case the president of the senate assumes the president's responsibilities.

The constitution of the Republic of South Africa contains a provision under which the President may be removed from office on the ground of misconduct or inability to perform efficiently the duties of his office.[13] The first step in the procedure to remove the President is a petition by not less than thirty members of the House of Assembly, requesting the appointment of a joint committee of the House and Senate to consider the removal. After its appointment the joint committee studies the matter and then submits a report of its findings to both Houses. The report is considered, after which both Houses may then pass a resolution declaring the President removed from office on the ground of misconduct or inability. The constitution also provides that whenever the office of President is vacant or the President is unable to perform his duties, the President of the Senate shall serve as acting President.

A State Tenure Law of 1951 in Israel contains a provision by which the Knesset (Parliament), upon a proposal of three-fourths of the House Committee, may declare by a vote of three-fourths of its members that "for reasons of health the President is unable to carry out his functions."[14] The chairman of Knesset then acts as President. If three-fourths of the House Committee find only a temporary disability, the Chairman acts until the expiration of the period fixed by the Committee in its decision, or sooner if the President says he is able to perform his duties, and the Committee agrees.

Conclusion

In its relatively brief existence the United States has evolved from a loose confederation of thirteen colonies to a complex and dynamic nation of nearly 200 million people. The growth of the country has been accompanied by a parallel development in the office of President. The presidency has become the single most powerful office in the world. Its occupant is the commander-in-chief of the armed forces of the United States, the chief architect of domestic and foreign policy, the moving force of the national administration —in short, the pillar upon which the freedom of the country and of a large part of the world depends.

In the preceding pages have been described the various occasions when the government of the United States has been put to the supreme test—its ability to effect an orderly transfer of power upon the death of the President. The smooth and systematic manner by which presidential power passed from one hand to another upon the deaths in office of eight Presidents has demonstrated one remarkable feature of our government—its continuity. The shock and grief attendant upon the death of each President were lessened by the realization that the government remained intact. In every case succession was swift and unquestioned. No gap occurred at the helm because there was a successor and no doubt as to his constitutional right and duty to assume the presidential powers. For this we are indebted to a few lines in the Constitution.

Since the presidency of the United States is so important, there must never be any doubt about the adequacy of the country's laws on succession to that office. Experience has shown that when such doubt exists the continuity of government and, perhaps, the very survival of the nation are seriously threatened. In the history of the United States the lack of clear procedures for dealing with presidential inability has proven to be the greatest deficiency in the succession mechanism. The devising of such procedures as well as procedures for filling a vacancy in the vice-presidency is an important step in eliminating some great gaps in the system. The statutory line

310

of succession should be re-examined, and clarification of the legal succession in the period before inauguration should be considered.

The central figure in the succession mechanism of the United States has been and will continue to be the Vice-President. Since the Vice-President might one day succeed to the presidency, it is essential that he be chosen as if he were actually to be President. It is equally vital that the Vice-President be an integral member of the administration and that he be thoroughly familiar with the great issues of the day. Since he is the person best able to prepare himself for possible succession to the presidency, it is only fitting that the office of Vice-President continue to expand and its occupant share with the President a gradually larger decision-making role in the government. It is not unreasonable to expect that the Vice-President will eventually become the actual first assistant to the President. This is the proper role for the second officer in the land.

APPENDICES

APPENDIX A

1. Deaths of Presidents

PRESIDENT	TERM FOR WHICH ELECTED	DATE OF DEATH	VICE-PRESIDENT WHO SUCCEEDED	DATE PRESIDENTIAL OATH TAKEN	LENGTH OF UNEXPIRED PRESIDENTIAL TERM†		
					YEARS	MONTHS	DAYS
1. William H. Harrison	March 4, 1841–1845	April 4, 1841	John Tyler	April 6, 1841	3	11	0
2. Zachary Taylor	March 4, 1849–1853	July 9, 1850	Millard Fillmore	July 10, 1850	2	7	23
3. Abraham Lincoln*	March 4, 1865–1869	April 15, 1865	Andrew Johnson	April 15, 1865	3	10	17
4. James A. Garfield*	March 4, 1881–1885	September 19, 1881	Chester A. Arthur	September 20, 1881 and September 22, 1881	3	5	13
5. William McKinley*	March 4, 1901–1905	September 14, 1901	Theodore Roosevelt	September 14, 1901	3	5	18
6. Warren G. Harding	March 4, 1921–1925	August 2, 1923	Calvin Coolidge	August 3, 1923 and August 21, 1923	1	7	2
7. Franklin D. Roosevelt	January 20, 1945–1949	April 12, 1945	Harry S. Truman	April 15, 1945	3	9	8
8. John F. Kennedy*	January 20, 1961–1965	November 22, 1963	Lyndon B. Johnson	November 22, 1963	1	1	29
				TOTAL:	23	10	20

* Presidents whose deaths were by assassination.
† The computation is based on the dates of the Presidents' deaths.

Appendix A (cont.)

II. Vice-Presidential Vacancies

VICE-PRESIDENT	PERIOD FOR WHICH ELECTED	TERMINATION OF SERVICE*	REASON FOR TERMINATION	LENGTH OF VICE-PRESIDENTIAL VACANCY		
				YEARS	MONTHS	DAYS
1. George Clinton	March 4, 1809–1813	April 20, 1812	Death		10	12
2. Elbridge Gerry	March 4, 1813–1817	November 23, 1814	Death	2	3	9
3. John C. Calhoun	March 4, 1829–1833	December 28, 1832	Resignation		2	4
4. John Tyler	March 4, 1841–1845	April 4, 1841	Succession	3	11	0
5. Millard Fillmore	March 4, 1849–1853	July 9, 1850	Succession	2	7	23
6. William R. King	March 4, 1853–1857	April 18, 1853	Death	3	10	14
7. Andrew Johnson	March 4, 1865–1869	April 15, 1865	Succession	3	10	17
8. Henry Wilson	March 4, 1873–1877	November 22, 1875	Death	1	3	10
9. Chester A. Arthur	March 4, 1881–1885	September 19, 1881	Succession	3	5	13
10. Thomas A. Hendricks	March 4, 1885–1889	November 25, 1885	Death	3	3	7
11. Garrett A. Hobart	March 4, 1897–1901	November 21, 1899	Death	1	3	11
12. Theodore Roosevelt	March 4, 1901–1905	September 14, 1901	Succession	3	5	18
13. James S. Sherman	March 4, 1909–1913	October 30, 1912	Death		4	5
14. Calvin Coolidge	March 4, 1921–1925	August 2, 1923	Succession	1	7	2
15. Harry S. Truman	January 20, 1945–1949	April 12, 1945	Succession	3	9	8
16. Lyndon B. Johnson	January 20, 1961–1965	November 22, 1963	Succession	1	1	29
			TOTAL:	37	3	2

* In the case of a Vice-President who succeeds to the Presidency, the date of the President's death is treated as the date of termination (see p. 92).

APPENDIX B

United States Constitution
Article II, Section 1, Clause 6

In Case of the Removal of the President from Office, or of his Death, Resignation, or Inability to discharge the Powers and Duties of the said Office, the Same shall devolve on the Vice President, and the Congress may by Law provide for the Case of Removal, Death, Resignation or Inability, both of the President and Vice President, declaring what Officer shall then act as President, and such Officer shall act accordingly, until the Disability be removed, or a President shall be elected.

APPENDIX C

Succession Law of 1947 (3 U.S.C. §19 [1958])

(a) (1) If, by reason of death, resignation, removal from office, inability, or failure to qualify, there is neither a President nor Vice-President to discharge the powers and duties of the office of President, then the Speaker of the House of Representatives shall, upon his resignation as Speaker and as Representative in Congress, act as President.

(2) The same rule shall apply in the case of the death, resignation, removal from office, or inability of an individual acting as President under this subsection.

(b) If, at the time when under subsection (a) of this section a Speaker is to begin the discharge of the powers and duties of the office of President, there is no Speaker, or the Speaker fails to qualify as Acting President, then the President pro tempore of the Senate shall, upon his resignation as President pro tempore and as Senator, act as President.

(c) An individual acting as president under subsection (a) or subsection (b) of this section shall continue to act until the expiration of the then current presidential term, except that—

(1) If his discharge of the powers and duties of the office is founded in whole or in part on the failure of both the President-elect and the Vice-President-elect to qualify, then he shall act only until a President or Vice-President qualifies; and

(2) If his discharge of the powers and duties of the office is founded in whole or in part on the inability of the President or Vice-President, then he shall act only until the removal of the disability of one of such individuals.

(d) (1) If, by reason of death, resignation, removal from office, inability, or failure to qualify, there is no President pro tempore to act as President under subsection (b) of this section, then the officer of the United States who is highest on the following list, and who is not under disability to discharge the powers and duties of the office of President shall act as President: Secretary of State, Secretary of the Treasury, Secretary of Defense, Attorney General, Postmaster General, Secretary of the Interior, Secretary of Agriculture, Secretary of Commerce, Secretary of Labor.

(2) An individual acting as President under this subsection shall continue so to do until the expiration of the then current presidential term, but not after a qualified and prior-entitled individual is able to act, except that the removal of the disability of an individual higher on the list contained in paragraph (1) of this subsection or the ability to qualify on the part of an individual higher on such list shall not terminate his service.

(3) The taking of the oath of office by an individual specified in the list in paragraph (1) of this subsection shall be held to constitute his resignation from the office by virtue of the holding of which he qualifies to act as President.

(e) Subsections (a), (b), and (d) of this section shall apply only to such officers as are eligible to the office of President under the Constitution. Subsection (d) of this section shall apply only to officers appointed, by and with the advice and consent of the Senate, prior to the time of the death, resignation, removal from office, inability, or failure to qualify, of the President pro tempore, and only to officers not under impeachment by the House of Representatives at the time the powers and duties of the office of President devolve upon them.

(f) During the period that any individual acts as President under this section, his compensation shall be at the rate then provided by law in the case of the President.

APPENDIX D

American Bar Association
Conference Consensus

The Conference considered the question of action to be taken in the event of inability of the President to perform the duties of his office. It was the consensus of the Conference that:

1. Agreements between the President and Vice President or person next in line of succession provide a partial solution, but not an acceptable permanent solution of the problem.

2. An amendment to the Constitution of the United States should be adopted to resolve the problems which would arise in the event of the inability of the President to discharge the powers and duties of his office.

3. The amendment should provide that in the event of the inability of the President the powers and duties, but not the office, shall devolve upon the Vice President or person next in line of succession for the duration of the inability of the President or until expiration of his term of office.

4. The amendment should provide that the inability of the President may be established by declaration in writing of the President. In the event that the President does not make known his inability, it may be established by action of the Vice President or person next in line of succession with the concurrence of a majority of the Cabinet or by action of such other body as the Congress may by law provide.

5. The amendment should provide that the ability of the President to resume the powers and duties of his office shall be established by his declaration in writing. In the event that the Vice President and a majority of the Cabinet or such other body as Congress may by law provide shall not concur in the declaration of the President, the continuing inability of the President may then be determined by the vote of two-thirds of the elected members of each House of the Congress.

The Conference also considered the related question of Presidential succession. It was the consensus that:

1. The Constitution should be amended to provide that in the event of the death, resignation or removal of the President, the Vice

President or the person next in line of succession shall succeed to the office for the unexpired term.

2. It is highly desirable that the office of Vice President be filled at all times. An amendment to the Constitution should be adopted providing that when a vacancy occurs in the office of Vice President, the President shall nominate a person who, upon approval by a majority of the elected members of Congress meeting in joint session, shall then become Vice President for the unexpired term.

APPENDIX E

Times during which either the Speaker
or President pro tempore (or both)
were from a different party than
that of the President

CONGRESS	PRESIDENT AND PARTY	SPEAKER AND PARTY*	PRESIDENT PRO TEMPORE AND PARTY
20th, 1827–1829	John Quincy Adams—C (DR)	Andrew Stevenson—J	Samuel Smith—J
28th, 1843–1845	John Tyler—W	John W. Jones—D	Willie P. Mangum—W
30th, 1847–1849	James K. Polk—D	Robert C. Winthrop—W	David R. Atchison—W
31st, 1849–1851	Zachary Taylor ⎱ W Millard Fillmore ⎰	Howell Cobb—D	David R. Atchison—W William R. King—D
32nd, 1851–1853	Millard Fillmore—W	Linn Boyd—D	William R. King—D David R. Atchison—W
34th, 1853–1857	Franklin Pierce—D	Nathaniel P. Banks—R	Jesse D. Bright—D Charles E. Stuart—D James M. Mason—D
36th, 1859–1861	James Buchanan—D	William Pennington—R	Benjamin Fitzpatrick—D Jesse D. Bright—D Solomon Foot—R

Appendix E (*cont.*)

CONGRESS	PRESIDENT AND PARTY	SPEAKER AND PARTY	PRESIDENT PRO TEMPORE AND PARTY
44th, 1875–1877	Ulysses S. Grant—R	Michael C. Kerr—D Samuel J. Randall—D	Thomas W. Ferry—R
45th, 1877–1879	Rutherford B. Hayes—R	Samuel J. Randall—D	Thomas W. Ferry—R
46th, 1879–1881	Rutherford B. Hayes—R	Samuel J. Randall—D	Allen G. Thurman—D
48th, 1883–1835	Chester A. Arthur—R	John G. Carlisle—D	George F. Edmunds—R
49th, 1885–1887	Grover Cleveland—D	John G. Carlisle—D	John Sherman—R
50th, 1887–1889	Grover Cleveland—D	John G. Carlisle—D	John J. Ingalls—R
52nd, 1891–1893	Benjamin Harrison—R	Charles F. Crisp—D	Charles F. Monderson—R
54th, 1895–1897	Grover Cleveland—D	Thomas B. Reed—R	William P. Frye—R
62nd, 1911–1913	William H. Taft—R	Champ Clark—D	William P. Frye—R Charles Curtis—R Augustus O. Bacon—R Jacob H. Gallinger—R Henry Cabot Lodge—R Frank B. Brandegee—R
66th, 1919–1921	Woodrow Wilson—D	Frederick H. Gillett—R	Albert B. Cummins—R
72nd, 1931–1933	Herbert C. Hoover—R	John Nance Garner—D	George H. Moses—R
80th, 1947–1949	Harry S. Truman—D	Joseph Martin, Jr.—R	Arthur Vandenberg—R
84th, 1955–1957	Dwight D. Eisenhower—R	Sam Rayburn—D	Walter F. George—D
85th, 1957–1959	Dwight D. Eisenhower—R	Sam Rayburn—D	Carl Hayden—D
86th, 1959–1961	Dwight D. Eisenhower—R	Sam Rayburn—D	Carl Hayden—D

* The party abbreviations are as follows: C—Coalition; D—Democratic; DR—Democratic-Republican; J—Jacksonian; R—Republican; W—Whig. (Source: *Encyclopedia Britannica* (1964), XXII, 799; *Biographical Directory of the American Congress 1774–1961* (Washington, 1961).

APPENDIX F

Republican Party Procedure

RESOLVED, That the Republican National Committee be and is hereby authorized and empowered to fill any and all vacancies which may occur by reason of death, declination or otherwise in the ticket nominated by this Convention and that, in voting in said Committee, the Committee members representing any State, the District of Columbia, Puerto Rico and the Virgin Islands shall be entitled to cast the same number of votes as said State, the District of Columbia, Puerto Rico and the Virgin Islands was entitled to cast in the . . . Republican National Convention or that the National Committee, in its judgment, may call a National Convention for the purpose of filling such vacancy.

APPENDIX G

Democratic Party Procedure

In the event of the death, resignation or disability of a nominee of the party for President or Vice President, the Democratic National Committee is authorized to fill the vacancy or vacancies, by a majority vote of a total number of votes possessed by the States and Territories at the preceding National Convention; the full vote of each State and Territory shall be cast by its duly qualified member, or members, of the National Committee. Should the two members disagree, each shall cast one-half of the full vote of the State.

APPENDIX H*

Line of Succession in the Fifty States

(See explanation at end of chart)

	LEGISLATIVE OFFICIALS					EXECUTIVE OFFICIALS						
STATE	LT. GOV.	PRES. OF SEN.	PRES. PRO TEM.	SPEAKER	OTHER	SEC'Y OF STATE	ATT'Y GEN.	AUDITOR	TREASURER	COMPTROLLER	OTHER	ADDITIONAL
Ala.	1		2	3		6	4	5	7			
Alaska						1					Successor to Secretary of State	
Ariz.						1	2	3	4		5	
Ark.	1		2	3		5	4		6			
Calif.	1		2	3		4	5		6	7		Gov. names 4–7 citizens
Colo.	1		2	3								
Conn.	1		2									
Del.	1		4	5		2	3					
Fla.		1		2		3	4		6	5	7–8	
Ga.	1			2								
Hawaii	1											
Idaho	1		2	3		4		5	6			
Ill.	1		2	3		4	5		6		7–8	
Ind.	1		2									
Iowa	1		2	3		5	4	7	6			
Kansas	1		2	3		4	5					Chanc. of U. of Kan. & Pres. of Kan. State U. of Agr. & Appl. Sci.

Appendix H (*cont.*)

	LEGISLATIVE OFFICIALS					EXECUTIVE OFFICIALS						
STATE	LT. GOV.	PRES. OF SEN.	PRES. PRO TEM.	SPEAKER	OTHER	SEC'Y OF STATE	ATT'Y GEN.	AUDI-TOR	TREAS-URER	COMP-TROLLER	OTHER	ADDITIONAL
Ky.	1		2			3						
La.	1		2			3						
Me.		1		2		3	4	5	6			
Md.		1		2			4			3		
Mass.	1					2	3	6	4			
Mich.	1					2	3	5	4		5	Gov. designates 3 successors
Minn.	1		2	3		4	7	5	6			
Miss.	1		2	3								
Mo.	1		2	3								
Mont.	1		2	3								
Neb.	1		2	2	Chmn. of Various Legis. Committees							
Nev.	1		2	3		4						
N.H.		1		2			3					
N.J.		1		2			3				4	Person desig. by available Legislators
N.M.	1		3	4		2	5	6	8		7	
N.Y.	1		2	3		11	4	6		5	6-10	
N.C.	1		2	3		4	8	5	6		7, 9-11	
N.D.	1		4	3		2	5					Former Govs.
Ohio	1		2	3		4	7	6	5			
Okla.	1		2	3		4	6	5	7		8-16	
Ore.		1		2		3			4			Senior circuit judge available

Appendix H (*cont.*)

LEGISLATIVE OFFICIALS   EXECUTIVE OFFICIALS

STATE	LT. GOV.	PRES. OF SEN.	PRES. PRO TEM.	SPEAKER	OTHER	SEC'Y OF STATE	ATT'Y GEN.	AUDITOR	TREAS-URER	COMP-TROLLER	OTHER	ADDITIONAL
Pa.	1		2	3								
R.I.	1		2									
S.C.	1		2	3		4	6		5			
S.D.	1		3	2	4	5						Gov. designates 3–7 interim successors
Tenn.		1		2		3						
Tex.	1		2	3			4			4		Ch. Just. of Cts. of Civil Appeals
Utah		2		3		1	4	5	6			
Vt.	1		3	2		4			5			
Va.	1		4	3	Chmn. of Committees of House and Senate		2					Former Govs., Ch. Just. of Sup. Ct. of App., Sr. Judge of Ct. of Record
Wash.	1		9	8		2	5	4	3		6–7	
West Va.		1		2			3	4				Former Govs.
Wisc.	1		6	5		2	3		4			
Wyo.	2		3		7–8	1		4	5		6	

Explanation: The numbers running across the page from left to right indicate the order of succession in each state.

* A chart alignment of the succession provisions in the fifty state constitutions can be found in the author's article, "The Problem of Presidential Inability—Will Congress Ever Solve It?" 32 *Fordham Law Review* 129–34 (October, 1963), the citations for which are at pages 102–05 of the article. Additional information about the state succession laws can be found in the author's article, "The Vice-Presidency and the Problems of Presidential Succession and Inability," 32 *Fordham Law Review* 485 & n. 166 (March, 1964).

FOOTNOTES

Chapter 1 (Pages 3–20)

1. *Report of the President's Commission on the Assassination of President John F. Kennedy* (Washington, 1964), p. 42.
2. *Ibid.,* 63.
3. *Ibid.,* 55.
4. *The Washington Post,* November 23, 1963, p. A1.
5. *Ibid.,* November 23, 1963, p. A4.
6. *Ibid.,* November 23, 1963, p. A4.
7. 109 Cong. Rec. 22693 (1963).
8. *The New York Times,* November 23, 1963, p. 6.
9. *The Washington Post,* November 23, 1963, p. 1.
10. *The New York Times,* November 23, 1963, p. 2.
11. See *The New York Times,* November 23, 1963, pp. 8, 12; *Daily News,* November 23, 1963, p. 4.
12. *U.S. News & World Rep.,* January 6, 1964, p. 7.
13. *Report of the President's Commission on the Assassination of President John F. Kennedy* (Washington, 1964), p. 59.
14. *The Washington Post,* November 24, 1963, p. A9.
15. *The New York Times,* March 16, 1964, p. 18.
16. *The Washington Post,* November 23, 1963, p. 4.
17. *The New York Times,* November 23, 1963, p. 1.
18. *Ibid.,* March 16, 1964, p. 18.
19. *Ibid.,* March 16, 1964, p. 18.
20. *Ibid.,* November 24, 1963, p. 1.
21. *New York Herald Tribune,* November 26, 1963, p. 2.
22. *Newsweek,* December 9, 1963, p. 21.
23. *The New York Times,* November 27, 1963, p. 1.
24. *Ibid.,* November 28, 1963, p. 20.
25. *Ibid.,* November 29, 1963, p. 20.
26. *New York Post,* November 26, 1963, p. 5.

Chapter 2 (Pages 23–38)

1. See Leonard Woods Labaree, *Royal Government in America* (New Haven, 1930), pp. 7–21, 95–96; *Royal Instructions to British Colonial Governors,* Labaree, ed. (New York, 1935), 2 vols.

329

Footnotes

2. Labaree, *Royal Government in America,* pp. 84–91.
3. *Ibid.,* p. 96.
4. Evarts B. Greene, *The Provincial Governor in the English Colonies of North America* (New York, 1898), pp. 54–55.
5. *Ibid.,* pp. 67–68.
6. Alf. J. Mapp, Jr., *The Virginia Experiment* (Richmond, 1957), pp. 17–25; see Herbert L. Osgood, *The American Colonies in the Seventeenth Century* (Gloucester, 1957), I, 46–55.
7. See Richard L. Morton, *Colonial Virginia* (Chapel Hill, 1960), I, 28–55.
8. Thomas Hutchinson, *The History of the Colony and Province of Massachusetts,* Mayo, ed. (Cambridge, 1936), II, p. 355 & n.
9. For text, see *The Federal and State Constitutions, Colonial Charters and Other Organic Laws,* Thorpe, ed. (Washington, 1909), III, 1852.
10. *The Public Records of the Colony of Connecticut* (Hartford, 1850), I, 147.
11. Thorpe, I, 528.
12. *The Records of the Colony of Rhode Island and Providence Plantations* (Providence, 1856), I, pp. 100, 101, 112.
13. *Ibid.,* 42.
14. Thorpe, I, 531; VI, 3214.
15. See *The Public Records of the Colony of Connecticut* (Hartford, 1850–1890), V, 38–39; VI, 483; VIII, 416–17; XIII, 171, 285; Samuel Greene Arnold, *History of the State of Rhode Island and Providence Plantations* (New York, 1878), I, 440, 441, 532; II, 54, 83, 93, 113, 119, 126, 202, 211, 248.
16. E. B. O'Callaghan, *History of the New Netherland* (New York, 1848 ed.), II, 561.
17. Paul A. W. Wallace, *Pennsylvania* (New York, 1962), p. 55.
18. William Hand Browne, *Maryland* (Boston, 1897), p. 75; Matthew Page Andrews, *The Founding of Maryland* (Baltimore, 1933), p. 229.
19. Thorpe, V, 2535.
20. John E. Pomfret, *The Province of East Jersey* (Princeton, 1962), pp. 227–28.
21. *Ibid.,* p. 330.
22. Thorpe, V, 2756.
23. W. F. Dunaway, *A History of Pennsylvania* (New York, 1935), p. 63.
24. Herbert L. Osgood, *The American Colonies in the Eighteenth Century* (New York, 1924), IV, 67–68.
25. Greene, p. 264.
26. *Ibid.,* p. 44.
27. Hutchinson, III, 126–28.
28. Thorpe, III, 1884–85.
29. Greene, p. 55 & n.4.
30. *Ibid.,* 56.
31. Labaree, p. 128.
32. *Ibid.,* p. 129.
33. *Ibid.,* p. 126.
34. Andrews, pp. 331–37.

Footnotes

35. See, generally, Osgood, *The American Colonies in the Eighteenth Century,* II, 49–54.
36. Greene, pp. 53–54.
37. *Ibid.,* p. 53.
38. William H. Fry, *New Hampshire as a Royal Province* (New York, 1908), p. 88.
39. *Ibid.,* p. 89.
40. *Ibid.,* pp. 90–92.
41. *Ibid.,* pp. 92–93.
42. Greene, p. 43.
43. Robert C. Newbold, *The Albany Congress and Plan of Union of 1754* (New York, 1955), p. 187.
44. See Allan Nevins, *The American States During and After the Revolution, 1775–1789* (New York, 1924).
45. For the text of these succession provisions, see John D. Feerick, "The Problem of Presidential Inability—Will Congress Ever Solve it?" 32 *Fordham Law Review* 79–80 &nn. 25–37 (October 1963).

Chapter 3 (Pages 39–56)

1. See Andrew C. McLaughlin, *A Constitutional History of the United States* (New York, 1935), p. 147.
2. See Frederic A. Ogg and P. Orman Ray, *Essentials of American Government* (New York, 1932), p. 31.
3. See John D. Feerick, "The Problem of Presidential Inability—Will Congress Ever Solve It?," 32 *Fordham Law Review* 81 & n. 39 (October, 1963).
4. Charles Warren, *The Making of the Constitution* (Boston, 1928), p. 55.
5. Henry E. Davis, "Inability of the President," S. Doc. 308, 65th Cong., 3d Sess. (1918); Robert F. Kennedy, 42 *Opinions of the Attorneys General* No. 5, pp. 3–4 (Washington, 1961); Ruth C. Silva, *Presidential Succession* (Ann Arbor, 1951), p. 4.
6. Max Farrand, *The Records of the Federal Convention of 1787* (New Haven, 1911 and 1937), III, 588.
7. *The Debates in the Several State Conventions, on the Adoption of the Federal Constitution,* Jonathan Elliot, ed. (Philadelphia, 1861 ed.), V, 577–78.
8. Lucia Von Lueck Becker, *The Pinckney Plan for the Federal Constitution* (Ph.D. Thesis, University of Chicago, 1911); John Franklin Jameson, "Studies in the History of the Federal Convention of 1787," in *American Historical Association, Annual Report For 1902* (Washington, 1903), I, 111–32.
9. Farrand, I, 288.
10. Farrand, III, 625.
11. Farrand, II, 85, 95, 97, 106.

12. *Ibid.*, p. 186.
13. *Ibid.*, pp. 137 & n. 6, 146.
14. *Ibid.*, pp. 163 & n. 17, 172.
15. *Ibid.*, p. 427.
16. *Ibid.*, pp. 473, 481.
17. *Ibid.*, pp. 493, 495.
18. *Ibid.*
19. *Ibid.*, p. 499.
20. *Ibid.*, p. 535.
21. *Ibid.*
22. *Ibid.*, pp. 536–37.
23. *Ibid.*, p. 537.
24. *Ibid.*
25. *Ibid.*
26. Warren, p. 635.
27. Farrand, II, 547, 554.
28. *Ibid.*, 573, 575.
29. *Ibid.*, 598–99.
30. *Ibid.*, p. 65.
31. *Ibid.*, p. 69.
32. See George Ticknor Curtis, *Constitutional History of the United States* (New York, 1889 ed.), I, 569.
33. Farrand, II, 626.
34. See, generally, Silva, pp. 31–34.
35. The best treatise on the meaning of the succession provision is Silva, *Presidential Succession* (Ann Arbor, 1951).
36. *The Federalist and Other Constitutional Papers,* Scott, ed. (Chicago, 1894), I, 376.
37. *Ibid.*, II, 628.
38. *Ibid.*, p. 573.
39. *Ibid.*, p. 613.
40. *Ibid.*, p. 856.
41. *Ibid.*, p. 898.
42. See Feerick, pp. 87–88.
43. Elliot (Philadelphia, 1866 ed.), IV, 26.
44. *Ibid.*
45. *Ibid.*
46. *Ibid.*, pp. 26–27.
47. *Ibid.*, III, 486–87.
48. *Ibid.*, p. 487.
49. *Ibid.*, p. 490.
50. *Ibid.*, II, 538.
51. *Ibid.*, IV, 42.
52. *Ibid.*, p. 43.
53. *Ibid.*, p. 107.
54. *Ibid.*, III, 487–88.
55. *Ibid.*, II, 85.

56. *Ibid.*, p. 408.
57. *Ibid.*, III, 498.
58. *Ibid.*, I, 378.
59. *Ibid.*, III, 490.
60. *Ibid.*, IV, 44.

Chapter 4 (Pages 57–62)

1. Annals of Congress, 1st Cong. (1790), II, 1813.
2. *Ibid.*, pp. 1853–56.
3. Annals of Congress, 2d Cong. (1791), p. 31.
4. *Ibid.*, p. 36.
5. *Ibid.*, p. 278.
6. *Ibid.*, p. 281.
7. *Ibid.*, p. 282.
8. *Ibid.*, p. 281.
9. *Ibid.*, p. 82.
10. *Ibid.*, p. 422.
11. *Ibid.*, pp. 406–07.
12. *Ibid.*, pp. 417–18.
13. 1 Stat. 239 (1792).
14. *The Works of Alexander Hamilton,* Lodge, ed. (New York, 1886), VIII, 261.
15. William C. Rives, *History of the Life and Times of James Madison* (Boston, 1868), III, 223.
16. *The Works of Fisher Ames,* Seth, ed. (Boston, 1854), I, 114.
17. *Writings of James Madison,* Hunt, ed. (New York, 1906), VI, 95 & n.1.
18. *Ibid.*

Chapter 5 (Pages 63–75)

1. U.S. Const., art. II, § 1, cl. 1.
2. U.S. Const., art. II, § 1, cl. 5.
3. Page Smith, *John Adams* (New York, 1962), II, 744.
4. *Ibid.*
5. 1 Stat. 23 (1789).
6. Smith, p. 781.
7. William Maclay, *The Journal of William Maclay* (New York, 1927), p. 2.
8. *Ibid.*, pp. 2–3.
9. *Ibid.*, p. 3.

Footnotes

10. *Ibid.,* p. 37.
11. *Ibid.,* pp. 38–39.
12. *Ibid.,* p. 2; see also Smith, pp. 751–52, 758, 788–89.
13. Smith, p. 789.
14. *The Works of John Adams,* C. F. Adams, ed. (Boston, 1850), I, 460.
15. Annals of Congress, 1st Cong. (1790), I, 646–56.
16. *Ibid.,* p. 646.
17. *Ibid.,* p. 649.
18. *Ibid.,* p. 650.
19. *Ibid.,* pp. 650–51.
20. *Ibid.,* pp. 646–47.
21. *Ibid.,* pp. 648–49.
22. *The Writings of George Washington,* Fitzpatrick, ed. (Washington, 1939), XXXI, 272–73.
23. *The Writings of Thomas Jefferson,* Bergh, ed. (Washington, 1903), I, 278–79.
24. Helen R. Rosenberg, *The Vice-Presidency of the United States* (Ph.D. Thesis, University of California, 1930), p. 82.
25. Henry B. Learned, "Casting Votes of the Vice-Presidents, 1789–1915," 20 *American Historical Review* 571 (April, 1915).
26. Smith, p. 846.
27. Charles O. Paullin, "The Vice-President and the Cabinet," 29 *American Historical Review* 497 (April, 1924).
28. *The Writings of Thomas Jefferson,* Ford, ed. (New York, 1896), VII, 120.
29. *The Writings of Thomas Jefferson,* Bergh, ed. (Washington, 1907) IX, 368.
30. *The Life and Correspondence of Rufus King,* King, ed. (New York, 1895), II, 167.
31. *The Works of John Adams,* Adams, ed. (Boston, 1853), VIII, 538–39.
32. *The Writings of Thomas Jefferson,* Ford, ed., VII, 120.
33. See Edgar Waugh, *Second Consul* (Indianapolis, 1956), pp. 41–48.
34. Annals of Congress, 8th Cong., 1st Sess. (1804), pp. 21–22.
35. *Ibid.,* p. 84.
36. *Ibid.,* p. 672.
37. *Ibid.,* p. 673.
38. *Ibid.,* p. 535.
39. *Ibid.,* pp. 143, 144.
40. *Ibid.,* p. 155.
41. *Ibid.,* p. 674.
42. *Ibid.,* p. 692.
43. *Ibid.,* p. 733.
44. E.g., *ibid.,* pp. 668–70, 693, 707, 710, 718, 726, 739, 753, 771.
45. E.g., *ibid.,* pp. 136, 139, 187, 198, 492, 535, 702–03, 750.
46. E.g., *ibid.,* pp. 91, 143–45, 529.
47. E.g., *ibid.,* p. 21.
48. E.g., *ibid.,* pp. 170, 173, 694–96, 710, 734, 766–71.

Footnotes

Chapter 6 (Pages 79–88)

1. See Irving G. Williams, *The American Vice-Presidency; New Look* (Garden City, 1954), p. 5.
2. Allen C. Clark, *Life and Letters of Dolly Madison* (Washington, 1914), p. 130.
3. Frank Monaghan, "George Clinton," in 4 *Dictionary of American Biography* 228 (New York, 1930).
4. *The Memoirs of John Quincy Adams,* C. F. Adams, ed. (Philadelphia, 1874), I, 385.
5. *William Plumer's Memorandum of Proceedings in the United States Senate,* Brown, ed. (New York, 1923), p. 634.
6. *Ibid.,* p. 450.
7. E. Wilder Spaulding, *George Clinton* (New York, 1938), p. 291.
8. Irving Brant, *James Madison* (Indianapolis, 1953), IV, 429. See also, Spaulding, pp. 287–88.
9. See Brant, pp. 430–31; Spaulding, pp. 289–90.
10. Brant, p. 423.
11. Spaulding, p. 295.
12. James T. Austin, *The Life of Elbridge Gerry* (Boston, 1829), p. 383.
13. James Schouler, *History of the United States of America* (New York, 1885), III, 198.
14. Annals of Congress, 16th Cong., 2d Sess. (1820), III, 118.
15. S. Doc. 74, 16th Cong., 2d Sess. (1821).
16. William E. Smith, "Martin Van Buren," in 19 *Dictionary of American Biography* 154 (New York, 1936).
17. Marquis James, *Andrew Jackson* (New York, 1937), pp. 390–91.
18. Proceedings of the National Democratic Convention, 1840, p. 19.
19. Letter of Andrew Jackson to Martin Van Buren dated April 3, 1840, in *Van Buren Papers* (Library of Congress); see Charles A. McCoy, *Polk and the Presidency* (Austin, 1960), p. 31.

Chapter 7 (Pages 89–98)

1. *Daily National Intelligencer,* March 5, 1841, p. 3.
2. James D. Richardson, *Messages and Papers of the Presidents, 1789–1897* (Washington, 1897), IV, 22.
3. *Ibid.,* p. 31.
4. *Ibid.,* p. 21.
5. *Ibid.,* pp. 22–23.
6. Ruth C. Silva, *Presidential Succession* (Ann Arbor, 1951), pp. 16–17.
7. Herbert W. Horwill, *Usages of the American Constitution* (London, 1925), pp. 70–71.
8. Lyon G. Tyler, *Letters and Times of the Tylers* (Richmond, 1885), II, 12; Silva, p. 17.

Footnotes

9. Richardson, pp. 31–32.
10. Hugh R. Fraser, *Democracy in the Making* (New York, 1938), p. 159; Robert J. Morgan, *A Whig Embattled; The Presidency Under John Tyler* (Lincoln, 1954), p. 59 & n. 8; Robert Seager II, *And Tyler Too, A Biography of John and Julia Gardiner Tyler* (New York, 1963), p. 149.
11. Fraser, pp. 159–60; Morgan, p. 59 & n. 8; Seager, p. 149.
12. Richardson, p. 37.
13. *New York American,* April 16, 1841, p. 2.
14. *The Memoirs of John Quincy Adams,* C. F. Adams, ed. (Philadelphia, 1877), X, 463–64.
15. *Ibid.,* 456.
16. See Silva, pp. 15–16 & n. 8.
17. Tyler, p. 72.
18. *Daily National Intelligencer,* April 15, 1841, p. 3.
19. Cong. Globe, 27th Cong., 1st Sess. (1841), p. 3.
20. *Ibid.,* pp. 3–4.
21. *Ibid.,* p. 4.
22. *Ibid.,* pp. 4–5.
23. *Ibid.,* p. 5.
24. *Ibid.*
25. *Ibid.*
26. Seager, pp. 204–05.

Chapter 8 (Pages 99–116)

1. *Polk: The Diary of a President, 1845–1849,* Nevins, ed. (New York, 1952), p. 29.
2. Charles J. Biddle, *Eulogy Upon the Hon. George Mifflin Dallas* (Philadelphia, 1865), p. 34.
3. Cong. Globe, 29th Cong., 1st Sess. (1846), p. 1156.
4. Washington *Republic,* July 9, 1850.
5. *Weekly National Intelligencer,* July 13, 1850, p. 2.
6. James D. Richardson, *Messages and Papers of the Presidents, 1789–1897* (Washington, 1897), V, 51.
7. *Ibid.,* p. 52.
8. *Ibid.,* p. 64.
9. See Charles O. Paullin, "The Vice-President and the Cabinet," 29 *American Historical Review* 497–98 (April, 1924).
10. Roy F. Nichols, "William Rufus Devane King," in 10 *Dictionary of American Biography* 407 (New York, 1933).
11. Walter M. Jackson, *Alabama's First United States Vice-President— William Rufus King* (Decatur, 1952), p. 39.
12. Philip Shriver Klein, *President James Buchanan* (Pennsylvania, 1962), p. 220.
13. Jackson, p. 42; *New York Evening Post,* April 12, 1853, p. 3.
14. Richardson, p. 225.

15. See 25 *The Congressional Digest* 71 (1946).
16. Cong. Globe, 34th Cong., 1st Sess. (1856), p. 1476.
17. S. Rept. 260, 34th Cong., 1st Sess. (1856).
18. Howard Carroll, "He Served the State," in *Twelve Americans—Their Lives and Times* (New York, 1883), p. 148.
19. Carl Sandburg, *Abraham Lincoln; The Prairie Years and the War Years* (New York, 1926), p. 219; Carroll, p. 151.
20. Carroll, p. 154.
21. Cong. Globe, 36th Cong., 2d Sess. (1860), p. 142.
22. Reinhard H. Luthin, *The Real Abraham Lincoln* (New Jersey, 1960), p. 618.
23. *Ibid.*
24. Ida M. Tarbell, *The Life of Abraham Lincoln* (New York, 1920), II, 244.
25. Robert G. Caldwell, *James A. Garfield* (New York, 1931), p. 155.
26. Richardson, VI, 284–85.
27. *Ibid.*, pp. 305–06.
28. See David Miller Dewitt, *The Impeachment and Trial of Andrew Johnson* (New York, 1903), pp. 390–93.
29. Cong. Globe, 39th Cong., 2d Sess. (Supplement, 1867), pp. 411–15.
30. Elias Nason and Thomas Russell, *The Life and Public Services of Henry Wilson* (Boston, 1876), p. 416.
31. Henry Wilson, *History of the Rise and Fall of the Slave Power in America* (Boston, 1872–1877), 3 vols.
32. Nason and Russell, pp. 418–19.

Chapter 9 (Pages 117–139)

1. *The New York Times,* July 3, 1881, p. 1.
2. *Ibid.,* July 3, 1881, p. 1.
3. *Ibid.,* July 3, 1881, p. 1.
4. *Ibid.,* July 3, 1881, p. 5.
5. *Ibid.,* July 3, 1881, p. 1.
6. *Ibid.,* July 3, 1881, p. 2.
7. Quoted in *The New York Times,* July 3, 1881, p. 5.
8. *The New York Times,* September 20, 1881, p. 2.
9. *Ibid.,* July 3, 1881, p. 7.
10. Benson J. Lossing, *A Biography of James A. Garfield* (New York, 1882), pp. 636–38.
11. *The New York Times,* July 4, 1881, p. 5.
12. George F. Howe, *Chester A. Arthur* (New York, 1957), p. 150.
13. *The New York Times,* July 5, 1881, p. 1.
14. Robert G. Caldwell, *James A. Garfield* (New York, 1931), p. 355.
15. See "Official Bulletin of the Autopsy on the Body of President Garfield," in James D. Richardson, *The Messages and Papers of the Presidents, 1789–1897* (Washington, 1897), VIII, 24–25.

Footnotes

16. *The New York Times,* July 8, 1881, p. 1.
17. *Ibid.,* August 2, 1881, p. 5.
18. *Ibid.,* August 11, 1881, p. 1.
19. Caldwell, p. 354.
20. *The New York Times,* August 28, 1881, p. 1.
21. *Ibid.,* July 23, 1881, p. 1, col. 2.
22. *Ibid.,* August 16, 1881, p. 1.
23. *Ibid.,* August 27, 1881, p. 4.
24. Richardson, p. 14.
25. *Ibid.,* pp. 33–34.
26. See, e.g., *The New York Times,* July 8, 1881, p. 4; September 21, 1881, p. 4; September 27, 1881, p. 4; October 11, 1881, p. 4.
27. See *The New York Times,* December 8, 1881, p. 4.
28. Symposium—"Presidential Inability," 133 *North American Review* 442–43 (1881); see also *The New York Times,* October 22, 1881, p. 4.
29. *The New York Times,* September 2, 1881, p. 1.
30. *New York Herald,* September 15, 1881, p. 6.
31. *New York Daily Tribune,* September 6, 1881, p. 4; see also *New York Daily Tribune,* August 11, 1881, p. 4; September 14, 1881, p. 4.
32. *The New York Times,* September 15, 1881, p. 1. See *New York Herald,* September 5, 1881, p. 8.
33. Symposium—"Presidential Inability," 418–21.
34. *Ibid.,* pp. 422–24.
35. 13 Cong. Rec. 124, 142–43, 191–93 (1882); see *The New York Times,* September 8, 1881, p. 1; December 16, 1881, p. 1.
36. Quoted in *The New York Times,* September 4, 1881, p. 1.
37. *New York Herald,* September 13, 1881, p. 5.
38. *New York Herald,* September 17, 1881, p. 6.
39. *New York Daily Tribune,* September 6, 1881, p. 4; see *New York Daily Tribune,* August 11, 1881, p. 4; August 30, 1881, p. 4; September 14, 1881, p. 4.
40. *The New York Times,* September 2, 1881, p. 1.
41. Symposium—"Presidential Inability," pp. 418–21.
42. *New York Herald,* December 16, 1881, p. 6.
43. *Ibid.,* September 10, 1881, p. 2.
44. *Ibid.,* September 3, 1881, p. 6.
45. Henry Flanders, *An Exposition on the Constitution* (Philadelphia 2d ed., 1874), pp. 165–66.
46. Joseph Story, *Commentaries on the Constitution of the United States* (Boston, 4th ed., 1873), II, § 1482.
47. James Kent, *Commentaries on American Law* (Boston, 12th ed., 1873), I, 278–79.
48. See Guy M. Boustead, *The Lone Monarch* (London, 1940), pp. 239–46, 263–83; Beckles Wilson, *George III as Man, Monarch and Statesman* (London, 1907), pp. 443–60, 548–67.
49. Howe, p. 153.
50. Richardson, p. 65.

Footnotes

Chapter 10 (Pages 140–146)

1. *New York Herald,* November 26, 1885, p. 3.
2. *Ibid.,* November 29, 1885, p. 9.
3. *Ibid.,* November 30, 1885, p. 4.
4. 13 Cong. Rec. 22, 123, 193 (1881).
5. S. 350 and S. 2035, 47th Cong., 1st Sess. (1881).
6. *New York Herald,* December 10, 1881, p. 6.
7. 14 Cong. Rec. 1014 (1883).
8. 15 Cong. Rec. 661 (1883).
9. James D. Richardson, *Messages and Papers of the Presidents, 1789–1897* (Washington, 1897), VIII, 365.
10. 17 Cong. Rec. 252 (1885).
11. 24 Stat. 1 (1886).
12. See 13 Cong. Rec. 122, 129–33, 137–39 (1881); 14 Cong. Rec. 688–89, 876–88, 913, 954, 965 (1883); 17 Cong. Rec. 214–16, 220–21, 686 (1885).
13. Annals of Congress, 5th Cong., 3d Sess. (1798), II, 2245–415.
14. E.g., U.S. Const., art. II, § 1, cl. 2, § 2, cl. 1, § 3; Amend. 14, § 3.
15. 14 Cong. Rec. 689 (1883).
16. 14 Cong. Rec. 688–89 (1883).
17. See Charles S. Hamlin, "The Presidential Succession Act of 1886," 18 *Harvard Law Review* 183 (1905).
18. Ruth C. Silva, *Presidential Succession* (Ann Arbor, 1951), pp. 146–47; Hamlin, pp. 183, 190.
19. Hamlin, p. 191.

Chapter 11 (Pages 147–151)

1. Allan Nevins, *Grover Cleveland* (New York, 1962), p. 528.
2. W. W. Keen, "The Surgical Operations on President Cleveland in 1893," 190 *The Saturday Evening Post* 24 (September 22, 1917).
3. *Ibid.*
4. *Ibid.,* p. 53.
5. Nevins, p. 533.
6. Keen, pp. 25, 55.

Chapter 12 (Pages 152–161)

1. David Magie, *Life of Garret Augustus Hobart—Twenty-Fourth Vice-President of the United States* (Boston, 1947), p. 79.
2. *Ibid.,* p. 169.
3. *Ibid.*

4. *Ibid.*
5. 33 Cong. Rec. 743–44 (1900).
6. 33 Cong. Rec. 738 (1900).
7. *The Autobiography of Theodore Roosevelt,* Andrews, ed. (New York, 1958), p. 153.
8. *Ibid.,* pp. 168–69.
9. Henry F. Pringle, *Theodore Roosevelt* (New York, 1931), p. 218.
10. Noel F. Busch, *T. R.; The Story of Theodore Roosevelt and His Influence on Our Times* (New York, 1963), pp. 143–45.
11. *Ibid.,* p. 143.
12. Charles S. Olcott, *The Life of William McKinley* (Boston, 1916), II, 274.
13. Busch, pp. 146–47.
14. H. Wayne Morgan, *William McKinley and His America* (Syracuse, 1963), p. 518.
15. *Ibid.,* p. 522.
16. *Ibid.*
17. *Ibid.,* p. 523.
18. *The Autobiography of Theodore Roosevelt,* p. 192.
19. Noel F. Busch, T.R.; *The Story of Theodore Roosevelt and His Influence on Our Times* (New York, 1963), p. 151.
20. *Ibid.*
21. James D. Richardson, *Messages and Papers of the Presidents, 1789–1905* (Washington, 1907), X, 399.
22. *Ibid.*
23. *The New York Times,* September 15, 1901, p. 2.
24. *The Autobiography of Theodore Roosevelt,* pp. 193–94.
25. Busch, p. 152.
26. Henry F. Pringle, *The Life and Times of William Howard Taft* (New York, 1939), I, 350.
27. *Ibid.,* p. 354.
28. *Ibid.*
29. *Ibid.,* pp. 354–55.
30. Busch, p. 274.

Chapter 13 (Pages 162–180)

1. Gene Smith, *When the Cheering Stopped; The Last Years of Woodrow Wilson* (New York, 1964), p. 101.
2. Herbert Eaton, *Presidential Timber* (London, 1964), pp. 244–45.
3. Alben W. Barkley, *That Reminds Me* (Garden City, 1954), p. 207.
4. Thomas R. Marshall, *Recollections of Thomas R. Marshall* (Indianapolis, 1925), p. 229.
5. *Ibid.,* p. 233.
6. *Ibid.*
7. Barkley, p. 221.

Footnotes

8. Marshall, p. 201.
9. See Silas Bent McKinley, *Woodrow Wilson* (New York, 1957), pp. 253, 262; Smith, p. 106.
10. Joseph P. Tumulty, *Woodrow Wilson As I Know Him* (Garden City, 1921), p. 435.
11. Elizabeth Jaffray, *Secrets of the White House* (New York, 1927), p. 69.
12. *The New York Times,* October 3, 1919, p. 1.
13. *Ibid.,* October 7, 1919, p. 1.
14. *New York World,* October 8, 1919, p. 12.
15. *The New York Times,* October 12, 1919, p. 1.
16. *Ibid.,* October 13, 1919, p. 1.
17. *The Sun And The New York Herald,* February 11, 1920, p. 1.
18. See John Dos Passos, *Mr. Wilson's War* (Garden City, 1962), pp. 492–93; Herbert Hoover, *The Ordeal of Woodrow Wilson* (New York, 1958), p. 271; David F. Houston, *Eight Years With Wilson's Cabinet* (Garden City, 1926), II, 36–37.
19. Smith, p. 97.
20. *New York Tribune,* October 14, 1919, p. 1.
21. Houston, p. 37.
22. Tumulty, pp. 443–44.
23. *The Cabinet Diaries of Josephus Daniels,* Cronon, ed. (Lincoln, 1963), p. 115.
24. Houston, p. 38.
25. *Ibid.*
26. *Ibid.,* p. 39.
27. *The New York Times,* October 7, 1919, p. 1.
28. *New York Herald,* October 7, 1919, p. 12.
29. CBS Reports. "The Crisis of Presidential Succession" (Columbia Broadcasting System Network, January 8, 1964).
30. Edith Bolling Wilson, *My Memoir* (Indianapolis, 1939), p. 290.
31. Hoover, pp. 271–72.
32. *The Cabinet Diaries of Josephus Daniels,* pp. 452–53; George Sylvester Viereck, *The Strangest Friendship in History* (New York, 1932), p. 314; Smith, p. 131.
33. *The New York Times,* December 6, 1919, p. 1.
34. William Allen White, *Woodrow Wilson; The Man, His Times, and His Task* (Boston, 1929), p. 45.
35. Smith, pp. 161–62.
36. CBS Reports.
37. Smith, p. 130.
38. *The New York Times,* February 14, 1920, p. 1.
39. Tumulty, p. 445.
40. H. J. Res. 297 and H. R. 12609, 66th Cong., 2d Sess. (1920).
41. H. R. 12609, 66th Cong., 2d Sess. (1920).
42. House Committee on the Judiciary, 66th Cong., 2d Sess. hearings on H. R. 12609, 12629, 12647, and H. J. Res. 297 (1920).
43. Houston, p. 70.

Footnotes

Chapter 14 (Pages 181–189)

1. Claude M. Fuess, *Calvin Coolidge* (Boston, 1940), p. 263.
2. *The New York Times,* December 17, 1920, p. 1.
3. Fuess, p. 278; Calvin Coolidge, *The Autobiography of Calvin Coolidge* (New York, 1929), p. 155.
4. Harry M. Daugherty, *The Inside Story of the Harding Tragedy* (New York, 1932), p. 278.
5. Coolidge, p. 161.
6. Fuess, p. 293.
7. Samuel G. Blythe, "A Calm View of a Calm Man," in 193 *The Saturday Evening Post* 3 (July 28, 1923).
8. See Samuel Hopkins Adams, *Incredible Era; The Life and Times of Warren Gamaliel Harding* (Boston, 1939), pp. 378–84; Gaston B. Means, *The Strange Death of President Harding* (New York, 1930).
9. Willis Fletcher Johnson, *The Life of Warren G. Harding* (1923), p. 236.
10. Fuess, pp. 309–10.
11. Coolidge, p. 175.
12. Daughterty, p. 280; Fuess, p. 315.
13. Coolidge, p. 164.
14. Louis C. Hatch and Earl L. Shoup, *A History of the Vice-Presidency of the United States* (New York, 1934), p. 45.

Chapter 15 (Pages 190–203)

1. Bascom N. Timmons, *Garner of Texas* (New York, 1948), p. 223.
2. Herbert Eaton, *Presidential Timber* (London, 1964), p. 402.
3. John Gunther, *Roosevelt in Retrospect* (New York, 1950), p. 349.
4. Eaton, p. 402.
5. *Ibid.,* p. 405.
6. *Ibid.,* p. 407.
7. Karl C. Wold, *Mr. President—How Is Your Health?* (Milwaukee, 1948), p. 191; see Charles W. Robertson, "Some Observations on Presidential Illnesses," 8 *The Boston Medical Quarterly* 85 (June, 1957); and Gunther, p. 361 & n. 1.
8. Robertson, p. 85.
9. Samuel I. Rosenman, *Working With Roosevelt* (New York, 1950), pp. 411–12.
10. Gunther, p. 365.
11. *Ibid.,* p. 374.
12. *Ibid.,* p. 373.
13. James Roosevelt and Sidney Shalett, *Affectionately, F. D. R.* (New York, 1959), pp. 354–55; see Gunther, p. 364.
14. Edward R. Stettinius, Jr., *Roosevelt and the Russians* (New York, 1949), p. 203.

Footnotes

15. Harry S. Truman, *Memoirs* (Garden City, 1955), I, 2.
16. Gunther, pp. 371–72.
17. Truman, p. 5.
18. *Ibid.*, p. 9.
19. *Ibid.*, pp. 9–10.
20. *Ibid.*, p. 12.
21. *Ibid.*, pp. 12–13.
22. *Ibid.*, p. 55.
23. *Ibid.*, pp. 53–55.
24. Alben W. Barkley, *That Reminds Me* (New York, 1954), p. 206.
25. *Ibid.*, pp. 207–08.
26. Truman, p. 57.
27. Barkley, p. 209.
28. *Ibid.*

Chapter 16 (Pages 204–210)

1. 25 Congressional Digest 87 (March, 1946).
2. 91 Cong. Rec. 6272 (1945).
3. H.R. 3587, 79th Cong., 1st Sess. (1945)
4. See 91 Cong. Rec. 7011–12, 7016 (1945).
5. 91 Cong. Rec. 7015, 7017–18, 7022 (1945).
6. 91 Cong. Rec. 7010 (1945).
7. 91 Cong. Rec. 7020 (1945).
8. S. 564, 80th Cong., 1st Sess. (1947).
9. 93 Cong. Rec. 7767–70 (1947).
10. 93 Cong. Rec. 7776–77 (1947).
11. 93 Cong. Rec. 7781 (1947).
12. 93 Cong. Rec. 7783–84 (1947).
13. 93 Cong. Rec. 7786 (1947).
14. 93 Cong. Rec. 7696, 8626 (1947); 91 Cong. Rec. 7009 (1945).

Chapter 17 (Pages 211–229)

1. Dwight D. Eisenhower, *The White House Years* (Garden City, 1963), p. 46.
2. Richard M. Nixon, "The Second Office," in *1964 Year Book,* World Book Encyclopedia, p. 82.
3. *Ibid.*
4. *Ibid.*, p. 91.
5. Eisenhower, p. 537.
6. *U.S. News & World Rep.*, October 7, 1955, p. 68 ("When Ike's Heart Faltered").

Footnotes

7. *The New York Times,* September 25, 1955, p. 41.
8. *U.S. News & World Rep.,* October 7, 1955, p. 78.
9. Eisenhower, p. 538.
10. *The New York Times,* September 27, 1955, p. 26.
11. *Ibid.,* p. 21.
12. *The New York Times,* September 28, 1955, p. 1.
13. Robert J. Donovan, *Eisenhower; The Inside Story* (New York, 1956), p. 372.
14. Sherman Adams, *Firsthand Report; The Story of the Eisenhower Administration* (New York, 1961), p. 186.
15. Eisenhower, p. 540.
16. Donovan, p. 373.
17. Eisenhower, p. 538.
18. *Ibid.,* p. 541.
19. Address to National Forum on Presidential Inability and Vice-Presidential Vacancy Sponsored by American Bar Association (May 25, 1964).
20. Ezra Taft Benson, *Cross Fire; The Eight Years With Eisenhower* (Garden City, 1962), p. 282.
21. Adams, p. 185.
22. Eisenhower, p. 542.
23. Adams, p. 192.
24. CBS Reports, "The Crisis of Presidential Succession" (Columbia Broadcasting System Network, January 8, 1964).
25. Richard M. Nixon, *Six Crises* (Garden City, 1962), p. 143.
26. Adams, p. 192.
27. Eisenhower, p. 545.
28. *The New York Times* (The News of the Week in Review), June 10, 1956, p. 1.
29. *The New York Times,* June 10, 1956, p. 60.
30. Nixon, *Six Crises,* p. 168.
31. Adams, p. 196.
32. Nixon, *Six Crises,* p. 171.
33. *U.S. News & World Rep.,* December 6, 1957, p. 108.
34. Adams, p. 198.
35. *Ibid.,* p. 200.
36. *Ibid.,* p. 200–01.
37. Nixon, *Six Crises,* p. 177.
38. White House Press Release, March 3, 1958.

Chapter 18 (Pages 230–233)

1. Richard M. Nixon, "The Second Office," in *1964 Year Book,* World Book Encyclopedia, p. 89.
2. William S. White, *The Professional: Lyndon B. Johnson* (Boston, 1964), p. 232.

Footnotes

3. James Reston, "Eisenhower to Johnson: Take It Easy," *The New York Times* (The News of the Week in Review), January 12, 1964, p. 12 E.
4. *The New York Times,* April 24, 1964, p. 14.
5. *Ibid.,* July 31, 1964, p. 8.

Chapter 19 (Pages 237–257)

1. CBS Reports: "The Crisis of Presidential Succession" (Columbia Broadcasting System Network, January 8, 1964).
2. S. Con. Res. 50, 79th Cong., 2d Sess. (1946).
3. See Staff of the House Committee on the Judiciary, 84th Cong., 2d Sess., Presidential Inability (Committee Print, 1956).
4. *Ibid.*
5. Hearings Before Special Subcommittee to Study Presidential Inability of the House Judiciary Committee, 84th Cong., 2d Sess., ser. 20 (1956).
6. See House Judiciary Committee, 85th Cong., 1st Sess., Presidential Inability: An Analysis of Replies to a Questionnaire and Testimony at a Hearing on Presidential Inability (Committee Print, 1957).
7. Hearing Before the Special Subcommittee on Study of Presidential Inability of the House Judiciary Committee, 85th Cong., 1st Sess. (1957).
8. *The New York Times,* June 24, 1957.
9. Hearings Before the Subcommittee on Constitutional Amendments of the Senate Judiciary Committee, 85th Cong., 2d Sess. (Washington, 1958).
10. S.J. Res. 161, 85th Cong., 2d Sess. (1958).
11. House Judiciary Committee, 85th Cong., 1st Sess., Presidential Inability: An Analysis of Replies to a Questionnaire and Testimony at a Hearing on Presidential Inability 10 (Committee Print, 1957).
12. S. Rep. 1382, 88th Cong., 2d Sess. (1964), p. 18.
13. Hearings Before the Subcommittee on Constitutional Amendments of the Senate Judiciary Committee, 88th Cong., 1st Sess. (Washington, 1963), p. 10.
14. Hearings Before the Subcommittee on Constitutional Amendments of the Senate Judiciary Committee, 88th Cong., 2d Sess. (Washington, 1964), p. 22.
15. S. J. Res. 139, 88th Cong. 2d Sess. (1964).
16. CBS Reports.
17. Hearings Before the Subcommittee on Constitutional Amendments of the Senate Judiciary Committee, 85th Cong., 2d Sess. (Washington, 1958), p. 14.
18. Herman Wouk, *The Caine Mutiny* (Garden City, 1951).
19. Hearings Before the Subcommittee on Constitutional Amendments of the Senate Judiciary Committee, 88th Cong., 2d Sess. (Washington, 1964), p. 232.
20. *Ibid.,* pp. 161, 164.

21. *Ibid.*, p. 3.
22. 110 Cong. Rec. 22288 (1964).
23. *New York Herald Tribune,* June 9, 1964, p. 20.

Chapter 20 (Pages 258–263)

1. Hearings Before the Subcommittee on Constitutional Amendments of the Senate Judiciary Committee, 88th Cong., 2d Sess. (Washington, 1964), pp. 1–2.
2. *The New York Times,* March 16, 1964, p. 18.
3. Hearings Before the Subcommittee on Constitutional Amendments of the Senate Judiciary Committee, 88th Cong., 2d Sess. (Washington, 1964), p. 240.
4. *Ibid.*, p. 164.
5. *Ibid.*, p. 5.
6. S. J. Res. 140, 88th Cong., 2d Sess. (1964).
7. Richard M. Nixon, "We Need a Vice President Now," in 237 *The Saturday Evening Post* 6 (January 18, 1964).
8. Hearings Before the Subcommittee on Constitutional Amendments of the Senate Judiciary Committee, 88th Cong., 2d Sess. (Washington, 1964), p. 188.
9. *Ibid.*, pp. 207–08.

Chapter 21 (Pages 264–269)

1. CBS Reports: "The Crisis of Presidential Succession" (Columbia Broadcasting System Network, January 8, 1964).
2. *The New York Times,* March 16, 1964, p. 18.
3. CBS Reports.
4. *Ibid.*
5. *Ibid.*
6. *Ibid.*
7. Silva, "The Presidential Succession Act of 1947," 47 *Michigan Law Review* 451, 463–64 (1949).

Chapter 22 (Pages 270–279)

1. For the various views, see *New York World Telegram & The Sun,* August 25, 1964, p. 21; *New York Herald Tribune,* October 4, 1964, p. 11; *The Wall Street Journal,* August 28, 1964, p. 6; and *U.S. News & World Rep.,* November 9, 1964, p. 44.
2. Cong. Globe, 42d Cong., 3d Sess. (1873), pp. 1285–1305.
3. Robert Bendiner, "The Changing Role of the Vice-President," 137 Collier's 53 (February 17, 1956).

Footnotes

4. Public Papers of the Presidents of the United States, 1955, (Washington, 1959), p. 557.
5. Bendiner, p. 53.
6. *The New York Times,* August 27, 1964, p. 20.
7. See *New York Journal American,* November 9, 1964, p. 15; *New York World Telegram & The Sun,* August 31, 1964, p. 8.
8. See Oliver P. Field, "The Vice-Presidency of the United States," 56 *American Law Review* 365, 398–400 (May–June, 1922); Clinton L. Rossiter, "The Reform of the Vice-Presidency," 63 *Political Science Quarterly* 383 (September, 1948).
9. Albert J. Beveridge, "The Fifth Wheel in Our Government," 79 *Century Magazine* 208 (December, 1909).
10. Lucius Wilmerding, Jr., "The Presidential Succession," 179 *The Atlantic Monthly* 91 (May, 1947); see Wilmerding, Jr., "The Vice Presidency," 68 *Political Science Quarterly* 17 (March, 1953).
11. Hearings Before the Subcommittee on Reorganization of the Senate Committee on Government Operations, 84th Cong., 2d Sess. (Washington, 1956), p. 57.
12. Herman Finer, *The Presidency: Crisis and Regeneration* (Chicago, 1960), p. 30.
13. *The New York Times,* November 29, 1964, p. 69.

Chapter 23 (Pages 280–290)

1. Ariz. Laws 1964, ch. 56.
2. *The New York Times,* August 23, 1964, p. 61.
3. See *Barnard v. Taggart,* 66 N.H. 362, 29 Atl. 1026 (1890); Louis Wyman, "When a President is Too Ill to Handle the Job," in *U.S. News & World Rep.,* March 9, 1956, p. 44.
4. 66 N.H. at 368, 29 Atl. at 1031.
5. See, generally, Clyde F. Snyder, "Gubernatorial Disability," 8 *The University of Chicago Law Review* 521 (April, 1941).
6. Facts are taken from *The New York Times* of May and June, 1959.
7. *The New York Times,* June 1, 1959, p. 21.
8. *Ibid.,* June 18, 1959, p. 20.
9. *Ibid.,* June 20, 1959, p. 11.
10. *Ibid.,* June 18, 1959, p. 20.
11. La. Att'y Gen. Op., June 22, 1959.
12. *The New York Times,* June 20, 1959, p. 1.
13. *Ibid.,* June 24, 1959, p. 20.
14. Ala. Const. art. V, § 128.
15. Mich. Const. art. V, § 26.
16. Miss. Const. art 5, § 131.
17. N.J. Const. art. V, § 1, ¶ 8.
18. Neb. Laws 1961, ch. 452, §§ 1–4, at 1379–81.
19. Ore. Rev. Stat. §§ 176.040, 176.050 (1959).

Footnotes

Chapter 24 (Pages 291–306)

1. *The New York Times,* October 11, 1963, pp. 1–2.
2. See *The New York Times,* October 19, 1963, p. 2.
3. 1 Edw. 8 & 1 Geo. 6, c. 16.
4. *Time,* December 6, 1963, p. 36.
5. *The New York Times,* April 23, 1964, p. 2.
6. *Ibid.,* October 16, 1964, p. 14.
7. *Ibid.,* January 9, 1964, p. 1.
8. *Ibid.,* January 9, 1964, p. 1.
9. *Ibid.,* March 19, 1964, p. 11.
10. *Ibid.,* August 11, 1964, p. 2.
11. *Ibid.,* December 7, 1964, p. 3.
12. Pak. Const. pt. III, ch. 1, art. 14(1)–(9).
13. S. Afr. Const. § 10(1) (b).
14. Amos J. Peaslee, *Constitutions of Nations* (The Hague, 2d ed., 1956), I, 475.

A SELECTED BIBLIOGRAPHY

1. COLONIES

Andrews, Charles M. *The Colonial Period of American History*. 4 vols. New Haven: Yale University Press, 1934–1938.

Bishop, Cortlandt F. *History of Elections in the American Colonies*. New York: Columbia College, 1893.

Dickerson, Oliver M. *American Colonial Government, 1696–1765*. New York: Russell and Russell, Inc., 1962.

Greene, Evarts Boutell. *The Provincial Governor in the English Colonies of North America*. New York: Longmans, Green, and Co., 1898.

Labaree, Leonard Woods, ed. *Royal Instructions to British Colonial Governors 1670–1776*. 2 vols. New York: D. Appleton-Century Co., Inc., 1935.

—————. *Royal Government in America*. New Haven: Yale University Press, 1930.

Osgood, Herbert L. *The American Colonies in the Eighteenth Century*. 4 vols. New York: Columbia University Press, 1924.

—————. *The American Colonies in the Seventeenth Century*. 3 vols. Massachusetts: Peter Smith, 1957.

Poore, Benjamin P., Comp. *The Federal and State Constitutions, Colonial Charters, and Other Organic Laws of the United States*. 2 vols. Washington: United States Government Printing Office, 1878.

Thorpe, Francis N., Comp. *The Federal and State Constitutions, Colonial Charters, and Other Organic Laws of the States, Territories, and Colonies*. 7 vols. Washington: United States Government Printing Office, 1909.

2. CONSTITUTION

Curtis, George Ticknor. *Constitutional History of the United States*. 2 vols. New York: Harper and Brothers, 1896–1899.

Elliot, Jonathan. *The Debates in the Several State Conventions, on the Adoption of the Federal Constitution*. 5 vols. Philadelphia: J.B. Lippincott and Co., 2d ed., 1866.

Farrand, Max. *The Records of the Federal Convention of 1787*. 4 vols. New Haven: Yale University Press, 1911 and 1937.

Foster, Roger. *Commentaries on the Constitution*. Boston: Boston Book Co., 1895.

Horwill, Herbert W. *The Usages of the American Constitution*. London: Oxford University Press, 1925.

Kent, James. *Commentaries on American Law*. Vol. I. Holmes, ed. Boston: Little, Brown and Co., 12 ed., 1873.

Scott, E. H., ed. *The Federalist and Other Constitutional Papers*. Vol. II, Chicago: Albert, Scott & Co., 1894.

Stevens, C. Ellis. *Sources of the Constitution of the United States*. New York: Macmillan and Co., 1894.

Story, Joseph. *Commentaries on the Constitution of the United States*. 2 vols. Boston: Little, Brown and Co., 4th ed., 1873.

Wilson, Woodrow. *Constitutional Government in the United States*. New York: Columbia University Press, 1908.

Warren, Charles. *The Making of the Constitution*. Boston: Little, Brown and Co., 1928.

3. PRESIDENTS

Abbott, Lawrence F. *Impressions of Theodore Roosevelt*. Garden City: Doubleday, Page & Co., 1919.

Adams, Charles Francis, ed. *The Memoirs of John Quincy Adams*. 12 vols. Philadelphia: J.B. Lippincott and Co., 1874–1877.

———. *The Works of John Adams*. 10 vols. Boston: Little, Brown and Co., 1850–1856.

Adams, Samuel Hopkins. *Incredible Era; The Life and Times of Warren Gamaliel Harding*. Boston: Houghton Mifflin Co., 1939.

Adams, Sherman. *Firsthand Report; The Story of the Eisenhower Administration*. New York: Harper & Brothers, 1961.

Andrews, Wayne, ed. *The Autobiography of Theodore Roosevelt*. New York: Charles Scribner's Sons, 1958.

Baker, Ray S. *Woodrow Wilson*. 8 vols. New York: Doubleday, Page & Co., 1927–1939.

Benson, Ezra Taft. *Cross Fire; The Eight Years With Eisenhower*. Garden City: Doubleday & Co., Inc., 1962.

Bishop, Joseph Bucklin. *Theodore Roosevelt and His Time Shown in His Own Letters*. New York: Charles Scribner's Sons, 1920.

Brant, Irving. *James Madison*. 6 vols. Indianapolis: Bobbs-Merrill Co., Inc., 1941–1961.

Brogan, D. W. *The Era of Franklin D. Roosevelt; A Chronicle of the New Deal and Global War*. New Haven: Yale University Press, 1951.

Bibliography

Bundy, J. M. *The Life of James Abram Garfield.* New York: A. S. Barnes & Co., 1881.

Busch, Noel F. *T. R.; The Story of Theodore Roosevelt and His Influence on Our Times.* New York: Reynal & Co., 1963.

Caldwell, Robert Grantville. *James A. Garfield.* New York: Dodd, Mead & Co., 1931.

Chitwood, Oliver P. *John Tyler: Champion of the Old South.* New York: D. Appleton-Century Co., 1939.

Cleaves, Freeman. *Old Tippecanoe: William Henry Harrison and His Time.* New York: Charles Scribner's Sons, Ltd., 1939.

Coolidge, Calvin. *The Autobiography of Calvin Coolidge.* New York: Cosmopolitan Book Corp., 1929.

Corwin, Edward S. *The President; Office and Powers, 1787–1957.* New York: New York University Press, 4th rev. ed., 1957.

Cronon, E. David. *The Cabinet Diaries of Josephus Daniels 1913–1921.* Lincoln: University of Nebraska Press, 1963.

Daniels, Jonathan. *The Man of Independence.* Philadelphia: J. B. Lippincott Co., 1950.

Daniels, Josephus. *The Wilson Era: Years of War and After.* Chapel Hill: University of North Carolina Press, 1946.

————. *The Life of Woodrow Wilson, 1856–1924.* Philadelphia: John C. Winston Co., 1924.

Daugherty, Harry M. *The Inside Story of the Harding Tragedy.* New York: The Churchill Co., 1932.

Dewitt, David Miller. *The Impeachment and Trial of Andrew Johnson.* New York: The Macmillan Co., 1903.

Donovan, Robert J. *Eisenhower; The Inside Story.* New York: Harper & Brothers, 1956.

Dyer, Brainerd. *Zachary Taylor.* Baton Rouge: Louisiana State University Press, 1946.

Eisenhower, Dwight D. *The White House Years.* Garden City: Doubleday & Co., Inc., 1963.

Fraser, Hugh Russell. *Democracy in the Making; The Jackson-Tyler Era.* Indianapolis: Bobbs-Merrill Co., 1938.

Fuess, Claude. *Calvin Coolidge.* Boston: Little, Brown and Co., 1940.

Gilman, Daniel C. *James Monroe in His Relations to the Public Service During Half a Century, 1776 to 1826.* Boston: Houghton, Mifflin & Co., 1883.

Goebel, Dorothy. *William Henry Harrison: A Political Biography.* Indianapolis: Historical Bureau of the Indiana Library and Historical Department, 1926.

Green, Horace. *The Life of Calvin Coolidge.* New York: Duffield & Co., 1924.

Bibliography

Griffis, William E. *Millard Fillmore*. Ithaca: Andrus & Church, 1915.

Gunther, John. *Roosevelt in Retrospect*. New York: Harper & Brothers, 1950.

Hamilton, Holman. *Zachary Taylor, Soldier in the White House*. Indianapolis: Bobbs-Merrill Co., Inc., 1951.

Hatch, Alden. *Franklin D. Roosevelt*. New York: Henry Holt and Co., 1947.

Hesseltine, William B. *Ulysses S. Grant*. New York: Dodd, Mead & Co., 1935.

Hoover, Herbert. *The Ordeal of Woodrow Wilson*. New York: McGraw-Hill Book Co., Inc., 1958.

Houston, David F. *Eight Years With Wilson's Cabinet*. 2 vols. Garden City: Doubleday, Page & Co., 1926.

Howe, George Frederick. *Chester A. Arthur*. New York: Frederick Ungar Publishing Co., 1957.

Hughes, Charles Evans. *Warren G. Harding; Memorial Address*. Washington: United States Government Printing Office, 1924.

James, Marquis. *Andrew Jackson*. Indianapolis: Bobbs-Merrill Co., 1937.

Johnson, Willis Fletcher. *The Life of Warren G. Harding*. William H. Johnston, 1923.

Keen, W. W. "The Surgical Operations on President Cleveland in 1893," *The Saturday Evening Post* (September 22, 1917).

Klein, Philip Shriver. *President James Buchanan*. Pennsylvania: The Pennsylvania State University Press, 1962.

Lawrence, David. *True Story of Woodrow Wilson*. New York: George H. Doran, 1924.

Leech, Margaret. *In the Days of McKinley*. New York: Harper & Brothers, 1959.

Lossing, Benson J. *A Biography of James A. Garfield*. New York: Henry S. Goodspeed & Co., 1882.

Luthin, Reinhard H. *The Real Abraham Lincoln*. New Jersey: Prentice-Hall, Inc., 1960.

Marx, Rudolph. *The Health of the Presidents*. New York: G. P. Putnam's Sons, 1960.

McClure, Alexander K. *The Authentic Life of William McKinley*. Washington: W. E. Scull, 1901.

McCoy, Charles A. *Polk and the Presidency*. Austin: University of Texas Press, 1960.

McKinley, Silas B. *Woodrow Wilson*. New York: Frederick A. Praeger, Inc., 1957.

Morgan, H. Wayne. *William McKinley and His America*. Syracuse: Syracuse University Press, 1963.

352

Bibliography

Morgan, Robert J. *A Whig Embattled; The Presidency Under John Tyler.* Lincoln: University of Nebraska Press, 1954.

Morrel, Martha McBride. *"Young Hickory"; The Life and Times of President James K. Polk.* New York: E. P. Dutton & Co., Inc., 1949.

Nevins, Allan. *Grover Cleveland.* New York: Dodd, Mead & Co., 1962.

Nevins, Allan, ed. *Polk: The Diary of a President, 1845–1849.* New York: Longmans, Green & Co., 1952.

Newman, Ralph G., ed. *Lincoln For the Ages.* Garden City: Doubleday & Co., Inc., 1960.

Nichols, Roy F. *Franklin Pierce: Young Hickory of the Granite Hills.* Philadelphia: University of Pennsylvania Press, 2d ed., 1958.

Ogilvie, J. S. *History of the Attempted Assassination of James A. Garfield.* New York: J. S. Ogilvie & Co., 1881.

Olcott, Charles S. *The Life of William McKinley.* Boston: Houghton Mifflin Co., 1916.

Perkins, Frances. *The Roosevelt I Know.* New York: The Viking Press, 1946.

Pringle, Henry F. *The Life and Times of William Howard Taft.* 2 vols. New York: Farrar & Rhinehart, 1939.

————. *Theodore Roosevelt.* New York: Harcourt, Brace and Co., 1931.

Randall, James G. *Lincoln the President.* 4 vols. New York: Dodd, Mead & Co., 1945–1955.

Rayback, Robert J. *Millard Fillmore.* Buffalo: Henry Stewart, Inc., 1959.

Report of the President's Commission on the Assassination of President John F. Kennedy. Washington: United States Government Printing Office, 1964.

Richardson, James D. *Messages and Papers of the Presidents.* 10 vols. Washington: United States Government Printing Office, 1897.

Rhodes, James Ford. *The McKinley and Roosevelt Administrations, 1897–1909.* New York: The Macmillan Co., 1922.

Robertson, Charles W. "Some Observations on Presidential Illnesses," 8 *The Boston Medical Quarterly* 33 (June, 1957); *ibid.,* 76 (September, 1957).

Roosevelt, Elliott. *As He Saw It.* New York: Duell, Sloan and Pearce, 1946.

Roosevelt, James, and Shalett, Sidney. *Affectionately, F. D. R.* New York: Harcourt, Brace & Co., 1959.

Rovere, Richard H. *The Eisenhower Years.* New York: Farrar, Straus and Cudahy, 1956.

Royall, Margaret Shaw. *Andrew Johnson—Presidential Scapegoat.* New York: Exposition Press, 1958.

Bibliography

Sandburg, Carl. *Abraham Lincoln; The Prairie Years and the War Years.* New York: Harcourt, Brace & Co., 1926.

Savage, John. *The Life and Public Services of Andrew Johnson, Seventeenth President of the United States.* New York: Derby & Miller, 1866.

Schlesinger, A. M. *The Age of Roosevelt.* 3 vols. Boston: Houghton Mifflin Co., 1957–1960.

Seager, II, Robert. *And Tyler Too, A Biography of John and Julia Gardiner Tyler.* New York: McGraw Hill Book Co., Inc., 1963.

Sherwood, Robert E. *Roosevelt and Hopkins: An Intimate History.* New York: Harper & Bros., 1948.

Smith, Gene. *When the Cheering Stopped; The Last Years of Woodrow Wilson.* New York: William Morrow and Co., 1964.

Smith, Page. *John Adams.* 2 vols. Garden City: Doubleday & Co., Inc., 1962.

Snow, Jane Elliott. *The Life of William McKinley.* Cleveland: The Gardner Printing Co., 1908.

Spielman, William C. *William McKinley.* New York: Exposition Press, 1954.

Steinberg, Alfred. *The Man From Missouri; The Life and Times of Harry S. Truman.* New York: G. P. Putnam's Sons, 1962.

Stryker, Lloyd P. *Andrew Johnson.* New York: The Macmillan Co., 1929.

Tarbell, Ida M. *The Life of Abraham Lincoln.* 2 vols. New York: The Macmillan Co., 1920.

Truman, Harry S. *Memoirs.* 2 vols. Garden City: Doubleday & Co., Inc., 1955.

———. *Mr. Citizen.* New York: Bernard Geis Associates, 1953.

Tully, Grace. *F. D. R. My Boss.* New York: Charles Scribner's Sons, 1949.

Tumulty, Joseph P. *Woodrow Wilson As I Know Him.* Garden City: Doubleday, Page & Co., 1921.

Tyler, Lyon G. *The Letters and Times of the Tylers.* 3 vols. Richmond: Whittet and Shepperson, 1884–1896.

Van Buren, Martin. "The Autobiography of Martin Van Buren," in *American Historical Association Annual Report For 1918.* Vol. 2. Washington, 1920.

Viereck, George Sylvester. *The Strangest Friendship in History; Woodrow Wilson and Colonel House.* New York: Liveright, Inc., 1932.

White, William Allen. *A Puritan in Babylon; The Story of Calvin Coolidge.* New York: The Macmillan Co., 1939.

———. *Woodrow Wilson.* Boston: Houghton Mifflin Co., 1925.

White, William S. *The Professional; Lyndon B. Johnson.* Boston: Houghton Mifflin Co., 1964.

Wilson, Edith Bolling. *My Memoir.* Indianapolis: Bobbs-Merrill Co., 1939.

Wold, Karl C. *Mr. President—How is Your Health?* Milwaukee: Bruce Publishing Co., 1948.

4. VICE-PRESIDENTS

Austin, James T. *The Life of Elbridge Gerry.* 2 vols. Boston: Wells and Lilly, 1828–1829.

Barkley, Alben W. *That Reminds Me.* Garden City: Doubleday & Co., Inc., 1954.

Biddle, Charles J. *Eulogy Upon Hon. George Mifflin Dallas.* Philadelphia: M'Laughlin Bros., 1865.

Carroll, Howard. "He Served the State—Hannibal Hamlin," in *Twelve Americans—Their Lives and Times.* New York: Harper & Brothers, 1883.

Dawes, Charles G. *Notes As Vice President.* Boston: Little, Brown, and Co., 1935.

de Toledano, Ralph. *Nixon.* New York: Henry Holt and Co., 1956.

Flitcroft, John E. "Garrett Augustus Hobart," in 9 *Dictionary of American Biography* 92. New York: Charles Scribner's Sons, 1932.

Gordon, Jr., Armistead C. "Daniel D. Tompkins," in 18 *Dictionary of American Biography* 583. New York: Charles Scribner's Sons, 1936.

Hamlin, Charles E. *The Life and Times of Hannibal Hamlin.* Cambridge: The Riverside Press, 1899.

Haynes, George H. "Henry Wilson," in 20 *Dictionary of American Biography* 322. New York: Charles Scribner's Sons, 1936.

Jackson, Walter M. *Alabama's First United States Vice-President—William Rufus King.* Decatur: Decatur Printing Co., 1952.

Keogh, James. *This is Nixon.* New York: G. P. Putnam's Sons, 1956.

Levin, Peter R. *Seven By Chance.* New York: Farrar, Straus, and Co., 1948.

Lord, Russell. *The Wallaces of Iowa.* Boston: Houghton Mifflin Co., 1947.

Magie, David. *Life of Garret Augustus Hobart—Twenty-Fourth Vice-President of the United States.* New York: G. P. Putnam's Sons, 1910.

Marshall, Thomas R. *Recollections of Thomas R. Marshall.* Indianapolis: Bobbs-Merrill Co., 1925.

Mazo, Earl. *Richard Nixon: A Political and Personal Portrait.* New York: Harper & Brothers, 1959.

Memorial Addresses on the Life and Character of Thomas A. Hendricks. Washington: United States Government Printing Office, 1886.

Monaghan, Frank. "George Clinton," in 4 *Dictionary of American Biography* 226. New York: Charles Scribner's Sons, 1930.

Morison, Samuel Eliot. "Elbridge Gerry," in 7 *Dictionary of American Biography* 222. New York: Charles Scribner's Sons, 1931.

Morris, Gouverneur. *An Oration . . . in Honor of the Memory of George Clinton.* New York: Hardcastle and Van Pelt, 1812.

Nason, Elias, and Russell, Thomas. *The Life and Public Services of Henry Wilson.* Boston: B. B. Russell, 1876.

Nichols, Roy F. "George M. Dallas," in 5 *Dictionary of American Biography* 38. New York: Charles Scribner's Sons, 1930.

———. "William Rufus Devane King," in 10 *Dictionary of American Biography* 406. New York: Charles Scribner's Sons, 1933.

Nixon, Richard M. *Six Crises.* Garden City: Doubleday & Co., Inc., 1962.

Smith, Edward Conrad. "James Schoolcraft Sherman," in 17 *Dictionary of American Biography* 82. New York: Charles Scribner's Sons, 1935.

Spaulding, E. Wilder. *His Excellency George Clinton.* New York: The Macmillan Co., 1938.

Timmons, Bascom Nolly. *Garner of Texas.* New York: Harper & Brothers, 1948.

Woodburn, James A. "Thomas A. Hendricks," in 8 *Dictionary of American Biography* 534. New York: Charles Scribner's Sons, 1932.

Young, Klyde and Middleton, Lamar. *Heir Apparent.* New York: Prentice-Hall, 1948.

5. SUCCESSION AND INABILITY

ABC News Reports. "Shadow Over the White House," American Broadcasting Company Network (June 18, 1964).

An Analysis of Replies To a Questionnaire and Testimony at a Hearing on Presidential Inability, H. R. Committee on the Judiciary, 85th Cong., 1st Sess. Washington: United States Government Printing Office, 1957.

Bayh, Jr., Birch. "Our Greatest National Danger," 28 *Look* 74 (April 7, 1964).

Brewer, F. M. "Succession to the Presidency," *Editorial Research Report* 195 (September 20, 1945).

Bibliography

Brownell, Jr., Herbert. "Presidential Disability: The Need For a Constitutional Amendment," 68 *The Yale Law Journal* 189 (December, 1958).

CBS Reports. "The Crisis of Presidential Succession," Columbia Broadcasting System Network (January 8, 1964).

"Congress Seeks Key to Succession Problem," 26 *Congressional Digest* 17 (January, 1947).

Davis, Henry E. "Inability of the President," *Senate Document.* 308, 65th Cong., 3d Sess. (1918).

Eisenhower, Dwight D. "When the Highest Office Changes Hands," *The Saturday Evening Post* (December 14, 1963).

Feerick, John D. "The Problem of Presidential Inability—Will Congress Ever Solve It?," 32 *Fordham Law Review* 73 (October, 1963).

———. "The Vice-Presidency and the Problems of Presidential Succession and Inability," 32 *Fordham Law Review* 457 (March, 1964).

———. "The Problem of Presidential Inability—It Must Be Solved Now," 36 *New York State Bar Journal* 181 (June, 1964).

———. "Presidential Inability: The Problem and a Solution," 50 *American Bar Association Journal* 321 (May, 1964).

Frelinghuysen, Jr. Peter. "Presidential Disability," 308 *Annals of the American Academy of Political and Social Science* 144 (September, 1956).

Gasperini, Edwin L. "The Presidential Inability Riddle," 31 *New York State Bar Journal* 258 (July, 1959).

Gilliam, Armistead W., and Sloat, Jonathan W. "Presidential Inability," 24 *George Washington University Law Review* 448 (March, 1956).

Green, Theodore F. "Presidential Succession," 61 *Dickinson Law Review* 323 (June, 1957).

Hamlin, Charles S. "The Presidential Succession Act of 1886," 18 *Harvard Law Review* 182 (January, 1905).

Hansen, Richard H. *The Year We Had No President.* Lincoln: University of Nebraska Press, 1962.

Hearings on S. J. Res. 13, S. J. Res. 28, S. J. Res. 35, S. J. Res. 84, S. J. Res. 138, S. J. Res. 139, S. J. Res. 140, S. J. Res. 143, S. J. Res. 147. S. Committee on the Judiciary, 88th Cong., 2d Sess. Washington: United States Government Printing Office, 1964.

Hearings on S. J. Res. 28, S. J. Res. 35 and S. J. Res. 84. S. Committee on the Judiciary, 88th Cong. 1st Sess. Washington: United States Government Printing Office, 1963.

Hearings on S. J. Res. 100, S. J. Res. 133, S. J. Res. 134, S. J. Res. 141, S. J. Res. 143, S. J. Res. 144, S. 238 and S. 3113. S. Committee on the Judiciary, 85th Cong., 2d Sess. Washington: United States Government Printing Office, 1958.

Bibliography

Hearing on Presidential Inability, H. R. Committee on the Judiciary, 85th Cong., 1st Sess. Washington: United States Government Printing Office, 1957.

Hearings on Proposal to Create Position of Administrative Vice President. S. Committee on Government Operations, 84th Cong., 2d Sess. Washington: United States Government Printing Office, 1956.

Hearings on Problem of Presidential Inability. H. R. Committee on the Judiciary, 84th Cong., 2d Sess. Washington: United States Government Printing Office, 1956.

Heinlein, J. C. "The Problem of Presidential Inability," 25 *University of Cincinnati Law Review* 310 (Summer, 1956).

Hofstadter, Samuel H., and Dinnes, Jacob M. "Presidential Inability: A Constitutional Amendment is Needed Now," 50 *American Bar Association Journal* 59 (January, 1964).

Hyman, Sidney. "The Issue of Presidential Inability," *The New York Times Magazine,* February 26, 1956, p. 13.

"If a Presidential Nominee or President-Elect Dies," 22 *Congressional Quarterly* 2466 (October 16, 1964).

Kallenbach, Joseph E. "The New Presidential Succession Act," 41 *American Political Science Review* 931 (October, 1947).

Kennedy, Robert F. 42 *Opinions of Attorneys General* No. 5. Washington: United States Government Printing Office, 1961.

Kirby, Jr., James C. "A Breakthrough on Presidential Inability: The ABA Conference Consensus," 17 *The Vanderbilt Law Review* 463 (March, 1964).

"Legislative Analysis: Presidential Disability and Vice-Presidential Vacancies," American Enterprise Institute (August 3, 1964).

————. "Resolutions and Bills Relating to the Inability of the President to Discharge the Duties of His Office," American Enterprise Institute (March 31, 1958).

Longgood, William. "Our Fuzzy Succession Rules," *New York World-Telegram and The Sun,* August 25, 1964, p. 21.

Morris, Richard B. "The Muddled Problem of the Succession," *The New York Times Magazine,* December 15, 1963, p. 11.

"Moves to Change Presidential Succession," 43 *Congressional Digest* 130 (May, 1964).

Nixon, Richard M. "We Need A Vice President Now," *The Saturday Evening Post* (January 18, 1964).

Otten, Alan L. "What Happens If A Nominee Dies," *The Wall Street Journal,* August 28, 1964, p. 6.

Rankin, Robert S. "Presidential Succession in the United States," 8 *The Journal of Politics* 44 (February, 1946).

Bibliography

Silva, Ruth C. *Presidential Succession.** Ann Arbor: University of Michigan Press, 1951.

————. "Presidential Inability," 35 *Detroit Law Journal* 139 (December, 1957).

————. "The Presidential Succession Act of 1947," 47 *Michigan Law Review* 451 (February, 1949).

Symposium—"Presidential Inability," 133 *North American Review* 417 (November, 1881).

"The Question of Adequate Legal Provision for Presidential Disability," 37 *Congressional Digest* 1 (January, 1958).

"The Question of Amending the Presidential Succession Act," 25 *Congressional Digest* 67 (March, 1946).

Transcript of Proceedings at a National Forum on Presidential Inability and Vice Presidential Vacancy Sponsored by the American Bar Association (May 25, 1964).

"What Happens in Election If Death Intrudes," *New York Herald Tribune,* October 4, 1964, p. 11.

Wickersham, Cornelius W. "Presidential Inability: Procrastination, Apathy and the Constitution," 7 *Villanova Law Review* 271 (Winter, 1961–62).

Wilmerding, Jr., Lucius. "The Presidential Succession," 179 *The Atlantic Monthly* 91 (May, 1947).

Works, Lewis R. "The Succession of the Vice-President Under the Constitution—an Interrogation," 38 *American Law Review* 500 (August, 1904).

Wyman, Louis C. "When a President is Too Ill to Handle the Job: Precedent in New Hampshire," 40 *U. S. News and World Report* 44 (March 9, 1956).

6. VICE-PRESIDENCY

Bendiner, Robert. "The Changing Role of the Vice-President," 137 *Collier's* 48 (February 17, 1956).

Beveridge, Albert J. "The Fifth Wheel in Our Government," 79 *The Century Magazine* 208 (December, 1909).

Broder, David S. "The Triple-H Brand on the Vice-Presidency," *The New York Times Magazine,* December 6, 1964, p. 30.

Burns, James MacGregor. "A New Look at the Vice Presidency," *The New York Times Magazine,* October 9, 1955, p. 11.

---

* This is the outstanding treatise on the subject of presidential succession.

Bibliography

Bush, Irving T. "Needed—A Business Manager," 65 *Collier's* 13 (March 13, 1920).

Clark, Walter. "The Vice-President: What to Do With Him," 8 *Green Bag* 427 (October, 1896).

Durham, G. Homer. "The Vice-Presidency," 1 *The Western Political Quarterly* 311 (September, 1948).

Field, Oliver P. "The Vice-Presidency of the United States," 56 *American Law Review* 365 (May-June, 1922).

Garner, John Nance. "This Job of Mine," 118 *American Magazine* 23 (July, 1934).

Hatch, Louis C., Shoup, Earl L. *A History of the Vice Presidency of the United States.* New York: American Historical Society, 1934.

Learned, Henry Barrett. "Casting Votes of the Vice-Presidents, 1789–1915," 20 *American Historical Review* 571 (April, 1915).

———. "Some Aspects of the Vice-Presidency," 7 *American Political Science Review* (Supplement) 162 (February, 1913).

———. "The Vice-President's Oath of Office," 104 *The Nation* 248 (April, 1917).

May, Samuel C., and McKinley, John R. "The Vice Presidency and Proposals for Strengthening the Office," Bureau of Public Administration, University of California (Unpublished Outline, July 27, 1948).

Menez, Joseph F. "Needed: A New Concept of the Vice-Presidency," 30 *Social Science* 143 (June, 1955).

Nixon, Richard M. "The Second Office," in *1964 Year Book,* World Book Encyclopedia.

Paullin, Charles O. "The Vice-President and the Cabinet," 29 *American Historical Review* 496 (April, 1924).

Roosevelt, Franklin D. "Can the Vice President Be Useful?," *The Saturday Evening Post* (October 16, 1920).

Roosevelt, Theodore. "The Three Vice-Presidential Candidates and What They Represent," 14 *Review of Reviews* 289 (September, 1896).

Rosenberg, Helen R. *The Vice-Presidency of the United States.* (Ph.D. Thesis, University of California, 1930).

Ross, Earl D. "The National Spare Tire," 239 *The North American Review* 3 (March, 1935).

Rossiter, Clinton L. "The Reform of the Vice-Presidency," 63 *Political Science Quarterly* 383 (September, 1948).

Waugh, Edgar W. *Second Consul.* Indianapolis: Bobbs-Merrill & Co., 1956.

Williams, Irving G. *The Rise of the Vice Presidency.* New York: Public Affairs Press, 1956.

———. *The American Vice Presidency: New Look.* Garden City: Doubleday & Co., 1954.

Wilmerding, Jr., Lucius. "The Vice Presidency," 68 *Political Science Quarterly* 17 (March, 1953).

7. STATES

Abernathy, Byron R. "The Office of the Lieutenant Governor," in *Some Persisting Questions Concerning the Constitutional State Executive.* Lawrence: The University of Kansas Publications Governmental Research Series, 1960.

Hansen, Richard H. "Executive Disability—A Void in State and Federal Law," 40 *Nebraska Law Review* 697 (June, 1961).

Isom, Warren R. "The Office of Lieutenant-Governor in the States," 32 *American Political Science Review* 921 (October, 1938).

Lipson, Leslie. *The American Governor From Figurehead to Leader.* Chicago: The University of Chicago Press, 1939.

Nispcl, Bcnjamin. *Reform of the Office of Lieutenant Governor.* Washington: Public Affairs Press, 1958.

Snyder, Clydc F. "Gubcrnatorial Disability," 8 *The University of Chicago Law Review* 521 (April, 1941).

Index

Index

364

Index

365

Index

Morgenthau, Henry Jr., 196, 199n., 204
Moro, Aldo, 305
Morris, Gouverneur, 39, 44–45, 47–49
Moyers, William D., 11, 13

Nadar, Kumaraswami Kamaraj, 302–04
Nebraska, inability procedure, 293
Nehru, Jawaharlal, 302–03
Neustadt, Richard, 255
New Hampshire, inability of governor, 286–87; lieutenant governor in colony, 30, 34–35
New Jersey, Concessions and Agreements of 1664, 30; succession in colony, 30; inability procedure, 292–93
New York, succession in colony, 29; lieutenant governor in royal colony, 30
Nixon, Richard M., 9, as Vice-President, 211–13, 216–23, 225–28, 230–31; views on inability agreements, 246; views on inability procedure, 254; views on filling vice-presidential vacancy, 259–60; 272

O'Brien, Lawrence F., 10, 16, 18
O'Donnell, Kenneth P., 3, 9, 10, 18
Oregon, inability procedure, 293
Oswald, Lee Harvey, 13n., 18n.

Pakistan, inability procedure, 308
Patterson, William, 40, 42
Penn, William, 29
Persons, Wilton D., 216–19, 227
Pierce, Franklin, 104–05
Pinckney, Charles, 39, 41–42
Platt, Thomas C., 120, 131, 154
Polk, James K., 87, 99–100
Pompidou, Georges, 299
Powell, Lewis F., Jr., 244
Powell, Lewis Thornton, 108–10
Proprietary colonies, succession in, 29–30

Randolph, Edmund, 39, 41, 43, 46, 47
Rayburn, Sam, 197–98, 200n., 203n., 205n., 227–28, 231
Republican Party, procedure for filling vacancy in national ticket, Appendix F
Rhode Island, union of Portsmouth and Newport, 28; confederation of 1647,

28; Rhode Island and Providence Plantations Charter of 1663, 28; deputy governor in colony of, 28–29.
Rockefeller, Nelson A., 262, 263n.
Rogers, William P., 217, 228, 241
Roosevelt, Franklin D., as vice-presidential candidate, 181–82, 189; attempted assassination, 190; as President, 191–98; death, 196–98; 203, 255, 278
Roosevelt, Mrs. Franklin D., 192, 196–97, 199
Roosevelt, Theodore, nomination for vice-presidency, 154–55; succession to presidency, 156–60; 278
Root, Elihu, 129, 154, 157–58, 159n.
Rossiter, Clinton, 255
Royal colonies, 24, succession in, 30–35
Ruby, Jack, 15
Rusk, Dean, 7, 8, 13–14, 18
Rutledge, John, 39, 43, 44

Salinger, Pierre, 7, 13, 15, 18, 268
Saragat, Giuseppe, 305
Sato, Eisaku, 306
Schoonmaker, Augustus, 134–35
Schrank, John N., 160
Sedgwick, Theodore, 57, 59, 69
Segni, Antonio, 305
Seward, William H., 109–11
Shastri, Lal Bahadur, 302–04
Sherman, James Schoolcraft, as Vice-President, 159–60; death, 161; 271n.
Sherman, Roger, 39, 45–47, 52, 58
Silva, Ruth, 254, 259, 268
Smith, William L., 57–58, 68, 70
Snyder, Howard McC., 214–15, 223–26
Snyder, Murray, 214, 216, 219
Sorensen, Theodore C., 7, 13–14, 18
South Africa, inability procedure, 309
Southard, Samuel L., 96–97
Soviet Union, succession in, 299–301
Stanton, Edwin M., 111–13
State Ratifying Conventions, 51–56
States, succession in, 283–93, Appendix H
States, the thirteen original, succession in, 36–38
Stelle, John, 287–88
Stettinius, Edward R., Jr., 196, 199n., 204
Stevenson, Adlai E. (1835–1914), 147–48, 150n., 152

Index